THE INKLINGS

Also by Humphrey Carpenter

A Thames Companion
(WITH MARI PRICHARD)

Tolkien: A Biography

THE INKLINGS

C. S. Lewis, J. R. R. Tolkien,
Charles Williams,
and their friends

by
Humphrey Carpenter

Boston
HOUGHTON MIFFLIN COMPANY 1979

First American Edition 1979

Copyright © 1978 by George Allen & Unwin (Publishers) Ltd.

Library of Congress Cataloging in Publication Data

Carpenter, Humphrey.
　The Inklings.
　Bibliography: p.
　Includes index.
　1. Lewis, Clive Staples, 1898–1963—Friends and
associates. 2. Tolkien, John Ronald Reuel, 1892–1973—
Friends and associates. 3. Williams, Charles, 1886–
1945—Friends and associates. 4. Authors, English—
20th century—Biography. 5. Oxford—Biography.
6. England—Intellectual life—20th century. I. Title.
PR6023.E926Z613　1979　823'.9'12　[B]　　78–26042
ISBN 0–395–27628–4

Printed in the United States of America

V 10 9 8 7 6 5 4 3 2 1

Dedicated to the memory of
the late Major W. H. Lewis
('Warnie')

CONTENTS

ILLUSTRATIONS

PREFACE

C. S. Lewis died in 1963, J. R. R. Tolkien in 1973, Charles Williams in 1945. In recent years the books of the first two have been immensely popular on both sides of the Atlantic, while Williams, though his name is far less well known, continues to exercise a considerable fascination to those who have encountered his writings.

These three men knew each other well. Lewis and Tolkien met in 1926 and soon achieved an intimacy which lasted for many years. Around them gathered a group of friends, many of them Oxford dons, who referred to themselves informally and half jestingly as 'The Inklings'. When in 1939 Charles Williams found himself obliged to move from London to Oxford he was quickly taken into this circle, and was on close terms with Lewis and the others until his death.

The Inklings achieved a certain fame – or even notoriety, for they had their detractors – during the lifetime of the group. And when some years later it was noted that *The Lord of the Rings, The Screwtape Letters,* and *All Hallows' Eve* (to name but three of many books) had this in common, that they were first read aloud to the Inklings, it became something of a fashion to study the writings of Lewis, Tolkien, and Williams on the assumption that they were members of a clearly defined literary group with a common aim. Such an assumption may or may not stand up to serious investigation. But in the meanwhile there has been no attempt to write any collective biography of the Inklings. This book tries to fill that gap.

It is based largely on unpublished material, and I am much in the debt of the various people who have made this material available to me. My acknowledgements to them and to the many others who have helped me will be found in Appendix D. As to quotations, their sources are fully identified in Appendix C, by a system which I feel is less intrusive than the conventional method of numerals referring to notes.

The book is largely concerned with C. S. Lewis; for, as I have argued in it, the Inklings owed their existence as a group almost entirely to him. I have also given an account, necessarily highly compressed, of the life and writings of Charles Williams. Of J. R. R. Tolkien's life and work outside the Inklings I have said very little, because he has been the subject of an earlier book of mine, to which I have little to add.

I have tried to show the ways in which the ideas and interests of the

Inklings contrasted sharply with the general intellectual and literary spirit of the nineteen-twenties and thirties. This has necessitated some discussion of their writings, particularly Lewis's. In this sense the book sometimes strays from 'pure' biography into literary criticism. But I have deliberately avoided making any general judgement of these men's achievement, for I think it is too early to try to do so. I have merely tried to tell their story.

H.C.
Oxford, 1978.

'*O my heart, it is all a very odd life.*'

Charles Williams in a letter to his wife, 12 March 1940

PART ONE

I

'Oh for the people who speak one's own language'

From the nursery window of the big house there could be seen a line of long, low mountains. Often the view was blurred by a slight mist, for the weather was generally damp, and on many days the sight of the hills was shut out entirely by slanting rain. Then, all that the boy could see were the wet fields that sloped down towards Belfast, where the tall cranes marked the shipyards whose hum could be heard even at this distance.

Even on wet days there was plenty to be done. Outside the nursery door were long upstairs corridors, attics to be explored, games to be played among the gurgling water-tanks where the wind blew under the slates. Or if the boy tired of that, there were pictures to be drawn and stories to be invented, and his diary of the holiday to be written up.

'My Life during the Exmas Holydays of 1907, by Jacks or Clive Lewis. Author of "Building of the promenad", "Toyland", "Living races of mouse-land" etc. I begin my life after my 9th birthday. On which I got a book from Papy and a post card album from Mamy. Warnie (my brother) was coming home and I was looking forward to him and the Xmas holydays.'

The boy had been christened Clive, but he always called himself Jacks or Jack. His brother Warnie, whose real name was Warren, was three years older than him, and went to a boarding-school in England. Jack always looked forward to Warnie's return, because then they could paint pictures together or make up stories. Warnie liked stories about steamships and trains and India, while Jack liked to write about animals who did heroic deeds. But they usually managed to fit all this into the same story. While Warnie was away at school, Jack carried on with the stories by himself, when he was not learning things from Miss Harper, his governess, or from his mother, who taught him French and Latin.

'Mamy is like most middle-aged ladys, stout, brown hair, spectaciles, knitting her cheif industry etc. etc. Papy of course is the master of the house, and a man in whom you can see strong Lewis features, bad temper, very sensible, nice wen not in a temper. I am like most boys of 9 and I am like Papy, bad temper, thick lips, thin, and generaly weraing a jersey.'

His father, who worked as a solicitor in Belfast, was changeable in mood, and Jack felt more comfortable with his mother, who behaved in the same calm affectionate way all the time. On the other hand it was his father who had bought all the hundreds of books which lined the study and the drawing-room and the cloakroom, and were stacked two deep in the landing bookcase, and filled the corridors and the bedrooms. Jack turned the pages of most of them in turn. One day he found these lines in a book of poetry by Longfellow:

> I heard a voice that cried
> Balder the beautiful
> Is dead, dead.

He had never heard of Balder, but the words gave him an extraordinary feeling, a notion of great cold expanses of northern sky. He could not understand exactly what he felt, and the more he tried to recapture the feeling the more it slipped away.

There were lots of other books to read: the Beatrix Potter tales, *Gulliver's Travels* in a big illustrated volume, and stories by Conan Doyle and Mark Twain and E. Nesbit. In the summer there were picnics on the hills and days by the sea, and there was always something to be done in the big house; so that the time passed quickly in a steady humdrum happiness.

Then one night not very long after his ninth birthday he woke with a headache, and when he cried, his mother did not come to him. There were lights in her room and a bustle of doctors and nurses. She had cancer. Jack prayed that God would make her better, but she went on being ill. On the day she died, the calendar in her room (which had a Shakespearian quotation for each day) bore the words: *Men must endure their going hence, even as their coming hither*. After that, everything changed. Jack would still have moments of happiness, but the old unshakeable comfort had gone. As he himself said, 'It was sea and islands now. The great continent had sunk like Atlantis.'

First came the discomfort of being crammed into Eton collar, knickerbockers and bowler hat; then the *clop clop* of the four-wheeler driving him and his brother to the quay in Belfast; then the sea crossing, followed by his first sight of England, which seemed a sadly flat landscape after the Irish hills; then school.

Wynyard School in Hertfordshire had been moderately good when Warnie was first sent there, but by the time Jack joined his elder brother it was deteriorating as its headmaster became insane. For the next two years Jack had to endure grossly incompetent teaching, bad food, stinking sanitation, arbitrarily inflicted beatings and perpetual fear. It was a terrible introduction to the outer world, and its only good result was to drive the two brothers closer together for mutual protection. By the time the school finally collapsed and the headmaster was certified mad, Warnie had already moved on to Malvern College; the younger boy was sent briefly to a school in Belfast, then to another in England.

Meanwhile Jack continued to read voraciously. He had discovered most of the English poets by the time he was fifteen. He found *The Faerie Queene* in a big illustrated edition and loved it. He was delighted by the romances of William Morris. Best of all, one day he chanced across an Arthur Rackham illustration to *Siegfried and the Twilight of the Gods,* and felt the same sensation as he had known when he first read the Longfellow lines about Balder. 'Pure "Northernness" engulfed me,' he said; and he began a quest for everything 'Northern'. Books of Norse myths, a synopsis of the *Ring* operas, Wagner's music itself, all were food to his imagination. Soon he was writing his own poem on the Nibelung story, rhyming 'Mime' with 'time' and 'Alberich' with 'ditch' because he knew no better. He worked hard at his school-books, too, showing considerable aptitude for Latin and Greek. Yet there was no sense of stability, no ultimate feeling of safety, neither in the school term nor at home during the holidays, when even his brother's companionship could not entirely lighten the oppressiveness of the big house, with its stuffy routine now dictated entirely by his father.

At the age of fourteen he won a classical scholarship to Malvern College.

*

'Not only does this persecution get harder to bear as time goes on, but it is actually getting more severe.' Fifteen-year-old Jack Lewis was writing home to his father from Malvern. 'All the prefects detest me and lose no opportunity of venting their spite. Today, for not being able to find a cap which one gentleman wanted, I have been sentenced to clean his boots every day after breakfast for a week. It is after breakfast that the form goes through their translation together. From this I am cut off. When I asked if I might clean them in the evening (an arrangement which you observe would have made no difference to him), I received a refusal, strengthened by being kicked downstairs. So we go on.'

Malvern was no worse than most English public schools of the time, but it was no better. Warnie had been happy there – he left just as Jack arrived – but the elder boy was, at this stage in their lives, the more resilient. Jack almost immediately took a dislike to the place. It was not that the teaching was bad: far from it, for he was encouraged by a first-rate form master and was commended for excellent work. But academic study and the opportunity to read books seemed to play such a small part in the life of the place. Almost all the day it was bells ringing, feet running, shouted commands from older boys, little sleep and no privacy. Two things in particular alarmed him. One was homosexuality, especially the flirtations of the older boys with the younger. The other was the fact that Malvern, like many other public schools, was run not so much by the staff as by an unofficial clique of senior boys called 'the Bloods'. Admission to this clique was not through formal qualification, but through being 'the right sort of person' and knowing 'the right people'. Moreover once a senior boy became a Blood he had considerable power over his fellows. Bloods who had any tendency to be bullies would pick on those who showed resentment of their power. Jack Lewis did show such resentment. He was soon selected as an ideal victim, and after just two terms of persecution he had seen enough. What he was going through was no worse than what thousands of other boys at English public schools were enduring, but he had no intention of staying firm and enduring it. He was not that sort of person. When faced with something he hated, he did not tolerate it but went to war on it. And since he could not take on the Malvern Bloods single-handed he decided that he had better get away. He wrote to his father: 'Please take me out of this, as soon as possible.'

His father, a man of peculiarly disjointed thinking, was usually notable for making the wrong decisions. But for once he did the right thing. He removed Jack from Malvern and sent him to the man who had been his own headmaster, and who was now retired in Surrey and taking one or two private pupils. W. T. Kirkpatrick, tall and muscularly lean, was a strict atheist who nevertheless put on his best suit to dig the garden on Sunday. This, however, was his only recorded piece of illogical behaviour: in every other particular his life was ruled by strictly rational principles. He was fearsome in conversation, for no sentence passed his lips that was not ruthlessly logical. When Jack Lewis first met his new teacher on arrival at the railway station, the boy attempted some small talk, remarking that the Surrey countryside was more wild than he had expected. 'Stop!' shouted Kirkpatrick. 'What do you mean by *wildness*, and what grounds had you for not expecting it?' Jack did his best, but answer after answer was rejected as being the product of inadequate thought. 'Do you not see', Kirkpatrick concluded, 'that your remark was meaningless?'

Under the tuition of 'Kirk' in the two years that followed, the boy learnt to phrase all remarks as logical propositions and to defend his opinions by argument. Not that 'opinion' was a term admissible in that household. 'I have', Kirkpatrick would exclaim with raised hands, 'no *opinion* on any subject whatsoever.'

Soon, Jack Lewis was learning to match his teacher's mind with dialects of his own, especially in his letters to a Belfast friend, Arthur Greeves, who was prone to vague and illogical statements and who in consequence found himself on the receiving end of Kirk-like arguments. Greeves adhered to the religious beliefs of his childhood, and when he mentioned this in a letter to Lewis there came back a tirade. 'I had thought that you were gradually being emancipated from the old beliefs,' Lewis declared. 'You know, I think, that *I* believe in no religion. There is absolutely no proof for any of them, and from a philosophical standpoint Christianity is not even the best. All religions, that is all mythologies to give them their proper name, are merely man's own invention – Christ as much as Loki.' And Lewis offered his own interpretation of Christianity: 'After the death of a Hebrew prophet Yesua (whose name we have corrupted into Jesus), he became regarded as a god, a cult sprang up, which was afterwards connected with the ancient Hebrew Jahweh-worship, and so Christianity came into being – one mythology among many.'

This atheism was in fact not the result of Kirkpatrick's teaching. Knowledge of his tutor's opinions and access to the rationalist books in the house did encourage Jack, but he had begun to abandon religious belief some years earlier, partly because he found it impossible to make his prayers sincere, partly because he did not think that Christianity had much relation to the largely unhappy world around him, and partly because the Bible did not appeal to him as a story. Or rather, it was when reading pagan stories, especially the myths of the Norsemen, that he experienced his most profound sensations of delight. He began to write a tragedy about the Norse gods. It was in Greek form, under the title 'Loki Bound', and it was an attempt to express both the appeal of Northern myth and his contempt for the Christian view of the universe; for in the play Loki sets himself in opposition to Odin the creator of the world, declaring that such creation was wanton cruelty. Lewis also wrote short poems on this theme, picturing God as a brutish force whose hatred has scarred men's lives.

Yet his own life now was remarkably unscarred. Placid days succeeded one another. He read Homer under Kirkpatrick's tuition, he walked in the Surrey countryside, he wrote poetry, and he sent for innumerable parcels of books from London shops. 'How one does want to read everything,' he remarked to Arthur Greeves, and soon

7

there was little in English literature that he had not encountered. For an atheist, he found delight in unlikely places. Of Malory's account of the Grail he remarked to Greeves, 'Those mystic parts are very good to read late at night when you are drowsy and tired and get into a sort of "exalted" mood.' And when he discovered George MacDonald's 'faery' novel *Phantastes* on a station bookstall he declared that reading it was 'a great literary experience'. Meanwhile his progress at academic work was good; indeed it was clear that he was suited for an academic career – and for that only. 'While admirably adapted for excellence,' Kirkpatrick wrote to Lewis's father, 'and probably for distinction in literary matters, he is adapted for nothing else. You may make up your mind on that.'

At the end of 1916 Jack Lewis won a scholarship to University College, Oxford.

*

It was the summer of 1917. Lewis's first term as an Oxford under-graduate had been interrupted, not unexpectedly, by his call-up papers, and he was now a cadet in uniform. His battalion was quartered just down the road, in Keble College. Cadets were billeted two to a set of rooms, and the allocations were made in alphabetical order. As a result, *Lewis C. S.* found himself sharing sleeping quarters with *Moore E. F. C.* Many years later, Jack Lewis's brother remarked in his diary, 'Lewis and Moore: it might just as easily have been Lewis and Sergeant Muggins, or Lewis and Lord Molineux, and the very fact would have been forgotten by now – but it was Lewis and Moore, and when the clerk filled in the names he permanently and almost immediately altered the course of several lives.'

Jack Lewis did not particularly care for his room-mate; he found 'Paddy' Moore rather childish. But Paddy's mother, an Irishwoman who had been separated from her husband for many years, was living in lodgings close by, so as to be near her son; and when they met she and Jack got on very well, so well that he was soon spending week-ends in her company. Later, when he got a month's leave, he stayed for most of it with the Moores at their Bristol home, going home to his father in Belfast only for the final few days. His father was surprised and hurt at this division of Jack's time.

Once or twice there had already been incipient romances in Jack's life. During his Surrey days he had been attracted to a Belgian refugee girl who was staying in the neighbourhood, and had talked about her in his letters to Arthur Greeves – 'I don't think I've ever been so bucked about anything in my life, she's an awfully decent sort.' Later, in his first few months at Oxford, he had been very friendly with a young woman from Belfast, who was in the city with her mother. But before any real romance could begin he met Mrs Janie Moore.

She was aged forty-five, Irish, and lively. She was poorly educated and her conversation was largely illogical nonsense, so in this respect she was a very odd friend for Jack; but something made him enjoy her company. Perhaps it was in large part simply the fact that she made him feel at home. He was never at ease at his real home in Belfast; his father lived according to an enervating daily routine, and was also perpetually inquisitive into his sons' lives. This made Warnie and Jack draw apart from their parent. Now, when Jack's military training was over and he was about to embark for the front line in France, he telegraphed to his father asking him to come over to England and say goodbye. His father, typically failing to understand the telegram, did not come. It was little wonder that Jack turned to Mrs Moore for affection.

By the time that Jack left for France he and Mrs Moore were behaving to each other like mother and son. As for the real son, Jack once remarked (years later, to his brother) that Mrs Moore and Paddy 'hadn't got on at all well'. In the spring of 1918, Paddy was reported missing in action, and when his death was officially confirmed Mrs Moore wrote to Lewis's father that Paddy had asked Jack 'to look after me if he did not come back'. This became the public explanation for what followed, but probably Jack would have looked after her whether Paddy had come back or not.

*

Jack Lewis's time in the trenches was short, and though he found it horrific he was not deeply shaken by the experience. He had, after all, lived with the knowledge of the war for more than three years before going out to the front line himself. It was something he knew he would have to endure, and (unlike public school) nobody expected him to like it. When he finally reached the front line he found that it was as bad as he had anticipated, but no worse.

Certainly he would always remember what he described as 'the horribly smashed men still moving like half-crushed beetles, the sitting or standing corpses'. And just once he put something of this into his poetry:

> 'What, brother, brother,
> Who groaned?' – 'I'm hit. I'm finished. Let me be.'
> – 'Put out your hand, then. Reach me. No, the other.'
> – 'Don't touch. Fool! Damn you! Leave me.' – 'I can't see.
> Where are you?' Then more groans. 'They've done for me.
> I've no hands. Don't come near me. No, but stay,
> Don't leave me . . . O my God! Is it near day?'

(These lines are from his narrative poem *Dymer*, written not long after the war.) Lewis himself was wounded by a shell a few months after going into the front line. But when he came to write an autobiography he devoted three heated chapters to the horrors of public school and only part of one – entitled 'Guns and Good Company' – to his war experiences. Two remarks about the war, in that book, sum up his attitude. After recording his memories of the animal horror of the trenches, he says: 'It is too cut off from the rest of my experience and often seems to have happened to someone else.' The other remark describes his response to hearing for the first time the whine of a bullet: 'At that moment there was something not exactly like fear, much less like indifference: a little quavering signal that said, "This is War. This is what Homer wrote about." '

*

When Jack Lewis was sent home wounded from the trenches in the spring of 1918, Mrs Moore came to London to be near his hospital. Later, he chose to convalesce in Bristol where she lived. After he had recovered and had re-entered army life, she spent the rest of the war following him from camp to camp, setting up temporary homes as near to him as possible. And when in the autumn of 1918 the war ended and he went back to Oxford as an undergraduate, she packed up her house in Bristol and came too.

They found a furnished house in Warneford Road in east Oxford, and shared the rent between them, Jack making use of an allowance from his father and Mrs Moore depending chiefly on money from her estranged husband, whom she called 'the Beast'. Officially, Jack was living in University College where he was an undergraduate reading Classics, but in reality he spent as much time as possible in 'our hired house', as he described it. 'After lunch,' he told Arthur Greeves, 'I work until tea, then work again until dinner. After that, a little more work, talk and laziness and sometimes bridge, then bicycle back to College at 11. I then light my fire and work or read till 12 o'clock when I retire to sleep the sleep of the just.' This may have been his routine on an ideal day, but more often his time at Warneford Road was occupied with one of the innumerable domestic chores which Mrs Moore was in the habit of devising for him: helping her to make jam and marmalade, scrubbing the floors, washing up, walking the dog, mending broken furniture, taking messages and doing shopping errands. It was not that she did not try to do any of these things herself, but she was easily exhausted – or at least Jack believed that she was – and, though they were generally able to afford a maid, Mrs Moore was suspicious of servants and did not like to trust the girl with these tasks. She used to say of Jack, 'He is as good as an extra maid.' As for Jack, he developed the ability to work at his desk in the middle of domestic mayhem. Only a few minutes would pass in an afternoon at Warneford Road without Mrs Moore's strident voice summoning him to some job or other; he would lay down his pen patiently, go and do what was wanted (however trivial) and then come back and resume work as if nothing had happened. He called this 'the hopeless business of trying to save D. from overwork'. 'D.' was how he referred to Mrs Moore in his diary; to other people he called her 'Minto'. Both names are inexplicable.

Remarkably, this disturbed way of life did no harm to his studies. Long before, in Surrey days, his tutor Kirkpatrick had reported to Jack's father, 'He has read more classics than any boy I ever had – or indeed I might add than any I ever heard of, unless it be an Addison or Landor or Macaulay.' Kirkpatrick had also said of Jack's enthusiasm for his work, 'He is a student who has no interest except in reading and study. The very idea of urging him or stimulating him to increased exertion makes me smile.' Nevertheless, given the distractions of life with 'Minto', Jack Lewis did very well to take a First Class in Classical Moderations in March 1920.

Meanwhile his friends and relatives were puzzling over his strange involvement with Mrs Moore. It was easy to explain the mother–son element in it by the losses of real mother and real son which they had suffered. But was that all? Some people perhaps suspected a romantic-sexual element in the liaison, and possibly this was what Jack's father had in mind when he referred to it as 'Jack's affair'. This sort of speculation was, if anything, fostered by the silence of Jack himself, who refused to discuss the matter with any of his close friends. On the only occasion Warnie Lewis asked his brother about the relationship he was told to mind his own business. In particular Jack tried to keep his father as much in the dark about it as possible, pretending to him that he was living in ordinary 'digs' with other undergraduates, and disguising a holiday spent with 'Minto' as a walking tour with a college friend. None of this helped to make it seem entirely respectable.[1]

On the other hand nobody who knew Jack Lewis supposed seriously

[1] Warnie Lewis was never able to explain the relationship. On 23 November 1948 he wrote in his diary, of a conversation with one of the maids at the Kilns: 'I cut the thing short, for I saw I was going to be asked the question I am so tired of, and to which I shall never find the answer, viz. how anyone so nice as J. ever came to make himself the slave of such a woman? It's a very odd thing how impossible it is to be believed when you are telling the truth. I have been asked the question by all the Inklings, by Parkin [a friend from army days], by many of our "lady helps" and servants: and when I reply, perfectly truthfully, that I don't know, and that J. and I never discuss this side of his life, I always see that I am suspected of an honourable reticence.'

that Mrs Moore was his mistress. Certainly he discussed sex in his letters to Arthur Greeves, but only in relation to masturbation, and this was probably all that he meant by the rather veiled and arch references he made (in the books he was later to write) to his sexual experience as a young man. On the practical level, a sexual relationship with Mrs Moore would have been difficult without servants' gossip, let alone the fact that another member of the household was Mrs Moore's daughter Maureen, who was eight years younger than Paddy and still a child.

After this strange ménage had been established in Oxford for a little over a year, Jack was able to move out of college and make the home with 'Minto' his official lodgings. But they were obliged to leave the Warneford Road house, and there began a long search for a permanent home in which they could use Mrs Moore's own furniture. Unfurnished houses at a moderate rent seemed impossible to find, and for two long years they moved from one place to another, renting furnished rooms or being lent the use of a house for a few weeks while the owner was away. Between 1918 and 1923 they lived at nine different addresses, 'most of them vile', as Jack remarked in his diary. At one time during this period Mrs Moore told him that 'she was quite convinced that she would never again live in a house of her own'.

*

Until 1918 Jack Lewis had gone on writing poems that were deeply pessimistic, flinging accusations at a cruel God. They were not particularly good as poetry, so he was lucky to have a volume of them published by Heinemann in 1918 under the title *Spirits in Bondage*. They attracted almost no attention, and Lewis brought no reputation as a poet when he came up to Oxford. Indeed, tastes were already changing, and he discovered that many of his fellow undergraduates who were interested in poetry admired T. S. Eliot and other exponents of modern verse. 'I'm afraid I shall never be an orthodox modern,' Lewis wrote to Arthur Greeves in October 1918. 'I like lines that will scan and do not care for descriptions of sea-sickness.'

He was not alone in disliking modern verse: he soon made friends with several other undergraduates who shared his views, and who (like him) wanted to go on writing poetry uninfluenced by the new movement. Among these was a young man at Wadham College, Owen Barfield. He and Lewis and several others conceived the rather grand idea of issuing a yearly collection of their verses; but this idea petered out. However, they continued to read each other's poetry with interest, and to offer criticisms.

By the time that Lewis began to read for the second part of the Classics course, 'Greats' (Ancient History and Philosophy), he had abandoned the pessimistic viewpoint of his early poems. He also decided to turn his back on the sensations of delight that he had received from Norse mythology, Malory, George MacDonald, and many other books. Privately he still sometimes felt such sensations, though not so often as before; but these he now labelled 'aesthetic experience' and said that they were valuable but not really informative. As to the existence of God, he adopted the attitude that 'it really made no difference whatever whether there was such a person or no'. All this he called his New Look. It certainly harmonised with the Oxford approach to philosophy at the time; the ruthlessly analytical Logical Positivism had not yet made its appearance, but there was a prevailing tone of scepticism which Lewis gladly adopted.

In 1922 he took a First Class in 'Greats'.

*

Shortly after this, he and Mrs Moore finally found a house that offered a hope of permanence, 'Hillsboro', a villa in the Oxford suburb of Headington which was available as an unfurnished letting. Out came Mrs Moore's furniture from store; Jack spent endless days painting and laying linoleum; and they moved in. This, however, did not mean domestic tranquillity, for 'Minto' still found more than enough for Jack to do, partly thanks to her habit of quarrelling with servants. Jack noted in his diary that the incompetence of one maid had become 'the exclusive subject of conversation' with Mrs Moore, remarking, 'I do not blame D. for this in the least, but of course it makes things very miserable.'

Jack now hoped for a teaching appointment at Oxford. But there were no university jobs available in Philosophy, his strong subject in 'Greats'; so, as his father was good-naturedly prepared to continue financial support for a time, he decided to read English Language and Literature, tackling the full course in just one year, a mere third of the time that most undergraduates devoted to it. This meant learning Anglo-Saxon and studying the principles of philology, besides reading literature from the medieval period to the nineteenth century. He was, of course, far from ignorant in this field already, but there was still a lot of ground to cover, and it was amazing that he managed to do it in the moments he could spare from domestic life. During the months while he was racing through the English syllabus he was teaching Latin to Mrs Moore's daughter Maureen and to her music-mistress in lieu of Maureen's fees, tutoring a neighbour's child in return for Maureen's lessons with its mother, and washing up after almost every meal. For two weeks he was, by day and night, looking after Mrs Moore's brother, who was having a severe nervous breakdown in the house.

13

He was also coping with a perpetual series of what he called 'Minto's mare's nests' – imaginary crises of every conceivable kind – and with a stream of visitors and paying guests. The most remarkable thing was that he did this with almost unvarying good humour. This was perhaps partly because he knew that the whole thing was very nearly his fault anyway, and if he complained it could be justly retorted that the household owed its existence to him. But really it was his immense fund of good nature that kept him going. He was already practised at coping with domestic oddities, thanks to the strangeness of family life with his father in Belfast; and in any case he was not a complainer by nature. Far from it: he derived immense amusement from the odd visitors who came to the house, to whom he and Mrs Moore gave nicknames: 'the Blackguard' for a grotesque French lodger, and 'Smudge' for the inoffensive and rather indistinct music teacher. Only when the question was raised of his brother Warnie coming to live with them did Jack warn him openly of 'the perpetual interruptions of family life – the partial loss of liberty'. And even then he qualified it by adding: 'This sounds as if I were either sick of it myself or else trying to make you sick of it: but neither is the case. I have definitely chosen and don't regret the choice. Whether I was right or wrong, wise or foolish, to have done so originally, is now only an historical question: once having created expectations, one naturally fulfils them.'

*

He was not very impressed by his first experiences when reading English Language and Literature at Oxford. 'The atmosphere of the English school', he wrote in his diary after attending a lecture, 'is very different from that of Greats. Women, Indians, and Americans predominate and – I can't say how – one feels a certain amateurishness in the talk and look of the people.' He thought poorly of many of the lectures, and felt no enthusiasm for the study of philological niceties such as glottal stops and vowel shifts, of which he remarked, 'Very good stuff in its way, but why physiology should form part of the English school I really don't know.' He was comfortable, however, in the company of the Martlets, the literary society of University College, which met to listen to papers read by its members. Lewis often contributed monographs on his favourite authors. He gave a talk on William Morris and another on Spenser. After the paper there would be a discussion, which sometimes turned into intellectual pyrotechnics; for like Lewis many of the Martlets were well read in philosophy. They enjoyed showing off their command of logic, as did Lewis, for he believed that his mind was well trained in argument. He was always in the forefront of any dialectical battle that concluded a Martlets evening, and he also liked to go for brisk walks with fellow members, during which they would continue an intricate argument from the previous Martlets meeting. This kind of talk was often an intellectual duel for the sake of the sport, and Lewis judged his and his opponent's performance as much on method as on content. 'In spite of many well contested points I was gravelled in the end,' he recorded after one such contest which was conducted while he and a friend strode across the meadows on the edge of Oxford, adding, 'We were neither of us in really good dialectical form.'

It was not only among the Martlets that he engaged in logical argument. It was indeed a form of conversation that he sought wherever it could be found, not least perhaps because it was a relief from Mrs Moore's illogical chatter; and he judged his acquaintances by their capacity for it, despising men who talked only in anecdotes or merely peddled facts. Nor did he care for men who were flippant or cynical. To get on with Lewis you had to argue with feeling as well as with your brain; you had to hold your opinions passionately and be prepared to defend them with logic. Not surprisingly, few people came up to the mark.

One who did was a fellow Irishman, Nevill Coghill, who like Lewis was reading the English course in one year, having previously graduated in History. Each found the other a good companion for energetic country walks, and while striding together over Hinksey Hill they would talk excitedly about what they had been reading that week. Coghill never forgot how on one such walk Lewis, who had just encountered the Anglo-Saxon *Battle of Maldon*, boomed out some lines from the end of the poem:

> 'Hige sceal þe heardra, heorte þe cenre,
> mod sceal þe mare, þe ure maegen lytlað.'

'Will shall be the sterner, heart the bolder, spirit the greater as our strength lessens.'

In the summer of 1923 Lewis was awarded a First Class in the English School He now had three Firsts to his name, and was determined to get an academic job, but the days were over when a clever young man could walk out of examinations into a college fellowship. There was plenty of competition and few jobs. Certainly Lewis had a wider choice than some men, for he could teach Philosophy as well as English Literature, but even so there were not many opportunities. For a year he could find nothing at all and, though his father generously continued to pay an allowance despite his suspicions (or perhaps because of his ignorance) about Jack's life with Mrs Moore, it was a

15

worrying time. Jack occupied himself by reading and by writing poetry. He was now at work on a long narrative poem which he called *Dymer*, about a young man who escapes from a totalitarian society, begets a monster on an unseen and mysterious bride, and is eventually killed by the monster, which becomes a god. Lewis declared that he had no idea what its meaning might be. 'Everyone may allegorise or psycho-analyse it as he pleases,' he said; and certainly one episode in the poem does seem to relate closely to his own life at the time of its composition. When Dymer wakes after his night of love in the dark room with the unseen girl, he wanders out into the daylight and explores the mysterious palace in which he has found her. After a few moments he returns to seek her, but the way to the room is now blocked by the witch-like shape of an old woman squatting on the threshold. Whichever way Dymer takes through the corridors, still the way is barred by this 'old, old matriarchal dreadfulness', so that in the end he is forced to leave the palace and abandon his lover, whom he never sees again. When Lewis began to write *Dymer* in 1922 he had been living with Mrs Moore for three years, and now that she had come into his life he took no further romantic interest in girls of his own age.

Dymer was more contemporary in tone than Lewis's 1918 anthology, being rather in the style of John Masefield. While Lewis was working on it, he often showed the manuscript to his undergraduate friend Owen Barfield. Barfield was generally very complimentary about the poem, and when he showed his own verse to Lewis he received equal praise.

Barfield, too, graduated with a First in English, and then tried to earn a living by contributing to London literary journals. Meanwhile Nevill Coghill, was awarded a fellowship at Exeter College, where he had been an undergraduate. Lewis himself continued to wait, applying for several jobs without success. After a year the position improved when he was given some part-time work teaching Philosophy at University College for a don who was temporarily in America. Then in the spring of 1925 a fellowship in English Language and Literature was advertised at Magdalen College. Lewis applied, though without much hope.

The weeks that followed were anxious. He continued to give tutorials and lectures at University College, generally walking home afterwards to save the bus fares. His afternoons spent striding across the Oxford-shire countryside with friends like Coghill had made him a practised walker, and the mere mile and a quarter from the town to Headington was nothing to him. He could be seen on most days, coming down the steps from the main entrance of his college, a heavily built young man with a florid face and a flop of dark hair, dressed in baggy flannel trousers and an old blazer with a University College badge, and wearing

1 (a) Left to right: Jack Lewis, Warnie Lewis, and their father in 1910.

1 (b) Maureen Moore, Jack Lewis, and Mrs Moore on holiday in Cornwall, 1927.

2 (a) Jack Lewis, Maureen Moore, and Mrs Moore on holiday in Cornwall, 1927.

2 (b) Left to right: Jack Lewis, Mrs Moore and Warnie Lewis at the Kilns in 1930.

a battered hat and a shabby mackintosh if the weather was not warm. 'Several Univ. people whom I don't know passed me,' he noted one morning. 'One of them, noticing my blazer, must have asked another who I was, for I heard him answer "Heavy Lewis".'

On 22 May 1925 *The Times* announced that 'The President and Fellows of Magdalen College have elected to an official Fellowship in the College as Tutor in English Language and Literature, for five years as from next June 25, Mr Clive Staples Lewis.'

*

Lewis settled into his new college during the Long Vacation of 1925. He had been allocated rooms in the eighteenth-century New Buildings, with windows overlooking the tower and lawns on one side and the Grove with its herd of deer on the other. Few people in Oxford had a finer view. Lewis reported to his father that it was 'beautiful beyond compare'.

By the time the Michaelmas term began he had bought the few pieces of furniture necessary for his rooms, choosing the very plainest because he did not think that such things mattered much. In fact he could have afforded a few extravagances, had they been to his taste, for he would have a good income from the fellowship and plenty of security. The appointment at Magdalen was nominally for five years only, but fellows were almost always re-elected when that period was over. It would only be necessary to keep on good terms with the other Magdalen dons and to do his job fairly conscientiously to be secure for the rest of his working days.

The snag was that one of these conditions – keeping on good terms with his colleagues – did not look as if it was going to be particularly easy. Some of them seemed pleasant enough; he liked and admired Frank Hardie, a don of about the same age as himself;[1] but he could not come to the same opinion about many of the others. 'I am beginning to be rather disillusioned about my colleagues,' he told his father. 'There is a good deal more intrigue and mutual back-scratching and even direct lying than I ever suspected possible: and what worries me most of all is that the decent men seem to be all the old ones (who will die) and the rotters seem to be all the young ones (who will last my time).' Among the older men were P. V. M. Benecke, the Ancient History tutor, and J. A. Smith, the moral philosopher, both of them Victorians in ideas as well as appearance. Lewis took to having his breakfast with

[1] The brother of Colin Hardie. In earlier accounts of Lewis's life the two have been confused. After one year at Magdalen, Frank Hardie moved to Corpus Christi College, of which he eventually became President. Colin Hardie arrived at Magdalen in 1936.

them, partly as a way of avoiding the younger dons. To a couple of these he responded with horrified fascination. Of one, the historian H. M. D. Parker, he wrote in his diary: 'He thinks of himself as a plain man with no nonsense about him, and hopes that even his enemies regard him as an honest fellow at bottom. The desire to be always exercising this shrewd practical commonsense leads him to endless discussions on everything that happens: he will draw anyone who listens into a corner and stand there exchanging husky confidences about his pupils and colleagues. He always implies that "we two (or three or four) are the only people in College who understand this matter and we must hold together". The very same people against whom he marshals his confidants on Wednesday will themselves be taken into council on Thursday. He believes all that he says for the moment, but being weak as water, takes a new colour from every group that he falls into.' In sharp contrast was another of the younger dons at Magdalen, T. D. ('Harry') Weldon, the Philosophy tutor, who was a militant atheist and who soon became the leader of the more radical dons. Of him, Lewis wrote: 'He has great abilities, but would despise himself if he wasted them on disinterested undertakings. He would be capable of treachery and would think the victim a fool for being betrayed. He preaches what he practises: tells you openly that anyone who believes another is a fool, and holds that Hobbes alone saw the truth: tells me I am an incurable romantic and is insolent to old men and servants. He is very pale, this man, good-looking, and drinks a great deal without getting drunk. I think he is the best of our younger fellows and I would sign his death-warrant to-morrow, or he mine, without turning a hair.'

When term began, Lewis's duties in Magdalen consisted of giving an hour's tutorial each week, together with any extra teaching he thought necessary, to those undergraduates in the college who were reading English In his first years as a tutor he rarely had more than half a dozen pupils; and as they came to him either singly or in pairs for their tutorials, this meant some six or eight hours of teaching a week. In addition to this he gave courses of lectures to the University as a whole, which meant another hour or two's work each week, plus the time taken to prepare the lectures. In some academic years he would also be required to serve as an examiner, which occupied a good deal of time. But much of his day was still his own, to use as he liked for private research, for helping Mrs Moore with domestic chores (which he continued to do each afternoon), and for meeting his friends.

Lewis did not find the Magdalen undergraduates much more attractive than many of the dons. He told his father that in his opinion the college was no more than 'a country club for all the idlest "bloods" of Eton and Charterhouse', adding, 'I really don't know what gifts the

18

public schools bestow on their nurslings, beyond the mere surface of good manners: unless contempt of the things of the intellect, extravagance, insolence, self-sufficiency, and sexual perversion are to be called gifts.' Certainly there was a Magdalen tradition of recruiting undergraduates from the smarter public schools; but here again, Lewis's own schooling had left him sensitive to such things, particularly to homosexuality.

As to the undergraduates, this is how one Magdalen freshman responded to his surroundings in that Michaelmas term of 1925:

> Balkan Sobranies in a wooden box,
> The college arms upon the lid; Tokay
> And sherry in the cupboard; on the shelves
> The *University Statutes* bound in blue,
> *Crome Yellow, Prancing Nigger,* Blunden, Keats . . .
> Privacy after years of public school;
> First college rooms, a kingdom of my own:
> What words of mine can tell my gratitude?
> No wonder, looking back, I never worked.

The undergraduate who wrote these lines was among Lewis's first pupils that term, and they did not get on well. 'Betjeman and Valentin came for Old English,' Lewis wrote in his diary. 'Betjeman appeared in a pair of eccentric bedroom slippers and said he hoped I didn't mind them as he had a blister. He seemed so pleased with himself that I couldn't help saying that I should mind them very much myself but that I had no objection to *his* wearing them – a view which I believe surprised him. Both had been very idle over the O.E. and I told them it wouldn't do.'

John Betjeman found Magdalen a blessed relief after schooldays at Marlborough, where he had endured just as much discomfort as Lewis at Malvern. He was certainly prepared to pay a little desultory attention to English literature, but he had not bargained for Old English (Anglo-Saxon), nor for such a tutor. Lewis, who was going to be responsible for teaching his pupils the whole English School syllabus from *The Battle of Maldon* to Blake, had decided to do his best to make the early part of the course palatable by organising evenings of 'Beer and Beowulf' and by inventing mnemonics to teach his pupils the laws of sound-changes. Betjeman, whose taste was for Swinburne, Firbank and the Gothic Revival, could scarcely be expected to respond enthusiastically to Lewis chanting over the beer-jug:

> Thus Æ to E they soon were fetchin',
> Compare such forms as þÆC and þECCEAN.

19

(The last word is pronounced approximately as *thetchen* and so provides a rhyme.) Betjeman absented himself from this ordeal whenever possible, slipping away to friends who had an exotic country house at Sezincote near Moreton-in-Marsh:

> I cut tutorials with wild excuse,
> For life was luncheons, luncheons all the way.

'While in College,' Lewis wrote in his diary, 'I was rung up on the telephone by Betjeman speaking from Moreton-in-Marsh, to say that he hadn't been able to read the Old English, as he was suspected for measles and forbidden to read a book. Probably a lie, but what can one do?'

When Betjeman was not lunching at Sezincote he could usually be found at the George Restaurant in Oxford with Harold Acton and the Etonian set from Christ Church, or at Wadham College in the group of young men who gathered around Maurice Bowra. But if Bowra's hospitality and wit showed Betjeman that dons were sometimes prepared to treat undergraduates as more than pupils, Betjeman found nothing of this reflected in his relationship with his tutor. The instant the tutorial hour was over, Lewis showed Betjeman to the door, generally with a fierce admonition to work harder. It was not that Lewis behaved in this way to all his pupils: he began to make friends with one or two who liked brisk walks and whose ideas interested him. But most undergraduates found him formal and fierce, and certainly he kept his distance from those whose behaviour had overtones of homosexuality – a fashionable mannerism among Oxford undergraduates at the time. Lewis's own attitude to homosexuality is hard to define; it was perhaps a mixture of revulsion, due to his Ulster upbringing which encouraged an Old Testament severity towards sexual deviation, and fear, even suppression, due to the fact that his own feelings for his male friends were so warmly affectionate. At all events, while many of the 'Georgoisie' (as Betjeman named his friends) ate their dinners in loose-knotted shantung ties and pastel shirts, Lewis seemed to be taking almost exaggerated care to be shabby, with his regular uniform of dung-coloured mackintosh and old cloth hat.

John Betjeman was sent down from Magdalen after only a few terms for failing the obligatory University examination in Divinity. He sought out Lewis 'in his arid room', but was told bluntly, 'You'd have only got a Third.'

Some years later, Betjeman turned the tables on his tutor. In his volume of poems *Continual Dew* (1937), he wrote in the preface that he was 'indebted to Mr C. S. Lewis for the fact on page 256'. The book consisted of only forty-five pages. And in one of the poems contained in it, 'A Hike on the Downs' – which might indeed be a deliberate parody of Lewis's whole way of life – there is this stanza, supposedly spoken by a young don:

'Objectively, our Common Room
Is like a small Athenian State –
Except for Lewis: he's all right
But do you think he's *quite* first rate?'

*

Betjeman and his set were enthusiastic about modern poetry. Lewis was becoming less and less sympathetic to it. In fact he was now thoroughly vehement about T. S. Eliot.

In the early months of 1926, while Betjeman was still his pupil, he borrowed a volume of Eliot's verse from him, and after studying it began to organise an anti-Eliot campaign among his friends. It was to take the form of a parody of modern verse which would be sent to the *Criterion*, which Eliot edited, in the hope that it would be mistaken for serious poetry and published as such. Lewis acquired several collaborators: his Magdalen colleague Frank Hardie, his pupil Henry Yorke (who had already published his first novel as 'Henry Green'), and Nevill Coghill. They wrote some appropriate verses and agreed to send them to Eliot under the names of a brother and sister, Rollo and Bridget Considine. 'Bridget is the elder,' wrote Lewis in his diary, 'and they are united by an affection so tender as to be almost incestuous. Bridget will presently write a letter to Eliot (if we get a foothold) telling him about her own and her brother's life. She is incredibly dowdy and about thirty-five. We rolled about in laughter as we pictured a tea party where the Considines should meet Eliot: Yorke would dress up for Bridget and perhaps bring a baby. The poems are to be sent from Vienna where Hardie has a friend. We think Vienna will decrease suspicion and is a likely place for the Considines to live in. Hardie and Coghill are in it for pure fun, I from burning indignation, Yorke chiefly for love of mischief.' The venture gained momentum when Lewis's acquaintance William Force Stead, the American clergyman and man of letters who knew Eliot and in 1927 baptised him a member of the Anglican Church, was shown one of the parodies without being told that it was parody, and expressed a serious enthusiasm for it. But this seemed to indicate not so much that the parody was good poetry as that Stead was a hopeless judge, and shortly after this the prank petered out.

*

Lewis's long narrative poem *Dymer* was now finished. It was offered to Heinemann, who had published his 1918 volume of verse, and Lewis was badly shaken when they rejected it. He asked Nevill Coghill for an opinion of the poem. Coghill was quite enthusiastic, liking *Dymer* enough to pass it to a friend who worked for J. M. Dent; and he and Lewis were delighted when Dent's expressed admiration and agreed to publish it. When it was issued in 1926 it earned some good reviews. But almost nobody bought it, and Lewis now doubted whether he would achieve success as a poet. He still believed that poetry was his 'only real line', but though he went on writing verse it took up a smaller part of his attention. Another factor in this was that old friends from undergraduate days, such as Owen Barfield, were no longer at hand to give advice and criticism. Indeed there were many ways in which Lewis felt the need for more companionship. In a letter to another friend from undergraduate days who had now left the University, A. K. Hamilton Jenkin, Lewis described the idyllic setting of his college rooms and went on: 'I wish there was anyone here childish enough (or *permanent* enough, not the slave of his particular and outward age) to share it with me. Is it that no man makes real friends after he has passed the undergraduate age? Because I get no forr'arder, since the old days. I go to Barfield for sheer wisdom and a sort of richness of spirit. I go to you for some smaller and yet more intimate connexion with the feel of Things. But the question I am asking is why I meet no such men now. Is it that *I* am blind? Some of the older men are delightful: the younger fellows are none of them men of understanding. Oh for the people who speak one's own language.'

*

Professors and college tutors at Oxford do not necessarily meet often in the course of duty, even if they are members of the same faculty. It was not until Tuesday 11 May 1926, after he had been in residence at Magdalen for two terms, that Lewis had a chance to talk at any length to the new Professor of Anglo-Saxon, who had started work in the University at the same time as himself. On that day he went to an 'English Tea' at Merton College for a discussion of faculty business.

At the tea there was some discussion of the General Strike, but not much was said about it, for Oxford had scarcely been affected. Then came some business involving the lecture lists. After that (Lewis recorded in his diary) 'Tolkien managed to get the discussion round to the proposed English Prelim. I had a talk with him afterwards. He is a smooth, pale, fluent little chap – can't read Spenser because of the forms – thinks the language is the real thing in the school – thinks all literature is written for the amusement of *men* between thirty and forty –

we ought to vote ourselves out of existence if we were honest – still the sound changes and the gobbets are great fun for the dons. His pet abomination is the idea of "liberal studies". Technical hobbies are more in his line. No harm in him: only needs a smack or so.'

2

'What? You too?'

John Ronald Reuel Tolkien was aged thirty-four, young by the standard of Oxford professors. He had been an Oxford undergraduate between 1911 and 1915, reading Classical Moderations and then English, specialising in the 'language' side of the course; that is, Anglo-Saxon, Middle English, and philology. After marrying, serving in France during the war, and working briefly in Oxford on the New English Dictionary, he had been appointed Reader in English Language at Leeds University. While teaching in Leeds he had built up a 'language' side to the English syllabus that was notable for its imagination and liveliness. Now that he was back in Oxford, he was determined to remodel the Oxford English School's 'language' side on the lines that had been successful in Leeds.

He put his proposals to the Faculty not long after Lewis's first conversation with him. Lewis was among those who voted against him.

*

In declaring to Lewis that 'the language is the real thing in the school', Tolkien was in fact reviving an old Oxford quarrel, which had split the Honour School of English Language and Literature ever since its foundation at the end of the nineteenth century.

It was a quarrel about what a university course in 'English' should consist of. One faction believed that it ought to be based on ancient and medieval texts and their language, with at most only a brief excursion into 'modern' literature – by 'modern' they meant anything later than Chaucer. These people wanted an English course that was as severe a discipline as a study of the classics. On the other side were those who thought the most important thing was to study the whole range of English literature up to the present day.

The two factions had different ancestors. The people who were in favour of ancient and medieval studies and philology (all known familiarly as 'language', though a good deal more than linguistics was involved) were the cultural descendants of the traditional Oxford classical scholarship, and more recently of nineteenth-century comparative philologists such as Max Müller. The 'literature' people (those in favour of the study of post-Chaucerian writers) were in general a new breed of teachers and literary critics who believed that the study of recent vernacular literature was just as important as reading Latin and Greek or other ancient writings. Indeed many of these people thought that, in a time of broadening educational opportunities, recent literature had a far greater future than 'dead' languages as an academic discipline. Some of them (more notably at Cambridge than at Oxford) were also beginning to form the idea that by reading English literature a student could in some way improve his character as well as his knowledge. It was this view which Tolkien attacked so vehemently when he told Lewis that he abominated 'liberal studies'.

There were several reasons why Tolkien took this attitude. First, he himself had never studied post-Chaucerian literature more than cursorily, for 'English' had scarcely been taught at his school (King Edward's, Birmingham), and as an undergraduate he had concentrated on the 'language' side of the English course. Moreover, although he had many favourites among later writers, he took an impish delight in challenging established values, saying that he found *The Faerie Queene* unreadable because of Spenser's idiosyncratic treatment of the language, and declaring that Shakespeare had been unjustifiably deified. But a deeper and more important reason was that his own mind and imagination had been captivated since schooldays by early English poems such as *Beowulf, Sir Gawain and the Green Knight,* and *Pearl,* and by the Old Icelandic *Völsungasaga* and *Elder Edda.* These were all the literature that he needed.

Lewis's view was rather different. For him the great works of post-Chaucerian literature had, after all, been a source of joy since boyhood. Spenser was a particular favourite with him. He knew comparatively little Anglo-Saxon literature, and though he was deeply attached to Norse mythology he did not know more than a few words of Old Icelandic itself. So the notion that the earliest part of the course was of special importance – or, as Tolkien put it, that 'the language is the real thing' – seemed an exaggeration. There was thus every reason for him to vote against Tolkien.

On the other hand the changes proposed by Tolkien were quite logical. At that time the Oxford syllabus was, in his view, gravely deficient in that it did not encourage a *literary* approach to early and medieval writings; and Tolkien did believe passionately that Anglo-Saxon and Middle-English prose and poetry should be treated as literature and not merely as a quarry for 'gobbets' (passages set in

25

examinations) and for teaching the rules of sound-changes. He was annoyed that students were required by the syllabus to learn off pat such linguistic rules as Grimm's and Verner's Laws, but did not have to read any Old or Middle-English literature other than short pieces in anthologies. He thought it absurd, in other words, that Lewis's pupils were having to learn rules by rote ('Thus Æ to E they soon were fetchin' ') while they scarcely knew any of the literature to which these rules applied. Lewis in fact had realised the absurdity of this situation. Hence his 'Beer and Beowulf' evenings, in which his pupils actually did some reading beyond the syllabus.

This state of affairs applied to the men and women who chose the course which specialised in post-Chaucerian literature – in fact about ninety per cent of the undergraduates reading English Nor were conditions much better for the few who opted for early and medieval studies, for they had to spend a good deal of time – wasted time, thought Tolkien – away from their special field, reading Shakespeare and Milton. Tolkien was determined to end this, and to get the Faculty to accept a re-modelled syllabus, in which everyone would be expected to read widely in early English literature, while the early and medieval specialists could pursue their chosen work without having to turn aside and study later writers.

Few people in the Faculty quarrelled with these notions as such. The trouble was that in order to make room for a more thorough study of the early period some other part of the syllabus would have to be abandoned or made optional. Tolkien recommended, in an article in the *Oxford Magazine*, 'jettisoning certainly the nineteenth century (unless parts of it could appear as an "additional subject")', and suggested that the compulsory papers should stop at 1830.

The notion of improving the study of ancient literature by curtailing the reading of modern writers had a certain appeal at Oxford. The English Faculty had always been embarrassed by those in the University – and there were many – who alleged that undergraduates could read English literature in their baths, and did not need dons to teach it to them any more than they needed nursemaids to wipe their noses. (Lewis himself shared this view.) The study of recent writers was particularly open to this charge; so there was some attraction in amputating the nineteenth century from the syllabus, particularly if it was to give place to what was indubitably a more scholarly pursuit in Oxford's eyes, the reading of Anglo-Saxon and Middle English. This is perhaps why, though Tolkien's proposal to finish the syllabus at 1830 was strongly resisted by many of the 'literature' dons, it was not quashed, but became the subject of considerable argument in the English Faculty during the months following Tolkien's first meeting with

Lewis; years, indeed, rather than months, for it was not until 1931 that the issue was settled.

*

At first, Lewis was among the opponents of Tolkien's proposals. But soon he began to come round to Tolkien's side in the English School faction fight. This was due in the beginning to the Coalbiters.

Tolkien had decided to form a club among the dons to read Icelandic sagas and myths. Among his proposals for syllabus reform was the suggestion that Old Icelandic, also known as Old Norse, should be given a more prominent place among early and medieval studies, at least for the specialists; and he thought that the best way to proselytise would be to show his colleagues how enjoyable the reading of Icelandic can be. So the Coalbiters came into existence.

Their Icelandic name was *Kolbítar*, a jesting term meaning 'men who lounge so close to the fire in winter that they bite the coal'. Tolkien founded the club in the spring term of 1926. Its first members included several men with a reasonable knowledge of Icelandic: R. M. Dawkins, the Professor of Byzantine and Modern Greek; C. T. Onions of the Dictionary; G. E. K. Braunholtz, the Professor of Comparative Philology; and John Fraser, the Celtic Professor. But another founder-member was Nevill Coghill, who knew no Icelandic; and soon he was joined by others who were similarly ignorant and were merely enthusiastic beginners. These included John Bryson, the English tutor at Balliol College; George Gordon, the Professor of English Literature and later President of Magdalen (who had been Tolkien's head of department at Leeds); and two Magdalen dons, Bruce McFarlane, the historian, and C. S. Lewis.

The suggestion that Lewis be invited to join may have come from John Bryson, a fellow Ulsterman, or from George Gordon, who had taught Lewis as an undergraduate and had been influential in getting him the Magdalen fellowship (Gordon was a great intriguer and campaigner: he had also had a hand in Tolkien's election as Professor of Anglo-Saxon). Or maybe it was Tolkien himself who discovered that Lewis was keen to join the club. At all events by January 1927 Lewis was attending the *Kolbítar*, and was finding it invigorating.

Like Coghill and several of the others he could not, when he first joined, read more than a few words of Icelandic without a dictionary. But this did not matter. During the evening, those present would take turns to translate from the text they were reading. Tolkien, who was of course expert in the language and knew the text well, would improvise a perfect translation of perhaps a dozen pages. Then Dawkins and others who had a working knowledge of Icelandic would translate

27

perhaps a page each. Then the beginners – Lewis, Coghill, Bryson and the others – would work their way through no more than a paragraph or two, and might have to call on Tolkien for help in a difficult passage. The learners certainly found it hard going; as John Bryson remarked, 'When we were enrolled we never realised that it was going to be such a business.' He recalled that on one occasion 'a certain scholar, who must remain nameless, was actually caught using a printed "crib" under the table as he translated his passage apparently impromptu. He was not invited back again!' But most of them took it seriously, especially Lewis.

For someone who had been devoted to Norse myths and legends since adolescence it was exhilarating to be reading them in the original language. 'Spent the morning partly on the Edda,' Lewis wrote in his diary in February 1927: the Coalbiters were working their way through the *Younger Edda*, which contains a version of the great Norse myths. 'Hammered my way through a couple of pages in about an hour, but I am making some headway. It is an exciting experience when I remember my first passion for things Norse under the initiation of Longfellow. It seemed impossible then that I should ever come to read these things in the original. The old authentic thrill came back to me once or twice this morning: the mere names of god and giant catching my eye as I turned the pages of Zoega's dictionary were enough.'

The Coalbiters met once every few weeks in term-time, progressing through the sagas towards their eventual goal of the *Elder Edda*. But not until three years had passed did Lewis begin to realise that the thrill he received from Norse mythology was shared by Tolkien.

On 3 December 1929 Lewis wrote to Arthur Greeves: 'One week I was up till 2.30 on Monday, talking to the Anglo Saxon professor Tolkien, who came back with me to College from a society and sat discoursing of the gods and giants of Asgard for three hours, then departing in the wind and rain – who could turn him out, for the fire was bright and the talk good.'

It was the beginning of a friendship: the moment, as Lewis once remarked, when someone who has till then believed his feelings to be unique cries out, 'What? You too? I thought I was the only one.'

*

Tolkien entirely shared Lewis's love for 'Northernness'. He too had first discovered the taste in childhood[1] when he found in a book of

---

[1] Tolkien was an orphan. His father had died when he was four and his mother when he was twelve. For a brief summary of his early life see Appendix A. A full account is given in the present writer's *J. R. R. Tolkien: a biography* (1977).

fairy stories the tale of Sigurd the Völsung who slew the dragon Fafnir. Reading it, the young Tolkien fell under the spell of what he called 'the nameless North'. He 'desired dragons with a profound desire'. At school in Birmingham he taught himself the Norse language and began to read the myths and sagas in their original words. Like Lewis, he fell under the spell of William Morris. And, just as Lewis during adolescence had begun to write his own Norse-style poetry and drama, Tolkien at about the age of eighteen conceived the idea of recreating the 'Northern-ness' that delighted him by writing a cycle of myth and legend. But it was a far more ambitious task than anything Lewis attempted, for whereas Lewis had merely written a pastiche of existing Norse stories, Tolkien began to create a whole new mythology out of his imagination. And while Lewis soon passed on from his adolescent 'Northern' writings to other kinds of poetry, Tolkien continued to work at his cycle year after year. It remained the centre of his imaginative life.

During the First World War he began to write in prose form the tales which were the principal elements of his cycle, and by the time he moved from Leeds to Oxford in 1925 these tales had long since been sketched out. But he did not organise them into an entirely continuous or consistent narrative, partly because his attention was taken up with a series of invented languages which were closely related to the myth-ology, being spoken by 'elvish' peoples; in fact these languages and the need to provide a 'history' for them had been a major motive for beginning the whole project. Tolkien also delayed drawing up a finished version of *The Silmarillion,* as he came to call his cycle, because he wanted to recast two of the principal stories into verse. Like Lewis he regarded himself chiefly as a poet. During his time at Leeds he began to write two long narrative poems, one telling the story of Túrin Túram-bar the dragon-slayer and the other recounting the romantic tale of Beren and Lúthien, the mortal man and the elven maid whom he loves, and for whose sake he goes on a terrible quest.

Tolkien kept this occupation a very private matter, rarely mentioning it to anyone. In 1925 he did send parts of the two poems to a retired schoolmaster who had once taught him, and he was disappointed when they were criticised rather severely. For a long time afterwards he consulted nobody.

It was early in December 1929, a few days after their late-night conversation about the Norse gods and giants, that he decided to show the Beren and Lúthien poem to Lewis. It was very long and still unfinished; its title was 'The Gest of Beren and Lúthien', and it was in rhyming couplets. Here is part of the description, in the version Tolkien showed to Lewis, of the 'elder days' of the elven kingdom of Doriath:

> There once, and long and long ago,
> before the sun and moon we know
> were lit to sail above the world,
> when first the shaggy woods unfurled,
> and shadowy shapes did stare and roam
> beneath the dark and starry dome
> that hung above the dawn of Earth,
> the silences with silver mirth
> were shaken, and the rocks were ringing –
> the birds of Melian were singing,
> the first to sing in mortal lands.

On 7 December 1929 Lewis wrote to Tolkien:

My dear Tolkien,

Just a line to say that I sat up late last night and have read the *geste* as far as to where Beren and his gnomish allies defeat the patrol of the orcs above the sources of the Narog and disguise themselves in the reaf. I can quite honestly say that it is ages since I have had an evening of such delight: and the personal interest of reading a friend's work had very little to do with it – I should have enjoyed it just as well if I'd picked it up in a bookshop, by an unknown author. The two things that come out clearly are the sense of reality in the background and the mythical value: the essence of a myth being that it should have no taint of allegory to the maker and yet should *suggest* incipient allegories to the reader. So much at the first flush. Detailed criticisms (including grumbles at individual lines) will follow.

Yours,
C. S. Lewis.

When Lewis's 'detailed criticisms' of the poem arrived, Tolkien found that Lewis had, in jest, annotated its text as if it were a celebrated piece of ancient literature, already heavily studied by scholars with such names as 'Pumpernickel', 'Peabody', 'Bentley', and 'Schick'; he alleged that any weaknesses in Tolkien's verses were the result of scribal errors or corruptions in the manuscript. Sometimes Lewis actually suggested entirely new passages to replace lines he thought poor, and here too he ascribed his own versions to supposedly historical sources. For example, he suggested that the lines about the 'elder days' quoted above could be replaced by the following stanza of his own, which he described as 'the so called *Poema Historiale*, probably contemporary with the earliest MSS of the *geste*':

There was a time before the ancient sun
And swinging wheels of heaven had learned to run
More certainly than dreams; for dreams themselves
Had bodies then and filled the world with elves.
The starveling lusts whose walk is now confined
To darkness and the cellarage of the mind,
And shudderings and despairs and shapes of sin
Then walked at large and were not cooped within.
Thought cast a shadow: brutes could speak: and men
Get children on a star. For spirit then
Threaded a fluid world and dreamed it new
Each moment. Nothing was false or new.

Lines like these showed how greatly Lewis's poetic imagination differed from Tolkien's. Tolkien wrote unaffectedly and simply, sometimes lapsing into slack diction or banality but often producing lines that were terse and dramatic; his unadorned style showed no particular 'influence'. Lewis's lines – and indeed all his poems – were more complex philosophically and stylistically, and more sure in diction and metre, but they often hovered on the borders of pastiche. Perhaps it was Lewis's enormous knowledge of English poetry through the centuries that encouraged him to copy earlier models rather than to find a style of his own; at all events this fondness for pastiche was arguably the major reason why his poetry was in the end a failure.

Tolkien did not agree with all Lewis's emendations of his poem. When Lewis suggested that Tolkien's couplet 'Hateful thou art, O Land of Trees!/My flute shall fingers no more seize' would be better as 'Oh hateful land of trees, be mute!/My fingers, now forget the flute', Tolkien scribbled in the margin, 'Frightful 18th century!!!' Worse still, where Tolkien's lines describing the three great and sacred elvish jewels had read 'The peerless Silmarils; and three/alone he made', Lewis suggested that this would be better as 'The Silmarils, the shiners three'. Tolkien, upon reading this, contemptuously underlined the last three words and scribbled a large exclamation mark beside them. But he was greatly encouraged by Lewis's enthusiasm, and took considerable notice of his criticisms, marking for revision almost all the lines that Lewis thought were inadequate, and in a few cases actually adopting Lewis's proposed emendations, including several whole lines. Eventually, indeed, he came to rewrite the whole poem, renaming it 'The Lay of Leithian'; though this was chiefly because of a wish to harmonise it with later developments in *The Silmarillion*.

Tolkien now began to read more of *The Silmarillion* aloud to Lewis, having noticed that he had a fondness for being read to. So Lewis was

31

permitted to explore the vast imaginary terrain of 'Middle-earth', aided by the maps Tolkien had drawn to accompany the stories. Lewis was delighted, for Tolkien's poems and prose tales reminded him in many ways of the romantic writings of Malory and William Morris in which he and Arthur Greeves had revelled during adolescence. At the end of January 1930 he wrote to Greeves: 'Tolkien is the man I spoke of when we were last together – the author of the voluminous metrical romances and of the maps, companions to them, showing the mountains of Dread and Nargothrond the City of the Orcs. In fact he *is*, in one part of him, what we were.'

It was not a very accurate description of Tolkien's work. The stories were by no means all 'romances', and the majority were in prose and not 'metrical', while Nargothrond was a city not of orcs but of elves. Yet if Lewis was not precise in these details he was as enthusiastic as Tolkien could ever have hoped. And this enthusiasm proved to be crucial. 'The unpayable debt that I owe to him', Tolkien wrote of Lewis years later, 'was not "influence" as it is ordinarily understood, but sheer encouragement. He was for long my only audience. Only from him did I ever get the idea that my "stuff" could be more than a private hobby.' His growing friendship with Lewis was also deeply important to him for reasons quite apart from his literary work. His marriage, never easy, had begun to go through a long period of extreme difficulty caused largely by his wife's resentment of his Roman Catholicism, and by other factors that went back to the broken childhoods they had both endured in Birmingham. By 1929 the Tolkiens were bringing up four children at their north Oxford house, but this if anything increased rather than lessened the strains of their marriage. It was thus with much feeling that Tolkien wrote in his diary, 'Friendship with Lewis compensates for much.'

3
Mythopoeia

The friendship was not quite so important to Lewis as it was to Tolkien. Late in 1931 Lewis, writing to Arthur Greeves, described Tolkien as 'one of my friends of the second class'. In the first class, as he explained in the same letter, were Greeves himself and Owen Barfield.

To anyone studying Lewis's life, Arthur Greeves is constantly present in the background: a shadowy figure who actually played no part in the action but was the constant recipient of confidences and reflections from Lewis. There is in fact little to be said about him. His family were neighbours of the Lewises in Belfast. Arthur himself was slightly older than Jack Lewis but distinctly less mature: rather childlike, in fact, brought up in perpetual anxiety about his health and, because of his poor constitution and plentiful family funds, soon abandoning any attempt to earn his living. He was so different from Lewis that the friendship seems rather surprising, yet they corresponded regularly, Lewis using Greeves as a mixture of father-confessor and spiritual pupil. With Arthur Greeves he discussed, in adolescent days, questions relating to sex – Greeves later scored out these passages in the letters – and to Greeves he was also something like frank on the topic of Mrs Moore. In fact Greeves burnt several pages which may have contained a full account of Lewis's relationship with her. On the other hand he often lectured Greeves on weak spelling or poor morale, taking a condescending line with his friend. It was altogether an odd and distinctly schoolboyish correspondence.

Lewis's friendship with Owen Barfield was of a very different nature, for he regarded Barfield as in every way an intellectual equal and in some respects superior to himself. Of smaller and lighter build than Lewis, Barfield was lithe and nimble – he thought at one time of earning his living as a dancer – and though almost equally adept at logical argument he had none of Lewis's rather heavy-handed dogmatism.

Lewis and Barfield often took holidays together, and from 1927

33

onwards they went on a walking tour with a couple of friends almost every spring.

*

It was an idyllic way to spend three or four days. Footpaths were plentiful, motor traffic rarely disturbed the quiet of the countryside, roads were often unmetalled and comfortable to the feet, inns were numerous and cheap, so that reservations for the night were not often necessary, and pots of tea and even full meals could be bought in most villages for the smallest sums. Much of rural England was in fact still as it had been in the nineteenth century.

In April 1927 Lewis and Barfield, together with two friends from undergraduate days, Cecil Harwood and W. O. Field (known as 'Woff' from his initials), walked along the Berkshire and Wiltshire downs, through Marlborough and Devizes, and then across the edge of Salisbury Plain to Warminster. A year later their walking tour was across the Cotswolds, and in 1929 they made a four day journey from Salisbury to Lyme Regis. But though the route was different every year their habits were almost unvarying. They did not attempt to cover vast distances each day, in the manner of fanatical hikers – Lewis said he disliked the word 'hiking' because it was unnecessarily self-conscious for something so simple as going for a walk – but they certainly set a good pace, and would reckon to do perhaps twenty miles a day, maybe a little more on easy country or rather less if the going was rough. Lewis refused to allow the party to take packed meals, insisting on plenty of stops at pubs. He and his friends always made a mid-morning halt for beer or draught cider, and there was more beer at lunch time as an accompaniment to bread and cheese. Lunch was always concluded by a pot of tea, and more tea was drunk at an inn or cottage in mid-afternoon. Indeed Lewis cared for his tea just as much as for his beer, if not more so. Meals were simple but usually excellent. On Salisbury Plain in 1929 they were 'given tea by a postmistress, with boiled eggs and bread and jam ad lib., for which she wanted to take only sixpence', and for supper that night at Warminster they had 'ham and eggs, cider, bread, cheese, marmalade and tea'.

Sometimes things went wrong. Of the Cotswolds trip in 1928 Lewis reported to his brother: 'This time we committed the folly of selecting a billeting *area* for the night instead of one good town: i.e. we said "Well here are four villages within a mile of one another and the map marks an inn in each so we shall be sure to get somewhere." Your imagination can suggest what this results in by about eight o'clock of an evening, after twenty miles of walking, when one is just turning away from the first unsuccessful attempt and a thin cold rain is beginning to fall. Yet these hardships had their compensations: thin at the time, but very rich in memory. One never knows the snugness and beauty of an English village twilight so well as in the homelessness of such a moment: when the lights are beginning to show up in the cottage windows and one sees the natives clumping past to the pub – clouds meanwhile piling up "to weather" Our particular village was in a deep narrow valley with woods all round it and a rushing stream that grew louder as the night came on. Then comes the time when you have to strike a light (with difficulties) in order to read the maps: and when the match fizzles out, you realise for the first time how dark it really is: and as you go away, the village fixes itself in your mind – for enjoyment ten, twenty, or thirty years hence – as a place of impossible peace and dreaminess.'

Occasionally – very occasionally indeed – Lewis and his friends would abandon a walk because of bad weather. But nothing short of a continuous downpour would stop them. Lewis himself was particularly determined to carry on through all but impossible conditions, maintaining stoutly that every kind of weather has its attractions. On Exmoor in 1930 the companions woke up in the morning to find a thick fog. 'Some of the others were inclined to swear at it,' wrote Lewis, 'but I (and I soon converted Barfield) rejoiced to meet the moor at its grimmest. In the afternoon the fog thickened but we continued in spite of it to ascend Dunkery Beacon as we had originally intended. There was of course not a particle of view to be seen.'

He was similarly determined to enjoy every kind of landscape, however dull it might seem to other people. His brother Warnie recorded of a journey they made near Plymouth in 1933: 'We had a long, tiresome, and very hot walk of about ten miles in hot sunken lanes, from which one occasionally got a glimpse of a dull, commonplace countryside, peppered with bungalows. J. and I argued briskly about the country we had walked through, J. contending that not to like *any* sort of country argues a fault in oneself: which seems to me absurd. He also said that my description of what we had seen – "lacking in distinction" – was "almost blasphemous". But I suspect that he was talking for victory.'

There was a certain amount of this 'talking for victory' on the walking holidays, for Lewis liked to argue with his companions as they walked. They were all of them well matched. Lewis, writing to 'Woff' Field, defined their characteristics as 'Owen's dark, labyrinthine pertinacious arguments, my bow-wow dogmatism, Cecil's unmoved tranquillity, your needle-like or greyhound keenness'. But too much serious talk was discouraged. One year when Lewis's pupil Griffiths (later Dom Bede Griffiths) joined them, he offended protocol by engaging Barfield in a lengthy and profoundly serious theological battle. Equilibrium was badly upset, nor was it restored until the party had him cracking jokes along with the rest of them. The kind of day they really liked was one such as in Dorset when they 'got through the serious arguments in the ten miles before lunch and came down to mere fooling and school-boy jokes as the shadows lengthened.'

*

Lewis and Barfield were at this time engaged in a battle of ideas.

Barfield had for several years been a disciple of Rudolf Steiner's Anthroposophy, a form of religious philosophy which offers a very idiosyncratic account of the nature of the world and of the relationship between God and Man.[1] Lewis was at first alarmed at his friend's enthusiasm for Steiner's teachings, with their occasional use of the word 'occult' and their inclusion of such doctrines as a belief in reincarnation. But he discovered that at close quarters Anthroposophy radiated, at least in his opinion, what he called 'a re-assuring Germanic dullness which would soon deter those who were looking for thrills'. However, he was still disturbed that Barfield should adopt any kind of super-

---

[1] It is entirely unfair to Steiner and his followers to attempt to define Anthroposophy in one paragraph. Nevertheless here is a brief and highly simplified outline of its principal doctrines. (a) Human thought is part of a larger extrapersonal process. 'The idea which Plato conceived and the like idea which I conceive are not two ideas. It is one and the same idea . . . In the higher sense Plato's head and mine interpenetrate each other; all heads interpenetrate which grasp one and the same idea . . . and the heads all go to one and the same place in order to have this idea in them' (Rudolf Steiner, *Mystics of the Renaissance*, New York, 1911, pp. 27-8). (Compare Charles Williams's 'Co-inherence' which has certain similarities.) (b) The Darwinian view of physical evolution leading ultimately to human consciousness is wrong. Consciousness has evolved in quite a different way, through identifiable stages: (i) 'Original participation' in which there was an extrasensory link between man and the power that created him; (ii) the age of the 'Intellectual soul' (the Graeco-Roman period) in which conceptual thinking began and developed, leading to the stage where human thought was completely subjective; (iii) the age of the 'Consciousness soul', in which we still are at present; the human microcosm is now completely cut off from the macrocosm; this may lead to a too literal acceptance of the world as it appears to us, whereas what is needed is a movement towards (iv) 'Final participation' in which man regains his at-one-ment with the principle of creation, only now in full self-consciousness as a self-contained Ego. (c) This 'final participation' is to be achieved by man becoming more fully aware of the workings of the imagination – more specifically by turning his attention to direct inspiration and inner revelation or intuition. (d) Anthroposophy does not of itself demand any specific religious observances; Steiner interpreted Christianity in his own fashion, but did not in any way deny its fundamental truth, and many Anthroposophists are practising Christians of one denomination or another. For further discussions of Steiner's teaching see, of course, the works of Owen Barfield, especially *Romanticism Comes of Age* and *Saving the Appearances*.

naturalism, for he himself was trying to be utterly rational in his philosophical outlook and to exclude any notion of the 'other' from his view of the universe. He was prepared to admit the existence of the imaginative thrill or romantic longing which he had experienced since childhood, and which he called 'Joy'; but he refused to admit that it had anything to do with objective truth. He declared to Barfield: 'Imaginative vision cannot be invoked as a source of certainty – for any one judgment against another.' In other words, it was splendid to have sensations of delight when you saw a sunset or read a poem, but this told you nothing objective about the world. The imaginative must be kept strictly apart from the rational.

Barfield disagreed utterly. Besides following Steiner's teachings, he had for many years admired and studied Coleridge's writings on the Imagination; and he began to argue this point with Lewis, both on the walking tours and in a correspondence that they soon named 'The Great War'. In particular, Barfield tried to persuade Lewis that purely rational argument of the kind that he had used since he was tutored by Kirkpatrick often depended on artificial terms and had little to do with the actual business of life. Barfield also did his best to convince Lewis that imagination and aesthetic experience did lead, if not automatically to objective truth, then at least to a better understanding of the world.

Lewis did not accept all Barfield's points. But as a result of the 'Great War' he ceased to separate his emotional experiences from his intellectual process, and came to regard 'Joy' and poetic vision, in their way, as truthful as rational argument and objective fact.

*

If Greeves and Barfield were one degree higher than Tolkien in Lewis's hierarchy of friends, his brother Warnie was above even them.

After leaving school, Warnie had become an army cadet, and served in the Royal Army Service Corps for the entire First World War. After the war he remained in the army as a regular officer, serving in England and overseas, and using the Lewis family house in Belfast as a home base – for like Jack he had remained unmarried. In 1929 their father died, and the Belfast house was sold. As a result, Warnie needed another home, especially as he was approaching his middle thirties and planned to leave the army soon on retirement pay, which, together with small private means, would be sufficient to keep him. Jack and Mrs Moore invited him to make his home with them, and Warnie accepted readily, though privately there were feelings of caution on both sides. Warnie knew that 'Minto' could be very demanding, while she and Jack felt in their turn that it was a sacrifice of their privacy.

37

But the two brothers were chiefly delighted at the prospect of each other's company.

Warnie and Jack were fairly similar physically, both being heavily built with broad faces, though Warnie was more thickset and was tanned from his years abroad. They dressed similarly in baggy flannel trousers and tweed jackets, and they shared a liking for pipe tobacco and beer and country walks. Warnie's formal education had stopped far short of Jack's, but he kept up his reading and was widely know-ledgeable in English literature and even more so in French history, particularly of the seventeenth century. In English literature he regarded himself as a mere amateur, but his sheer enthusiasm, uncomplicated by any preconceived notions of what he ought or ought not to like, made him a discerning critic. Jack much appreciated this quality in his brother. After receiving a letter from Warnie on service abroad, enthusing about *The Faerie Queene*, he wrote to him: 'I wonder can you imagine how reassuring your bit about Spenser is to me who spend my time trying to get unwilling hobble-de-hoys to read poetry at all? One begins to wonder whether literature is not, after all, a failure. Then comes your account of the *Faerie Queene* on your office table, and one remembers that all the professed "students of literature" don't matter a rap.' In the next few years Jack Lewis was to develop a persona as the 'plain man' of literary criticism. Perhaps that role was influenced by the unaffectedly 'plain' qualities of his brother's taste.

Not that Warnie Lewis was in any sense intellectually crude. But there was something 'simple' about him in the best and most positive sense of the word. 'Dear Warnie,' Jack remarked to Arthur Greeves, 'he's one of the simplest souls I know in a way: certainly one of the best at getting simple pleasures.'

It was largely this quality of getting the best out of ordinary life that made Warnie Lewis a first-rate diarist. He kept a record of daily events intermittently throughout his adult years. Here, for example, is his entry for 21 December 1932, shortly after he had come from foreign service and had at last retired from the army:

To-day, I got up early, and went to the hall door where I found *The Times* containing the announcement which I have been dreaming of for years – 'Capt. W. H. Lewis retires on ret. pay (Dec. 21)'. And so, after eighteen years, two months, and twenty days, my sentence comes to an end, and I am able to say, like Wordsworth, that I have

> shaken off
> The heavy weight of many a weary day
> Not mine, and such as were not made for me.

But so far from grousing, I am deeply, and I hope devoutly thankful. It has been a good bargain: how many men are there, who, before they are forty, can struggle free, and begin the business of living?

In 1930 the Lewis-Moore ménage moved to the Kilns, a house at the foot of Shotover Hill not far outside Oxford city and on the edge of the village of Headington Quarry. The house was named after the brick kilns that stood nearby; the garden was the size of a small park, with eight acres of land rising steeply up a wooded hillside, and broken by a lake which could be used for bathing and even punting. Chiefly thanks to funds from the sale of the Belfast house, the Lewis brothers and Mrs Moore were able to raise the sum asked for the property, and it became their home late in 1930. After settling in with Jack and 'Minto', Warnie took stock of his new life, of the house in its idyllic setting, of the undeniable domestic tensions, and also of the pleasant daily routine that he envisaged. 'I reviewed the pros and cons', he wrote in his diary, 'and came to the conclusion that on balance, I prefer the Kilns at its worst to army life at its best: the only doubtful part being "Have I seen the Kilns at its worst?"'

*

By the beginning of September 1931 eleven years had passed since Jack Lewis had stopped being a dogmatic atheist.

As long ago as 1920 his study of philosophy had led him 'to postulate some sort of God as the least objectionable theory', though he added, 'of course we *know* nothing'. The notion of an ultimate truth made sense to him because, as he remarked in 1924 when commenting on Bertrand Russell's free-thinking idealism, 'our ideas are after all a natural product', and there must be some objective standard, some ultimate fact to explain them. On the other hand 'God' still seemed a crude and nursery-like word, and for several years Lewis used other terms to describe his notion of fundamental truth. During this time he was, like most of those who studied philosophy at Oxford in the early nineteen-twenties, still accepting the work of Hegel and his disciples, and as a result he chose Hegelian expressions such as 'the Absolute Mind' or just 'the Absolute'.

But when he spent the year 1924–5 teaching Philosophy at University College he discovered that this 'watered Hegelianism' was inadequate for tutorial purposes. The notion of an unspecified Absolute simply could not be made clear to his pupils. So he resorted to referring to fundamental truth as 'the Spirit', distinguishing this (though not really explaining how) from 'the God of popular religion', and emphasising that there was no possibility of being in a personal relationship with this

Spirit. Meanwhile he adopted a benevolent but condescending attitude to Christianity, which he said was a myth conveying as much of the truth as simple minds could grasp.

This was all very well, but among those 'simple minds' were men whose thinking he profoundly admired in other respects: Malory, Spenser, Milton, Donne and Herbert, Johnson, and the author whose romance *Phantastes* he had discovered in adolescence, George Mac-Donald. It was annoying to love the writings of these men without being able to accept the central premise of their thought, Christianity. Moreover, many of his friends were Christians. Tolkien was a Catholic, and Greeves and Coghill were Anglicans, while Barfield, though an Anthroposophist, accepted the principal ideas of Christianity. So, in the company of those whom he most liked, Lewis was the outsider.

His ideas changed again when, as a result of their 'Great War', Barfield managed to persuade him to accept the experience of 'Joy' as relevant to his thinking, and not to dismiss it as merely subjective emotional sensation. 'Joy was not a deception,' he now decided. 'Its visitations were rather the moments of clearest consciousness we had.'

He was going through this stage during 1926 and 1927, and the admission of something as irrational as Joy into his ruthlessly logical thinking threw him into confusion. 'All my ideas are in a crumbling state at present,' he wrote in his diary in May 1926. He realised that he had let his rational side dominate his emotions too long, remarking in the diary, 'One needn't be asking questions and giving judgments *all* the time.' But while this realisation was refreshing, he recorded (in January 1927) that he was frightened of what he called 'the danger of falling back into the most childish superstitions', by which he presumably meant belief in God and Christianity. He still had immense resistance to the idea of returning to anything so nursery-like.

Three weeks after this he stopped keeping a diary and never resumed, declaring that it was a foolish waste of time. It was also perhaps because he was unwilling to make public (he often read his diary to Mrs Moore and showed it to Warnie, so it was really a public document) the sensations of the supernatural which he was now experiencing; for he had begun to feel that it was not he himself who was taking the initiative but something outside him. As he expressed it to Owen Barfield, the 'Spirit' was 'showing an alarming tendency to become much more personal and is taking the offensive'. One day while going up Heading-ton Hill on a bus he 'became aware that I was holding something at bay, or shutting something out'. There was a choice to open the door or keep it shut. Next moment he found that he had chosen to open it. From this, which happened in 1927 or 1928, it was only a matter of time before he 'admitted that God was God', a step that he finally took in the summer of 1929. It was then that he 'gave in and knelt and prayed'. But even so he had done no more than accept Theism, a simple belief in God. He was not able to perceive the relevance of Christ's death and resurrection, and he told a friend, Jenkin: 'My outlook is now definitely religious. It is not precisely Christianity, though it may turn out that way in the end.'

*

Apart from the last stage, when he had admitted some kind of supernatural experience, Lewis had reached this position entirely through logical argument. Even his acceptance of 'Joy' as a factor had only been conceded after elaborate reasoning by Barfield. But now he began to realise that reasoning would not take him any further. The acceptance of God did not lead him automatically to the acceptance of Christianity. He was becoming certain that he wanted to accept it: he examined other religions, but found none that was acceptable; meanwhile his present state of simple Theism was inadequate. On the other hand he did not know how he could argue himself into specifically Christian beliefs. Even if he were to accept the historicity of the Christian story – and he could see no particular barrier to it – he could not understand how the death and resurrection of Christ were relevant to humanity.

*

By the time that Lewis had come to believe in God (but not yet in Christ), Owen Barfield had done something for him that would later bear fruit. He had shown Lewis that Myth has a central place in the whole of language and literature.

Barfield's arguments were printed in *Poetic Diction*, a short book by him that appeared in 1928 – though by that time Lewis knew its ideas well. Barfield examined the history of words, and came to the conclusion that mythology, far from being (as the philologist Max Müller called it) 'a disease of language', is closely associated with the very origin of all speech and literature. In the dawn of language, said Barfield, speakers did not make a distinction between the 'literal' and the 'metaphorical', but used words in what might be called a 'mythological' manner. For example, nowadays when we translate the Latin *spiritus* we have to render it either as 'spirit' or as 'breath' or as 'wind' depending on the context. But early users of language would not have made any such distinction between these meanings. To them a word like *spiritus* meant something like 'spirit-breath-wind'. When the wind blew, it was not merely 'like' someone breathing: it was the breath of a god. And when an early speaker talked about his soul as *spiritus* he did not merely mean that it was 'like' a breath: it was to him just that, the breath of life.

Mythological stories were simply the same thing in narrative form. In a world where every word carried some implication of the animate, and where nothing could be purely 'abstract' or 'literal', it was natural to tell tales about the gods who ruled the elements and walked the earth.

This, in greatly simplified form, is what Barfield argued in *Poetic Diction*. He was not the only person to come to this conclusion: for example in Germany, Ernst Cassirer had said much the same thing independently. But it was said with particular force by Barfield, and his book impressed not just Lewis but also Tolkien. Not long after the book's publication, Lewis reported to Barfield: 'You might like to know that when Tolkien dined with me the other night he said *à propos* of something quite different that your conception of the ancient semantic unity had modified his whole outlook and that he was always just going to say something in a lecture when your conception stopped him in time. "It is one of those things," he said "that when you've once seen it there are all sorts of things you can never say again." ' Perhaps it was as a result of reading Barfield's book that Tolkien made an inversion of Müller's remark. 'Languages', he declared, 'are a disease of mythology.'

So it was that by 1931 Lewis had come to understand that mythology has an important position in the history of thinking. It was a realisation that helped him across his last philosophical hurdle.

*

On Saturday 19 September 1931 Lewis invited two friends to dine with him in Magdalen. One was Tolkien. The other was Hugo Dyson.

Henry Victor Dyson Dyson, always known as 'Hugo', lectured in English Literature at Reading University. He was a couple of years older than Lewis. He had been severely wounded in the First World War, had read English at Oxford, and was a practising member of the Church of England. He was also exuberant and witty. Lewis had been introduced to him in July 1930 by Nevill Coghill, and 'liked him so much that I determined to get to know him better'. On further acquaintance he found Dyson to be 'a man who really loves truth: a philosopher and a religious man; who makes his critical and literary activities depend on the former – none of your dammed dilettanti'.

On this Saturday night in 1931, after they had dined, Lewis took his guests on a walk through the Magdalen grounds. They strolled along Addison's Walk (the path which runs beside several streams of the River Cherwell) and here they began to discuss metaphor and myth.

Lewis had never underestimated the power of myth. Far from it, for one of his earliest loves had been the Norse myth of the dying god

Balder. Now, Barfield had shown him the crucial role that mythology had played in the history of language and literature. But he still did not *believe* in the myths that delighted him. Beautiful and moving though such stories might be, they were (he said) ultimately untrue. As he expressed it to Tolkien, myths are 'lies and therefore worthless, even though breathed through silver'.

No, said Tolkien. *They are not lies.*

Just then (Lewis afterwards recalled) there was 'a rush of wind which came so suddenly on the still, warm evening and sent so many leaves pattering down that we thought it was raining. We held our breath.'

When Tolkien resumed, he took his argument from the very thing that they were watching.

You look at trees, he said, and call them 'trees', and probably you do not think twice about the word. You call a star a 'star', and think nothing more of it. But you must remember that these words, 'tree', 'star', were (in their original forms) names given to these objects by people with very different views from yours. To you, a tree is simply a vegetable organism, and a star simply a ball of inanimate matter moving along a mathematical course. But the first men to talk of 'trees' and 'stars' saw things very differently. To them, the world was alive with mythological beings. They saw the stars as living silver, bursting into flame in answer to the eternal music. They saw the sky as a jewelled tent, and the earth as the womb whence all living things have come. To them, the whole of creation was 'myth-woven and elf-patterned'.

This was not a new notion to Lewis, for Tolkien was, in his own manner, expressing what Barfield had said in *Poetic Diction*. Nor, said Lewis, did it effectively answer his point that myths are lies.

But, replied Tolkien, man is not ultimately a liar. He may pervert his thoughts into lies, but he comes from God, and it is from God that he draws his ultimate ideals. Lewis agreed: he had, indeed, accepted something like this notion for many years. Therefore, Tolkien continued, not merely the abstract thoughts of man *but also his imaginative inventions* must originate with God, and must in consequence reflect something of eternal truth. In making a myth, in practising 'mythopoeia' and peopling the world with elves and dragons and goblins, a storyteller, or 'sub-creator' as Tolkien liked to call such a person,[1] is actually fulfilling God's purpose, and reflecting a splintered fragment of the true light. Pagan myths are therefore never just 'lies': there is always something of the truth in them.

---

[1] '*Sub*-creator' in that he is under God, the prime Creator. For Tolkien's exposition of this term, and for a full account of his views about the truth of myth, see his essay 'On Fairy-Stories', which is printed in *Essays Presented to Charles Williams* (ed. C. S. Lewis) and in Tolkien's own *Tree and Leaf*.

They talked on, until Lewis was convinced by the force of Tolkien's argument. But he had another question to put to his friends, and as it was late they decided to go indoors to Lewis's rooms on Staircase III of New Buildings. There, he recorded, 'we continued on Christianity'.

*

Lewis had a particular reason for holding back from Christianity. He did not think it was necessarily untrue: indeed he had examined the historicity of the Gospels, and had come to the conclusion that he was '*nearly* certain that it really happened'. What was still preventing him from becoming a Christian was the fact that he found it irrelevant.

As he himself put it, he could not see 'how the life and death of Someone Else (whoever he was) two thousand years ago could help us here and now – except in so far as his example could help us'. And he knew that Christ's example as a man and a teacher was not the centre of the Christian story. 'Right in the centre,' he said, 'in the Gospels and in St Paul, you keep on getting something quite different and very mysterious, expressed in those phrases I have so often ridiculed – "propitiation" – "sacrifice" – "the blood of the Lamb".' He had ridiculed them because they seemed not only silly and shocking but meaningless. What was the point of it all? How could the death and resurrection of Christ have 'saved the world'?

Tolkien answered him immediately. Indeed, he said, the solution was actually a development of what he had been saying earlier. Had he not shown how pagan myths were, in fact, God expressing himself through the minds of poets, and using the images of their 'mythopoeia' to express fragments of his eternal truth? Well then, Christianity (he said) is exactly the same thing – with the enormous difference that the poet who invented it was God Himself, and the images He used were real men and actual history.

Do you mean, asked Lewis, that the death and resurrection of Christ is the old 'dying god' story all over again?

Yes, Tolkien answered, except that here is a *real* Dying God, with a precise location in history and definite historical consequences. The old myth has become a fact. But it still retains the character of a myth. So that in asking what it 'meant', Lewis was really being rather absurd. Did he ask what the story of Balder or Adonis or any of the other dying gods in pagan myth 'meant'? No, of course not. He enjoyed these stories, 'tasted' them, and got something from them that he could not get from abstract argument. Could he not transfer that attitude, that appreciation of *story*, to the life and death of Christ? Could he not treat it *as* a story, be fully aware that he could draw nourishment from it which he could never find in a list of abstract truths? Could he not realise that it *is* a myth, and make himself receptive to it? For, Tolkien said, if God is mythopoeic, man must become mytho*pathic*.

*

It was now 3 a.m., and Tolkien had to go home. Lewis and Dyson came downstairs with him. They crossed the quadrangle and let him out by the little postern gate on Magdalen Bridge. Then, Lewis recorded, 'Dyson and I found more to say to one another, strolling up and down the cloister of New Building, so that we did not get to bed till 4.'

Twelve days later Lewis wrote to Arthur Greeves: 'I have just passed on from believing in God to definitely believing in Christ – in Christianity. I will try to explain this another time. My long night talk with Dyson and Tolkien had a good deal to do with it.'

4

'The sort of thing a man might say'

Actually it was not quite so easy or so sudden as that. Arthur Greeves wrote to Lewis saying he was delighted that his friend had at last accepted Christianity. After reading this letter from Greeves, Lewis began to feel that 'perhaps I had said too much'. He told Greeves cautiously: 'Perhaps I was not nearly as clear on the subject as I had led you to think. But I certainly have moved *a bit*, even if it turns out to be a less bit than I thought.'

He had in fact reached the point where rational argument failed, and it became a matter of belief rather than of logical proof. Tolkien and Dyson's argument about Christianity as 'a true myth which is nevertheless a myth' had a lot of imaginative force, but it was a questionable proposition in terms of strict logic.

Lewis could not go on thinking it over for ever. He realised that some sort of 'leap of faith' was necessary to get him over the final hurdle. 'There must', he said, 'perhaps always be just enough lack of demonstrative certainty to make free choice possible, for what could we do but accept if the faith were like the multiplication table?'

So he became a Christian. He made his Communion for the first time since childhood days on Christmas Day 1931, in his parish church at Headington Quarry. But he did not forget to maintain in his mind the distinction between the two questions: the existence of God, which he believed he could prove by logical argument, and the truth of Christianity, which he realised was not subject to rational proof. Indeed his doubts about the Christian story never entirely ceased. There were, he remarked, many moments at which he felt 'How could I – I of all people – ever have come to believe this cock and bull story?' But this, he felt, was better than the error of taking it all for granted. Nor was he utterly alarmed at the notion that Christianity might after all be untrue. 'Even assuming (which I most constantly deny)', he said, 'that the doctrines of historic Christianity are merely mythical, it is the myth which is the vital and nourishing element in the whole concern.[1]

*

One reason for Lewis's holding back from conversion for so long was his inability to find the Gospel story attractive. It evoked none of the imaginative response that was aroused in him by pagan myths. As he told Greeves, 'the *spontaneous* appeal of the Christian story is so much less to me than that of Paganism'. This was perhaps one reason why he now began to create his own fictional setting for Christianity.

He had already made two attempts to write an account of his conversion. The first, in prose, had been begun while he was a Theist but not yet a Christian, and it was soon abandoned. In the spring of 1932, shortly after returning to the practice of Christianity, he tried again, this time in verse. But again he quickly abandoned the project. Then, in August of the same year, he suddenly found the right method.

He had been at work for some time on a projected book about the allegorical love-poetry of the Middle Ages, and in consequence he had made a thorough study of the workings of allegory. Though Bunyan's *Pilgrim's Progress* was outside the scope of his project, he had known and loved it since childhood, and now its example rose before him. While staying with Arthur Greeves in Belfast he began to write what he called *The Pilgrim's Regress: An Allegorical Apology for Christianity, Reason, and Romanticism*. As he himself said of Bunyan's book, 'Now, as never before, the whole man was engaged'. In a fortnight this witty and often moving allegory of a modern pilgrim's journey to Christianity was finished.

The writing of stories in prose came almost incredibly easy to Lewis. 'It's such fun after sweating over verse,' he said, 'like free-wheeling.' He worked fast, managed to write almost everything in one draft, and never made more than minimal revisions. This was in marked contrast to Tolkien who, though he *wrote* fast, took endless pains over revision

---

[1] For a full exposition of Lewis's views on the Christian story as myth-that-is-true, see his article 'Myth became Fact', printed in the collection of his essays entitled *Undeceptions*, which is known in America as *God in the Dock*. Owen Barfield remarks, in a letter to the present writer: 'The proposition, that in the Incarnation and Resurrection, "myth became fact", is simply taken for granted by every Anthroposophist, and had been so for years before Lewis's essay. It would be an accurate sub-title for Rudolf Steiner's book *Christianity as Mythical Fact*, published in German in 1902.'

G. K. Chesterton expounds the view that pagan mythologies express in crude form some fragment of divine truth in the fifth chapter of *The Everlasting Man*. Austin Farrer explores the notion of Christianity as a 'true myth' in his essay 'Can Myth be Fact?', printed in *Interpretation and Belief* (1976).

and regarded it as a continuing process that was not necessarily complete when the book was published. The two men were also very different in their attitudes to the manuscripts of their work. Tolkien invariably kept all his drafts and his notes; Lewis just as invariably tore his up as soon as the book reached print. He also tore up other people's. Tolkien recalled: 'He was indeed accustomed at intervals to throw away papers and books – and at such times he destroyed those that belonged to other people. He "lost" not only official documents sent to him by me, but sole MSS. of at least two stories.'

The most important fact about *The Pilgrim's Regress* is one that can easily be missed because it is so obvious. Less than a year after he had become a Christian, Lewis already felt capable of telling other people about his own experiences, capable of being an 'apologist', a defender of Christianity by argument. There was to be no novitiate, no period in which he would wait for his understanding of his religion to mature and deepen. He must begin right away.

Nor was the book just to be a defence of Christianity. In it he also championed the two things which he believed had helped him along the road to belief: Reason, and 'Romanticism', by which he specifically meant the search for 'Joy'. And in defending these two things he launched, in *The Pilgrim's Regress*, a forceful and often bitter attack against almost every other form of thinking current in his time. For in describing the snares which the pilgrim encounters on his journey, Lewis enumerates not only traditional intellectual or emotional dangers (Ignorantia, Superbia, Orgiastica, Occultica, and so on) but also brings more contemporary enemies into the tale. At least, to him they were enemies.

Lewis had conceived a profound dislike not merely for T. S. Eliot's poetry but for the whole modernist movement in the arts. In *The Pilgrim's Regress* his hero lands in the middle of 'the Clevers', allegorical figures representing what Lewis thought were the objectionable features of the nineteen-twenties art forms. In a later edition of the book he added running headlines identifying the various members of the Clevers as 'The poetry of the Silly Twenties', 'The swamp-literature of the Dirty Twenties', and 'The gibberish-literature of the Lunatic Twenties'. And it is not only the arts that come under attack in the book. Freudianism and Marxism are among the many other dangers that the pilgrim encounters, and Lewis's feelings towards the whole era are summed up at the moment in the story when Reason attacks and slays the *Zeitgeist* or Spirit of the Age.

After the pilgrim has escaped from 'darkest Zeitgeistheim' he spends the night at the house of 'Mr Sensible', a learned but utterly shallow dilettante who undoubtedly represents Lewis's view of many of his

3 (a) J. R. R. Tolkien, circa 1935.

3 (b) C. S. Lewis, circa 1935.

4 (a) Owen Barfield and C. S.
Lewis, circa 1950.

4 (b) Addison's Walk, in the
grounds of Magdalen
College, Oxford: the
scene of Lewis's 'long
night talk' with Tolkien
and Dyson.

Oxford colleagues – well-read men, able to produce witty aphorisms for every occasion, but adhering to no religion or philosophy and living a shallow life; the kind of man in fact that Lewis was thinking of when he said that, in contrast, Hugo Dyson was 'none of your damned dilettanti'. Then, from the house of Mr Sensible, the pilgrim John journeys into sterner regions of the mind; and here the book launches an attack on another of Lewis's enemies.

Sheltering in a hut and attempting to survive by extreme asceticism are three Pale Men, 'Humanist', 'Neo-Classical', and 'Neo-Angular'. The first two profess no religion, but Neo-Angular is a believer in 'the Landlord', the figure that stands for God in the allegory. His practice of religion, however, is a very different thing from the orthodoxy which John eventually embraces. 'My ethics are based on dogma, not on feeling,' he tells John, and he disapproves of John's search for 'the Island', the allegorical representation of 'Joy', telling him that it is the wrong reason for the pilgrimage. He also declares that John should not speak directly to 'Mother Kirk' (the Church) but should 'learn from your superiors the dogmata in which her deliverances have been codified for general use'. Lewis explained this part of the allegory in a letter to a friend: 'What I am attacking in Neo-Angular is a set of people who seem to me to be trying to make of Christianity itself one more highbrow, Chelsea, bourgeois-baiting fad. T. S. Eliot is the single man who sums up the thing I am fighting against.'

Eliot's conversion to Christianity had by this time become a matter of public knowledge, but it had not endeared him to Lewis, who felt that Eliot's form of religion was 'High and Dry', not merely sectarian in its Anglo-Catholicism but also emotionally barren and counter-romantic. So in *The Pilgrim's Regress* a character dismisses the fact that Neo-Angular is a Christian by suggesting that he may be only 'poacher turned gamekeeper'.

The book's title is explained in the last section. John the pilgrim, after crossing by Mother Kirk's aid the chasm of original sin, has no sooner become regenerate as a Christian than he is told to retrace his steps. This he does, passing once more through the regions of the mind and seeing them for the delusions they really were. He comes at last to his childhood home of Puritania, and it is from the gate of his parents' cottage that he finally climbs the foothills towards the mountain where stands the Landlord's Castle, the City of God. He has come at last to true 'Joy', and has found it in – of all places – the religion of his childhood.

This element of revisiting childhood, combined with the attack on contemporary ideas, did not escape the notice of the critics. 'Though Mr Lewis's parable claims to reassert romanticism,' remarked *The Times*

Literary Supplement reviewer when the story was published in 1933, 'it is the romanticism of homesickness for the past, not of adventure towards the future, a "Regress" as he candidly avows.'

Among Lewis's friends there was one who gradually began to think that the book's title was particularly significant, though in rather a different way. Tolkien admired *The Pilgrim's Regress*, but many years later he wrote of it: 'It was not for some time that I realized that there was more in the title *Pilgrim's Regress* than I had understood (or the author either, maybe). Lewis would regress. He would not re-enter Christianity by a new door, but by the old one: at least in the sense that in taking it up again he would also take up, or reawaken, the prejudices so sedulously planted in boyhood. He would become again a Northern Ireland protestant.'

*

Was Lewis an Ulster Protestant? In *Surprised by Joy* he denies that he had been brought up in any particularly puritanical form of religion, and he was very angry when a Catholic publisher who reissued *The Pilgrim's Regress* identified 'Puritania' with Ulster. 'My father', declared Lewis, 'was, by nineteenth-century and Church of Ireland standards, rather "high".' However, his diary of life at Wynyard School, written when he was ten years old, gives a rather different impression:

> We were obliged to go to St John's (Watford), a church which wanted to be Roman Catholic, but was afraid to say so. A kind of church abhorred by respectful [*sic*] Irish Protestants. In this abominable place of Romish hypocrites and English liars, the people cross themselves, bow to the Lord's Table (which they have the vanity to call an altar), and pray to the Virgin.

Twenty-two years later when Lewis resumed the practice of religion he was still rather evangelical in his approach, making his Communion only at major festivals and generally preferring to attend Matins. After a time he increased his frequency of Communion to monthly intervals. Eventually he adopted the habit of communicating weekly and on major saints' days. Indeed as the years passed he became distinctly more 'Catholic' in his practices. He began to make regular confessions, and came to believe in the importance of prayers for departed souls. Yet these things did not play a large part in his religious thought, or at least not in his Christian writings, where he rarely discussed them. Indeed, he tried to avoid anything that would classify him as 'Anglo-Catholic' or 'Evangelical'. He hated such terms and maintained that to say that you were High Church or Low Church was to be wickedly schismatical.

For him, the real distinction lay elsewhere, not between High and Low at all but between religious belief that was orthodox and supernatural on the one hand, and 'liberal' and 'demythologised' on the other. He had been on a long journey before he arrived at Christianity, and now that he had arrived he was determined to accept the traditional doctrines of the Church; he wanted not to argue about them or to reinterpret them but to defend them. As a result he was highly critical of the 'broad church' as he called it, the liberalism which he believed to be the canker in modern Christianity. Among the targets for attack in *The Pilgrim's Regress* is 'Mr Broad', who though a 'Steward' (a clergyman) doubts the necessity of actual conversion. 'I wouldn't for the world hold you back,' he tells John. 'At the same time there is a very real danger at your age of trying to make these things too definite. These great truths need reinterpretation in every age.' Lewis thought he saw this attitude growing in the contemporary church, and he took a stand firmly in opposition. For him, the great truths did *not* need reinterpretation. They needed to be championed, to be defended as much against 'liberalisers' as against unbelievers. In this attitude he was in agreement with two ultra-orthodox defenders of the faith, G. K. Chesterton, whose apologetic writings had been an influence on him during his conversion, and Tolkien.

Tolkien was a devout Roman Catholic. He had hoped that Lewis too might become a Catholic, and he was disappointed that he had returned to membership of the Church of England (the equivalent of the Church of Ireland in which Lewis had been baptised). Tolkien was strongly unsympathetic towards the Church of England, not least because during his childhood his own mother, a Catholic convert, had been treated harshly by relatives who belonged to it – indeed he believed that this 'persecution' had hastened her death. As a result he was particularly sensitive to any shade of anti-Catholic prejudice.

Unfortunately Lewis retained more than a trace of the Belfast Protestant attitude to Catholics. In unguarded moments he and his brother Warnie might refer to Irish Catholics as 'bog-trotters' or 'bog-rats', and, though they usually avoided such crude remarks in Tolkien's presence, there were moments of tension. 'We were coming down the steps from Magdalen hall,' Tolkien recalled, 'long ago in the days of our unclouded association, before there was anything, as it seemed, that must be withheld or passed over in silence. I said that I had a special devotion to St John. Lewis stiffened, his head went back, and he said in the brusque harsh tones which I was later to hear him use again when dismissing something he disapproved of: "I can't imagine any two persons more dissimilar." We stumped along the cloisters, and I followed feeling like a shabby little Catholic caught by the eye of an

51

"Evangelical clergyman of good family"[1] taking holy water at the door of a church. A door had slammed. Never now should I be able to say in his presence:

> Bot Crystes mersy and Mary and Jon,
> Thise arn the grounde of alle my blysse

– *The Pearl*, 383–4; a poem that Lewis disliked[2] – and suppose that I was sharing anything of my vision of a great rood-screen through which one could see the Holy of Holies.'

Tolkien wrote this thirty years later, when other events had soured his recollections. In the early days of the friendship such moments were rare, and for the most part he was profoundly grateful for Lewis's conversion. In October 1933 he wrote in his diary that friendship with Lewis, 'besides giving constant pleasure and comfort, has done me much good from the contact with a man at once honest, brave, intellectual – a scholar, a poet, and a philosopher – and a lover, at least after a long pilgrimage, of Our Lord'.

*

'On Saturday last, I started to say my prayers again after having discontinued doing so for more years than I care to remember: this was no sudden impulse, but the result of a conviction of the truth of Christianity which has been growing on me for a considerable time.'

This was written not by Jack Lewis but by his brother Warnie. During the months when Jack was returning to Christianity, Warnie too was resuming the religious beliefs and practices of his childhood. Like Jack he had in boyhood drifted away from the Church. Now in 1931 his return to Christianity was different in manner from his brother's. He indulged in few philosophical speculations, merely recording in his diary that his new-found belief was 'a conviction for which I admit I should be hard put to find a logical proof, but which rests on the inherent improbability of the whole of existence being fortuitous, and the inability of the materialists to provide any convincing explanation of the origin of life'.

While he was at home at the Kilns early in 1931, Warnie went to Matins at the local church with Jack. But the brothers scarcely discussed their changing views, and soon afterwards Warnie was posted to

[1] Lewis's own term (intended a little sarcastically) for his own grandfather, in *Letters to Malcolm, Chiefly on Prayer*, Chapter 2. It ought to be added that in the next chapter of that book Lewis says that he has no objection to devotions to saints, though he adds 'I am not thinking of adopting the practice myself.'
[2] But Lewis does quote from *The Pearl* at the head of Chapter 8 of *Surprised by Joy*.

Shanghai for his final months of army service. It was there, and without any knowledge that his brother was doing the same, that he made his Communion for the first time for many years on Christmas Day 1931. A few weeks later a letter from Jack reported that he too had made his Communion on that day. 'I am delighted,' Warnie wrote in his diary. 'Had he not done so I, with my altered views, would have found – hardly a barrier between us, but a lack of complete identity of interest which I should have regretted.' Jack, when he learnt of Warnie's full return to Christianity, made the same comment: 'What a mercy that the change in his views (I mean as regards religion) should have happened in time to meet mine – it would be awkward if one of us were still in the old state of mind.'

The brothers' new 'identity of interest' was reflected when, after Warnie's retirement from the army and his return to the Kilns as a permanent member of the household, the two of them almost immediately set off on a walking tour, their first together, up the Wye Valley. Warnie, despite his army training, was nervous about carrying a heavy pack for twenty miles or more a day, but he was soon being pleasantly surprised at the ease of it all, and at the end of their journey he judged it to be one of the best holidays he had ever had. This was in January 1933, and for many years afterwards a January walking tour was a regular fixture for the two brothers, quite independent of Jack's annual walk with Barfield and the other friends of that set, which usually took place just after Easter. Warnie and Jack were at their happiest on these walks, talking about anything from beer to theology. 'We discussed', Warnie noted in January 1935 when he and Jack were walking in the Chilterns, 'how useful it would be if there were a *beer map* of England, showing the areas controlled by each Beer Baron.' Another day they argued about the nature of personal immortality. Warnie was less well-read than Jack, but with his speculative imagination and his common sense he was an excellent companion for his brother.

At home too they spent a lot of time together. In term, Jack now slept in his college rooms, partly so that he could go to chapel early in the morning and begin work immediately after breakfast. (Mrs Moore declared herself to be an atheist and was inclined to mock at the brothers' return to Christianity.) But in the afternoons Jack came out to the Kilns, where he and Warnie took the family dogs for a walk, or worked in the garden, rebuilding paths and planting saplings, which they called 'public works'. Warnie had a bedroom at the Kilns, but he kept most of his books in Magdalen, in one of his brother's two sitting-rooms; and he usually spent the morning there, sorting out and typing transcripts of the Lewis family papers, a task that took him several years. In fact it became his chief occupation, for his army pension together with small private means meant that he did not need to take a paid job. He was able to spend much of his time going to concerts, and reading, which he did a great deal. He also got to know Jack's friends when they dropped in at Magdalen.

He was typing one morning in February 1933 when (he wrote in his diary) 'in came J's friend Dyson from Reading – a man who gives the impression of being made of quick silver: he pours himself into a room on a cataract of words and gestures, and you are caught up in the stream – but after the first plunge, it is exhilarating. I was swept along by him to the Mitre Tap in the Turl (a distinct discovery this, by the way) where we had two glasses of Bristol Milk apiece and discussed China, Japan, staff officers, Dickens, house property as an investment, and, most utterly unexpected, "Your favourite reading's *Orlando Furioso* isn't it?" (deprecatory gesture as I got ready to deny this). "Sorry! Sorry! my mistake." As we left the pub, a boy came into the yard and fell on the cobbles. Dyson (appealingly): "Don't do that my boy: it hurts you and distresses us." '

Hugo Dyson, on his visits to Oxford from Reading, became a frequent and most welcome interrupter of Warnie Lewis's mornings: 'At about half past eleven when I was at work in the front room in College, in burst Dyson in his most exuberant mood. He began by saying that it was such a cold morning that we would have to adjourn almost immediately to get some brandy. I pointed out to him that if he was prepared to accept whiskey as an alternative, it was available in the room. Having sniffed it he observed "it would be unpardonable rudeness to your brother to leave any of this" and emptied the remains of the decanter into the glass. After talking very loudly and amusingly for some quarter of an hour, he remarked airily "I suppose we can't be heard in the next room?" then having listened for a moment, "Oh, it's all right, it's the pupil talking – your brother won't want to listen to him anyway". He next persuaded me to walk round to Blackwell's with him, and here he was the centre of attraction to a crowd of undergraduates. Walking up to the counter he said: "I want a second hand so-and-so's Shakespeare; have you got one?" The assistant: "Not a *second hand* one, sir, I'm afraid." Dyson (impatiently): "Well, take a copy and rub it on the floor, and sell it to me as shop soiled." '

*

Tolkien too was a regular caller while Warnie Lewis was at work in Magdalen. He and Jack were in the habit of spending an hour together on Monday mornings, generally concluding their conversation with a pint of beer in the Eastgate Hotel opposite the college. 'This is one of the pleasantest spots in the week,' remarked Jack. 'Sometimes we talk

English School politics; sometimes we criticize one another's poems; other days we drift into theology or "the state of the nation"; rarely we fly no higher than bawdy or puns.'

By 'bawdy' Lewis meant not obscene stories but rather old-fashioned barrack-room jokes and songs and puns. For example, he greatly relished one of his pupils' perfectly serious description of courtly love as 'a vast medieval erection', and in meetings of the Coalbiters he and the other members of that club listened with delight to scurrilous jests composed in Icelandic by Tolkien, who was a past master of bawdy in several languages. Lewis believed that to be acceptable, bawdy 'must have nothing cruel about it. It must not approach anything near the pornographic. Within these limits I think it is a good and wholesome *genre.'*

As to 'English School politics', these became less turbulent after 1931 when – chiefly thanks to Lewis's part in the campaign – Tolkien's syllabus reforms were accepted by the Faculty, with the result that the Anglo-Saxon and Middle English parts of the course became much more attractive to undergraduates, and the study of Victorian literature was virtually abandoned. Lewis was delighted at this victory, which as he put it 'my party and I have forced upon the junto after hard fighting'.

Shortly after the new syllabus was put into effect, Lewis and Tolkien were both doing duty as examiners in the English School, together with Tolkien's friend and former colleague from Leeds, E. V. Gordon. Lewis lost no opportunity of writing a jibe in the *Beowulf* metre at the two philologists' performance in the *viva voce* examination sessions:

> Two at the table in their talk borrowed
> Gargantua's mouth. Gordon and Tolkien
> Had will to repeat well-nigh the whole
> That they of Verner's law and of vowel sorrows,
> Cares of consonants, and case endings,
> Heard by hearsay.
>   Never at board I heard
> Viler vivas.

'In fact', Tolkien remarked of these lines, 'during the sessions C. S. L.'s voice was the one most often heard.'

Outside term time, Tolkien and Lewis sometimes went for afternoon walks together. Warnie Lewis liked to enjoy as much of his brother's company as possible, and he was not always pleased about this. 'Confound Tolkien!' he wrote in his diary on one such occasion. 'I seem to see less and less of J. every day.' Knowing Warnie's feelings, Jack took a great deal of trouble not to leave his brother out of anything and, when Tolkien and he decided to spend an evening reading aloud the libretto of Wagner's *Die Walküre*, Warnie was asked to join them even though he knew no German and could only take part by using an English translation. They began after tea, broke off for supper at the Eastgate – 'where we had fried fish and a savoury omelette, with beer' – and then returned to Jack's rooms in Magdalen 'and finished our play (and incidentally the best part of a decanter of very inferior whiskey),' recorded Warnie. 'Arising from the perplexities of Wotan we had a long and interesting discussion on religion which lasted until about half past eleven.'[1]

Warnie was with Jack at a dinner in July 1933 when Tolkien and Hugo Dyson acted as joint hosts at Exeter College, of which they were both old members. 'Dyson and Tolkien were in exuberant form,' recorded Warnie. 'I should like to have seen more of a man on the opposite side of the table, Coghill: big, pleasant, good looking.' Later 'the party broke up, Tolkien, Dyson, J., a little unobtrusive clergyman, and myself walking back to Magdalen where we strolled about in the grove, where the deer were flitting about in the twilight – Tolkien swept off his hat to them and remarked "Hail fallow well met".'

There were also quite a few gatherings of this sort at which Warnie Lewis was not present. The English School 'junto' led by Lewis and Tolkien began to hold informal dinners. This was quite a large group, known as 'the Cave' and including a number of college tutors besides the nucleus of Lewis and his friends.[2] Sometimes a similar group, 'the Oyster Club', would gather to celebrate the end of examination-marking by eating oysters. Meanwhile the Coalbiters continued to meet, until at last they had read the major Icelandic sagas and both Eddas, when they were dissolved.

Such semi-formal groups were a regular feature of Oxford life, and there was certainly nothing remarkable about them. Nor was there anything particularly notable about a literary society in which Lewis and Tolkien were both involved for a few terms. It met at University College, where Lewis still taught a few pupils (though in English Literature now, rather than Philosophy). Its founder and organiser, like

[1] Priscilla Tolkien recalls that her father and Lewis also attended a performance of one of the *Ring* operas at Covent Garden, where they found themselves to be almost the only members of the audience in their part of the theatre not in evening dress.

[2] The Cave was named after the Cave of Adullam in which David organised the conspiracy against Saul (I Samuel xxii, 1–2), the implication being that Lewis's junto was conspiring against what had been, at least until 1931, the reigning party in the English School, and in particular David Nichol Smith the Professor of English Literature. The Cave's members included Lewis, Tolkien, Coghill, Dyson, Leonard Rice-Oxley, and H. F. B. Brett-Smith. It was still in existence during the nineteen-forties.

most of the members, was an undergraduate, Edward Tangye Lean, who edited the university magazine *Isis* and published a couple of novels while still studying for his degree. There were also a few dons present at the meetings. The club existed so that members could read unpublished compositions aloud, and ask for comments and criticisms. Tangye Lean named it 'The Inklings'.

No record of its proceedings survives, though Tolkien recalled that in its original form the club soon died, probably when Tangye Lean left Oxford in 1933 for a career in journalism and broadcasting. Tolkien also remembered that among the unpublished works read aloud at its meetings was his own poem 'Errantry'. That poem (which begins 'There was a merry passenger, A messenger, a mariner') was published soon afterwards in the *Oxford Magazine*. Warnie Lewis read it, admired it, and declared it to be 'a real discovery', not least because of its unusual metre. Meanwhile Jack Lewis had recently finished reading a longer work by Tolkien. On 4 February 1933 he wrote to Arthur Greeves: 'Since term began I have had a delightful time reading a children's story which Tolkien has just written. I have told you of him before: the one man absolutely fitted, if fate had allowed, to be a third in our friendship in the old days, for he also grew up on W. Morris and George MacDonald. Reading his fairy tale has been uncanny – it is so exactly like what we would both have longed to write (or read) in 1916: so that one feels he is not making it up but merely describing the same world into which all three of us have the entry.' The story was called *The Hobbit*.

Tolkien had invented it partly to amuse his own children, and certainly without any serious thought of publication. He had not even bothered to finish typing out a fair copy, but had left it broken off some way before the end. Lewis, much as he liked the story, was by no means certain of the measure of Tolkien's achievement. 'Whether it is really *good*', he remarked to Greeves, 'is of course another question: still more, whether it will succeed with modern children.'

*

Tolkien ought, on the face of it, to have been an ideal companion for Lewis and Barfield on their walking tours. But when he did accompany them he found that twenty miles or so a day, carrying a heavy pack, was more than he liked.[1] Tolkien's own idea of a walk in the countryside involved frequent stops to examine plants or insects, and this

[1] This walk took place in April 1937, and was in the West Country, where the party walked in the Quantocks. The date is known from a postcard sent by Tolkien to his daughter Priscilla, who believes that her father also joined Lewis for another walking tour, to Lyme Regis.

irritated Lewis. When Tolkien spent some time at Malvern on holiday with the Lewis brothers in 1947, Warnie remarked: 'His one fault turned out to be that he wouldn't trot at our pace in harness; he will keep going all day on a walk, but to him, with his botanical and entomological interests, a walk, no matter what its length, is what we would call an extended stroll, while he calls us "ruthless walkers".'

Lewis once described an event that might be imagined to have happened on one of his and Tolkien's rural expeditions:

> We were talking of dragons, Tolkien and I
> In a Berkshire bar. The big workman
> Who had sat silent and sucked his pipe
> All the evening, from his empty mug
> With gleaming eye, glanced towards us;
> 'I seen 'em myself', he said fiercely.

The lines, however, were invented by Lewis simply as a demonstration of the alliterative metre, and Tolkien said that they had no basis in fact: 'The occasion is entirely fictitious. A remote source of Jack's lines may be this: I remember him telling me a story of Brightman, the distinguished ecclesiastical scholar, who used to sit quietly in Common Room (in Magdalen) saying nothing except on rare occasions. Jack said that there was a discussion on dragons one night and at the end Brightman's voice was heard to say, "I have seen a dragon." Silence. "Where was that?" he was asked. "On the Mount of Olives," he said. He relapsed into silence and never before his death explained what he meant.'

*

A great part of Lewis's time was of course taken up with giving tutorials and lectures to undergraduates. When teaching, he turned for a model to the method of his old tutor Kirkpatrick. But while 'Kirk's' ways had served well in their place, they were not liked by many of the undergraduates who climbed the stairs of Magdalen New Buildings for tutorials. Lewis (though he privately found tutorials boring) was conscientiously attentive to his pupils and to the essays they read aloud to him. But he rarely praised their work, preferring to engage them in heated argument about some remark they had made. This frightened all but the toughest-minded undergraduates. A few managed to fight back and even win a point – which was just what Lewis wanted them to do – but the majority were cowed by the force of his dialectic and went away abashed.

In the lecture room his manner was less fierce. He lectured clearly in a steady, even voice, and without dramatic gestures; though when he quoted, which he did a great deal, he read superbly. Sometimes, in his 'Prolegomena to Medieval Studies', he actually dictated important passages word by word to his audience, while all the time he cited *facts*, and this was what many undergraduates wanted. Other English School dons might be more entertaining – Nevill Coghill expounded Chaucer with urbane humour, and Tolkien's *Beowulf* lectures were famed for their striking recitations – but Lewis handed out information, and his lectures were very well attended for this reason.

He was becoming known as an expert in medieval literature, and his 'Prolegomena' lectures, setting out the background required for a study of the medieval period, were soon regarded as indispensable. In his spare time from teaching he was still at work on his study of the allegorical love-poetry of the Middle Ages. When it was published in 1936 as *The Allegory of Love* it was greatly admired, not least for Lewis's beautifully apt translations of medieval Latin and French poems into mock-medieval English verse of his own composition. Lewis did this to preserve the flavour of the originals, and also because he enjoyed writing pastiche. But fine as was the achievement of *The Allegory of Love,* he did not regard himself exclusively as a specialist in that period of literature. Indeed, as early as 1931 he had begun to take arms over a critical issue affecting the whole of English literature, an issue that was profoundly involved with his conversion to Christianity.

He believed that he saw a characteristic in literary criticism which was becoming more marked, and which disturbed him. This was the tendency for critics to discuss the personality of the writer as it could be deduced from his work, rather than the character of the writing. At best, Lewis believed, this produced a kind of pseudo-biography, at worst sheer psychological muck-raking. For example he quoted E. M. W. Tillyard saying that *Paradise Lost* 'is really about the true state of Milton's mind when he wrote it'. Lewis thought this was nonsense, and he wrote an essay attacking what he called 'The Personal Heresy in Criticism', declaring: 'A poet does what no one else can do: what, perhaps, no other poet can do; but he does not express his personality.' The essay was published in an academic journal; Tillyard replied, and a public controversy began between them.

Lewis's attack was partially justified. In its extreme form this 'biographical' tendency in criticism is objectionable. Yet there are also grounds for supposing that Lewis's attitude to it grew from something deep-seated in his own personality. In saying this one is of course falling into the very Personal Heresy that he attacked. Nevertheless it needs to be said.

He had always been shy of the emotions. He was aware of this himself, and he said it was because in his childhood he had been embarrassed by his father's ups and downs of mood. In reaction he tried to cultivate a detachment from passing shades of sorrow and happiness, and to maintain a calmly cheerful exterior. Taking this one stage further, he also abstained from speculations about his own psychological make-up and that of his friends. There was of course no reason why he *should* speculate about his own personality. On the other hand, given his strange and perhaps inexplicable attachment to Mrs Moore, there were perhaps reasons why he should not.

This attitude was held even more deeply by him after his conversion. He managed to incorporate it into his Christianity, declaring that it was a Christian's duty to get on with doing the will of God and not to waste time tinkering with his own psychology. 'To know how bad we are', he said, 'is an excellent recipe for becoming much worse.' His own motto for the conducting of his life was

> Man, please thy Maker and be merry,
> And set not by this world a cherry.

Was this deliberate lack of interest in his own personality the cause of an alteration in Lewis's manner after his conversion? At all events Owen Barfield gradually became aware that something was happening to Lewis during this period. 'Looking back over the last thirty years,' Barfield wrote shortly after Lewis's death, 'it appears to me that I have throughout all that time been thinking, pondering, wondering, puzzling over the individual essence of my old friend. The puzzlement has had to do above all with the great change that took place in him between the years 1930 and 1940 – a change which roughly coincided with his conversion but which did not appear, and does not appear in retrospect, to be inevitably or even naturally connected with it.'

In particular Barfield noticed that, once this change had occurred, Lewis had 'deliberately ceased to take any interest in himself except as a kind of spiritual alumnus taking his moral finals'. He also observed that something a little strange was happening to Lewis's manner as a writer.

One example in particular stuck in Barfield's memory. After Tillyard's rejoinder to the 'Personal Heresy' essay had been published, Lewis wrote a reply to that rejoinder which he called 'An Open Letter to Dr Tillyard'. Barfield was staying at the Kilns at the time and, when Lewis handed it to him, he read it with admiration, but also (he said) 'with a certain underlying – what is the word? – restlessness, *malaise*, bewilderment – that gradually increased until, when I came to the passage at the end:

As I glance through the letter again I notice that I have not been able, in the heat of argument, to express as clearly or continuously as I could have wished my sense that I am engaged with "an older and a better soldier". But I have little fear that you will misunderstand me. We have both learnt our dialectic in the academic arena where knocks that would frighten the London literary coteries are given and taken in good part; and even where you may think me something too pert you will not suspect me of malice. If you honour me with a reply it will be in kind; and then, God defend the right!

I am, my dear Sir, with the greatest respect,
Your obedient servant,
C. S. Lewis.

'I slapped down the book' (Barfield continued) 'and shouted: 'I don't believe it! It's *pastiche!*" '

It may of course have been *deliberate* pastiche, something that Lewis always enjoyed writing. Yet on that occasion he had no ready answer to Barfield's accusation – or at least none that Barfield could recall thirty years later – and all through the 'Personal Heresy' controversy there was something in his tone that seemed just subtly artificial. He attacked the tendency of critics to exalt poets because he said it disparaged what he called 'common things and common men'. He declared that the modern verse of the nineteen-twenties only succeeded in communicating a boredom and nausea that had little place in 'the life of the corrected and full-grown man'. And, laughing at the notion that poets are in any sense braver than ordinary men, he asked: 'What meditation on human fate demands so much "courage" as the act of stepping into a cold bath?'

This last remark seems more appropriate to G. K. Chesterton than to Lewis. It would not have been voiced by Lewis as a young man; he had taken the writing of poetry very seriously. But after his conversion this came more and more to be the kind of thing he said and the kind of attitude he took. Or rather, it was the kind of attitude he *thought* he took, or had decided to take. As Barfield expressed it, 'It left me with the impression, not of "I say this", but of "This is the sort of thing a man might say".'[1]

It was naturally a little disturbing, not least because sometimes the old Lewis would appear again. 'From about 1935 onwards I had the impression of living with, not one, but two Lewises,' said Barfield. 'There was both a friend and the memory of a friend; sometimes they

[1] Barfield actually made this remark not apropos of *The Personal Heresy* but of a poem written by Lewis in the nineteen fifties. See *Light on C. S. Lewis* p. xi, for the full context.

61

were close together and nearly coalesced; sometimes they seemed very far apart.'

*

If Barfield thought that Lewis's contribution to *The Personal Heresy* had something of a pose or posture about it, others observed that in the controversy Lewis took up a position that was specifically Christian. In his initial essay he declared that one of the reasons why he disliked paying too much attention to a poet's personality was that this implied that the personality *mattered*, which, he said, was the sort of view held by 'a half-hearted materialist'. He said that the modern critic failed to realise that if the materialistic view of the universe was true, then 'personality' was as meaningless as everything else. 'If the world is meaningless,' he said, 'then so are we; if we mean something, we do not mean alone.'

He himself of course did now believe that the universe 'meant something'. And he did not intend to keep his Christian view of the world out of his literary criticism. If his attitude in *The Personal Heresy* (which was eventually published as a book) was only Christian by implication, in a short article published soon afterwards he was much more open about what he thought.

The article was called 'Christianity and Literature'. It originated as a paper read to a religious society at Oxford, and it was printed in 1939 in Lewis's volume of essays *Rehabilitations*. In it, Lewis said he found 'a disquieting contrast between the whole circle of ideas used in modern criticism and certain ideas recurrent in the New Testament'.

'What', he asked, 'are the key-words of modern criticism? *Creative,* with its opposite *derivative*; *spontaneity*, with its opposite *convention*; *freedom,* contrasted with *rules*. We certainly have a general picture of bad work flowing from conformity and discipleship, and of good work bursting out from certain centres of explosive force – apparently self-originating force – which we call men of genius.' This, he said, was in conflict with the New Testament, where (he claimed) it is often implied that all 'creation' by men is at its best no more than imitation of God, and in no sense 'original' at all. From this he concluded that the duty of a Christian writer lies not in self-expression for its own sake, but in reflecting the image of God. 'Applying this principle to literature,' he said, 'we should get as the basis of all critical theory the maxim that an author should never conceive himself as bringing into existence beauty or wisdom which did not exist before, but simply and solely as trying to embody in terms of his own art some reflection of eternal Beauty and Wisdom. Our criticism would therefore from the beginning group itself with some existing theories of poetry against others. It would have affinities with the primitive or Homeric theory in which the poet is the mere pensioner of the Muse. It would have affinities with the Platonic doctrine of a transcendent Form partly imitable on earth; and remoter affinities with the Aristotelian doctrine of μιμησις and the Augustan doctrine about the imitation of Nature and the Ancients. It would be opposed to the theory of genius as, perhaps, generally understood; and above all it would be opposed to the idea that literature is self-expression.'

The argument of Lewis's 'Christianity and Literature' was paralleled by Tolkien's lecture on Fairy-Stories, delivered the same year (1939) that Lewis's essay was published. In this lecture Tolkien declared – as he had told Lewis on that September night eight years earlier – that in writing stories man is not a creator but a *sub*-creator who may hope to reflect something of the eternal light of God. In the lecture he quoted from the poem that he had written for Lewis, recording something of their talk that night under the trees in Addison's Walk:

> Man, Sub-creator, the refracted Light
> through whom is splintered from a single White
> to many hues, and endlessly combined
> in living shapes that move from mind to mind.
> Though all the crannies of the world we filled
> With Elves and Goblins, though we dared to build
> Gods and their houses out of dark and light,
> and sowed the seed of dragons – 'twas our right
> (used or misused), That right has not decayed:
> we make still by the law in which we're made.

Something of the same view was held by Hugo Dyson. In a British Academy lecture on Shakespeare's tragedies – not delivered until 1950 but presumably expressing ideas that he had held for some years – Dyson said: 'Man without art is eyeless; man with art and nothing else would see little but the reflections of his own fears and desires.' And Owen Barfield in *Poetic Diction* had expressed a similar notion when he said that in studying great poetry, 'our mortality catches for a moment the music of the turning spheres'.

These views could hardly have been more different from those held by one of the major and most influential literary critics of the time, F. R. Leavis. Indeed, Leavis and the contributors to his periodical *Scrutiny* were the group of critics whom Lewis was by implication attacking in *The Personal Heresy* and 'Christianity and Literature'. From the beginning of his work at Cambridge, Leavis campaigned for the recognition of 'culture' as the basis of a humane society, but did not believe that this culture should be based on any one objective standard, least of all Christianity. He declared that there was among educated persons 'sufficient measure of agreement, overt and implicit, about essential values to make it unnecessary to discuss ultimate sanctions, or to provide a philosophy, before starting to work'.

In answer to this, Lewis declared that Leavis and one of the other great critics of the period, I. A. Richards, were part of a 'tradition of educated infidelity' which could be traced to Matthew Arnold, were even indeed 'one phase in that general rebellion against God which began in the eighteenth century'. He also said that Leavis's position as a critic was fundamentally based on subjective judgement and nothing more, which he said was 'like trying to lift yourself by your own coat collar'; and he declared: 'Unless we return to the crude and nursery-like belief in objective values, we perish.' He said too that the 'personal heresy' in Leavis's and Richards's work could be traced to this subjectivism: 'Since the real wholeness is not, for them, in the objective universe, it has to be located inside the poet's head. Hence the quite disproportionate emphasis laid by them on the poet.' And he summed up the differences between them when he said: 'Leavis demands moral earnestness; I prefer morality.'

*

While Lewis was widening his reputation as a literary critic, Owen Barfield was tied to an office job in London. He had found that he could not make a living from literary work – he now had a wife and children to support – so he entered his father's legal firm in London and became a solicitor, hoping to continue writing in his spare time. But this proved to be a mirage. First there was the challenge of learning a new discipline, and then simply the exhaustion of the job. Though he still wrote poetry, none of it got into print, and for some years the total of his published works was a children's story, *The Silver Trumpet,* a short book entitled *History in English Words,* and *Poetic Diction.* Lewis often referred to this book and to Barfield's notions about myth and language in his lectures and in his own published writings, so often indeed that it became a jest among his pupils that Barfield was actually an *alter ego,* a figment of Lewis's imagination to whom Lewis chose to ascribe some of his own opinions.

To Barfield, the jest was perhaps rather hollow. He had not wanted to slide into this obscurity. Nor was there in his friendship with Lewis quite the same richness as there had once been. They still went on walking tours, until the increasing suburbanisation of the countryside and the outbreak of war brought that annual event finally to a halt. But they did not argue as before, at least not about fundamentals, for now that he had become a Christian Lewis ceased to discuss his beliefs with his old friend. This was rather to Barfield's regret, for he had found few people of weighty intellect in the Anthroposophical movement, and he would have been glad of a rational exchange of views. But Lewis shied away from real argument; he had made up his mind.

Meanwhile Barfield was obliged to continue in his London office, even when war seemed imminent, dealing with the petty grind of routine legal work. As he expressed it in a moment of fury:

> How I hate this bloody business,
>   Peddling property and strife
> While the pulse of Europe falters –
>   How I hate this bloody life!

*

The Hobbit was published in 1937. It had come to the notice of a London publisher, and Tolkien was persuaded to finish it in time for it to be issued in the autumn of that year. Lewis was delighted, and he helped the book on its way by giving it two glowing reviews, both in *The Times* and in *The Times Literary Supplement*. In the first he wrote: 'All who love that kind of children's book which can be read and re-read by adults should take note that a new star has appeared in this constellation. To the trained eye some characters will seem almost mythopoeic.' And he concluded by saying of Tolkien that he 'has the air of inventing nothing. He has studied trolls and dragons at first hand and describes them with that fidelity which is worth oceans of glib "originality".' In *The Times Literary Supplement* he classed the book with the works of his beloved George MacDonald, and remarked: 'No common recipe for children's stories will give you creatures so rooted in their own soil and history as those of Professor Tolkien – who obviously knows much more about them than he needs for this tale.'

By now Tolkien had read much of *The Silmarillion* to Lewis, and when at the end of 1937 he began to write a sequel to *The Hobbit* he passed his new chapters to Lewis. 'Mr Lewis and my youngest boy are reading it in bits as a serial,' Tolkien told his publishers when reporting on its progress. He also said that the boy (his third son, Christopher) and Lewis 'approve it enough to say that they think it is better than *The Hobbit*'.

By the time that Lewis began to read Tolkien's still untitled new story, he himself had turned his hand to fiction again. His new book began as a joint project, a kind of bargain or wager with Tolkien, who recalled of it: 'Lewis said to me one day: "Tollers, there is too little of what we really like in stories. I am afraid we shall have to write some ourselves." ' What they had in mind was stories that were 'mythopoeic' but were thinly disguised as popular thrillers. Tolkien began on 'The Lost Road', the tale of a journey back through time to the land of Númenor. Lewis decided to tackle space-travel because he wished to refute what he considered to be a prevalent and dangerous notion: that interplanetary colonisation by mankind was morally acceptable and even a necessary step forward for the human race. (He found this notion clearly expressed by J. B. S. Haldane in the final chapter of *Possible Worlds*.) He also wanted to do what he had attempted in *The Pilgrim's Regress,* to give the Christian story a fresh excitement by retelling it as if it were a new myth. His choice of science fiction as a form was also influenced by his admiration for H. G. Wells – or rather, for Wells's narrative powers, but not his ideology – and for David Lyndsay, whose *Voyage to Arcturus* (he said) 'first suggested to me that the form of "science fiction" could be filled by spiritual experiences'.

Lewis's *Out of the Silent Planet* was finished by the autumn of 1937. He submitted it to J. M. Dent, who had published *Dymer* and *The Pilgrim's Regress*; but they turned it down. Tolkien then came to Lewis's aid. He recommended the book in warm terms (though not without criticism) to his own publisher, Stanley Unwin, the chairman of Allen & Unwin who had published *The Hobbit*. 'I read the story in the original MS.,' he told Unwin, 'and was so enthralled that I could do nothing else until I had finished it. My first criticism was simply that it was too short. I still think that criticism holds, for both practical and artistic reasons. Other criticisms, concerning narrative style (Lewis is always apt to have rather creaking stiff-jointed passages), inconsistent details in the plot, and philology, have since been corrected to my satisfaction. The author holds to items of linguistic invention that do not appeal to me (*Malacandra, Maleldil* – *eldila* in any case I suspect to be due to the influence of the *Eldar* in *The Silmarillion* –) but this is a matter of taste.' And Tolkien concluded: 'I at any rate should have bought this story at almost any price if I had found it in print.'

Allen & Unwin's readers reported unfavourably on the book, and the firm turned it down. But Stanley Unwin passed it to The Bodley Head, of which he was also chairman, and they accepted it and brought it out a few months later, in the autumn of 1938. Many people were soon echoing Tolkien's enthusiasm for it. Not that he had been obliged to rely solely on his own judgement in recommending it, for, as he told Stanley Unwin in another letter, after reading the book in manuscript he had 'heard it pass rather a different test: that of being read aloud to our local club (which goes in for reading things short and long aloud). It proved an exciting serial, and was highly approved. But of course we are all rather like-minded.'

This was in February 1938. In June of the same year, Tolkien wrote (again to Unwin): 'You may not have noticed that on June 2 the Rev. Adam Fox was elected Professor of Poetry (at Oxford). He was nominated by Lewis and myself, and miraculously elected: our first public victory over established privilege. For Fox is a member of our literary club of practising poets – before whom *The Hobbit*, and other works (such as the *Silent Planet*) have been read. We are slowly getting into print.' Fox was a Magdalen don and had been a friend, though not an intimate, of Lewis for about ten years. As for the 'literary club of practising poets', neither of the Lewis brothers was keeping a diary at this time, and there is no mention of it in their papers until more than a year later when, on 11 November 1939, Jack Lewis wrote in a letter to Warnie: 'On Thursday we had a meeting of the Inklings'.

*

After the dissolution of Tangye Lean's 'Inklings' at University College, the name, Tolkien recalled, 'was then transferred (by C. S. L.) to the undetermined and unelected circle of friends who gathered about C. S. L. and met in his rooms at Magdalen'. There is no record of precisely when this happened – if indeed it was a precise event and not a gradual process. Tolkien seems to imply that it took place as soon as Tangye Lean's club broke up, which would be in about 1933. On the other hand there is no contemporary mention of it until Tolkien's report of their 'public victory' in the professorial election of 1938.

Lewis never explained why he transferred the name 'Inklings' from the undergraduate club to the group of his friends. Yet there was a certain attraction in its ambiguity. Tolkien said of it: 'It was a pleasantly ingenious pun in its way, suggesting people with vague or half-formed intimations and ideas plus those who dabble in ink.'

*

Lewis's walking tours with his brother and with Barfield came to an end with the outbreak of war. Warnie Lewis had acquired a small two-berth cabin cruiser which he moored at Salter's boatyard on the Thames in Oxford, and which he called *Bosphorus*. In August 1939 he arranged to take Jack and Hugo Dyson on a short holiday up the river. But war now seemed likely, and when the time came Warnie, who had rejoined the Royal Army Service Corps with the rank of Major, was obliged to report for army duty. Jack and Dyson had no wish to cancel their trip, but neither of them felt able to manage the practical side of a motor boat; so they enlisted the Lewis family doctor, R. E. Havard, as navigator, he being a man whom Lewis much liked and admired, a Catholic convert who would cheerfully allow Lewis to engage him in a philosophical conversation when they were supposed to be discussing medical symptoms. The party met at Folly Bridge at midday on Saturday 26 August. The pact between Germany and Russia had just been signed, and there was much anxiety about what would be the consequences. 'Yet', recalled Havard, 'our spirits were high at the prospect of a temporary break with politics and daily chores.'

They set off up the Thames from Oxford, following the river through low meadows and past riverside pubs ('Few of these', remarked Havard, 'escaped a visit from us'). On the first evening, after an hour or two spent at the Trout Inn at Godstow, Dyson and Lewis began a vigorous argument about the Renaissance, which Lewis contended had never happened at all, or if it had, hadn't mattered. They went on through the darkness to the Rose Revived at Newbridge; Lewis and Dyson slept in the inn while Havard spent the night on board. 'The next morning, Sunday,' recalled Havard, 'we moved on to Tadpole Bridge and separated on foot to our respective churches in Buckland a mile or so away. That afternoon after lunch we went on upstream and met, coming down, Robert Gibbings in a canoe, naked to the waist. His bearded figure was greeted rapturously by Lewis with a quotation:

> Have sight of Proteus rising from the sea;
> Or hear old Triton blow his wreathed horn.

At this, Gibbings picked up an enormous conch from the bottom of his canoe and attempted to blow a fanfare on it. After some lively talk, each craft went on its way. Gibbings later put some of the canoe trip into his book *Sweet Thames Run Softly*.

'We saw no papers' (continues Havard) 'and were cut off from all news except what Lewis and Dyson gathered from the inns where they slept at night. I remember an hour on a riverside lawn waiting for lunch to be ready at Radcot. I remember an evening meal at Lechlade and an expedition upstream for half a mile to Inglesham and the ruined opening into the disused Thames and Severn Canal. I remember little of the return downstream except that the engine broke down, as engines of small boats often do. Lewis and Dyson shared a tow rope on the river bank. I offered my own share, but neither of the other two seemed able to keep the boat out of the bank while it was being towed. So after a short spell ashore I was voted back again to the helm. About this time also the weather broke. Fortunately for tempers, the engine recovered and returned to duty.

'Our spirits revived until we heard at midday on the Friday that Hitler had invaded Poland. We knew then that war was imminent. The news broke on us, I think, at Godstow, and the return to Oxford was in an unnatural silence. We left *Bosphorus* at Salter's, and agreed to meet for a final dinner at the Clarendon in Cornmarket. At dinner Lewis tried to lighten the gloom by saying, "Well, at any rate we now have less chance of dying of cancer." '

*

War was declared the following Sunday. Lewis had been told that his college rooms, together with the whole of New Buildings, would be required for government use. Gloomily he and Warnie had moved all their books into the basement. A week after the war began it was announced that the building was not needed after all. Laboriously, he brought all the books back again. Indeed it soon appeared that the hostilities were unlikely to cause so very great a disruption in the life of the University – at least, the colleges would not be closing down to anything like the extent they had done in the First World War. Besides the undergraduates (comparatively few in number) who continued with their normal studies, there began some time later to be a steady flow of cadets who were sent to Oxford to spend a few terms reading 'shortened courses' before going off to active service. While some dons who, like Lewis, were above the age for military service were required to take on government jobs of various kinds, many remained to continue working much as they had done in peacetime. Lewis soon found that he and Tolkien and most of his Oxford friends were in the latter category. Meanwhile evacuee children were billeted at the Kilns, and, when on 17 September news came that Russian forces had crossed into Poland, Lewis reported that Mrs Moore 'regards this as sealing the fate of the allies – and even talks of buying a revolver'.

But, as he wrote to Warnie, 'along with these not very pleasant indirect results of the war, there is one pure gift – the London branch of the Oxford University Press has moved to Oxford, so that Charles Williams is living here.'

PART TWO

I

C.W.

'The telephone bell was ringing wildly, but without result, since there was no-one in the room but the corpse.'

It was a conventional beginning to what at first sight appeared to be a conventional detective story. An unidentified man is murdered in the offices of a publishing company. There are a number of suspects. Inspector Colquhoun investigates.

But, when the book was published in 1930, readers soon discovered that it was not exactly like that. The corpse, it appeared, was only the introduction to the real story: the discovery of the Holy Grail in a country church, its theft by a black magic enthusiast, and the attempt of an Anglican parson and a Roman Catholic Duke to rescue it. Nor did even this seem to be entirely what the story was about, for the pursuit of the Grail (or 'Graal' as the author spelt it) was soon giving place to visionary experiences and the contention of the forces of good and evil. As Inspector Colquhoun remarked in Chapter Sixteen, 'What an infernally religious case this is getting!'

The book was called *War in Heaven*, and it was the first novel to be published by Charles Williams.

*

By that time – 1930 – the name 'Mr Charles Williams' was a familiar sight on the list of evening classes arranged by the London County Council at the City Literary Institute and at Evening Institutes in many parts of the metropolis. Here, in bare buildings with naked light-bulbs, people of all ages and types and levels of education would come for a couple of hours each week, to sit in echoing lecture rooms and study the subject of their choice. Those who opted for English Literature would soon find themselves being lectured to by a thin man with round spectacles, a high forehead, and a long upper lip. He talked in a lower middle-class London accent, and the vowels of his speech seemed at first to contrast oddly with his manner, which was quite unlike that of any other Evening Institute lecturer. Sitting on a table and often moving his arms and hands in dramatic gestures, he spoke passionately and without ceasing. Most people gave up trying to take notes.

His lectures were usually on major poets, especially Milton, Shakespeare, and Wordsworth, though sometimes he talked about modern poetry or even (though the classes were supposed to be in English Literature) on Dante. People who came hoping for plain information were taken aback, for, though he chose his words with great precision, he mentioned few facts. Nor did he offer the usual sort of critical opinions. Indeed he did not really *discuss* the poetry at all. What he did was to communicate his feelings for it, or even his ability to participate *in* it. His lectures were full of quotations, always done from memory and never from notes or a text; or rather, they were not so much quotations as incantations, a kind of ritual chanting of lines from the poem he was talking about – or very likely from a totally different poem, for he might use a phrase from Milton to illustrate an ode of Keats, or a line of Wordsworth to comment on something in Dante. He seemed in fact to be able to express his own thoughts best by taking phrases from the great poets, seemed to think largely in poetry, so it was no surprise to learn from a casual remark he might drop in a lecture that he wrote poetry himself – though very few people had ever read any of it.

After the hour's lecture there would be (by the rules of the Evening Institutes) an hour's discussion, not the usual stilted question-and-answers which happen in those circumstances but – such was the enthusiasm with which he would pick up a hesitant remark from a member of his audience – a vital and involved conversation. And when the formal discussion was over there would always be somebody stopping to talk to him afterwards, maybe on the subject of poetry but more likely about some highly private problem of their own; for regular attenders at his classes had long ago discovered the very special kind of help he could give. He would treat someone's personal worry with the same vitality that he showed in the lecture, the same grave courtesy and fiery vision; so that it was easy to go home feeling that this was what it would have been like to meet Dante himself, or Blake, or even Shakespeare.

This too was the feeling he created at his place of work, which was in a small semi-private square lying under the shadow of the Old Bailey, hard by St Paul's Cathedral at the heart of the City of London. Here each weekday morning there would arrive, one by one, the staff of the London office of the Oxford University Press, which had its premises in Amen House. Promptness was a rule of the house, and the junior members of the firm would be in their places by the time the City clocks struck nine. In one of the smaller rooms, with a window looking out to the dome of the Old Bailey, a clerk would change the calendar and the date stamp which lay on the desk, ready for the occupant. Then, at 9.15 precisely, feet would run up the stairs and a figure would spring into the room. Hat, gloves and walking-stick would be hung up, and their owner would throw himself into his chair, swivelling and tilting it back so that he could put his feet on the desk. In this fashion, with a sixpenny writing pad balanced on his knee, he would finish the poem he had been thinking about while walking up Newgate Street from the Underground station; and all the time he would be talking to the clerk or to the man who shared the office with him, or to somebody who came in from another department. Soon, he would leave his own writing on one side and get down to the firm's work, perhaps reading a manuscript submitted by an author, or casting his eye over proofs, or discussing details of binding and typeface with the people who looked after the production of books. But even then he was often turning back to his own occupations, dashing off a letter to a friend in rather shaky handwriting (his hands trembled due to some slight nervous affliction), finishing a review for *Time & Tide*, and at lunch time rushing out for an appointment with another friend over a sandwich at Shirreff's Wine Vaults in Ludgate Hill. The only thing that could break the independence of his routine would be a summons to the inner sanctum where sat the Publisher himself, Sir Humphrey Milford; for when word came that 'Sir Humphrey wishes to see Mr Williams' there was never any delay or excuse, but an immediate journey down corridors to the big room with its ornate ceiling and heavy carved chairs. Here, and here only, Charles Williams ceased to be the poet, the critic, the visionary, and became a publisher's assistant who had been with the firm for a quarter of a century and would presumably remain with it to the end of his working days.

But soon he would be out of the Publisher's room, lighting a cigarette and bounding up the stairs two at a time to his own office; and then somebody would meet him on the staircase and would say something to him – perhaps just a casual greeting or remark – and he would immediately turn his full attention to that person, and they would embark on a conversation that might be hilarious but would also be deeply serious. So the day would pass, and soon he would be hurrying off to take an evening class. Not until a late hour would he return by Tube to Hampstead, where in a rented flat at the top of a dizzy staircase, with tall windows that looked out towards the lights of the West End and the City in the distance, he would drink a cup of tea and talk to his wife, say goodnight to his small son, and then settle down, with the pad balanced on his knee, to more writing. It might be the next chapter of a historical biography that had been commissioned by a publisher, or a book review, or the beginning of another novel, whose royalties he hoped would help to pay next year's bills. Or just possibly, if he was feeling self-indulgent, he might allow himself to spend an hour or two writing the only thing he really cared about: poetry. He would try not to stay up very late, but very likely he would not be able to sleep properly; and if that was the case (it happened quite often) he would be at work again as dawn came up over London.

*

His full name was Charles Walter Stansby Williams, and he was a Londoner born and bred, brought up not a Cockney (as some of his Oxford admirers later alleged) but at Holloway in the northern part of the city, an area characterised by railway goods yards, small shops and businesses, and endless terraces of drab brick houses.

He was born in 1886, the elder of two children, and for the first eight years of his life there was something like security. His father, a man of some education, worked as a clerk in the City but devoted much of his spare time to literature, reading widely and contributing poems and short stories to magazines, from which he made a few guineas. He and his wife were devout members of the Church of England; in his early years Charles caught their fervour and was always happy in church, where he chanted the psalms loudly in a most unmusical voice.

In 1894 there was a double crisis in the family. Mr Williams's firm was about to close, so he would lose his job, and at the same time he was warned by a doctor that his eyesight, never good and now fast deteriorating, would be irretrievably damaged if he did not move out of London to fresher air.

Somehow the family weathered the storm. The notion of living in 'the country' did not appeal in the least, for they were town dwellers by habit and inclination, so they compromised by moving to the city of St Albans, where they found a vacant shop which they decided to run as a business selling artist's materials. In the years that followed, this managed to produce an adequate if unreliable income, though the worries about money made a mark on Charles, who in adult life was never able to avoid worrying about his own finances.

The father's sight did not improve, and, though he never became totally blind, Mr Williams was soon unable to give much help with the shop or to continue with his literary hobbies. The frustration and misery of this was communicated to his son, so that for the rest of his life Charles Williams was largely pessimistic, and never indulged in shallow optimism. But it did mean that the father had much time to devote to the son, and the two went for long walks together in St Albans and the Hertfordshire countryside around, talking all the time. Outside the town they paid little attention to their surroundings, for neither of them could see well – Charles was very short-sighted – and in any case they were more interested in talk than scenery. Mr Williams was not only widely-read but totally undogmatic, teaching his son that there were many sides to every argument, and that it was necessary to understand the elements of reason in the other point of view as well as your own. Though a devout churchman, he encouraged Charles to appreciate the force of atheist rationalism and to admire such men as Voltaire and Tom Paine. Above all he insisted on accuracy, impressing on his son that one should never defend one's opinions by exaggeration or distortion of the facts. It was a remarkable education. It did not – which it perhaps might have done – encourage Charles to adopt an attitude of detachment. He learnt to be committed, in his case to Christianity; but he also learnt that the other side may have an equal force of argument. It was perhaps partly because of this that he never wavered from belief in God during his adolescence; or, to put it another way, his father had taught him to absorb doubt and disbelief into his beliefs.

His formal education was at day schools in St Albans, but his father was his real educational influence. Already Charles was developing a remarkably nimble and active mind. One of the St Albans Abbey clergy who prepared him for confirmation remarked that the boy 'had too many brains for him', and that he could not get to the bottom of what was going on in Charles's head.

In adolescence Charles began to write poetry, and such was his trust in his father that he showed it to him, and received both encouragement and constructive criticism. Indeed, at this stage of his life he shared his serious ideas with no one but his father. The only school friend that he asked to read his poetry found much of it beyond him. However, with this school friend's help Charles did regularly enact a private fantasy, a kind of continuing Ruritania-style drama which the boys performed at odd moments of the day, and in which Charles's sister Edith was enlisted to play the Princess. From this, Charles learnt the delight of living in a world of half-serious, half-comic assumed identities. These Ruritanian inventions also appealed to his growing love of ritual and ceremony, as did the historical pageants which were regularly performed at his school in St Albans. Indeed the school itself, which was in an old monastic building close to the Abbey, delighted him with its spiral staircases, vaulted roofs, tall dark classrooms, and the view of the Abbey itself, from which the bells rang out the quarters.

In 1901 Charles won an Intermediate Scholarship to University College, London, and began to study there before his sixteenth birthday, reading a general course which included Latin, French, and English history, but which did not offer any specialised training. He continued to live at home in St Albans, travelling by train into London each day, so that college life made comparatively little impression on him and seemed to be no more than an extension of school. Moreover after two years his family found that they could no longer afford to contribute to the cost of keeping him at the university, so he left without taking a degree, and at the age of eighteen he set about earning his living.

A clerk's post was found for him – for he was scarcely qualified for anything better – at a Methodist Bookroom in the Holborn district of London, and he began work there in 1904. He endured the menial work with patience and even with humour, and he might have continued there indefinitely had not the Bookroom closed in 1908, so that it was necessary for him to find another job. A friend, Frederick Page, told him that there was a post as a proof reader in the London office of the Oxford University Press. He applied, was accepted, and began there, still travelling to London daily from St Albans.

After the Methodist Bookroom the Press was majestic. Within its walls Charles Williams found stability, hierarchy, and order. The London office was largely independent of the University Press in Oxford, but it had much of the formality and academic grandeur of its Oxford parent. It has been described as 'rather like an ancient half-occupied half-ruined palace, where a number of people maintained a living ritual and ceremonial duties, and in whose vaulted roofs sounded the chant of Greek and Latin verse and the echo of venerated names'.

As the offices of the Press were in the City of London, Williams found the surroundings peculiarly appealing. Just as at St Albans he had been impressed by the sense of history and ritual conveyed by the Abbey and by the medieval buildings of his school, so he now found this expressed even more positively by the City. Or, rather, it was not so much the notion of history that the City conveyed to him as the idea of the perfect formal community.

Many other young men, chained like him to an office desk and a repetitive job, would not have shared his vision. But to Charles Williams the City, with its churches, its law-courts, its business houses, banks, libraries and printing presses, seemed the expression of an ideal order. The City's rigid hierarchies and rules, as well as its love of pageantry and ritual, delighted his imagination and seemed to him refreshingly stable and unshakeable after the uncertainties and worries of his parents' home. Indeed to him the City of London soon became an earthly expression of the ultimate city, the City of God.

At this time he began to find companions with whom he could share his poetry and his ideas. He made friends through a Working Men's College in London where he attended part-time classes, and with these, as well as with his old school friend in St Albans, he spent many hours in amiably contentious arguments, sometimes changing his own position half-way through a debate just to find out what sort of case he could put for the other side (a legacy of his father's training). From such evenings of talk came warm affection, recalled by him in a poem:

> O rooms and roads of gay contest,
> Journey and argument and jest,
> From Kew to Harpenden!
> Where, while the days made man of me,
> My love felt yours amazedly –
> Men splendid among men.

Not all Charles Williams's friendships were with other men. In 1908 he met Florence Conway, the daughter of a St Albans ironmonger and a helper at the Sunday School where he was teaching. 'For the first five minutes of our meeting', she recalled, 'I thought him the most silent, withdrawn young man I had ever met. For the rest of the evening I thought him the most talkative young man I had ever met, and still the nicest.' They became engaged to be married.

Florence did not pretend to be learned, nor did she share Charles's passionate intellectual interests. But she was shrewd and intelligent, and lively too, though she was sometimes embarrassed by her fiancé's exuberance, particularly his tendency to recite poetry loudly in public places; and she rebuked him for this. He in reply nicknamed her 'Michal', after Saul's daughter who mocked at David when he danced before the Lord. And 'Michal' she remained.

As for his feelings towards her, he declared that hers was 'a face which some pre-Raphaelite should have loved'; and there was a good deal of the pre-Raphaelite about the sequence of eighty-four sonnets that he wrote for her and thrust into her hands one night. She read them carefully. 'So lovely they seemed,' she said. But she also noted – and it puzzled her – that, though they were addressed to her, their theme was the renunciation of love.

Why should he have considered renouncing love? In part it was simply his awareness that marriage with its many obligations and strains might destroy love: he was never easily optimistic. But, more than this, he was discontented about the very ordinariness of 'being in love'. His mind was too subtle and self-aware, too capable of seeing endless possibilities in every human thought and action, for the state of loving to seem enough. He asked himself 'whether love were not meant for something more than wantonness and child-bearing and the future that closes in death'. He meditated on the notion of achieving some spiritual advancement through renunciation, speculating in the sonnets he wrote for 'Michal' whether they might not 'put off love for love's sake'. And there was another possibility. Turning to his Christian beliefs, he considered the idea that love for another human being might be a step towards God – 'the steep', as he expressed it in the sonnet sequence, 'whence I see God'. At this point he discovered Dante.

In 1910 the Oxford University Press reissued Cary's translation of the *Divine Comedy*. It was Charles Williams's task to correct the proofs. In this fashion he came to read Dante's account of how his love for Beatrice eventually brings him through Hell and Purgatory to Paradise and the Beatific Vision of the Trinity. Williams did not respond, as many commentators and critics had done, by speculating on what this could mean. He simply felt: 'But this is *true*.' It was exactly what he had been aiming towards in his own thoughts: the notion that human love can lead to a selfless love of the divine. In Dante he found confirmation of his hope that love for his own 'Michal' might not just be an end in itself but indeed the approach to spiritual ecstasy. And, having in mind this notion of earthly love being a ladder or staircase up to God, he called the sonnet sequence *The Silver Stair*.

Thanks to encouragement and financial help from the poet Alice Meynell and her husband Wilfrid, who happened to be friends of Williams's colleague at the Press, Fred Page, *The Silver Stair* was published in 1912. But it was not until 1917, when he was thirty and they had been betrothed for nine years, that he married Michal. It is difficult to say quite why they delayed so long. There may have been practical reasons such as concern over money or future prospects. Or perhaps it had something to do with a fundamental element in Charles Williams's character, the thing that he was trying to express when he told a friend: 'At bottom a darkness has always haunted me.'

*

What was this darkness? In part it was no more than a sense of potential chaos and despair. But it also, perhaps, had a connection with his habit from early years of changing sides in an argument. Behind every bad thing he could see something good, but also behind every good thing he could see darkness. Nor did he stop at the mere intellectual contemplation of it. There were reverse sides to two of the principal areas of his life. He was a devout member of the Church of England, but he was also interested in magic. He was a devoted lover, but he also enjoyed the notion of inflicting pain.

Probably he took at least a mild interest in magic during his childhood; certainly by the time he was in his late twenties he was making some study of the beliefs and practices of that semi-magical branch of Christianity known as Rosicrucianism. During this period he read books by the Rosicrucian writer A. E. Waite; he entered into correspondence with Waite, and at Waite's invitation was initiated (in

5 (a)   Charles Williams, circa 1917.

5 (b)   'Michal' Williams in
pageant costume, 1907.

6 (a) Charles Williams in
1935.

6 (b) Hugo and Margaret
Dyson in the early
years of their mar-
riage.

1917) into an organisation called the Order of the Golden Dawn.[1]

The line between religion and magic is sometimes hard to draw, and since its foundation thirty years earlier this Order had wavered rather uncertainly between the two. In its early days some of its members had certainly indulged in would-be magical practices. Among its first initiates was a coroner who allegedly performed necromantic rites over corpses obtained through his profession, while another early member was the black magician Aleister Crowley, the self styled Great Beast who (as Cyril Connolly once said) 'bridged the gap between Oscar Wilde and Hitler'. But the Order of the Golden Dawn also included persons of less outlandish ways, such as W. B. Yeats, whom Williams met during the period of his membership, one or two clergy with a taste for the mystical, and A. E. Waite himself, who though he was learned in the history of magic did not, it seems, practise it or encourage others to do so – Aleister Crowley called Waite 'a dull and inaccurate pedant without imagination or real magical perception'. There were many quarrels among the members of the Golden Dawn, and after a series of schisms Waite formed his own 'temple'. It was this group that Williams joined.

As a neophyte aspiring to be initiated into the Golden Dawn he would apparently have had to declare: 'My soul is wandering in the Darkness, seeking for the Light of Occult Knowledge, and I believe that in this Order the Knowledge of that Light may be obtained.' He also had to take an oath to keep the rites secret, on penalty of a 'hostile current' which would be set against him if he broke faith. The oath was kept, and neither Williams nor any other member ever divulged precisely what those rites were. Probably they were harmless enough, based as they seem to have been on Waite's enthusiasms for freemasonry, vaguely Christian mysticism, and Rosicrucianism, a system of occult beliefs which combines the symbolism of Christianity with the terminology of alchemy, and has the Rosy Cross as its central feature.[2]

[1] A letter from Waite to Williams, dated 6 September 1917, discusses arrangements for 'your Reception at the Autumnal Equinox'. (The letter is in the Wade Collection, Wheaton College, Illinois.)

[2] Waite's own explanation of Rosicrucianism comes as near to lucidity as does any account of this opaque subject: 'The Cross is the sign or symbol of Jesus Christ, of the Brotherhood in its inward dedication, of pure mystical wisdom. Its red colour represents the mystical and divine blood of Christ, which – according to the Apostle – cleanses from all sin . . . There is placed in its centre a Rose "of the colour of Blood" to indicate the work of Sacred and Divine Alchemy in the purification of that which is unclean.' (A. E. Waite, *The Brotherhood of the Rosy Cross* (William Rider, 1924), pp. 107–8.)

Waite suggested that the teachings of Rudolf Steiner were associated with Rosicrucianism: 'It has been reported that he derives from some German Order of the Rosy Cross.' (ibid., p. 618). Waite did not, however, investigate this possible link between his own beliefs and Anthroposophy.

Certainly membership of the Golden Dawn involved the performance of rituals, which Williams, with his love of rite and ceremony, entered into wholeheartedly: he told his friend Anne Ridler that he had always taken care to learn by heart the words of any Golden Dawn rite, so that he could participate with dignity, whereas many other members did not trouble to do so, and merely read the words from a card.

There does not seem to have been anything in Waite's 'temple' of the Golden Dawn which was opposed to Christianity. Indeed Waite, who had been brought up a Catholic, believed its practices to be part of what he called the 'Secret Tradition' of Christianity, the tradition that besides the overt meaning of Christian doctrine there is also a hidden series of truths revealed only to an elect few. Waite remarked of this gnostic tradition, and apparently of his 'temple', to which he here seems to be referring: 'It is not in competition with the external Christian Churches, and yet it is a Church of the Elect, a Hidden and Holy Assembly.' Its beliefs apparently involved, as a principal symbol, the 'Holy Graal' (as Waite spells it). Waite wrote, in a typically incomprehensible sentence: 'It is a House of the Holy Graal in the sanctity of a High Symbolism, where the sacred intent of the Order is sealed upon Bread and Wine.'

It was perhaps in Waite's writings that Williams first found mention of the 'Tetragrammaton', the Hebrew name of God which when used in ceremonies, especially in its reversed form, was supposed to have magical powers. Waite also made a special study of talismans and of the Tarot cards, particularly the 'Trumps Major', and the 'Graal' was a central symbol of his thought. These and other details of occult knowledge were to play a major part in Williams's novels. In one of Waite's books he also encountered the 'Sacred Tree of the Sephiroth', a symbolic diagram based on the Jewish mystical *Zohar*, in which various parts of the human body are associated with particular qualities of spirit and mind; Williams later made great use of this in his poetry. Perhaps, too, Williams's developing notions of human love as a ladder to God owed something to Waite's account of the concept of marriage in the *Zohar*, which pictures the nuptial union on earth as a type of, and path of approach to, the mystical union in heaven. And it was maybe also from Waite's writings that Williams acquired some of his knowledge of black magic.

Waite himself discouraged the Order of the Golden Dawn from practising 'Magia', the Renaissance term for white magic, and certainly he was opposed to any meddling in 'Goetia' or black magic. This was the chief reason why Aleister Crowley left the Order not long after its formation, preferring as he did to practise 'Goetia' combined with sexual promiscuity and drug taking. On the other hand Waite did write a good deal about all forms of magic, though he generally dismissed it, or pretended to dismiss it, as absurd and fantastic. His *Book of Ceremonial Magic* (1910) does include a number of spells, such as 'To Become Invisible', 'A Conjuration to Lucifer', and 'How to Cause the Appearance of Three Ladies or Three Gentlemen in One's Room after Supper'. But Waite presents this stuff in the form of a sceptical inquiry into magical procedure, and more probably Williams acquired his extensive knowledge of 'Goetia' from other sources, such as Aleister Crowley's extravagant novel *Moonchild* (1929) and the stories of 'Sax Rohmer' (A. H. Ward), a fellow Golden Dawn member whose 'Fu Manchu' thrillers Williams much enjoyed. Whatever the sources, by the late nineteen-twenties Williams was thoroughly acquainted with the terminology and practices of black magic.

A question which must strike anyone who reads his novels and notices the seriousness with which he presents magical events is: did he believe in it? It is very difficult to give a clear answer. Certainly he did not dismiss black magic as dangerous tomfoolery. To him it was as valid a form of symbolism as the symbols of Christianity. Whether it was more than symbolism to him, whether he thought it to be true, is difficult to say. To understand his attitude to magic one has to understand his attitude to the whole question of belief.

'No one can possibly do more than decide what to believe,' says a character in one of his novels, and that was exactly what Williams himself thought. He had decided to believe in Christianity, but it was a conscious choice. As far as witchcraft and black magic were concerned, he avoided making any such decision. He used them in his books, but he did not say, or ask his readers to say, 'true or false?' to such things. They were simply there. So, though he soon outgrew the Golden Dawn and left the Order (the date of this is not known), the symbolism and the knowledge of the occult that he had acquired during his membership remained valuable to him, not least because in its extreme form black magic was the polar opposite of Christianity; and his mind was always drawn to an awareness of the opposite pole of any argument or belief.

> Our Father who wert in heaven,
> A lonely road is Thine;
> Hardly after long travel
> Shall we reach to our design.

He wrote these lines in a poem called 'Witchcraft', a hymn to Satan which is an investigation of the 'oppositeness' of the devil to Christ. And, as so often in his writings about black magic, there seems to be something more than a calm intellectual interest.

> Envy and Anger and Lust
>   Are half the kin of Love,
> But Thy great throne is lifted
>   All lesser thrones above.
> Whose sole joy is to see
>   Love weep and bleed anew.
>
> O Terror! O Cruelty!
>   O Hate! O Anguish of Joy!
> Make our hearts one with Thine
>   To ravage and destroy.

Certainly a reader unfamiliar with the character of Williams might suppose this poem to be the work of someone with a potential for cruelty. And this would be true.

It was something that appeared more clearly in Williams's later years, when his writings and the nature of his friendships gave him more opportunity to display it; but a sadistic element occasionally appears in his earlier work, such as the poem 'Antichrist' where, on beholding his beloved's face grown unbearable, he declares:

> My mind possessed me with delight
>   To wrack her lovely head
> With slow device of subtle pain.

He was no Jekyll and Hyde: this sadistic element did not emerge at intervals to change his behaviour. Rather, it was constantly present, held in balance with the other aspects of his imagination.

*

Little is known about Charles and Michal Williams's early married life. They rented a flat in the Hampstead district of London; Michal Williams taught for a few years in an elementary school; a son, confusingly christened Michael, was born to them in 1922, their only child; and that is about all that can be said. Williams's poetry, of which three further volumes were published during these years, gives some idea of contented domesticity, but uses this only as a framework for theological preoccupations. So in the poem 'To Michal meditating a new Costume' he lovingly describes her dress but mentions this only because she is wearing it when they go 'To keep the Mass of our New Year'. A poem about bringing breakfast to her in bed becomes the vehicle for an imaginary journey to 'the land of the Trinity', Sarras in the Arthurian legend of the Grail. Williams often said that he was proud to be one of the few poets who had made marriage a principal subject of verse, but in fact he did not discuss his marriage more than peripherally in his poems. There are also disquieting hints that all was not well, such as in 'After Marriage' where he speaks of the beloved as withdrawn from him, while he himself is 'dispersed in ancient pain And into chaos plunged again'.

Through his writings during the nineteen-twenties ran an increasing element of supernaturalism. He had never fully accepted the conventional distinction between natural and supernatural, or 'Arch-natural' as he preferred to call it; and as the years passed he came to feel that no barrier really existed between the two states, and that the supernatural was constantly present, requiring only extra awareness from the beholder to make it visible. This idea runs through his early poetry. A motor bus lumbering down from Golders Green into Hertfordshire seems to be a long narrow coffin in which he rides, with Death as a fellow passenger. A city pavement may suddenly melt away and reveal the 'firmer under-stone' of the eternal City of God. A prearranged meeting with someone on a street corner may never take place because the other person has accidentally slipped into another time-scale. And in performing simple domestic chores – lighting a fire, having a bath, or going down to the cellar to fetch something – he encounters a host of apparitions. The cellar steps lead into Hell itself, the match he puts to the fire is the flame which kindled Joan of Arc's burning at the stake, and even the seemingly innocent bathwater is the sea in which men are drowning.

These last experiences are described in a poem ironically called 'Domesticity', and besides showing Williams's interest in the supernatural they are also a demonstration of something which was becoming very important in his thought. It had begun during the 1914–18 war, in which he had been unable to fight – he was declared unfit because of what was called 'lack of nervous co-ordination', the physical state that demonstrated itself in the trembling of his hands. During the war his two closest friends from the Working Men's College were killed. At the time Williams was greatly distressed that they should have sacrificed themselves (as it seemed) on his behalf. Worse still, because of his growing habit of ignoring conventional distinctions of time and space he could not feel that their deaths were something which had happened elsewhere and in the past, and were now over. To him the whole thing was constantly happening. The clink of teacups at his own breakfast table seemed to him to be the tin mugs passing from hand to hand while dying men were crying for drink in no-man's-land. This may seem like a casual poetic fancy, but it was not. Such was his imagination that he could feel it acutely. It ceased to be painful to him only

85

when he moved on to an awareness that all human action, whether death in war or the ordinary tasks of daily life, benefits or harms other human beings: all live in a greater framework in which every event has a bearing on something else. Expressed like this, it does not sound very remarkable. But it was important to Williams in that it became the basis of all his mature work.

*

In 1924 the Oxford University Press moved into larger premises. This was Amen House, in Warwick Square, a fine building partly dating from the Restoration. Its elegant formality delighted Williams and confirmed his vision of the Press and the City around it as part of some great ritual. This vision also gained strength from the character of the man who now ruled over the Press, Humphrey Milford.

To Charles Williams, Milford (who became the Publisher in 1913) seemed to contain in his person the perfect expression of authority. Changeable in manner, he could by turns be formal and friendly, approachable and chillingly remote. But at all times he bore himself with the hierarchical dignity appropriate to his almost imperial power in the Press. Williams soon began to refer to him, only half jestingly, as 'Caesar'.

The move to Amen House was accompanied by an increase in staff, and a significant inauguration: the Library, a showroom to house a copy of each of the books published by the Press. The Library occupied a central position in the building, and it became an informal meeting-place for conversation and the exchange of ideas among those working in Amen House. The moving energy in many of these conversations was Charles Williams.

By 1924 he was thirty-eight, and had already spent sixteen years with the Press. Though he had begun humbly as a proof reader, his wide knowledge of literature and his passionate devotion to poetry in particular had gradually gained him greater responsibilities, and he was now a valued member of the editorial department. But his office work at Amen House mattered much less to him than the friendships which grew from it.

There were many on the staff of the Press with whom he found it easy to be friendly. Indeed he would be intimate with anyone who responded to him, for at a first meeting he would talk as if he had known you for years, and as if it were the most natural thing in the world to discuss poetry or theology with you. All that was needed was for you to accept this manner, and respond in kind, and then a friendship would begin. Many of the new staff at Amen House (as well as the longer-serving people) did respond, and 'C. W.' – as he was known among them – soon became the centre of a circle of friends, changing a place of work into a place of talk and friendship and delight.

'C. W.' himself was soon giving formal expression to his pleasure at these friendships in *An Urbanity*, a long poem that he addressed to Phyllis Jones, a young woman who had joined the staff in 1924 to take charge of the Library at Amen House. In it he lamented the absence on holiday of their particular friends, whose identity he lightly masked beneath poetic names chiefly taken from the genre of pastoral verse. 'Dorinda' was Miss Peacock from the Production Department, 'Alexis' and 'Colin' were Gerard Hopkins (nephew of the poet) who worked in Publicity and Fred Page, Williams's office companion, while Phyllis Jones herself was 'Phillida' and Humphrey Milford was of course 'Caesar'.

An Urbanity was little more than an elegant jest. But it was soon followed by something that expressed Williams's feelings about Amen House and its friendships more deeply. Retaining the assumed identities for his friends, he cast them as characters in a masque. They performed it in the Library on Humphrey Milford's birthday in 1927, in front of a small invited audience presided over by Milford himself, for whom (by Williams's direction) there was set, slightly forward from the rest, a throne-like seat appropriate for 'Caesar'.

The Masque of the Manuscript, as it was named, delicately mocked the absurdities of the publishing business. A worthy but dull Manuscript is eventually made acceptable for publication by the combined efforts of Dorinda, Alexis, Colin and Phillida. Then Caesar gives his consent, and the Manuscript – played by a female member of the cast – is placed on a bier and prepared for death. At last she rises, printed and bound and published. But the Masque is more than mockery, for it is concerned with the pursuit of truth, and ends with an epilogue on the dissolution of all mortal things, 'Even the most precious talk of friends'.

The Masque was a remarkable success. It created an extraordinary sense of delight in Amen House; for, by making the daily tasks of publishing into the stuff of poetry and ritual, Williams had transmuted a chore into something seemingly of wider significance. Nor did it end at the finish of the hour's entertainment. In the months that followed, Williams continued to address his friends by their poetic names, so that they were caught up into a myth of his own devising. In the Library and on the staircase he would involve them in talk on a myriad of subjects, bringing out the best qualities in each of them. 'He found the gold in all of us and made it shine,' said one of them, Gerard Hopkins. 'By sheer force of love and enthusiasm he created about him an atmosphere that must be unique in the history of business houses.'

During the weeks immediately after the performance of *The Masque of the Manuscript,* Williams's life was in many respects full of gaiety and hope. At Amen House he was, as he well knew, the cause of great happiness. Outside working hours he was now a regular lecturer at Evening Institutes, where he had already won the admiration and friendship of many members of his classes. Three volumes of his poetry had been published by the Press itself. He could almost have said that all was well. Almost, but not quite, for privately his life was dominated by one thing. He was in love with the Librarian at Amen House, Phyllis Jones.

*

Probably the marriage between Charles and Michal Williams had been tempestuous from the start. They were persons of strong character, and of very different ideas. He was absorbed in poetry and theological speculations, while she was practical-headed and liked to talk mostly about family or domestic matters. Charles tried to make a virtue of his wife's domesticity, declaring his admiration for it; but it imposed a strain. Nor was their marriage greatly eased by the birth of their son in 1922, for Charles found the boy's upbringing difficult to conduct, and discovered that his own close friendship with his father could not be repeated. Yet to explain his falling in love with another woman by saying that he was unhappy at home would be to fall short of understanding him entirely.

He had never expected marriage to be blissful or easy. His outlook did not allow any such casual optimism. Indeed he may have made the opposite mistake of expecting and looking for the worst. In the poetry that he wrote during the long years of his betrothal to Michal he showed himself only too aware of her limitations, describing her as 'wilful, insolent', and 'part scornful, part obsequious to the world'. Perhaps by the time they married he was no longer romantically in love with her. Certainly he had made himself ready for a change in his feelings by developing his 'Romantic Theology', as he now called it, his Dantean notion that human love is a ladder reaching up to God; for it seemed understandable to him that in climbing the ladder he should pass beyond the lower rungs, the youthful state of loving. But this had not prepared him for falling in love all over again.

Phyllis Jones was in her early twenties when she joined the Press. She had been educated at London University and had worked as a teacher before being given a job by Humphrey Milford. As Librarian at Amen House she was based in the room where 'C. W.' conducted many of his most animated conversations. She was soon caught up in them, and soon too she began to find poems addressed to her and left on her desk. Gradually she discovered that Williams was in love with her.

At first she loved him in return, and it was this – though almost nobody working at Amen House knew it[1] – that was the immediate cause of *An Urbanity* and the Masque; or rather, Masques, for the first was soon followed by another in the same vein, *The Masque of Perusal*. In this second piece, when the vital question 'Why do you publish?' fails to find an answer it is Phillida (Phyllis Jones herself) who finally supplies the justification of the whole procedure, declaring that the Press serves the ends of 'labour and purity and peace'.

Perhaps Williams found a kind of peace in their love affair during these months. But it is difficult to imagine that he, given his nature and his view of the marriage vows, could ever have contemplated divorce or adultery. At all events neither took place.[2] The only immediate physical result of his love for 'Phillida' was the constant stream of poems that he addressed to her. In these, he veiled her identity still further under the name 'Celia', which he took from Marvell's 'The Match', a poem describing how one spark from Love sets aflame the whole of Nature. Because of this he called the experience of falling in love in this fashion 'the Celian moment'. But it did not last. The feelings of 'Celia' changed, and soon she was in love with another member of the staff at Amen House.

This had a remarkable effect on Williams. He was desolate: in fact he never entirely came to terms with it. But he was also spurred by it into beginning his mature work as a writer.

*

In the fifth act of Shakespeare's *Troilus and Cressida*, it suddenly becomes plain to Troilus that his beloved Cressida, of whose love he was until that moment utterly sure, is not the changeless and unchangeable creature he had believed her to be. She is mutable: in fact she is faithless, is dallying with Diomedes. Troilus observes this – and declares that he has seen the impossible. When asked to explain what Cressida has done, he replies:

Nothing at all, unless that this were she.

[1] Nor was it known by Alice Mary Hadfield, Williams's friend and biographer, when she wrote *An Introduction to Charles Williams* (1959).

[2] Williams discusses the problems of what he calls the 'Second Image' of romantic love, by which he means the experience of falling in love a second time, after the first 'Beatrician experience' of love, in *The Figure of Beatrice*, his study of Dante and Romantic Theology (Faber & Faber, 1943): 'The second image is not to be denied; we are not to pretend it is not there, or indeed to diminish its worth; we are only asked to free ourselves from concupiscence in regard to it . . . The first image was towards physical union; the second towards its separation. It repeats the first, in an opposite direction. But both movements are alike intense towards most noble Love: that is, towards the work of the primal Love in creation.' (p. 49).

The Cressida who has been faithless must be someone else. She cannot be the same Cressida who loves him. But she is. And Troilus 'undergoes an entire subversion of his whole experience'.

These last words are by Charles Williams, who wrote at some length on this passage in *Troilus and Cressida*. Indeed he regarded it as crucially important not merely for this play but for the whole of Shakespeare's work, declaring that in this one line Shakespeare achieves a hitherto unequalled complexity of expression. He also looked for, and found, similar moments of equal importance in the work of other great poets, and concluded that it is at such moments that we can observe 'the passing of the poetic genius from its earlier states into its full strength'. He developed this theory into the central argument of his book *The English Poetic Mind,* applying it to the work of Milton, Wordsworth, Keats and Tennyson. Sometimes it fits the evidence very well, sometimes less so. In fact Williams would probably not have pressed the theory so hard had it not related closely to his own experience.

Up to this time he had lived, on the whole, according to his own plan. His intellect rose above those of almost all around him, and he was able to direct his life largely on his own terms. Certain things such as worry about money or domestic crises might cause ripples on the surface of his existence, but they did not reach to the depths of his being. He was able to embrace everything – belief and doubt, hope and disillusion, love and hatred – within the secure irony that he had developed. That irony had served to encompass the breakdown of romantic love within his marriage; it had served to create a unique half-serious half-playful ceremony of friendships at Amen House; it had even perhaps served to explain the fact that he, who had believed himself to be the poet of married love, should find himself in love extramaritally. But it had not prepared him for action taken by another person – for his rejection by 'Celia'.

That she did reject him was in fact not surprising. She wrote long afterwards: 'When one reads of the unhappy love affairs of poets, one feels how mean were the objects of their affections, and why couldn't they have given more? But the reality of such situations is more difficult.' Two things in particular made her draw back from him. The first was that he wanted her not merely to accept the poems he addressed to her, but to respond to them with intelligence and vitality; and she found it impossible to sustain this kind of response with freshness when new poems arrived on her desk almost every day. There was also his fondness for inflicting pain, though this showed itself in a harmless way. He would set her mock 'examination papers' on the English poets, partly through a real wish to improve her knowledge, but also so that he could threaten that if 'the candidate' failed to achieve the desired mark, she would be spanked on the hand with a ruler. So she withdrew, and turned to another, whose office was, ironically, directly beneath Williams's; the sound of their voices, filtering through the floorboards, caused him agonies of jealousy. Though her rejection of him was not sudden or surprising – nor entirely one-sided, for his feelings towards her had changed a little because of her seeming indifference to his poetry – the distress of it did not leave him, not least because she was still one of his daily companions at Amen House, his friend and yet totally isolated from him, Celia and not Celia, Cressida and not Cressida.

This she? no, this is Diomed's Cressida.

'How dreadful', Williams wrote five years after the ending of the affair, 'is the exalted head of the beloved moving serenely above and apart from one! Well – here are five years of pain, and still the victory is unachieved, partly because the will is not yet converted.' In 1934 'Celia' left Amen House, was married, and went to Java with her husband. Yet Williams's feelings for her lasted for the rest of his life. In 1940 he wrote: 'There can be few people who have behaved to each other with the same criminal lunacy, the same insane fidelity of attachment, the same throwing over and the same continual returns, the same insults and injuries, and the same devotion and peace and need, as Celia and I.'

What Williams called the 'great period' of the love affair came to an end soon after the first Masque in 1927. Shortly afterwards, there began his enormous outpouring of books: seven novels, more than a dozen plays, three volumes of literary criticism, a handful of biographies, several books of theology, and a lengthy and complex cycle of Arthurian poetry.

*

The 'Celian experience' itself was the subject of one of his first writings after the event had occurred. This was *The Chaste Wanton*, of which the title was casually suggested by Williams's friend Gerard Hopkins as suitable for a mock-Elizabethan play. Mock-Elizabethan it certainly was, for Williams had not yet found his own poetic style, and he depended, as his first four volumes of poetry show, on borrowing techniques from those poets he admired. *The Chaste Wanton* was stylistically a pastiche of Shakespeare. Yet though its form was second-hand its content was highly personal.

Set in an Italian ducal town of the Renaissance, the play begins with the meeting of the Duchess, young and beautiful but restless and as yet unfulfilled in life, with the middle-aged alchemist Vicenzo. He arrives

91

at her court, falls in love with her, and works a great change in her. He teaches her (in fact) the true nature of love, showing her, as Williams showed 'Celia' and others, by means of his Romantic Theology, how the process of loving can be 'commerce with heaven', a ladder to beatitude. And at first the Duchess returns his love. But it would not be an appropriate marriage, between a Duchess and a mere alchemist. Meanwhile the Prince of Padua is asking for the Duchess's hand, and he of course is an ideal suitor, even though he could never have worked the great change which now capacitates her for love. She chooses, in the event, to accept Padua and to use what Vicenzo has taught her to illuminate her marriage to the prince. Vicenzo hears the marriage treaty proclaimed; then he is told, 'The Duchess, sir, requires you; follow to her.'

> *Vicenzo:* I – follow?
> *Adrian:* Sir, the Duchess bade –
> *Vicenzo:* There is none.
> None, none, no Duchess. It is Tartary
> you speak of; there are Khans and Khanims . . .

It is *Troilus* all over again: 'This she? no, this is Diomed's Cressida.' And now everything is lost for Vicenzo. 'I would be somebody in heaven,' he declares, 'and now I am forever nothing and in hell.'

This death of love is followed by physical death. Among those at the court is the Bishop, who when the marriage is announced talks to Vicenzo in absurd platitudes about how the youthful romantic love of the Duchess and Padua will eventually mature into 'good works and decent frame, Quiet moderation of a happy hearth'. This was the kind of banality that Williams often found to be characteristic of the official Church's attitude to love – the very opposite of his Romantic Theology with its belief that love can lead ever upwards to higher states of vision and experience. Vicenzo responds in a fury, crying out: 'The void! the void! the utterance of the void!' and leaps at the Bishop, who falls and strikes his head against a stone seat. It is not clear whether the Bishop dies as a result – in his plays, Williams was often very bad at explaining what was actually going on – but the incident is enough to condemn Vicenzo to death. The Duchess comes to him in his cell and, though she hesitates to do so, Vicenzo bids her sign his death warrant. She has killed their love, so it is a small matter by comparison to kill his body. She signs it, and they part.

At the conclusion of *The Chaste Wanton* Charles Williams turned away from love. This play – never performed during his lifetime – was his record of the delight and tragedy of his 'Celian experience'. The

experience was never repeated, for he did not fall in love again. Nor
did he ever again use romantic love alone as the central matter of his
writings. His Romantic Theology was to play a vital part in his work,
but merely human love never concerned him again for its own sake.
It was perhaps too painful; it was certainly a stage which he felt he had
now left behind. For though he still regarded the death of the love affair
with 'Celia' as a tragedy, he seems also to have thought of it as a refining
fire which had purged his imagination and fitted it for higher things.

The immediate result was a novel.

*

It was called *Shadows of Ecstasy*, and it was (as a character in it remarked)
'all such a mad mixture, purple rhetoric and precise realism, doctrines
of transmutation and babble about African witch-doctors and airships
and submarines'. Indeed it was one of the oddest books ever to go under
the name of novel.

Its lack of interest in ordinary character portrayal was striking –
though certainly one of the principal characters, Roger Ingram the
Professor of Applied Literature at London University, was recognisable
as bearing a superficial resemblance to Williams himself. Ingram is
committed to *applying* literature to his own and other people's lives,
rather than, as he puts it, 'embalming' it in the manner of many literary
critics. He declares of the study of poetry: 'You've nearly killed it, with
your appreciations and your fastidious judgements, and your lives of
this man and your studies in that. Love and poetry are powers. Power,
power, it's dying in you, and you don't hunger to feel it live.' It was the
first appearance of the theme of power, a theme which ran through all
Williams's early novels.

Ingram soon encounters someone who shares his recognition that
poetry is a living force or energy, someone who (and this is the central
point of the novel) can show him how to use that energy to give himself
strength. This is Considine, a man who claims to have conquered death,
and who has already lived for two hundred years. Considine has done
this, he says, by turning the force of all emotional experiences inward
upon himself, so that instead of pouring his energy out as other men
do in love and hate, joy and misery, he can convert the strength of these
feelings into a form of power which will infinitely prolong his physical
life. 'I have poured the strength of every love and hate into my own
life,' he tells Ingram, 'and now I need love and hate no more.' Considine explains that he learnt this in his youth when he was rejected by
a girl he loved, and, experiencing severe emotional pain, said to himself,
'If this pain were itself power . . .' Now he can transmute – and can
show others how to transmute – all sexual energy into such self-

strengthening power; and not just sexual energy, but all such forces of the emotions. Ingram hesitates, but eventually commits himself to becoming a disciple of this superman, and begins to experience the strengthening force of emotion turned back into his own life. However, Considine is murdered by a jealous follower, and at the end of the book Ingram is left desolate, wondering whether Considine can indeed conquer death and return to the living.

This is just the central matter of the plot. The other odd happenings, thrown into the story with a total disregard for plausibility, do indeed produce a 'mad mixture'; and understandably *Shadows of Ecstasy* at first failed to find a publisher. It is the least successful of Williams's novels. But it is also the most autobiographical; for what Considine teaches Ingram – that the emotions can be turned inwards to strengthen the personality – was what Williams now believed.

His next novel to be offered for publication was *War in Heaven*. In it, the theme of power is not yet fully developed. Certainly the central object in the story, the Holy Graal, contains stored supernatural power which may be released by an adept in black magic. But this is not of prime importance in the novel, which is really little more than a *jeu d'esprit* investigating the possibilities of the supernatural when used in 'thriller' form. Not that it is at all humorous or light-weight; the passages describing the magical practices are sometimes singularly and unpleasantly vivid, so that one wonders if Williams is not gratuitously enjoying them beyond the demands of the story. But in general the book's treatment of the supernatural is more like, say, Chesterton's *The Man Who Was Thursday* than anything Williams wrote later, while the character of the Archdeacon bears a marked resemblance to Chesterton's Father Brown.[1]

Perhaps because it could be recognised as belonging to an existing genre of novel, *War in Heaven* eventually (after several rejections) was

[1] Much of Williams's early (i.e. pre-*Taliessin through Logres*) poetry shows the influence of Chesterton; e.g. Williams's 'Taliessin's Song of Byzantion' printed in *Three Plays*, p. 65:

> In the gate of Santa Sophia, amid patriarchs and popes
> I saw the Emperor sitting, and the smoke of earthly hopes
> went up to him as incense, and the tapers shone around
> as prayers before the Emperor, sitting aureoled and crowned.
>
> As God sits in the pictures that the monks on parchment draw,
> in pavilions over Sinai, giving Israel the law,
> or thrusting seas in order and firmaments in place,
> and the little devils hiding from the terror of his face;
>
> in the gate of Holy Wisdom, so I saw the Emperor sit . . . (etc.)

accepted by Victor Gollancz and published in 1930. Its success was sufficient for three more novels by Williams to be published by the same firm shortly afterwards. He was writing fast now, partly in office hours at the Press. *War in Heaven* actually brought him some modest royalties, and the prospect of making money by writing encouraged him to continue in the same vein. Not that he had any absurd dream of riches, but there was a constant stream of household bills to be settled. His salary at the Press was not unreasonably low, but he was bad at managing money – he was always buying cups of coffee and glasses of sherry and meals for his friends – and in any case his memories of financial anxiety in his childhood left him in a constant state of worry about his bank-balance. So he went on writing novels specifically for the purpose of making money, and indeed he believed strongly that this was an excellent motive. He declared that it was the stimulus of potential poverty that had produced so many great writers from the ranks of the financially unstable lower middle classes. 'I saw Shake-speare', he wrote in a poem,

> In a Tube station on the Central London:
> He was smoking a pipe:
> He had Sax Rohmer's best novel under his arm
> (In a cheap edition)
> And the *Evening News.*
> He was reading in the half-detached way one does.
> He had just come away from an office
> And the notes for *The Merchant*
> Were in his pocket,
> Beginning (it was the first line he thought of)
> 'Still quiring to the young-eyed cherubins',
>
> But his chief wish was to be earning more money.

This poem shows Williams's total disregard for the conventional distinctions of time and space, the natural and the supernatural, and his habit of setting extraordinary events against mundane backgrounds. If he wanted to talk about seeing Shakespeare, why should it not happen in a Tube railway station? If he wished to write a novel about the magical properties of the Stone of Suleiman, then let it be set in modern London and let the participants include the Lord Chief Justice and his secretary. (This was *Many Dimensions*, published in 1931, and including in the character of the secretary Chloe something of a portrait of 'Celia'.) Or if the plot was to concern the appearance in the material world of 'huge and mighty forms', the Platonic archetypes themselves, then let those archetypes appear in the most ordinary landscape that he knew, the Hertfordshire countryside surrounding St Albans. (This was *The Place of the Lion*, published in the same year.) And, if his subject was to be the Tarot cards and their supernatural relation to the 'eternal dance' of the universe, let the terrifying results of the use and abuse of those cards be experienced by a modern middle-class citizen at a house on the South Downs. (This was *The Greater Trumps*, published in 1932. *Shadows of Ecstasy* was eventually issued a year later.)

These novels were all concerned with the rightful and wrongful use of power. And here somebody reading them may find himself in some confusion, for Williams's ideas of right and wrong often seem extremely odd. In *Shadows of Ecstasy* it is disturbing to find the 'hero' Roger Ingram becoming a disciple of the 'villain' Considine. In *War in Heaven* it is at first puzzling to discover that Williams seems to have almost as much enthusiasm for the cause of the black magicians as for the Arch-deacon and his friends. And in *The Greater Trumps*, when Aaron Lee and his grandson Henry use the Tarot cards to raise a great storm by which they hope to murder a man, Williams seems to take sides with them as much as with Coningsby, their intended victim. What has happened to his moral sense?

The answer is that in these novels he was not principally concerned with moral issues. The question of the nature of good and evil occupied his mind, but he did not discuss it in depth in the novels, reserving it for his religious dramas and his theological study *He Came Down From Heaven*. For the moment he was content to leave it somewhat on one side, and to judge the characters in his novels not by such terms as 'good' and 'bad' but by differentiating their attitudes to the super-natural. Low in the scale come such people as Damaris Tighe in *The Place of the Lion*, who merely *studies* the history of supernatural beliefs without considering what she herself should believe. Low too in the scale are those – and there are many in the novels – who desire to use supernatural powers for their own ends; but though this may be evil it does show a proper awareness of those powers. Higher are those persons such as Lord Arglay in *Many Dimensions* and Sir Bernard Travers in *Shadows of Ecstasy* who are true agnostics, having decided neither to believe nor to disbelieve but to remain with open minds; and their unruffled scepticism, characteristic of one aspect of Williams himself, in its way admits that belief is possible. Highest of all come those few – there is rarely more than one in each novel – who commit themselves fully to the supernatural, resigning themselves utterly into its hands, even if the result is (as it sometimes is) physical death.

Even this bare summary of some of the elements in the novels shows how unusual they are, a 'mad mixture' even by the side of conventional occult or supernatural fiction. Not surprisingly, when they were first published a lot of people found them unreadable, or dismissed them as 'painfully incredible' (J. B. Priestley's comment on *The Greater Trumps*.) However, some readers admired them greatly. Among these admirers was T. S. Eliot.

'There are no novels anywhere quite like them,' wrote Eliot. 'He makes our everyday world much more exciting, because of the supernatural which he finds always active in it. He really believes in what he is talking about. And seeing all persons and all events in the light of the divine, he shows us a significance, in human beings, human emotions, human events, to which we had been blind.'

Eliot had been told to read *War in Heaven* and *The Place of the Lion* by Lady Ottoline Morrell, and shortly afterwards (in 1934) she invited Williams to one of her London tea parties to meet Eliot. 'I remember a man in spectacles,' recalled Eliot of the occasion, 'who appeared to combine a frail physique with exceptional vitality. He appeared completely at ease in surroundings with which he was not yet familiar, and which had intimidated many; and at the same time was modest and unassuming to the point of humility. One retained the impression that he was pleased and grateful for the opportunity of meeting the company, and yet that it was he who had conferred a favour – more than a favour, a kind of benediction, by coming.'[1]

By the time the two men met, Williams had already published his opinion of Eliot's poetry. This was in *Poetry at Present*, a volume (based on his evening classes) of brief critical studies of contemporary poets – or rather, critical *enthusiasms*, for typically Williams used the essays to point out strengths rather than to lay bare weaknesses. Although in his own poetry he had as yet shown little interest in post-1914 styles, he found much to admire in modern verse. Indeed, only in one major instance did he fail to show much understanding. 'I feel a real apology is due to Mr Eliot,' he wrote, 'for whose work I profess a sincere and profound respect, though I fail to understand it.' He declared himself disturbed by what he called Eliot's 'unmeaning', and said: 'If only we

[1] Among those of Lady Ottoline's guests who were 'intimidated' was Hugo Dyson. He was invited to Garsington Manor on several occasions when he was an undergraduate. Recalling these visits (in a radio broadcast fifty years later) he said that at Garsington he had encountered 'all the people whom secretly one would have most desired to meet – and, as so often happened to a shy insignificant person, when one did meet them one was filled with a kind of terror. They were kindly enough, but I found them alarming. They weren't, most of them, my weight. I do remember finding Virginia Woolf immensely beautiful and immensely frightening; and one of my *fears* – I don't think I was quite alone in this – was that she would speak to me one day (but she never did).' (In conversation with Roger Green, BBC Radio Oxford, May 1971.)

could neglect it, and go back to our sound traditional versifiers!' Yet of those versifiers he said, referring to Eliot's 'Sweeney Among the Nightingales', 'Which of them has, in their own way, ever done anything half so good?'

On the basis of this puzzled respect by Williams, and Eliot's enthusiasm for Williams's novels, a slightly restrained friendship began between them. They enjoyed each other's company when they met, which was perhaps once or twice a year; but there was only a limited understanding between them, and their most profound ideas were not shared. They might, in fact, have achieved a real exchange of thought, for as Christian poets their work was largely a matter of related opposites: Williams wrote about such 'affirmative' aspects of Christianity as the Dantean approach to romantic love, while Eliot was concerned largely with the 'negative' or ascetic rejection of the world. There were indeed certain small influences on each side: Williams showed a few traces of Eliot's style in some of his later poems, and Eliot by his own admission took the 'still point of the turning world' in *Burnt Norton* from the Fool in Williams's *The Greater Trumps*. Perhaps too the moment in *The Cocktail Party* when Reilly quotes Shelley's lines about a *doppelgänger* was suggested by a similar use of those lines in Williams's *Descent into Hell*. But such things did not show any fundamental understanding between the two men. Their differences far exceeded any such slight similarities, and they largely failed to communicate with each other.

*

The fame of Williams's novels was never great, and such as it was it spread slowly. It was early in the nineteen-thirties that R. W. Chambers, Professor of English at London University, read and admired those of them that had been published. Chambers knew C. S. Lewis, and he mentioned to Lewis that he ought to read one of these 'spiritual shockers' by Williams. But at first Lewis did not do anything about it.

It was not until February 1936, when he was calling on Nevill Coghill in Exeter College and heard his host eloquently praising *The Place of the Lion*, that Lewis borrowed Coghill's copy, took it home, and read it. Perhaps it was fortunate that it was this book rather than any other of the early novels that formed his introduction to Williams's work. Not only did one of its themes – the necessity of taking philosophical and religious studies utterly seriously and not merely using them as 'research' – agree with what Lewis himself often said, but the book lacked any of the unpleasantness which sometimes seemed to be beneath the surface of the black magic and 'sexual energy' in *War in Heaven* and *Shadows of Ecstasy*.

On 26 February 1936 Lewis wrote to Arthur Greeves: 'I have just read what I think a really great book, *The Place of the Lion* by Charles Williams. It is based on the Platonic theory of the other world in which the archetypes of all earthly qualities exist: and in the novel these archetypes start sucking our world back. The lion of strength appears in the world and the strength starts going out of houses and things into him. The archetypal butterfly (enormous) appears and all the butterflies of the world fly back into him. But every man contains and ought to be able to rule these forces: and there is one man in the book who does. It is not only a most exciting fantasy, but a deeply religious and (unobtrusively) a profoundly learned book. The reading of it has been a good preparation for Lent as far as I am concerned: for it shows me (through the heroine) the special sin of the abuse of intellect to which all my profession are liable, more clearly than I ever saw it before. I have learned more than I ever knew yet about humility. In fact it has been a big experience. Do get it, and don't mind if you don't understand everything the first time. It deserves reading over and over again. It isn't often now-a-days you get a *Christian* fantasy.'

As it happened, Lewis's *Allegory of Love,* then provisionally titled *The Allegorical Love Poem,* was at this time in the hands of the Oxford University Press and awaiting publication. The book was the concern of the academic division of the Press in Oxford, but the London branch had some responsibility for sales, and Humphrey Milford was given a set of proofs so that he could get one of his staff to write a descriptive paragraph about it. He passed these proofs to Williams, who read them through at speed, and was delightedly amazed to find Lewis praising Dante's 'noble fusion of sexual and religious experience'.

Williams had no sooner finished reading the book and had written a paragraph praising it than he heard from Milford that Lewis had been saying complimentary things about *The Place of the Lion.* A day later he received a letter from Lewis saying that he thought the novel remarkable. Williams replied by return of post:

12 March 1936

My dear Mr Lewis,

If you had delayed writing another 24 hours our letters would have crossed. It has never before happened to me to be admiring an author of a book while he at the same time was admiring me. My admiration for the staff work of the Omnipotence rises every day.

To be exact, I finished on Saturday looking – too hastily – at proofs of your *Allegorical Love Poem.* I regard your book as practically the only one that I have ever come across, since Dante, that shows the slightest understanding of what this very peculiar identity of love and religion means. As to your letter, what can I say? The public for these novels has been so severely limited (though I admit in some cases passionate) that it gives me very high pleasure to feel that you liked the *Lion*. You must be in London sometimes. Do let me know and come and have lunch or dinner.

Very gratefully yours,
Charles Williams.

2

'A tremendous flow of words'

Lewis did not often come to London. Business rarely took him there, and he saw in the capital city little of the significance that Williams perceived, finding it to be mostly chaos where Williams could distinguish order. But he did sometimes have to make a journey up from Oxford, and next time this happened he accepted Williams's invitation and had lunch with him. He was as fascinated by Williams the man as he had been by *The Place of the Lion*.

'He is', he told Arthur Greeves, 'of humble origin (there are still traces of Cockney in his voice), ugly as a chimpanzee but so radiant (he emanates more *love* than any man I have ever known) that as soon as he begins talking he is transfigured and looks like an angel. He sweeps some people quite off their feet and has many disciples. Women find him so attractive that if he were a bad man he could do what he liked either as a Don Juan or a charlatan.'

*

By this time Williams did indeed have 'disciples', largely as a result of lecturing for the Evening Institutes. After a bravura performance in the lecture itself, he would lead a discussion which electrified his audience into believing that they themselves were almost as clever and interesting as he was. An inevitable result was that many of them stayed behind to talk to him afterwards; and an inevitable result of that was a long conversation, usually conducted as he sat with his pupils in a tea shop or strolled with them through the London streets – the habit of peripatetic talking had remained with him since the childhood walks with his father. Nor did it end there, for a number of friends he made in this fashion ceased to be contented with a once-weekly meeting at an evening class, and began to search him out at the Press. At Amen

House, 'C. W.'s young women' (as they were known) soon made up a large proportion of the visitors.

The majority of those who sought him out were indeed young women, and, as Lewis noted, they found him extremely attractive. Not that he was good-looking in a conventional way; one female admirer spoke disparagingly of the shape of his mouth, and of 'his curious accent and the unpleasing timbre of his voice'. But she added: 'Of all these details I was unconscious. His was a dignity which out-soared absurdity; as his was an attractiveness so potent that it turned the ugliness of his voice and features to no account.'

The source of this potent attraction was hard to define. It was partly the manner of his movements, the way he would sweep himself up-stairs, whirl a visitor into a room, and offer a greeting or conduct a farewell with Elizabethan courtesy, bending over the hand of a female friend and kissing it lightly. It was also the intensity of his gaze; and it was the blend of sympathy, as he listened to an outpouring of troubles and personal problems, with *command*; for he would answer any such outpouring with a firm instruction, holding the friend by the wrist and counting on her fingers as he spoke: 'Love – obey – pray – play – and be intelligent.' It was also his lack of self-consciousness, which allowed him to call unblushingly to a young woman friend across a crowded railway carriage: 'God bless you, child. Under the Protection.'

There was, in other words, a good deal of personal magnetism. And there was also something in his manner that is best described as in-cantatory. The benediction called across the railway carriage and the rhythmic phrase tapped out on the fingers were manifestations of this; as were his lectures, in which he chanted lines of verse almost as if they were magical formulae. They were not always lines that made any great sense out of context – 'And thus the Filial Godhead answering spake' from *Paradise Lost* and 'Felt in the blood and felt along the heart' from Wordsworth's 'Tintern Abbey' were among his favourites – but he did not believe that the actual meaning of such lines was especially import-ant. 'There has been a great deal too much talking of what the poets *mean*,' he wrote in *The English Poetic Mind*. And in another context he said: 'It isn't what poetry says, it is what poetry *is*.' What poetry was to him was a storehouse of emotional or even supernatural power. He believed he could come into contact with that power by chanting lines of great verse. Like Roger Ingram in *Shadows of Ecstasy* he 'submitted his obedience to the authority of Milton and Wordsworth, waiting for the august plenitude of their poetry to be manifested within him'.

This was not the usual stuff of London County Council evening classes, but many of his audience found it magnificent. And if they became friends with him, it was only the first of several metaphysical notions with which he presented them. Those who showed themselves particularly sympathetic to his ideas were told that they might like to regard themselves as one of the 'Companions of the Co-inherence'.

*

It was not Williams's own idea to form an Order. The impetus to establish it came from his disciples, and for a long time he was reluctant to do any such thing. But at last he agreed to permit those who desired it to call themselves members of a Company, and in time he came to like the idea. Some years later he expressed the nature of such a body in a poem which was part of his Arthurian cycle, 'The Founding of the Company':

Grounded in the Acts of the Throne and the pacts of the themes,
it lived only by conceded recollection,
having no decision, no vote or admission,
but for the single note that any soul
took of its own election of the Way; the whole
shaped no frame nor titular claim to place.

The 'Companions of the Co-inherence' (the name generally given to the group, though it was often referred to as 'the Household' or 'the Company') took their title from one of Williams's central ideas, which had first grown in his mind during the 1914–18 war, when his grief at the death of the two close friends of his Working Men's College days eventually persuaded him that all human beings are totally dependent on each other, that indeed 'no man is an Island', and that each thought or action has a bearing on other people. This idea he called Co-inherence, and he developed it further, suggesting that even evil actions will produce good and that many good things will lead to evil. There is, he believed, an enormous potential both for good and evil in every piece of human behaviour. Not that this argued against there being such a thing as sin. 'Sin', he said, 'is the preference of an immediately satisfying experience to the declared pattern of the universe'; and it is, he said, the Christian's duty to perceive that pattern ('the eternal dance' he called it in *The Greater Trumps*) and to act according to it.

Williams's 'Co-inherence' harmonised with orthodox Christian teaching. But others of his doctrines which the Companions were asked to observe and practise were less conventional.

First was Romantic Theology. He impressed upon those close to him that lovers should see in each other a reflection of God, that in the beauty of the beloved 'an explanation of the whole universe is being offered, and indeed in some sense understood; only it cannot be defined'.

103

Romantic Theology was not peculiar to Williams – he had found it, of course, in Dante – but it was more idiosyncratic than Co-inherence, and when he drafted a book on it in the early nineteen-twenties and offered it to the Press, Humphrey Milford was distinctly dubious, and sent the manuscript to an adviser for comment. Unfortunately for Williams that adviser was 'Tommy' Strong, the Bishop of Oxford, who was not only a bachelor but reputedly a misogynist. Not surprisingly Strong did not recommend that 'Outlines of Romantic Theology' be published, and the book remained in manuscript, its contents gradually being absorbed into Williams's other writings during the succeeding years.

The real gulf between Williams and such churchmen as Strong was not in their attitudes to women but in their approach to the Christian life. Indeed, Williams was steering a markedly different course from that chosen by the majority of Christian teachers over the centuries. Traditionally, the Church has more often emphasised asceticism and the rejection of worldly enjoyment than the alternative, the trans-mutation of the delights of the world into the Christian vision. But it was this last method which Williams adhered to. He called it The Way of Affirmation, as opposed to the ascetic Way of Rejection. His Romantic Theology was 'affirmative' in that it used worldly love as its starting-point rather than rejecting it in favour of an ascetic life; and there was Affirmation too in Williams's other principal doctrine which was practised by the Companions of the Co-inherence: the practice of 'Substitution' or 'Substituted Love'. This doctrine was not developed by Williams until some years after he had outlined Romantic Theology, and it was never communicated to Bishop Strong, which was perhaps just as well; for that ecclesiastical dignitary would undoubtedly have been highly perturbed by it.

The first notion of Substitution occurred to Williams in 1932. 'I have a point to discuss with you', he wrote to a young friend from the even-ing classes, Thelma Shuttleworth, 'which makes me wonder whether the New Testament may not be merely true in some of its advice. All about "bearing one another's burdens". I have an awful (full of awe) feeling that one can.'

In his thinking and writings Williams had already paid much atten-tion to the metaphorical implications of 'bear ye one another's burdens'. It was a natural development from Co-inherence to observe the degree in which human life depends on the principle of exchange, on the sharing of tasks and responsibilities. Mundane forms of this exchange include commerce (where money is offered in return for goods) and professional and business life (where members of the community undertake specialised responsibilities by which they serve others). These mundane exchanges can of course be seen in any city, and this helped to strengthen Williams's notion of cities in general and the City of London in particular as a type of the City of God, for he believed that Exchange was a heavenly principle. But as to the *literal* implications of St Paul's words about bearing one another's burdens, that was another matter.

Could personal burdens be born by others? Could, for example, someone racked by worry or anxiety pass that particular emotional burden to someone else who had agreed voluntarily to accept it? Williams came to believe that this could in fact be done, simply by a mutual pact, came to believe even that actual physical pain could be taken over by someone who was willing to substitute himself or herself for the sufferer. And this Substitution became an important activity of the Companions of the Co-inherence.[1]

*

Did it work? Certainly a number of responsible and sensible people who knew Williams were strongly persuaded that it did. It was after all in spirit entirely Christian – Williams regarded the Crucifixion as the ultimate Substitution, by which Christ offered his own suffering for the sins of the world. On the other hand, like so much of Williams's thought, it did have an air of the magical. And did Williams have any right to assume authority in it, instructing (as he sometimes did) one of the Companions to substitute herself for another who was going through some physical or emotional difficulty?

'Substitution' played quite a large part in Williams's letters to the Companions and to other friends and admirers. And though his letters did not deal only with such spiritual matters – he often discussed his poetry, or the absurdities of daily life, all with a delightfully wry wit[2] – they tended, as one of his disciples in the nineteen-forties, Lois Lang-Sims, remarked, to consist of 'a tremendous flow of words'. The letters were also open to misinterpretation. 'My dear Thelma,' he began one such letter,

> I very nearly adore you. In fact I do; so that you can say, as the Angel in the Apocalypse said to the Divine John, 'See thou do it

[1] It has been pointed out to me that Williams's concept of Substitution may have been suggested by Kipling's short story 'The Wish House', which was first published in 1924 and which tells the story of an old woman who makes a deal with a spirit or 'token' that she will bear all the pain of the man she loves, up to and including terminal cancer. Kipling's blend of the modern with the supernatural probably had a wide influence on Williams's imagination.

[2] For the breadth of subject-matter in Williams's letters, see the many examples quoted below, in Part Three, Chapter 5.

not'. But one may adore Love-in-Thelma, and think that the dwelling place of the Eternal that dwelleth in the heavens is a very transmuting one. Remember that you *are* more lucid, more beautiful, more Love. I add in a postscript that you are as divine a creature as I have ever known in this high pursuit of Love.

Thelma Shuttleworth was wise enough in the ways of Charles Williams to know that this was a demonstration of Romantic Theology rather than of erotic passion. She recalled of these years, 'We were together in love, though never with one another.' But others did not find it so easy to make the distinction, or did not care to. 'I was by this time', wrote Lois Lang-Sims of her growing feelings for Williams, ' "in love" with Charles in the sense that I wanted to be his mistress.'

He never took sexual advantage of any of his disciples who found themselves in this state of mind; or at least he did not do so in the conventional sense. His general rule, as C. S. Lewis observed, was 'to teach them the *ars honesta amandi* and then bestow them on other (younger) men'. On the other hand Lois Lang-Sims alleges that on one occasion he put his arms round her and 'held me in a strange stillness, a silence so unlike his usual loquacity, a motionlessness so unlike his usual excitement, that nothing could have been further from the kind of behaviour my previous knowledge of him had led me to expect'. At the time she was greatly puzzled, not to say alarmed. Later she thought she recognised in this behaviour a kind of ritual that was sometimes practised by magical sects, and even by some early Christians until the practice was strongly suppressed in the Church, a ritual that attempts to heighten consciousness and increase power by harnessing the sexual instinct, and achieving a kind of tension-of-polarity between desire and restraint. If Lois Lang-Sims was right,[1] Williams was actually putting into practice the kind of thing he had hinted at some years earlier in *Shadows of Ecstasy*, where a young lover sees in his mind the naked physical beauty of his beloved, but instead of aiming his desires towards sexual consummation 'seemed to control and compel them into subterranean torrents towards hidden necessities within him'.

Those of Williams's disciples who confessed to small failures or a general lapse of conduct would find that he imposed some small penance upon them; for instance, 'You'll copy out for me the first twelve verses of the 52nd chapter of Isaiah: you will do this *as soon as you can*, and

---

[1] In the first chapter of his book *The Descent of the Dove* Williams certainly mentions with some enthusiasm the *subintroductae* of the early church, women who slept with their male companions without sexual intercourse. He says: 'In some cases it failed. But we know nothing – most unfortunately – of the cases in which it did not fail.' He calls the practice 'dangerous but dangerous with a kind of heavenly daring'.

you'll learn the first three verses by heart.' Occasionally too there was evidence here of the sadistic element in his personality, for he would sometimes threaten a whipping as a punishment for misbehaviour. But this remained in the realm of fantasy.

Williams himself had no delusions about his own personality. 'God forbid I should call myself an apostle!' he told Thelma Shuttleworth. 'I am the least – O unworthy, unworthy! – of all.' But he believed firmly that his own failings made not a jot of difference to the validity of his teaching. 'St Paul knew that it is possible to preach to others and yet to be a castaway,' he wrote. 'Only – and this the fools sometimes forget – the preaching is true all the same.'

He often emphasised this point in his writings. Of the poet Peter Stanhope in the novel *Descent into Hell* – a character undoubtedly based on what Williams would have liked to be[1] – it is said: 'Whether his personal life could move to the sound of his own lucid exaltation of verse she [Pauline Anstruther] did not know. It was not her business; perhaps it was not even his.' And when discussing Dante and the Way of Affirmation (i.e. Romantic Theology), Williams declares: 'We do not know if, or how far, Dante himself in his personal life cared or was able to follow the Way he defined, nor is it our business.' These remarks ought to be remembered during any investigation of Williams's own life. Moreover, the personality expressed in his writings and remembered by his friends did show a positive quality of inner calm, of humility; so that it is possible to understand how T. S. Eliot could say of Williams, 'He seemed to me to approximate, more nearly than any man I have known familiarly, to the saint.'

*

'What finally convinced me that he has written a great poem was a transformation which my judgment underwent in reading it.' The periodical in which this review appeared was *Theology* for April 1939; the reviewer was C. S. Lewis. After long effort, Williams had published the first volume of his cycle of Arthurian poetry, *Taliessin through Logres*.

'I liked its "flavour" from the first,' wrote Lewis, 'but found it so idiosyncratic that I thought the book might be what Lamb called a "favourite", a thing not for all days or all palates, like *Tristram Shandy* or the *Arcadia*. But as I went on I found bit after bit of my "real world" falling into its place in the poem. I found pair after pair of opposites harmoniously reconciled. I began to see that what had seemed a deliciously

[1] Williams himself used 'Peter Stanhope' as a *nom de plume* for his religious drama *Judgement at Chelmsford*, and the character of Stanhope in *Descent into Hell* resembles Williams in many particulars. On the other hand Stanhope in the novel differs from Williams in that he enjoys success and fame almost on a par with Shakespeare.

private universe was the common universe after all: that this apparently romantic and even wilful poem was really "classic" and central. I do not think this can happen in a minor work.'

After their first meeting at which he had been captivated by Williams, Lewis continued to see him as often as possible, though the friendship was limited by the distance between Oxford and London. Occasionally Williams came down to visit Lewis at Magdalen; more often the meetings were in London, either in Williams's tiny office at Amen House or at his favourite lunch-place, Shirreff's under the railway arch in Ludgate Hill. Williams usually had nothing more than a sandwich for his lunch, but on one memorable occasion in 1938 Lewis brought his brother Warnie and Hugo Dyson with him from Oxford, and they all ate (said Lewis) 'kidneys enclosed, like the wicked man, in their own fat'. After lunch they walked about and sat in St Paul's churchyard, conducting what Lewis afterwards remembered as an 'almost Platonic discussion'.

Lewis and Williams continued to profess enthusiasm for each other's writings. When in 1938 Williams published what might be called a 'handlist' of his interpretations of Christian doctrine, *He Came Down From Heaven,* he referred in it to Lewis's *The Allegory of Love,* which he called 'one of the most important critical books of our time'. Lewis was equally enthusiastic about *Taliessin through Logres* when it appeared in the same year, and his support was especially valuable to Williams, because otherwise the book met with little success.

This was scarcely surprising, for the poems it contained were extremely difficult to understand, even by the standard of Williams's other writings. He paid little attention to the central events of the Arthurian story but concentrated on lesser-known details from Malory, and introduced other figures, most notably Taliessin, the poet of Celtic legend, whom he made King's Poet at Arthur's court – and whose character and role had a relation to Williams's own idea of himself. He named Arthur's kingdom 'Logres', using a Celtic word for Britain, and he made Logres a province of 'The Empire', by which he meant literally the Byzantine Empire and metaphorically the Kingdom of God on earth. Geographical features of his Arthurian landscape included not just Malory's 'Carbonek' (the Grail castle) and 'Sarras' (the earthly paradise or 'land of the Trinity') but also 'Broceliande', a forest of metaphysical rather than physical character, a 'place of making' from which both good and evil may come; and there was also 'P'o-l'u', the antipodean seat of a diabolical Anti-Emperor. This name was a private jest, though a sad one, for Williams had found 'P'o-l'u' on a map of Java, and it was to Java that his Celia had gone after her marriage. On top of all this was an extra layer of symbolism, by which different parts of the human body were chosen to represent different provinces of the Empire: the head for Logres, the breasts for Gaul, the buttocks for Caucasia; while these provinces themselves represented spiritual characteristics. Williams had adapted this idea from the Sephirotic Tree in A. E. Waite's *Secret Doctrine in Israel,* and he used it literally 'on top' of the geography of his Arthurian poems, for on the endpapers of *Taliessin through Logres* was printed a map of the Empire with a naked female body superimposed.

Taliessin went almost unnoticed. It was meant by Williams to be the finest expression of his thought, and he had taken many years over the development of the poems in it, the majority of which were far more modern in style than his earlier verse; they showed some influence of Gerard Manley Hopkins, the collected edition of whose poems he had revised for the Press, and they had also benefited from the advice of a friend, the young poet Anne Ridler. But for the most part they were incomprehensible to anyone not entirely conversant with Williams's ideas. '*Taliessin through Logres* contained some beautiful poetry,' wrote T. S. Eliot a year after the book was published, 'but also some of the most obscure poetry that was ever written.'

Williams was in fact having little popular success with any of his books, though this was not for lack of trying. During the nineteen-thirties his output was immense. Besides the poetry there were three volumes of literary criticism, several plays (including *Thomas Cranmer of Canterbury* which was performed at the Canterbury Festival the year after *Murder in the Cathedral*), two theological books (*He Came Down From Heaven* and *The Descent of the Dove*), innumerable book reviews for newspapers and for *Time & Tide,* and five historical biographies, of Henry VII, Elizabeth, James I, Bacon, and the Restoration poet Rochester. He also wrote a number of articles, edited *The New Book of English Verse* for Gollancz, revised the Bridges edition of Hopkins' poems, and contributed to several anthologies for the Oxford University Press. And on top of this there were the novels.

The historical biographies were the product of an intimate knowledge of their subjects and periods, but they were undertaken to earn money and were written in a hurry. Inevitably they often revealed themselves as pot-boilers. 'He always boiled an honest pot,' said T. S. Eliot of them; but too often Williams resorted to stylistic mannerisms. Graham Greene, reviewing *Rochester*, singled out this passage:

'The poor benefit of a bewildering minute' had a vivid place in the awareness of my lord's poetic genius. It is in the mere admiration of what, in the contrasting line of Mr T. S. Eliot, has been, with a larger but inclusive scope, called 'the infirm glory of the positive hour'. It was precisely the 'infirm glory' and 'the poor benefit' of which my lord's angry contempt was contendingly aware.

Graham Greene called this 'pretentious jargon', and said that one would hardly think it referred to a bawdy incident at the Customs. 'A great deal of the book is very badly written,' he added. 'Mr Williams loses himself hopelessly in abstractions.'

Even when Williams's work was good, the fact that his large output covered several different fields of literature meant that he did not make his name as a specialist. Until 1939 only his novels built up any substantial regular following, and even then their sales were small. Gollancz, who published the first five, were not encouraged, and when Williams offered them another novel in 1937 they rejected it.

This rejection was partly because the new book, *Descent into Hell,* was notably different from its predecessors, lacking their crisply dramatic opening chapters and having very little of the 'thriller' about it. It would probably not have been published at all had not T. S. Eliot accepted it on behalf of Faber & Faber, of which he was a director. Eliot said that he did not find it as enthralling as Williams's earlier novels; but he liked it enough to want to see it in print. In fact *Descent into Hell* was a remarkable piece of work, in many ways better than anything Williams had done before. It was slow to gather momentum but eventually achieved a terrifying sense of the damnation of one man. Yet when it was published its success in financial terms was no greater than that of its predecessors. By this time Williams had to resign himself to the fact that if he had not exactly failed as a writer, he had by no means achieved the success for which he had once perhaps hoped.

When war broke out in September 1939 he was fifty-two and not in the best of health – he had undergone a serious operation for a gastric disorder, intussuception, some years earlier. He was also very tired. He was, too, saddened by what had happened to the Press in the ten years since the Masques had been performed. The old sense of purpose had gone. Humphrey Milford, now Sir Humphrey, seemed more remote, and had withdrawn himself from all but necessary conversation (he was in fact suffering from an undiagnosed illness). And now, at the outbreak of war, the entire staff of Amen House were to be evacuated to Oxford. 'To think we said the Masque was God!' Williams wrote sadly.

> It was? My dear! How very odd!
> But if it was you must allow
> God is as dead as doornails now.

PART THREE

7 (a) Charles Williams
on the terrace of
the Spaldings'
house in Oxford,
1939.

7 (b) C. S. Lewis in an Oxford pub.

8 (a) Charles Williams in 193[9]

8 (b) The 'Bird and Baby'.

I

'They are good for my mind'

'Outside Lewis I never want to see anyone of Oxford or in Oxford again,' Charles Williams wrote to his wife on 4 October 1939.

He had moved down from London with his Oxford University Press colleagues a month earlier. Temporary office premises had been found for them in Southfield House, an unremarkable mansion on the Cowley Road to the east of the city, and things were very makeshift there. Most of the staff had to share cramped rooms and, though Williams was lucky enough to have an office to himself, that 'office' was a bathroom. Certainly it was a large bathroom, and somebody had fitted a cover to the bath so that it made a useful shelf for manuscripts and books. Nor was the view from the window at all bad: there was a gravel drive and a tall hedge, and beyond that were college playing-fields. But it was not the kind of view that Williams cared for. 'I was just saying to C. S. L.', he told his wife, 'that I have a nostalgia for walking round the block in London – the City and the Dome; the flat and you.'

At first it had been planned that his wife and son, Michal and Michael, should come and live in Oxford with him. They journeyed down from London just before war broke out, but Michal Williams did not much care for what she found. Charles had been offered accommodation by the Spalding family, who lived in a big house in South Parks Road near the centre of the city; they had got to know him some months earlier when his nativity play *Seed of Adam* was produced at the University Church by Ruth Spalding, a daughter of the family who worked for the Religious Drama Society. Ruth and her sister Anne were delighted to have him as a paying guest, and as their parents were in America there was room in the house to accommodate his wife and son until they could find something more permanent. But when the Williams family arrived, Michal was met almost on the doorstep by 'the

113

Aunt', a fearsome member of the Spalding household, who cried: 'Can you cook? Can you wash? Can you darn?' Michal, not caring for this, turned tail and went back to London, taking the boy.

'I sympathise with her,' remarked Charles in a letter to a friend. 'I wish I had the chance of doing the same thing!' He liked the Spaldings and could see that Ruth and Anne were doing their best to make him comfortable; they had given him their parents' bedroom, which allowed him plenty of space for working in the evenings. But there was no fire in the grate, so when the autumn turned to winter it was simply too cold to be more than tolerable, and he had to work downstairs in the drawing-room. This was certainly more cheerful, but it was also rather noisy, for Gerard Hopkins from the Press was also living in the house, and he would clatter away in the evenings on an ancient and loud typewriter. Williams managed to work against this background with his usual sixpenny writing-pad balanced on his knee, but he would certainly rather have been at home in the Hampstead flat.

He wrote to his wife every couple of days or so. Undoubtedly in many ways he was not sorry that sixty miles now separated him from Michal for at least five days a week (he usually went home to London at week-ends), for the marriage had not become any easier as the years passed. Michal had eventually learnt about 'Celia' and Charles's feelings for her; she also disliked the way that he had acquired a following of young women, and this too was a cause of some tension between them. But little of this was apparent in the letters that he now wrote her, letters that were full of affection and of nostalgia for the domesticity of their flat. Nor was this simply a pose adopted to placate Michal, for he really did miss that domesticity, and in particular the small snacks of tea and cake and sandwiches on which she had so often fed him while he was working late in the evening. 'I am in one of my periodical fits of loathing the food at South Parks Road, which is unfair enough!' he told her after a few months at the Spalding house, where the food was in the charge of rather old-fashioned servants who insisted on regular meal times. 'But does anyone ever say, at 9.30, "Wouldn't you like something to eat?" No. I even miss working to the sound of someone doing things about the place, and even being interrupted by a voice saying: "Darling, what about a cup of tea?" These things have been nine-tenths of my life.'

Cups of tea mattered particularly to him. Like Roger Ingram in *Shadows of Ecstasy*, 'if he had to choose for the rest of his life between wine and tea he had no kind of doubt where the choice would rest'. And as neither Southfield House where he was working nor South Parks Road where he was living afforded more than strictly limited supplies of tea, he was glad to discover somewhere that did. 'I have fled to C. S. Lewis's rooms,' he told his wife soon after arriving in Oxford. 'He is a great tea-drinker at any hour of the night or day, and left a tray for me with milk and tea, and an electric kettle at hand.'

It was of course not just tea that he needed. 'There is no-one here to whom I can talk about *Taliessin,*' he told Michal, though he added, 'there aren't many in London.' Certainly there were not. He badly needed criticism of a constructive kind, for he was writing more poetry for his *Taliessin* cycle, and even in London he knew few people whose knowledge of his work was sufficient and whose minds were sharp enough to be of much use. In Oxford he did not yet know of anybody who he thought could help. Lewis of course had admired the first volume of the cycle, *Taliessin through Logres,* but Williams still did not know Lewis very well.

Yet Williams gradually began to settle in. 'Things are not too bad down here,' he told a friend in mid-October 1939. 'I dislike the conditions – but only mildly.'

*

No sooner had Williams arrived in Oxford than Lewis persuaded him to join the group that met in his Magdalen rooms to read their 'work in progress' aloud to each other, the group that Tolkien called 'our literary club of practising poets', the Inklings. They generally met on Thursday evenings during the University term and sometimes in vacation, and by November 1939 Williams was a regular member. One of the first things that he read to the Inklings was his new nativity play, *The House by the Stable,* which he had just finished writing for Ruth Spalding's company to perform at the University Church. It was unconventional by the standard of most nativity plays (its characters included Pride and Hell), but it was a lucid piece of work, and Lewis, after listening to Williams reading it aloud to the Inklings, remarked that it was 'unusually intelligible' for Williams. On the other hand Lewis did not hesitate to criticise Williams's work severely when he thought fit. 'We had an unusually good Inklings on Thursday,' he recorded in May 1940, 'at which Charles Williams read us a Whitsun play, a mixture of very good stuff and some deplorable errors in taste.' The play was called *Terror of Light,* and its chief 'error in taste' was the invention of a romance between Mary Magdalen and St John.

Williams soon began to realise that Lewis's considerable admiration for his work was tempered with criticism which could often be severe. Lewis said of Williams: 'He is largely a self-educated man, labouring under an almost oriental richness of imagination ("Clotted glory from Charles" as Dyson called it) which could be saved from turning silly or even vulgar in print only by a severe early discipline which he never had.' Lewis was surely thinking of his own 'severe early discipline' under Kirkpatrick. He also wrote of Williams: 'He has an undisciplined mind and sometimes admits into his theology ideas whose proper place is in his romances.' Lewis attacked, too, what he considered to be one of Williams's chief failings, his obscurity. 'Don't imagine I didn't pitch into Charles Williams for his obscurity for all I was worth,' he told Owen Barfield a few years later. In fact Williams found in Lewis what he had almost entirely lacked up to this time – a friend of high intellectual ability who was fundamentally very enthusiastic about Williams's work, but was also extremely and beneficially critical.

In the weekly gatherings of the Inklings, Williams found something else of great value. Besides the reading aloud and the criticism, the Thursday evening sessions in Magdalen gave plenty of chances for good talk, and for the first time in many years Williams found himself arguing and discussing in the company of men who were his equals as debaters. It was true that in his early days there had been male friends at the Working Men's College with whom he had argued and walked about London for hours as they talked, 'men splendid among men' as he had called them. And some years later he had formed a strong friendship of this kind with Daniel Nicholson, a man of energetically sceptical mind who edited the *Oxford Book of English Mystical Verse* for the Press; Williams had found in him somebody who was fully his equal in conversation. But Nicholson died in 1935, and since then, though many of his friends had minds of equal calibre, there had been almost nobody who took the same delight in argument. The Inklings now began to fill that gap.

Indeed, in some respects Williams now found himself not just among intellectual equals but arguing with people whose knowledge was often greater than his own. He was himself, after all, not particularly learned. Lewis called him 'a cheering proof of how far a man can go with few languages and imperfect schooling'. His knowledge of classical authors and of the early Middle Ages was certainly not equal to Lewis's; on the other hand, as Lewis was quick to point out, his expertise in history, theology, comparative religions, and most of all English literature from Shakespeare onwards, was considerable. He could also quote with amazing fluency. 'Before he came,' said Lewis, 'I had passed for our best conduit of quotations: but he easily outstripped me. He delighted to repeat favourite passages, and nearly always both his voice and the context got something new out of them. He excelled at showing you the little grain of truth or felicity in some passage generally quoted for ridicule, while at the same time he fully enjoyed the absurdity: or, contrariwise, at detecting the little falsity or dash of silliness in a passage which you, and he also, admired.'

In *The Place of the Lion,* Williams wrote a passage which showed how much he valued the stimulus of such friendships as he found in the Inklings: 'Much was possible to a man in solitude, but some things were possible only to a man in companionship, and of these the most important was balance. No mind was so good that it did not need another mind to counter and equal it, and to save it from conceit and bigotry and folly.'

At one Inklings evening soon after Williams's arrival in Oxford, he, Lewis and Tolkien started to argue about the meaning of Christ's words *Narrow is the way and few be they that find it,* which Lewis called 'one of the most distressing texts in the Bible' because it suggested a universe where the majority of souls were damned. Also present was Tolkien's fellow Anglo-Saxonist Charles Wrenn, who sometimes came along to these Thursday meetings, and he took exception to what he considered to be Williams's thoroughly heretical views on the subject. Williams believed that 'the way' included not merely the holy life of an ascetic but also Affirmation, the knowledge of God through such things as Romantic Theology. This sort of thing seemed entirely inadmissible to Wrenn, who (Lewis reported) '*almost* seriously expressed a strong wish to burn Williams, or at least maintained that conversation with Williams enabled him to understand how inquisitors had felt it right to burn people'. Williams in fact found himself having to defend his opinions more strenuously than he had done for years. Writing to his wife, he declared of the Inklings: 'They are good for my mind.'

On the other hand the Inklings were not, ultimately, terribly important to him. The Thursday nights at Magdalen and the friendship with Lewis were stimulating, and very welcome, but such things did not really have much to do with the fundamentals of his mind. All his ideas had been developed long before he had come to Oxford, and the thing that occupied his imagination chiefly at the present time – the composition of more poems for *Taliessin* – was a private task to which the Inklings could not contribute. It was true that he did read some of his *Taliessin* verse aloud on Thursday nights, but everybody except Lewis found it incomprehensible. And even Lewis, whose manner tended to be heavyweight in such things, was not able to offer the particular level of sympathetic understanding that Williams needed. 'I brood on and off on the new poems but nothing much gets done,' he told his London friend Anne Ridler. 'No-one of a vivid brain ever talks to me about them – or at least no-one in the way I like. C. S. L. admires them and alludes to them, but . . .'

*

If Lewis was not ultimately very useful to Williams as a critic, he was able to do one valuable thing for him. He arranged for Williams to give a course of lectures in the University; and this was a form of official recognition which very much gratified Williams.

The idea occurred to Lewis during the Michaelmas term of 1939, when he had a chance to observe at first hand Williams's unique manner as a lecturer. In November he went to one of the women's colleges to hear Williams read a paper; 'or rather not "read" ', Lewis reported, 'but "spout" – i.e. deliver without a single note a perfectly coherent and impassioned meditation, variegated with quotations in his incantatory manner. A most wonderful performance and it impressed his audience, specially the young women, very much. And it really *is* remarkable how that ugly, almost simian, face, becomes transfigured.'

It was one thing for Williams to give an informal address to a group of undergraduates, but quite another for him to lecture formally for the English Faculty. In fact under normal conditions it might have proved impossible to arrange it, because Williams was not only unconnected with the University in any official capacity but was not a graduate, having broken off his formal education without taking a degree. Nevertheless Lewis was determined, as he put it, 'to smuggle him into the Oxford lecture list, so that we might have some advantage from the great man's accidental presence in Oxford'. And since in wartime there was a shortage of teaching staff Lewis managed to arrange it. Yet Oxford snobbery still had its say. 'The vulgarest of my pupils,' snorted Lewis, 'asked me, with an air, if Williams had a degree. The whelp!'

The course of lectures was to be on Milton, and the choice of subject was significant, for Lewis realised that Williams had much to say that was relevant to contemporary criticism of Milton's poetry. Attacks on Milton's style and on the supposedly unsympathetic character of *Paradise Lost* had been going on for more than two centuries. In recent times the attackers had included Middleton Murry, who said of Milton, 'We cannot make him real; he does not, either in his great effects or his little ones, trouble our depths', and T. S. Eliot, who declared that Milton's style had done damage to the English language, and said that he found the theology of *Paradise Lost* 'repellent'. Williams took a very different line, and Lewis (knowing this) was keen that what he had to say about Milton should be said in front of an Oxford audience.

On 28 January 1940 Williams told his wife: 'To-morrow I go to Magdalen at 10.45, where Lewis and Tolkien will put on their gowns and take me to the Divinity School. Of course there may be no-one there! but I suppose, in the grand Oxford Tradition, one lectures anyhow.'

There was in fact quite a sizeable audience, for Williams's name was known to at least some undergraduates. The first lecture, which was chiefly introductory, was successful if not startling. Afterwards Lewis took Williams and Tolkien, along with Gerry Hopkins from the Press who had come to listen, to the bar of the Mitre Hotel to celebrate the occasion. A week later the same people reassembled to hear the second lecture in the series, which was to be on Milton's masque *Comus*. Lewis described the occasion to his brother Warnie, who was now serving as a Major at a supply depot in one of the French ports:

'On Monday', he wrote, 'C. W. lectured nominally on *Comus* but really on Chastity. Simply as criticism it was superb because here was a man who really started from the same point of view as Milton and really cared with every fibre of his being about "the sage and serious doctrine of virginity" which it would never occur to the ordinary modern critic to take seriously. But it was more important still as a sermon. It was a beautiful sight to see a whole room full of modern young men and women sitting in that absolute silence which can *not* be faked, very puzzled, but spell-bound: perhaps with something of the same feeling which a lecture on *un*chastity might have evoked in their grandparents – the forbidden subject broached at last. He forced them to lap it up and I think many, by the end, liked the taste more than they expected to. It was "borne in upon me" that that beautiful carved room had probably not witnessed anything so important since some of the great medieval or Reformation lectures. I have at last, if only for once, seen a university doing what it was founded to do; teaching wisdom.'

Williams himself was pleased by the reception of the lecture, and in particular by the enthusiastic response of Lewis and his friends. Indeed it began to seem to him that he could number among his followers a band of *men*, as well as the young women who had till now been in the majority. 'Am I only to be followed by the feminine?' he asked his wife in one of his typically florid letters to her. 'No; you will be attended – you – by the masculine minds: great minds, strong males, brothers of our energy – those who know our work – Lewis – and Tolkien . . .'

2

'We had nothing to say to one another'

If Charles Williams thought that he could number Tolkien among his followers he was mistaken. From the beginning of their acquaintance Tolkien was to some extent suspicious of Williams. This was understandable, for while Williams and Lewis had got to know each other by admiring each other's books Tolkien simply had Williams thrust upon him. The first thing he knew about Williams was Lewis declaring that he had made the acquaintance of a most marvellous person, and that he (Tolkien) would undoubtedly love Williams as soon as he met him. The most generous-hearted person would have been a little suspicious of this, and Tolkien responded by becoming faintly jealous. Lewis's friendship meant very much to him, and he did not altogether care for the sudden arrival of Williams at a high place in Lewis's affections. From the beginning, therefore, he was on his guard; and of Lewis's feelings towards Williams, he said that Lewis was 'a very impressionable, too impressionable, man'.

Some years later, Lewis wrote that by 1939 Williams 'had already become as dear to all my Oxford friends as he had to me'. But next to these words in his own copy of the book in which they appeared, Tolkien wrote: 'Alas no! In any case I had hardly ever seen him till he came to live in Oxford.'

Now that Williams was in Oxford, Tolkien had to put up with something very like hero-worship on Lewis's part. For instance, Lewis told a friend: 'If you were going up the High in a bus and saw Charles Williams walking along the pavement among a crowd of people, you would immediately single him out because he looked godlike; rather, like an angel.' It so happened that the person to whom this remark was made, Lewis's pupil Peter Bayley, had indeed seen Williams from the top of an Oxford bus. 'To my eyes,' he said, 'he looked like a clerk or craftsman in a small line of business – perhaps a joiner or carpenter;

but I thought there was nothing godlike or angelic about him.'

Tolkien would have agreed. He liked Williams, but he did not regard him as even remotely angelic. Lewis declared of Williams: 'In every circle that he entered, he gave the whole man.' But Tolkien commented on this: 'No, I think not.' Tolkien was perhaps more perceptive than Lewis about Williams's character; he may have realised that behind Williams's ebullience in conversation there was an inner nature which rarely showed itself. Certainly he had distinct doubts about some of Williams's ideas.

'I was and remain wholly unsympathetic to Williams' mind,' Tolkien wrote in 1965. 'I knew Charles Williams only as a friend of C. S. L. whom I met in his company during the period when, owing to the War, he spent much of his time in Oxford. We liked one another and enjoyed talking (mostly in jest) but we had nothing to say to one another at deeper (or higher) levels. I doubt if he had read anything of mine then available; I had read or heard a good deal of his work, but found it wholly alien, and sometimes very distasteful, occasionally ridiculous. (This is perfectly true as a general statement, but is not intended as a criticism of Williams; rather it is an exhibition of my own limits of sympathy. And of course in so large a range of work I found lines, passages, scenes, and thoughts that I found striking.) I remained entirely unmoved. Lewis was bowled over. But Lewis was a very impressionable man, and this was abetted by his great generosity and capacity for friendship.'

Tolkien did not specify what it was in Williams's work that he found distasteful, but once in his old age he referred to Williams as 'a witch doctor'. Certainly he was aware – perhaps more than Lewis was – of the importance of black magic and devilry in some of Williams's books. Tolkien himself had a profound belief in the devil and all his works, and he did not think that such things should be bandied about in popular novels.

On the purely personal level, Tolkien was perhaps a little resentful of Williams's intrusion into the Monday morning talks with Lewis which he had enjoyed for nearly ten years. Since the early nineteen-thirties, Monday had been the day when the two men talked, and drank beer at the Eastgate; but now Williams generally made a third at these sessions. Moreover, the conversation became as a result more generally literary than Tolkien always cared for. He himself was not widely read in English literature after Chaucer, and he had few favourites among later writers. On the other hand Williams and Lewis liked almost everything. 'This morning I reached Magdalen at 11 a.m.,' Tolkien recorded one Monday, 'and spent two hours with C. S. L. and C. W. It was very enjoyable. We talked a good deal about "prosody" and (more

121

than I cared for) about C. Lamb: an author that I find no use for, I fear.'

On the other hand Tolkien's emphatic declarations that he and Williams had nothing in common intellectually, and had no sympathy for each other's work, were made long after the event. They were also prompted by the suggestion that he and Williams might have 'influenced' each other's work, a suggestion that Tolkien was very eager to contradict. There is in fact much to suggest that at the time the two men got on extremely well, and did have something to say to each other 'at deeper (or higher) levels'.

Certainly there were many meetings between them, more than there would have been had any real antipathy existed. They often drank beer together, especially in the Eagle and Child public house in St Giles, a favourite haunt of Lewis and his friends, which was generally known as 'The Bird and Baby' because of its signboard depicting the infant Ganymede being carried off by Jove's eagle. 'Had a glass and half an hour at the B & B with Charles Williams,' Tolkien noted one Tuesday morning, Tuesday being the day on which the Inklings had taken to gathering at lunch time in that pub; and such meetings between him and Williams were frequent. And there were certainly some occasions when the two men did talk seriously. One such was a Thursday night when Tolkien was walking home after a Magdalen session of the Inklings. As he lived in North Oxford his journey took him past Williams's front door in South Parks Road. 'I did not start home till midnight,' Tolkien recorded, 'and walked with C. W. part of the way, when our converse turned on the difficulty of discovering what common factors if any existed in the notions associated with *freedom* as used at present. I don't believe there are any, for the word has been so abused by propaganda that it has ceased to have any value for reason, and become a mere emotional dose for generating heat.' Williams had much to say on this subject, for he believed that the only way to find real freedom was to submit oneself to the rule of God. 'The only freedom,' he said, 'is a freedom to choose obedience'; and this formed the theme of one of the poems he was writing for a second *Taliessin* volume. The poem, 'The Departure of Dindrane', told how a slave-girl at Arthur's court is faced with a choice of continuing in servitude or of freedom to lead her own life; in the end she chooses servitude. 'In her heart,' wrote Williams,

> servitude and freedom were one and interchangeable.

Tolkien was not being fair if he meant to suggest, twenty years later, that Williams had no interest in his writings. The sequel to *The Hobbit*, already entitled *The Lord of the Rings*, was being read aloud to the

Inklings as Tolkien wrote it, and during the years in which he was a member of the group Williams heard most of it. He was in fact far more enthusiastic about it than were some of the other Inklings, and five years after he came to live in Oxford he borrowed the entire type-script, as far as it was then complete, so that he could refresh his memory. 'C. Williams who is reading it all', Tolkien noted at the time, 'says the great thing is that its *centre* is not in strife and war and heroism (though they are all understood and depicted) but in freedom, peace, ordinary life and good living. Yet he agrees that these very things require the existence of a great world outside the Shire – lest they should grow stale by custom and turn into the humdrum.'

On the other hand Tolkien's sympathy for Williams's work was certainly limited. He did not claim to understand more than the rudiments of Williams's poetry, nor did he find it attractive. The Byzantine setting of some of the *Taliessin* poems irritated him, while the overlaying of geography and symbolism made no impact on his imagination at all. Williams's use of such apparently unrelated geographical features as Logres, Mount Elburz and P'o-l'u was puzzling enough to him without the symbolism of the human body that was combined with it – the symbolism which for instance identified Caucasia with the buttocks. This was not the sort of myth making that seemed to have any 'truth' to Tolkien. Yet he listened with full attention when Williams read the poems aloud to the Inklings; and, if Williams's ideas did not appeal, then the man himself (he found) was undeniably charming – as Tolkien declared in this poem which he wrote some time during the war.

'Our dear Charles Williams many guises shows:
the novelist comes first. I find his prose
obscure at times. Not easily it flows;
too often are his lights held up in brackets.
Yet error, should he spot it, he'll attack its
sources and head, exposing ramps and rackets,
the tortuous byways of the wicked heart
and intellect corrupt. Yea, many a dart
he crosses with the fiery ones! The art
of minor fiends and major he reveals –
when Charles is on his trail the devil squeals,
for cloven feet have vulnerable heels.

'But heavenly footsteps, too, can Williams trace,
and after Dante, plunging, soaring, race
up to the threshold of Eternal Grace.

The limits of all fallen men, maybe,
(or mine alone, perhaps) explain why he
seems best to understand of all the three
Inferno's dark involved geography.

'Geography indeed! Here he again
exerts a subtle mind and labouring pen.
Geodesy say rather; for many a 'fen'[1]
he wrote, and chapters bogged in tangled rhymes,
and has surveyed Europa's lands and climes,
dividing her from P'o-L'u's crawling slimes,
in her diving buttocks, breast, and head
(to say no fouler thing), where I instead,
dull-eyed, can only see a watershed,
a plain, an island, or a mountain-chain.
In that gynecomorphical terrain
History and Myth are ravelled in a skein
of endless interchange. I do not hope
to understand the deeds of king or pope,
wizard or emperor;[2] beyond my scope
is that dark flux of symbol and event,
where fable, faith, and faërie are blent
with half-guessed meanings to some great intent
I cannot grasp. For Mount Elburz[3] to me
is but a high peak far beyond the sea
(and high and far I'd ever have it be).

'The Throne, the war-lords, and the logothetes,
the endless steps, the domes, the crowded streets,
the tolls, the taxes, the commercial fleets,[4]
Byzantium, New Rome! I love her less
than Rome the Old. For War, I must confess,

---

[1] *fen:* the name of a section in Avicenna's *Canon of Medicine*; also used by Chaucer in *The Pardoner's Tale*.

[2] *king or pope, wizard or emperor:* Arthur, the Pope, Merlin, and the Emperor are four of the principal figures in the *Taliessin* poems.

[3] *Mount Elburz:* mentioned by Williams several times in the poems. This is his own note on it: 'A Caucasian mountain: type of the lowness and height, fertility and chastity, verdure and snow, of the visible body.' (Quoted by Lewis in Chapter 2 of 'Williams and the Arthuriad', *Arthurian Torso*.)

[4] *The Throne, the war-lords etc.:* reminiscent of Williams's poem 'The Vision of the Empire' in *Taliessin through Logres*, except of course that to Williams these things are pleasing.

Eagles to me no more than Ravens bless,
no more than Fylfot, or Chrysanthemum
blown to a blood-red Sun.[1] Byzantium!
Praise her, ye slaves and eunuchs! I'll be dumb.
To me she only seems one greater hive,
rotting within while outwardly alive,
where power corrupts and where the venal thrive;
where, leeches on the veins of government,
officials suck men's blood, till all is spent.
If that is what by Law and Order's meant,
then any empire's over-lofty crown,
and vast drilled armies beating neighbours down
to drag them fettered through New Order's town,
to me's as good a symbol, or as ill,
of Rule that strangles and of Laws that kill,
of Man that says his Pride is Heaven's will.
O, Buttocks to Caucasia!'
                    'Tolkien, please!
What's biting you? Dog in the Manger's fleas?
Let others hear, although you have no mind,
or have not seen that Lewis has divined
and has expounded what you dully find
obscure. See here, some thirty lines you've squandered.
You came to praise our Charles, but now you've wandered.
Much else he wrote that has not yet been pondered.'

    'Quite true, alas! But still I'm rather puzzled.
There's Taliessin – no, I'll not be muzzled;
I'm writing this, not you; I won't be hustled –
there's Taliessin now: I'd always thought
that in the days of Cymbeline he wrought,[2]
ere Rome was Old or New, and that if aught
is now preserved of what he sang or said,
'tis but an echo times have edited
out of all likeness to his tongue long dead,
the ancient British, difficult and dark,
of a minor minstrel in an Outer Mark.
But here, it seems, a voyage in some swift bark
to that Black Sea (which now is mainly Red)

---

[1] *Fylfot, or Chrysanthemum . . . :* A 'fylfot' is a swastika; the Chrysanthemum and the Sun are Japanese emblems.

[2] The orthodox view is in fact that Taliessin was broadly speaking from the Arthurian period.

125

has much enlarged him, both in heart and head;[1]
but still I understand not aught he said!

  'A truce to this! I never meant to do it,
thus to reveal my folly. Now I rue it.
Farewell (for now) beloved druid-poet![2]
Farewell to Logres, Merlin, Nimue,
Galahad, Arthur! Farewell land and tree
heavy with fates and portents not for me!
I must pass by all else you wrote:
play, preface, life, short verse, review or note
(rewarded less than worth with grudging groat).
  'When your fag is wagging and spectacles are twinkling,
when tea is brewing or the glasses tinkling,
then of your meaning often I've an inkling,
your virtues and your wisdom glimpse. Your laugh
in my heart echoes, when with you I quaff
the pint that goes down quicker than a half,
because you're near. So, heed me not! I swear
when you with tattered papers take the chair
and read (for hours maybe), I would be there.
And ever when in state you sit again
and to your car imperial give rein,
I'll trundle, grumbling, squeaking, in the train
of the great rolling wheels of Charles' Wain.'[3]

---

[1] *a voyage in some swift bark . . . :* Williams takes the figure of Taliessin from Celtic legend and makes him contemporary with Arthurian Britain and also the Byzantine Empire. He also literally takes him (briefly and swiftly) on a journey to Byzantium itself.

[2] *beloved druid-poet:* In Williams's poems, Taliessin is associated with druidical origins. It has also been suggested that Williams himself was of Welsh descent, but his sister Edith Williams wrote: 'So far as I know there is no "Welsh descent" anywhere in the family.' (Charles Williams Society newsletter no. 3, autumn 1976, p. 12.)

[3] *Charles' Wain:* a name for the constellation more commonly called the Great Bear. It was also known as 'Arthur's Plough'.

3
Thursday evenings

The Inklings kept no minute-book, so there is no full record of the proceedings during Thursday nights in Lewis's rooms in Magdalen. It might easily have been otherwise, for Warnie Lewis was a good diarist and could have provided a detailed account. 'I would have played Boswell on those Thursday evenings,' he said regretfully many years later, 'but as it is, I am afraid that my diary contains only the scantiest material for reconstructing an Inklings.'

On the other hand Jack Lewis's letters to his brother during the first months of the war, when Warnie was serving abroad, do record quite a lot of what went on; while later in the war Tolkien wrote detailed diary-letters to this third son Christopher who was with the R.A.F., and these letters too record something of what happened at the Inklings. So from these, from the diaries that Warnie Lewis kept (they were not, in fact, so very scanty about the Inklings) and from the reminiscences of the people who attended on Thursday nights, it is possible to get some idea of the kind of thing that happened.

One way to convey the atmosphere of an Inklings evening is to describe an imaginary meeting. What follows is an artificial reconstruction, and entirely imaginary in that it is not based on any one particular evening. On the other hand the subjects of conversation are the kind of things that the Inklings discussed, while the remarks of the various people present are taken from their writings, both published and unpublished, which have been freely adapted to suit the context.[1] So while this must not be taken as an accurate record, it may perhaps catch rather more of the flavour of those Thursday evenings than any purely factual account could do. More, but not all; for no reconstruction can do more than hint at what the real thing was like.

*

[1] Lewis's comments on the Moria Gate section of *The Lord of the Rings* are my own invention, though they are based on changes that Tolkien did make in the manuscript.

Considering how fine a building they are in, Lewis's rooms are rather bleak. The effect is as if a school or some other institution had taken over a fine country house, for his plain (and in some cases downright shabby) furniture simply does not come up to the standard of the eighteenth-century panelling, the broad sash windows, and the high ceilings.

The main sitting-room is large, and though certainly not dirty it is not particularly clean. Lewis's 'scout', the college servant responsible for the rooms on this staircase, only has time to give it a quick flip of the duster early in the morning; and as for Lewis himself, he never bothers with ashtrays but flicks his cigarette ash (he smokes cigarettes as much as a pipe) on to the carpet wherever he happens to be standing or sitting. He even absurdly maintains that ash is good for carpets. As for chairs – there are several shabbily comfortable armchairs and a big Chesterfield sofa in the middle of the room – their loose covers are never cleaned, nor has it ever occurred to Lewis that they ought to be. Consequently their present shade of grey may or may not bear some relation to their original colour.

Apart from the chairs, there is not much furniture in the room. A plain table stands behind the Chesterfield. It was never a very good table; long ago when Lewis first moved into these rooms, his brother Warnie noticed that Jack had chosen the furniture just as he chose his clothes – by walking into a shop and taking the first thing that he was offered. The table now bears the scars of twenty years' ruthless use: ink stains, cigarette burns, and ring-shaped marks, the larger of which come from the beer jug that often stands here, and the smaller from ink bottles. Across the room are bookshelves, and (like the table) they are very plain and rather shabby; nor are the books themselves much to look at. Long before, in his adolescent days, Lewis and his friend Arthur Greeves were avid collectors of smart editions with fine bindings. But Lewis gave up this taste when he was a young man, partly because thanks to the expense of the ménage with Mrs Moore he could no longer afford it, and partly because when he began to move towards Christianity he ceased to think that such things were more than vanity. In consequence the books on the shelves are nothing very special, nor are there very many of them, for Lewis uses the Bodleian (the University library) for all but essential volumes. The few that are on his shelves are mainly cheap or second-hand copies of major works, both theological and literary. The *Summa Theologiae* of Aquinas stands near *Beowulf* and the *Roman de la Rose,* while notably absent are *The Allegory of Love* and *Out of the Silent Planet,* for Lewis takes no trouble to keep copies of his own books, and gives (or even throws) them away at the slightest opportunity. On the other hand *The Hobbit* is there, next to Barfield's children's story *The Silver Trumpet,* while there are several of Charles Williams's books here too. There are also books in the two smaller rooms that open off the main sitting-room. In one of these rooms Warnie Lewis works on weekday mornings, and several rarities can be found on the shelves here, for Warnie collects works relating to the Bourbon court and is always glad to lay his hands on a fine edition. In this room there is also a typewriter, which Warnie uses both for his own work (he is beginning to arrange material for a book of his own on the court of Louis XIV) and for typing his brother's letters, for he now acts as secretary to Jack. Lying by the typewriter is a packet of cheap typing paper and a large pair of scissors. Warnie dislikes wasting paper (especially under wartime economy conditions) and he refuses to use anything smarter than this stuff for Jack's correspondence. Moreover if the letter is a short one, Warnie will not use up a complete sheet of paper for it, but will cut off a strip just deep enough to hold the text and his brother's signature, and will send off this two- or three-inch slip complete with a reference number ('40/216') to make it clear to the recipient that Jack Lewis has already written two hundred and sixteen letters this year. Jack is faintly embarrassed by all this.

The other small room is Jack's bedroom. He sleeps here during term time, rising early on most mornings to go to college prayers before breakfast, or to Communion. The bedroom is bare and looks a little like a monastic cell, for there is nothing in it besides a washstand with a jug and basin, and a pile of books beside the bed. Yet those books include not just the Prayer Book and the Bible but one of the Waverley novels, Trollope's *The Warden,* and *The Wind in the Willows.*

It is dark, being about nine o'clock on a winter evening; and it is also cold, particularly in the big sitting-room which looks north on to Magdalen Grove. The only source of heat is the coal fire, which at the moment is burning very low in the grate, for it is a couple of hours since anyone has been in the room. A faded screen has been set up near the door which leads out on to the staircase, in the hope of muffling the draught; but it makes little difference.

Magdalen clock strikes nine, other college clocks preceding and following it in the distance. Now and then, feet run up and down the stairs outside the door; but it is not until after Great Tom at Christ Church half a mile away has sounded his hundred and one strokes at ten past nine that a more measured tread is heard on the stairs, and the door opens to reveal two men. The first takes off his hat and coat and throws them down on the nearest chair. Then he pulls down the blinds and draws the blackout curtains, after which his companion switches on the light.

The first man is broadly built, with a plump rather red face, a small moustache, and receding hair. He wears a tweed jacket and baggy flannel trousers. He is Warnie Lewis. In the first months of the war he was on active service, stationed at le Havre with the R.A.S.C., but it was soon decided that officers of his age were not needed, and he was allowed to go back on the retired list and return home. Now that he is back in Oxford he is spending a good deal of his time living on his motor boat *Bosphorus* and cruising up and down the river as part of the Upper Thames Patrol. He has painted his boat battleship-grey and has bought a naval style peaked cap, much to the amusement of Jack.

His companion is R. E. Havard, the Oxford doctor who looks after the Lewis and Tolkien households and who regularly comes to Magdalen on Thursday evenings. He is a few years younger than Warnie and is expecting to be called up for military service fairly soon, albeit as a medical officer. For some reason Havard has always attracted nicknames from the Inklings. Though his Christian names are Robert Emlyn he was once referred to by Hugo Dyson as 'Humphrey', either in pure error or because it alliterated with his surname. Some time later, Warnie Lewis was irritated one evening by Havard's failure to turn up with a car and give him a promised lift home, and dubbed the doctor 'a useless quack'; and 'The Useless Quack' or 'U.Q.' Havard has remained. How far this is from being an accurate description of the man may be gauged by Tolkien's remark to one of his sons: 'Most doctors are either fools or mere "doctors", tinkerers with machinery. Havard at any rate is a Catholic who thinks of people as people, not as collections of "works".'

When the light has been switched on, Warnie Lewis puts some coal on the fire, and grumbles to Havard about the shortage of beer in Oxford – beer is in low supply because of the war, and the Bird and Baby frequently has a 'No Beer' sign on its door. 'My idea of the happy life,' says Warnie, 'would be to buy a pub, put up one of those *No Beer* notices, lock the customers out, and drink the stuff myself.'

The two men talk about beer for a few minutes more, Warnie referring contemptuously to an inferior brew that he and Havard have just been drinking at a hotel down the road – he describes it as 'varnish', the term that he and Jack always use for bad beer.

There is no fixed hour at which the Inklings meet on Thursdays, but by general agreement people turn up at any time between nine and half past ten. Nor is there any formal system of membership or election, and in theory it is only necessary for one Inkling to obtain the approval of the others (particularly of Lewis) before introducing somebody new. But in practice this does not happen very often, and on most Thursdays the company consists solely of the Lewis brothers, Tolkien, Havard and Williams, sometimes with the addition of Hugo Dyson, who teaches at Reading University but is often in Oxford. Nevill Coghill used to be quite a regular member of the group, but he is in great demand as a producer of plays for the University dramatic society and other local groups, and he is now rarely seen in Lewis's rooms on Thursday nights. He is not the only Inkling to have dropped out: Adam Fox, the Magdalen chaplain who (thanks to the campaign conducted by Tolkien and Lewis) was elected Professor of Poetry in 1938 rarely comes now. Owen Barfield very occasionally turns up on his visits from London, where he still works as a solicitor; and sometimes Charles Wrenn looks in. But for the most part the Thursday party is a small group. A direct result is that usually the only people to read their work aloud are Tolkien, Lewis and Williams. Coghill has once or twice read light verses or lampoons, and Fox (when he comes) generally reads his poetry. Up to the present time Warnie Lewis has had nothing of his own to read to the Inklings, and as for Havard, he always emphasises that he is not a literary man, though he does occasionally contribute some small thing to the group. Readings therefore are in comparatively short supply. Hugo Dyson (when he attends) does not mind this at all, claiming that the conversation is far more enjoyable anyway. But Lewis insists that the readings – the original *raison d'etre* of the club – must be kept up. Sometimes, as chance will have it, a logical sequence appears, and one reading seems to lead naturally into the next. But this is by no means always the case.

Warnie begins to make tea – a regular ritual at the start of an Inklings – and in a few minutes Jack Lewis and Tolkien arrive; Lewis has been giving Tolkien dinner on High Table in Magdalen.

Both men are fairly certain of being able to remain in Oxford for the duration of the war. Tolkien is nearly fifty and will definitely not be required for active service; his contribution to the war effort is to take turns of duty as an air raid warden, spending one night every two weeks or so waiting by the telephone in a cheerless concrete hut in the grounds of St Hugh's College. Lewis is several years younger than Tolkien, but he does not expect to be called up. He declares that his personal war aims are exactly summed up by an entry in the *Peterborough Chronicle*: 'During all this evil time, Abbot Martin retained his abbacy.' However, he does duty with the Home Guard – and at this moment Havard is asking him how he takes to it.

'Merrily enough I suppose,' Lewis answers. 'I spend one night in nine mooching about the most depressing and malodorous parts of Oxford with a rifle. I think that Dyson has the right idea about the Home Guard. He says it should be conducted on the same principle as Dogberry's Watch in *Much Ado* – "Let us go sit on the church bench till two, and then all to bed." '

Warnie asks his brother if there is any beer to be had. Jack usually brings a big enamel jug of it up from the college buttery, but apparently tonight the college is as short of it as is the Bird and Baby. 'I think there's some rum in the cupboard if anybody would like some,' says Jack, and Warnie goes to look for it, while his brother declares:

'I think positively the *nastiest* kind of war service is the thing that Barfield is doing. He's just taken a part-time job in – would you believe it – the Inland Revenue, of all disgusting things! As I was saying to Tollers just now, he's very depressed because he's one of those people who really feels the miseries of the world, and the war is making him terribly gloomy.'

'One can hardly blame him for that,' says Tolkien. 'None of us here has exactly displayed a totally unruffled cheerfulness throughout the year.' He is thinking of the fall of France in June, when even Oxford's calm was shaken by what seemed the certain prospect of invasion, and of the Battle of Britain, in which his own son Michael was involved as an anti-aircraft gunner.

'No,' says Lewis, 'one can't, but that's not quite what I meant. What I'm trying to say is this: that there's Barfield, with more than enough in his own and his neighbours' personal lives to worry about, actually spending a good deal of time being miserable about the terrible sufferings which are being endured by people hundreds or thousands of miles away. Now, terrible as those sufferings are, I'm not quite sure whether it's really one's duty as a man and a Christian to be so vividly and continuously *aware* of them. Should we try, for instance, to be aware of what it's like, say, to be a fighter pilot being shot down in flames at this moment?'

'I should imagine Williams would think one ought to be very much aware of it indeed,' says Harvard. 'Isn't that part of his "Co-inherence"?'

'Yes, of course,' answers Lewis. (He talks emphatically – 'in italics' as a pupil puts it – but does not raise his voice even in the heat of argument. There is just a trace of Ulster still in the vowel-sounds.) 'Yes. I entirely accept the general principle. We must realise, as Williams would say, that we live in each other. But in purely practical terms, were we meant to know so much about the sufferings of the rest of the world? It seems to me that modern communications are so *fast* – with the wireless and the newspapers and so on – that there's a *burden* imposed on our sympathy for which that sympathy just wasn't designed.'

'Give an example,' says Tolkien.

'That's easy. Now, supposing the poor Jones family in your own street are having terrible troubles – sickness and so on – well then, obviously it's your duty to sympathise with them. But what about the morning paper and the evening news broadcasts on the wireless, in which you hear all about the Chinese and the Russians and the Finns and the Poles and the Turks? Are you expected to sympathise with *them* in the same way? I really don't think it's possible, and I don't think it's your duty to try.'

'You certainly can't do them any good by being miserable about them,' says Warnie.

'Ah, but while that's perfectly true it's not the point. In the case of the Jones family next door, you'd think pretty poorly of the man who felt nothing in the way of sympathy for them because that feeling "wouldn't do them any good".'

'Are you saying', asks Havard, 'that when we read the newspapers we shouldn't try to sympathise with the sufferings of people we don't know?'

'Jack is probably saying', remarks Warnie, 'that we shouldn't read the newspapers at all. You know he never bothers to look at anything other than the crossword.'

'Perfectly true,' answers his brother. 'And I have two very good reasons for it. First of all I deplore *journalism* – I can't abide the journalist's air of being a specialist in everything, and of taking in all points of view and always being on the side of the angels. And I hate the *triviality* of journalism, you know, the sort of fluttering mentality that fills up the page with one little bit about how an actress has been divorced in California, and another little bit about how a train was derailed in France, and another about the birth of quadruplets in New Zealand.'

'Well, I think it's irresponsible of you not to read the war news, at least,' says Warnie, and Havard grunts in agreement.

'It might be, if the news was in any way *accurate,* or if I was qualified to interpret it. But instead here I am, without any military knowledge, being asked to read an account of the fighting that was distorted before it reached the Divisional general, and was further distorted before it left him, and then was "written up" out of all recognition by a journalist, and which will all be contradicted next day anyway – well, I ask you!'

'Do you know,' chimes in Tolkien, 'I was coming back in a train from Liverpool the other week, and there was a Canadian and his wife in the opposite seat, and they drank neat gin out of aluminium cups all the way to Crewe, by which time their eyes had certainly become rather dewy.'

'What on earth has that got to do with journalism?' asks Lewis, who hates the conversation to degenerate into anecdote or mere chat.

'Only that the man was labelled "War Correspondent", so I shan't wonder in future why these people's despatches are so fatuous!'

Lewis roars with laughter.

'What's your other reason for not reading the papers?' asks Havard. 'I thought you said you had another?'

'It's this,' answers Lewis, 'though I'm almost ashamed to admit it. You see, I simply don't *understand* most of what I find in them. I reckon that the world as it's now becoming is simply *too much* for people of the old square-rigged type like me. I don't understand its economics, or its politics, or any damn thing about it.'

'Well, I imagine you understand its theology,' says Warnie, handing round cups of tea.

'Not a bit of it. In fact it's very distressing. I always thought that when I got among Christians I'd have reached somewhere that was safe from that horrid thing *modern thought*. But did I? Oh no, not at all. I blundered straight into it. I thought I was an upholder of the old stern doctrines against modern quasi-Christian slush, but it's beginning to look as if what *I* call sternness is slush to most of *them*. Or at least that's what it was like when I was talking to a group of Christian under-graduates the other day. They'd all been reading a dreadful man called Karl Barth, who seemed to be a kind of opposite number to Karl Marx. They all talked like Covenanters or Old Testament prophets. They don't think human reason or human conscience is of any value at all, and they maintain just as stoutly as Calvin that there's no reason why God's dealings should appear just to us, let alone merciful. They hold on to the doctrine that all our righteousness is just filthy rags so fiercely and sincerely that I can tell you it's like a blow in the face.'

'If there's really a religious revival, that's probably what it'll be like,' says Warnie. 'Does everyone want rum?'

'Oh, do we really need any?' answers his brother. 'I thought you needed blackcurrant or something to go with it.' The question of drink at an Inklings is a slightly delicate matter between the Lewis brothers. Warnie likes it to flow freely, but Jack maintains that regular drinking on Thursday nights alters the character of the club. (There is another factor, in that Jack is concerned about Warnie's occasional bouts of heavy drinking, which have been going on sporadically for some years.) But tonight as the bottle is already open and Tolkien suggests adding hot water to the rum, Warnie wins and the glasses are handed round.

'As Warnie says,' remarks Havard, 'if we do get a religious revival, it'll probably be just like that – very Calvinist.'

'I know,' answers Lewis. 'And will we like it? I mean, we've been delighted to see the churches almost full since the war began, and we talk enthusiastically of a Christian revival among the undergraduates, and there's certainly some sign of it happening. But I rather think that if it really comes, people like us won't find it nearly so agreeable as we'd expected. Of course, we ought to have remembered that if the real thing came it would make us sit up. Do you remember Chesterton? "Never invoke gods unless you really want them to appear. It annoys them very much." '

'But you don't think these people enthusing about Barth are necessarily wrong?' Havard asks.

'No, I don't. I think the young gentlemen are probably largely right. But between ourselves I have a hankering for the old and happier days, the days when politics meant Tariff Reform, and war was war against the Zulus, and Religion meant that lovely word *Piety* – you know, "The *decent* church that crowns the neighbouring hill", and "Mr Arabin sent the farmers home to their baked mutton very well satisfied".'

There is a pause while Lewis lights his pipe. 'Williams is coming later,' he says through the stem, 'but I don't think anyone else will be turning up. Has anyone got anything to read?'

Tolkien says that he has brought 'another Hobbit chapter' – for some reason he rarely refers to his new book by its formal title, and the Inklings generally know it as the New Hobbit.

'It's a pity Coghill doesn't come along on Thursdays much these days,' remarks Warnie. 'He liked Tollers' first hobbit book so much that I'm sure he'd enjoy this.'

'Of course,' says Tolkien, 'his "Producing" takes up a good deal of his time.'

'Do you remember Coghill's *Hamlet* about five years ago?' Lewis asks, as Tolkien gets his manuscript ready.

'It was pretty good stuff as such things go, as far as I remember,' says Warnie.

Jack grunts. 'I suppose it was, of its kind, but really I get next to no enjoyment out of these undergraduate productions. They act them in a way that fills one at first with embarrassment and pity, and finally with an unreasoning personal hatred of the actors – you know, "Why should that damned man keep on bellowing at me?" '

'*Hamlet* is a fine enough play,' says Tolkien, 'providing you take it just so, and don't start *thinking* about it. In fact I'm of the opinion that Old Bill's plays in general are all the same – they just haven't got any coherent ideas behind them.'

'It's Hamlet himself that I can't abide,' remarks Warnie. 'Whenever I see the play I find myself conceiving the most frightful antipathy to him. I mean, there's such an intolerable deal of him. Every few minutes all the other characters sneak off in a hard-hearted way and leave us at the mercy of this awful arch-bore for hundreds of lines. I remember

135

when I saw Coghill's version I thought the only dramatic merit had been supplied by him and not by Shakespeare.'

'You sound as if you want to rewrite the play,' says Havard.

'And why not?' answers Tolkien. 'You could show what a stinking old bore his father really was, before he became a ghost (to the relief of the Danish court), and how nice poor Claudius was by comparison.'

'And how the old man really died of some nasty disease and wasn't murdered at all,' adds Warnie.

'And then even in the grave couldn't keep from mischief,' continues Tolkien.

'. . . but had to come back with a filthy cock-and-bull story about a murder, which at first was too much even for his own son to swallow,' adds Jack Lewis, who admires *Hamlet* profoundly but cannot resist joining in this nonsense.

'. . . the son being a chip of the old blockhead, and quite as conceited as papa,' Tolkien concludes. 'But I suppose it won't ever get written.'

'It might make an opera,' muses Lewis.

'Wagner?'

'No, I think something more in the style of Mozart. We must have a go at it. But let's hear the new chapter.'

Tolkien begins to read from his manuscript.

It is the chapter which describes the arrival of the hobbits and their companions at the doors of the Mines of Moria, and which recounts the beginning of their journey through the darkness. Tolkien reads fluently. Occasionally he hesitates or stumbles, for the chapter is only in a rough draft, and he has some difficulty in making out a word here and there. The pages are closely covered – he has written it on the back of old examination scripts. One or two details are still uncertain: he explains that he has not yet worked out an Elvish version of the inscription over Moria Gate, and he reads it in English; he is uncertain whether the word of power with which Gandalf opens the doors should be *Mellyn* or *Meldir*; and here and there he points out that he has got the details of distance or time of day wrong, and will have to correct them. But such small details do not interfere with the concentration of his listeners, for though he reads fast and does not enunciate very clearly, the story quickly takes charge. It is more than an hour before he has finished. Meanwhile the fire burns low, and nobody bothers to throw coal on it. At last he comes to the end.

' "The Company passed under the northern arch and came through a doorway on their right. It was high and flat-topped, and the stone door was still upon its hinges, standing half open. Beyond it was a large square chamber, lit by a wide shaft in the far wall – it slanted upwards and far above a small square patch of sky could be seen. The light fell directly on a table in the midst of the chamber, a square block three feet high upon which was laid a great slab of whitened stone." ' He pauses and puts his manuscript aside. 'That's as far as it runs. The end is in rather a muddle, and there should have been a song earlier, in which Gimli recollects the ancient days when Moria was peopled by Durin's folk.'

'I don't think that's needed,' says Lewis. (Of Tolkien's poetry, he generally admires only the alliterative verse.) Tolkien does not reply. Instead he says:

'Did you realise that the faint patter of feet is Gollum following them? He is to reappear now, you see.'

'Oh yes, I think that's clear,' says Lewis. 'And the underground stuff is marvellous, the best of its kind I've ever heard. Neither Haggard nor MacDonald equal it. Perhaps you could just spread yourself a little more in the scene where that Thing comes out of the water and grabs at Frodo. It's a little unprepared at the moment – shouldn't there be ripples on the water when it starts to move?' Tolkien agrees and makes a note of this.

'I was struck,' says Warnie (offering more rum to the company), 'by that bit about the cats of Queen – what was her name?'

" 'He is surer of finding the way home in a blind night than the cats of Queen Berúthiel," ' quotes Tolkien. 'Yes. Do you know, I find that rather puzzling. Trotter just made the allusion to her without any forethought by me – she just popped up, in fact. Odd, isn't it?' ('Trotter' is the character who will later be renamed 'Strider'.)

'So you've no idea who she was?' asks Jack Lewis, putting more coal on the fire.

There is a gleam in Tolkien's eye. 'No, I didn't say that. I said she just popped up. Since she did, I do have a notion that she was the wife of one of the ship-kings of Pelargir.'

'Pelargir?' asks Warnie. 'I don't remember that.'

'No, you wouldn't: the story hasn't reached it yet. It was a great port, you see, and poor Berúthiel loathed the smell of the sea, and fish and gulls, like the giantess Skadi – do you remember her?' (he turns to Lewis). 'She came to the gods in Valhalla and demanded a husband in payment for her father's death. They lined everybody up behind a curtain and she selected the pair of feet that appealed to her most. She thought she'd got Balder, but it turned out to be Njord; and after she'd married him she got fed up with the seaside life, and the gulls kept her awake, and at last she went back to live in Jotunheim. Well, Berúthiel went to live in an inland city too, and she went to the bad – or returned to it: she was a black Númenórean in origin, I suspect – and she was one of those people who hate cats, but cats will jump on them and

137

follow them about (you know how they can pursue people who loathe them). I'm afraid she took to torturing them for amusement, but she trained some to go on evil errands by night, to spy on people or terrify them.' Tolkien stops and relights his pipe, and there is a respectful pause from his audience (though in fact a certain amount of what he said was not entirely audible to them, thanks to his speed and the pipe in his mouth).

'I don't know how you think of these things,' says Havard, who does not actually find it easy to appreciate *The Lord of the Rings*, but who certainly admires the fertility of Tolkien's imagination.

'How does any author think of anything?' answers Jack Lewis, quick as usual to turn the particular into the general. 'I don't think that conscious invention plays a very great part in it. For example, I find that in many respects I can't *direct* my imagination: I can only follow the lead it gives me.'

'Absolutely true,' says Warnie. 'I mean, when I picture the country house I'd like to have if I were a rich man, I can *say* that my study window opens on a level park full of old timbers, but I can only *see* undulating ground with a fir-topped knoll. I can fix my mind, of course, on the level park, but when I turn to the window again after arranging my books, there's that damn knoll once more.'

'That's exactly what I find when I'm writing a story,' declares his brother. 'I *must* use the knoll and can't force myself to use the level park.'

Havard asks: 'What do you suppose is the explanation, or the significance? I imagine Jung would ascribe it to the collective unconscious, whose dictates you are being obliged to follow.'

'Maybe,' Lewis says. 'Jung's archetypes do seem to explain it, though I'd have thought Plato's would do just as well. And isn't Tollers saying the same thing in another way when he tells us that Man is merely the *sub*-creator and that all stories originate with God?' Tolkien grunts in agreement. 'But the real point is not *how* it happens (because surely we can never be certain about that) but that it *does* happen. You see, I come more and more to the conclusion that all stories are *waiting*, somewhere, and are slowly being recovered in fragments by different human minds according to their abilities – and of course being partially spoiled in each writer by the admixture of his own mere individual "invention". Do you agree?' He turns to Tolkien.

'Of course, of course. Although you may feel that your story is profoundly "true", all the details may not have that "truth" about them. It's seldom that the inspiration (if we are choosing to call it that) is so strong and lasting that it leavens all the lump, and doesn't leave much that is mere uninspired "invention".'

'What about the new Hobbit book?' asks Havard. 'How much of that would you say was "true"?'

Tolkien sighs. 'I don't know. One hopes ... But you mean, I take it, how much of it "came" ready-made, and how much was conscious invention. It's very difficult to say. One doesn't, perhaps, identify the two elements in one's mind as it's happening. As I recall, I knew from the beginning that it had to be some kind of quest, involving hobbits – I'd got hobbits on my hands, hadn't I? And then I looked for the only point in *The Hobbit*, in the first book, that showed signs of development. I thought I'd choose the Ring as the key to the next story – though that was the mere germ, of course. But I want to make a big story out of it, so it had got to be *the* Ring, not just any magic ring. (I invented that little rhyme about *One Ring to rule them all*, I remember, in my bath one day.)'

'But all that part of it was, by the sound of it, mere invention,' says Lewis. 'Didn't you find when you actually began to write that things appeared largely of their own accord?'

'Of course. I met a lot of things on the way that astonished me. The Black Riders were completely unpremeditated – I remember the first one, the one that Frodo and the hobbits hide from on the road, just turned up without any forethought. I knew all about Tom Bombadil already, but I'd never been to Bree. And then in the inn at Bree, Trotter sitting in the corner of the bar parlour was a real shock – totally unexpected – and I had no more idea who he was than had Frodo. And I remember I was as mystified as Frodo at Gandalf's failure to appear at Bag End on September the twenty-second. What's more, I can tell you that there are quite a few unexplained things still lurking. *Seven stars and seven stones and one white tree*: now, what do you make of that? I know it will play some important part in the story, but I can't say what.'

'In the same sort of way,' says Lewis, 'I have a picture in my mind – it's been there for some time – of floating islands, islands that float. At present (if it interests you even remotely to know it) I'm trying to build up a world in which floating islands could exist.'

There is a moment's silence, broken by Warnie.

'Well, Tollers, whether it's inspiration or invention, I still don't know how you keep up your story so magnificently. It hasn't flagged for a moment. I can tell you without exaggeration that simply nothing has come my way for a long time which has given me such enjoyment and excitement.'

'Oh yes,' adds his brother. 'It's more than good: the only word I can use is *great*.'

Warnie continues: 'But how the public will take it, I can't imagine.

I should think, Tollers, you'd better prepare yourself for a lot of mis-understanding. I'm afraid some people will interpret it as a political allegory – you know, the Shire standing for England, Sauron for Stalin, and that kind of thing.'

'Whereas of course the truth', says Jack, 'is that no sooner had he begun to write it than the real events began to conform to the pattern he'd invented.'

'I know that Tolkien always reminds us that it isn't allegory,' Havard says, 'but I don't quite see why it's so silly at least to attempt to inter-pret it allegorically. I'm sure that some perfectly sensible people are bound to.'

'Of course they are,' answers Tolkien. 'And while, as you know, I dislike conscious and intentional allegory, it's quite true that any attempt to explain the purport of myth or fairytale must use allegorical language. And indeed the more "life" a story has, the more readily it will be susceptible of allegorical interpretations; while conversely, the better a *deliberate* allegory is, the more nearly it will be acceptable just as a story.'

Havard asks Tolkien: 'If you're prepared to admit the susceptibility of your Hobbit story to allegorical interpretation, what particular interpretations do you predict people will make?'

'Well,' Tolkien says, 'I suppose all my stuff – both this new story and the earlier mythology from which it derives – is mainly concerned with the Fall, with mortality, and with the Machine. The Fall is an inevitable subject in any story about *people*; mortality in that the consciousness of it affects anyone who has creative desires that are left unsatisfied by plain biological life – any artist must desire great longevity; and by the Machine I mean the use of all external plans or devices, instead of the development of *inner* powers and talents – or even the use of those talents with the corrupted motive of dominating, of bullying the world and coercing other wills. The Machine is merely our more obvious modern form. (By the way, did you know that a maker of motor bikes has named his product Ixion Cycles? *Ixion*, who was bound for ever in Hell on a perpetually revolving wheel!)'

'But can't you admire any machines? Havard asks. 'The advance of medicine depends greatly on the benefits that they can confer.'

'Maybe,' Tolkien replies. 'But it seems to me that the ultimate idea behind all machinery, however apparently beneficial its immediate function, is to create Power in *this* world. And that can't be done with any real final satisfaction – unlike art, which is content to create a new world, a secondary world in the mind.'

'Don't you approve of any labour-saving devices?' asks Warnie.

'Labour-saving machinery only creates endless and worse labour. The

Fall only makes these devices not just fail of their desire, but turn to new and horrible evil. Look how we've "progressed": from Daedalus and Icarus to the Giant Bomber. It isn't really man who is ultimately daunting and insupportable: it's the *man-made*. If a Ragnarök would burn all the slums and gasworks and shabby garages, it could (for me) burn all the works of art – and I'd go back to trees.'

'Certainly we seem to be progressing towards universal suburbia,' Lewis says. 'And while, as Havard suggests, the first stages of "Progress" may most certainly be beneficial, we have to know where to stop. And at the moment there doesn't seem much hope that we *will* stop.' He searches among his papers and takes out a sheet. 'I've called this "Evolutionary Hymn",' he says, and begins to read.

> 'Lead us, Evolution, lead us
>   Up the future's endless stair.
> Chop us, change us, prod us, weed us,
>   For stagnation is despair:
> Groping, guessing, yet progressing,
>   Lead us nobody knows where.
>
> 'To whatever variation
>   Our posterity may turn,
> Hairy, squashy, or crustacean,
>   Bulbous-eyed or square of stern,
> Tusked or toothless, mild or ruthless,
>   Towards that unknown god we yearn.
>
> 'Ask not if it's god or devil,
>   Brethren, lest your words imply
> Static norms of good and evil
>   (As in Plato) throned on high;
> Such scholastic, inelastic,
>   Abstract yardsticks we deny.
>
> 'Far too long have sages vainly
>   Glossed great Nature's simple text;
> He who runs can read it plainly:
>   "*Goodness* equals *what comes next*."
> By evolving, Life is solving
>   All the questions we perplexed.'

'Good,' says Havard. 'But I'm not clear whether it's scientific progress you're attacking, or Darwin. The objectives seem to have got a little muddled.'

'That's the whole point of the poem,' Lewis answers. 'What I'm saying isn't that Darwin was wrong – though incidentally I believe biologists are already contemplating a withdrawal from the Darwinian position – but that Evolution as popularly imagined, the modern concept of Progress, is simply a fiction supported by no evidence whatever. It's an older fiction than Darwin, in fact: you can find it in Keats's *Hyperion* and in Wagner's *Ring*, and it turns up in all sorts of forms, such as Shaw's Life-Force; and for most people it has now taken the place of religion.'

'But I still don't see precisely what you're attacking,' Havard says.

'Quite simply the belief that the very formula of universal process is from imperfect to perfect, from small beginnings to great endings. It's probably the deepest-ingrained habit of mind in the contemporary world. It's behind the idea that our morality springs from savage taboos, adult sentiment from infantile sexual maladjustment, thought from instinct, mind from matter, organic from inorganic, cosmos from chaos. It always seems to me immensely implausible, because it makes the general course of nature so very unlike those parts of it we can observe. You remember the old puzzle as to whether the first owl came from the first egg or the first egg from the first owl? Well, the modern belief in universal evolution is produced by attending exclusively to the owl's emergence from the egg. From childhood we're taught to notice how the perfect oak grows from the acorn; we aren't so often reminded that the acorn itself was dropped by a perfect oak. We're always remarking that the express engine of today is the descendant of the *Rocket*, but we don't equally remember that the *Rocket* didn't come from some even more rudimentary engine, but from something much more perfect and complicated than itself – a man of genius.'

'All right,' answers Havard. 'I understand your objection to the fact that progress is based on a misunderstanding of the process of development in nature. But does that mean that all progress is of necessity bad? I notice that you have no hesitation (nor does Tolkien for that matter) in using trains and cars when they're offered. (Though I note you usually prefer a slow local train to a main line express.) But surely you must allow *some* good in mechanical science, such as the invention of printing? Didn't that greatly expand culture and scholarship?'

'Possibly,' Lewis replies. 'But have I too fanciful an imagination when I say that I suspect that the flood of so-called "learned" books which was beginning to overwhelm us before the war (and which will undoubtedly return with peace) must inevitably mean recent inferior work pushing good old books out of the way? That is what we shall see, I'm sure.'

'And what about literature?' Warnie asks. 'You must allow of some improvement in *that* over the centuries.'

'Not at all, not as a general statement. Barfield proved years ago that what we have actually experienced is a *decay*, a breaking-up of the ancient unity in which myth could not have any "meaning" separated from it, into allegory, where the meaning can be distinguished and detached; and the ultimate result of this process is of course a literature that has no meaning at all! The other day I read a symposium on T. S. Eliot's "Cooking Egg" poem. There were seven contributors, all of them men whose lives have been devoted to the study of poetry for thirty years or so, and do you know there wasn't the slightest agreement between any of them as to what the poem meant!'

'I can well believe it,' says Tolkien.

'Yet to be fair, can you tell us what Tolkien's story means?' asks Havard.

'But that's the whole point!' Lewis answers. 'It doesn't *mean* anything, in the sense of abstracting a meaning from it. Tollers may regard it fundamentally as "about" the Fall and Mortality and the Machine, but that may not be how I read it. Indeed it seems to me (with due respect) a great mistake to try and attach any kind of abstract meaning to a story like his. Story – or at least a great Story of the mythical type – gives us an experience of something not as an abstraction but *as a concrete reality*. We don't "understand the meaning" when we read a myth, we actually encounter the thing itself. Once we try to grasp it with the discursive reason, it fades. Let me give you an example. Here I am trying to explain the fading, the vanishing of tasted reality when the reasoning part of the mind is applied to it. Probably I'm making heavy weather of it.'

'You are,' says Warnie.

'All right. Let me remind you instead of Orpheus and Eurydice, how he was supposed to lead her by the hand but, when he turned round to look at her, she disappeared. Now what was merely a principle should become imaginable to you.'

'I never thought of applying that meaning to the Orpheus story,' Warnie says.

'Of course not. You weren't looking for an abstract "meaning" in it at all. You weren't knowing, but *tasting*. But what you were tasting turns out to be a universal principle. Of course the moment we state the principle, we are admittedly back in the world of abstractions. It's only while receiving the myth *as a story* that you experience a principle concretely. Let's take an example from quite a different sort of story. Consider Mr Badger in *The Wind in the Willows* – that extraordinary amalgam of high rank, coarse manners, gruffness, shyness and goodness.

143

The child who has once met Mr Badger has got ever afterwards, in its bones, a knowledge of humanity and English social history which it certainly couldn't get from any abstraction. Now do you see what I mean?'

'This talk of "tasted reality",' says Tolkien, 'reminds me of an experience I had the other day, in which I think I encountered the same thing in a different fashion. It sounds rather ridiculous, but I was riding along on my bicycle past the Radcliffe Infirmary when I had one of those sudden clarities, the kind that sometimes come in dreams. I remember saying aloud with absolute conviction, "But of course! Of course that's how things really do work." But I couldn't reproduce the argument that had led to this, although the sensation was the same as having been convinced by reason (though without any reasoning). And I've since thought that one of the explanations as to why one can't re-capture the wonderful argument or secret when one wakes up is simply that there wasn't one, but there was some kind of direct appreciation by the mind without any chain of argument as we know it in our time-serial life.'

'I think that's fascinating,' Warnie says, 'and I'm sure I've experi-enced something of the same kind myself. But I'm a little worried still whether the people who read Tollers's new Hobbit story are going to appreciate all this. I'm sure that some critics will talk about it as simply "escapist" and "wish-fulfilment" and that sort of thing. You know the way these people go on.'

'Very probably they will,' answers Tolkien. 'Though anyone who in real life actually found himself, say, journeying through the Mines of Moria would, I imagine, wish to escape *from* that, to exchange it for almost any other place in the world! You see, I think that if there is any "escapism" involved, it's in being able to survey danger and evil (when we read a story) without any disturbance of our spiritual equilibrium. We're escaping from the limitations of our own personality, which wouldn't allow us to have any adventures because we'd be too fright-ened! And really, you know, these critics who are so sensitive to the least hint of "escapism" – well, what class of men would you expect to be so worked up about people escaping?' The company waits for an answer. 'Jailers!' says Tolkien.

'Yes,' adds Lewis, laughing. 'They're afraid that any glimpse of a remote prospect would make their own stuff seem less exclusively important.'

'But you must be aware', Havard remarks, 'that some people will find a story like Tolkien's to be deficient in the kind of detailed studies of complex human personalities that you find in Tolstoy or Jane Austen.'

The undersigned, having just partaken of your ham, have drunk your health:

C. S. Lewis. Fellow of Magdalen, sometime scholar of University College 2/Lt 13th Light Infantry

H. V. D. Dyson Fellow of Merton College, Lecturer of University College University Lecturer in English Literature. ~~Form~~ sometimes Commoner of Exeter College, Queen's Own Royal West Kent Regt 1915-19.

David Cecil Fellow of New College — exc. Fellow of Wadham College — University Lecturer in English Literature. Commoner of Christ Church.

W. H. Lewis. Royal Military College, Sandhurst, Regular Army 1914-1932, World War II 1939-45. Major. Retired pay.

Colin Hardie Fellow and Tutor in Classics of Magdalen College University Lecturer in Greek and Latin Literature, formerly Director of the British School at Rome, and Fellow, Scholar & Exhibitioner of Balliol College. Secretary of the Oxford Dante Society (founded 1876) Sector Warden ARP service Oxford.

Christopher·Reuel·Tolkien.:. B·A·.:. Undergraduate, of Trinity College.:. Late R.A.F.

R Emlyn Havard. M. A. : D.M. oxon. B.A. Cantab. Late Scholar & Research Fellow University of Oxford, Late Lecturer in Physiology Guy's Hospital. Demonstrator in Biochemistry University of Oxford, late Surgeon R.N.V.R.

John Ronald Reuel Tolkien. M.A. Merton Professor of English Language & Literature, later professor of Anglo-Saxon (Pembroke College), and exhibitioner of Exeter College. and of the Lancashire Fusiliers (1914-8) and father of the above-named C.R.T.

9   Signatures of some of the Inklings, sent to Dr Warfield M. Firor in 1948, after he had given them a ham.

10   Jim Dundas-Grant, Colin Hardie, 'Humphrey' Havard, and C. S. Lewis on the terrace at the Trout Inn, Godstow, circa 1947.

'Of course,' Lewis answers. 'But that isn't a criticism. It's merely saying that the Hobbit story is different. A critic who likes Tolstoy and Jane Austen and doesn't like Tolkien should stick to novels of manners and not attack the Hobbit book. His own taste doesn't qualify him to condemn a story which is primarily *not* about human behaviour. We mustn't listen to Pope's maxim about the proper study of mankind: the proper study of man is *everything*, everything that gives a foothold to the imagination and the passions.'

'Including elves and goblins?' asks Havard.

'Of course. They do the same thing that Mr Badger does: they're an admirable hieroglyphic which conveys psychology and types of character much more briefly and effectively than any novelistic presentation could do. Now, I know that Tolkien's story does lie on (or beyond) one of the frontiers of taste; what I mean is, if you ask someone, "Do you like stories about other worlds – or hunting stories – or stories of the supernatural – or historical novels?", you will always get an unalterable "yes" or "no" from the very depth of the heart. I don't know why; it's a very interesting literary fact which I've never seen discussed by any critic of merit, certainly not by Aristotle or Johnson or Coleridge. Anyway there it is, and Tollers's book will undoubtedly provoke that "yes" or "no" response. But the point is that the people who say "no" shouldn't try to stop other people from saying "yes". For a start, they may be proved entirely wrong by history: the book that they scorn today may be a classic for the intelligentsia of the twenty-third century. Very odd things may happen: our age may be known not as the age of Eliot and Pound and Lawrence but as the age of Buchan and Wodehouse, and perhaps Tolkien. You see, the trouble is that our map of literature is always drawn up to look like a list of examination results, with the honour candidates above that line and the pass people below. But surely we ought to have a whole series of vertical columns, each representing different *kinds* of work, and an almost infinite series of horizontal lines crossing these to represent the different degrees of goodness in each. For instance in the "Adventure Story" column you'd have the *Odyssey* at the top and Edgar Wallace at the bottom, and Rider Haggard and Stevenson and Scott and William Morris – and of course Tollers – placed on horizontal lines crossing "Adventure Story" at whatever heights we decide. But look, Tollers never answered Warnie's criticism about "wish-fulfilment".'

'It wasn't a criticism,' Warnie answers. 'I was merely suggesting that some people might say it.'

'Most certainly they will,' Tolkien says. 'But one can only ask, is the wish itself such a bad one? And in what sense is it fulfilled? Of course there are certain books which do arouse and imaginatively satisfy

145

certain wishes which ought to be left alone – pornography is the obvious example. But I'm quite certain that the longing for fairy-land is fundamentally different in character. As I've already suggested, we don't actually want to *experience* all the dangers and discomforts of the Mines of Moria, in the way that somebody susceptible to pornography wants to experience the things it describes. We don't want to be in Moria: but the story (I hope) does have an effect on us. It stirs us and troubles us.'

'That's right,' says Lewis. 'Far from *dulling* or *emptying* the actual, of reducing it to something very *low* as pornography does, it gives it a new dimension. Look, a child doesn't despise real woods just because he's been reading about enchanted woods. What he's read makes all real woods a little enchanted. And a boy who has any imagination enjoys eating cold meat, which he'd otherwise find dull, by pretending that it's buffalo-meat, which he's just killed with his own bow and arrow. As a result, the real meat tastes more savoury. In fact you might say that only then *is* it the real meat. This isn't a retreat from reality. It's a rediscovery of it.'

The Magdalen clock chimes the quarter. Warnie looks at his watch. 'Eleven-fifteen. We shan't be seeing Charles tonight, I'm afraid.' He turns to Tolkien. 'There's one thing I meant to ask. What actually happens at the end of that chapter? It seemed to stop a bit abruptly.'

'The Company discovers a great book,' Tolkien answers, 'in which is written the history of the reoccupation of Moria by the dwarves, under the leadership of Balin (you may remember him from my first hobbit story). I've delayed writing that bit because there are a number of linguistic problems relating to the text which they find. And they also discover a tomb, in which lies the body of Balin, slain by – well, we shall be coming to that.'

'Tomb?' asks Lewis doubtfully. 'Surely a pyre would be more likely?'

'No,' answers Tolkien. 'They buried their dead. Or rather, they laid them in tombs of stone, never in earth (as might be expected, considering their origins). Only in the most dire necessity did they resort to burning their dead – it happened once, after the great battle at Azanulbizar, when more were slain than they could possibly have entombed, and then they made pyres, but only reluctantly.'

'It does seem a little odd,' muses Lewis, 'or at least a little out of character with what you must admit is the Teutonic nature of your dwarves. Are we to take it from this that they believed in the resurrection of the body?'

'A difficult question,' Tolkien answers. 'But really, you know, it must be a tomb.'

146

'Why, Tollers?' Warnie asks. 'You don't object to cremation, do you?'

'Generally speaking, the Catholic Church forbids it,' says Havard, who has been a Catholic for about ten years. 'There are exceptions, I believe, when there is any special reason – a plague, for instance. But in general it is not allowed, because (of course) it rather goes against belief in bodily resurrection.'

'Oh, come now,' says Lewis. 'Your Church is perfectly entitled to practise what it chooses, but you can't say that cremation denies the resurrection of the body. Why should the resurrection of a *cremated* body be any less plausible than that of a *decayed* body?'

'That may be true,' says Tolkien, 'but you would find in fact that cremation is far more widely accepted by atheists than by adherents to any form of Christianity. It may not logically contradict the resurrection of the body, but it clearly *goes with* disbelief in it.'

'But why on earth should it?' asks Warnie. 'I just don't see that you're putting up any case against cremation whatever.'

'A corpse is a temple of the Holy Ghost,' Tolkien says.

'But you must admit, a *vacated* temple,' Lewis answers.

'Yes,' Havard says. 'But does that mean that it is right to destroy it? If a church has to be vacated for some reason, you don't immediately blow it up or burn it to the ground.'

'You would do,' Warnie answers, 'to prevent it being used, shall we say, by Communists. You'd surely rather see it destroyed then?'

'No,' Tolkien answers, 'I would not.'

Warnie persists: 'Why not?'

'It's very difficult to explain.' Tolkien shifts uncomfortably in his chair. ('I have no skill in verbal dialectic,' he has remarked to one of his sons, adding, 'I tend to lose my temper in arguments touching fundamentals, which is fatal.') He says: 'Take a slightly different example: if you knew that a chalice was going to be used by black magicians – as in that story of Williams's – you wouldn't regard it as therefore being your duty to destroy it, would you?'

'I think I would,' Warnie answers.

'Then you would be mentally guilty if you did so. It would be your business simply to reverence it, and what the magicians did to it afterwards would be theirs.'

'With due respect to your beliefs, Tollers,' declares Lewis, 'I think you are entirely missing the point.' He is uncomfortably aware that the two Anglicans and the two Catholics have ranged themselves rather belligerently against each other, but he cannot by his nature drop an argument half-way through. 'Surely the Incarnation is a key to what we should believe about the body? You remember the words of the

Athanasian Creed: *One; not by conversion of the Godhead into flesh . . .*'

Another voice, with a London accent, takes up his words from the doorway: '. . . *but by taking of the Manhood into God.*' Charles Williams has arrived after all. '*One altogether,*' he continues to chant, '*not by confusion of Substance; but by unity of Person.*' He crosses the room with brisk movements and throws himself down in the middle of the Chesterfield. '*For as the reasonable soul and flesh is one man; so God and Man is one Christ.*'

'We have been discussing,' says Lewis a little lamely, 'the subject of cremation.'

' "Those are pearls that were his eyes . . ." ' Williams replies. 'O, don't you think that would be the best sort of burial? "Nothing of him that doth fade, But doth suffer a sea-change Into something rich and strange." ' He closes his eyes and tilts his head back, crossing his legs, so that his grey suit becomes a little creased. (Eliot's description of Williams at Lady Ottoline Morrell's seems fitted to Williams among the Inklings: 'One retained the impression that he was pleased and grateful for the opportunity of meeting the company, and yet that it was he who had conferred a favour – more than a favour, a kind of benediction, by coming.')

'You're frightfully late, Charles,' says Warnie. 'I expect you'd like some tea. Where have you been?'

Williams sighs. 'I was asked by some undergraduates to address them on Malory. I assented. I did not quite like *not* to. But it was – to be frank . . .' He leaves the sentence unfinished.

'Well, I'm sure they were enthralled,' says Warnie. 'I know your lectures are being greatly valued.'

'That's an understatement,' adds his brother. 'It's a long time since anyone dropped on Oxford with such a cometary blaze.'

'O, but yes,' answers Williams. 'Yet – one does not live by reputations. I'm always a trifle worried by Our Lord's dictum, "Woe unto you when all men shall speak well of you." ' He turns to Lewis. 'By the way, your Mr Sampson has been talking to me on the telephone. He has in mind a book for his "Christian Challenge" series; and would I be open to a proposal? I would, of course. There is a novel that I feel I ought to be doing, but I do not know what it is to be about, and for the moment . . .' (Ashley Sampson is the publisher who commissioned Lewis's *The Problem of Pain.*)

'I gather', Lewis says, 'he wants you to write something about the forgiveness of sins.'

'He does,' Williams answers. 'It is, of course, something that we have often considered, and yet a good deal of thought is still required.' (He often uses the ceremonial 'we' instead of 'I', declaring it not to be conceit but showing an awareness of 'function'.) 'One thing particularly

148

nags: he wishes an entire chapter to be devoted to How We Should Forgive the Germans.' He sighs. 'It will not be easy.'

'Do you know,' Tolkien says, 'there was a solemn article in the local paper the other day seriously advocating the systematic extermination of the entire German nation as the only proper course after military victory because, if you please, they are all rattlesnakes, and don't know the difference between good and evil! Can you beat it?'

'Yes,' says Lewis. 'How do you begin to talk about forgiveness to the kind of person who writes that stuff?'

'On the other hand,' remarks Havard, 'I wonder how you'd feel about forgiving the Germans if you were a Pole or a Jew?'

'So do I,' Lewis says. 'I wonder very much. And I suppose that compared to them we have nothing to forgive, and shouldn't even begin to try.'

'Exactly,' says Williams. 'By the side of their sufferings it would be ridiculous for us to – O so laboriously – *forgive* the Germans for the small things they have inflicted on most of us: a slight financial loss, a personal separation or two. Without real personal injury, there can be little question of real forgiveness.'

'It seems to me,' says Tolkien, 'that in doing what that newspaper article did, we are in spirit doing exactly what the Germans have done. *They* have declared the Poles and Jews to be exterminable vermin, utterly subhuman. *We* now declare that all the Germans are snakes, and should be systematically put to death. We have as much right to say that, as they have to exterminate the Jews: in other words, no right at all, whatever they may have done.'

'Otherwise,' Lewis says, 'we will be no better than the Nazis.'

'Exactly. As Gandalf often says, you can't fight the Enemy with his own Ring without turning into an Enemy yourself.' Tolkien sighs.

Warnie shifts uncomfortably. 'This is getting a bit rarefied. I mean, in purely practical terms the best way to ensure that the Germans don't do it again, when the war is over, is to put their leaders to death. That's only practical common sense.'

'It does sound very much like it,' says Williams.

'And it seems to me', Warnie continues, 'that taking what Jack and Tollers were saying only just a little bit further, you land up in a kind of pacifist state of mind in which you're not going to fight anybody, however wicked and dangerous they are, because you know that potentially you're just as wicked and dangerous yourself. Now, don't get me wrong: I'm not attacking *real* pacifism, a real hatred of war. The only true pacifists I've met have been professional soldiers – they know too much about the game to be fire-eaters. What I'm attacking is the kind of woolly intellectual pacifism which we've all seen a good deal of.'

'Oh, of course,' says his brother. 'I don't think any of us is really remotely pacifist in the sense that we're uneasy at taking part in a war. Don't we all believe that it's lawful for a Christian to bear arms when commanded by constituted authority, unless he has a very good reason – which a private person scarcely can have – for believing the war to be unjust?'

'The notion that the use of physical force against another is always sinful', says Williams, 'is based on the belief that the worst possible sin is the taking of physical life. Which I'm sure none of us believes.'

'I know it's off the point,' Havard interjects, 'but I'd like to ask Williams what he *would* regard as the worst possible sin?'

Williams answers without a moment's hesitation: 'The exclusion of love.'

Havard nods.

'Certainly war is a dreadful thing,' Lewis continues, 'and I can respect an honest pacifist, though I think he's entirely mistaken. What I *can't* understand is the sort of *semi*-pacificism you get nowadays which gives people the idea that though you have to fight, you ought to do it with a long face, as if you were ashamed of it.'

'Oh yes,' Tolkien agrees. 'And it's a perfectly ridiculous attitude. I find it refreshing to discover at least some young men who have the opposite approach. I've met several, all of them airmen as it happens, to whom the war has offered the perfect round hole for a round peg – and they only found square holes before the war. What I mean is, the job of fighting demands a quality of daring and individual prowess in arms that I'd have thought was a real problem for a war-less world fully to satisfy.'

'All right,' says Warnie. 'You're not, any of you, supporting pacifism. You say it's all right to fight Hitler. But you're not in favour of exacting cold-blooded revenge after the war has been won. Is that it?'

'Yes,' says his brother. 'And I'd have thought that the prohibitions in the Sermon on the Mount supported that view – they don't prohibit war, but revenge.'

'You're certain, in fact, that it's our duty to forgive the Germans, both now and after the war?'

'Oh yes. We must love our enemies and pray for our persecutors. Our Lord made that perfectly clear.'

'And yet you say that in practical terms it's silly to try and forgive them for what they've done to *us*, because what we've suffered is nothing compared to the sufferings of the Jews and the Poles. So it would seem to me,' Warnie concludes, 'that our duty is to try and forgive them *on behalf of* the Jews and the Poles.'

'O but is it?' Williams asks. 'When we ask the Omnipotence to forgive Herr Hitler for what he has done to the Jews, are we not in fact reminding Him of how terrible Herr Hitler is? Are we really asking for forgiveness, or indulging our anger?'

'Isn't there such a thing as holy anger?' Havard asks.

'There is: O yes there is,' Williams answers. ' "The golden blazonries of love irate" – mingled with compassion. But, you know, holy anger is a very dangerous thing indeed for anyone who isn't a saint to play with. Supernatural indignation may be possible, but it springs from a supernatural root. Our business is surely to look for that root rather than to cultivate the anger?'

'All right then,' says Warnie. 'Why don't we just say we *pardon* them and have done with it?'

'A little facile,' Jack grunts.

'And anything other than a facile pardon would probably, in the circumstances, prove to be impossible,' Tolkien adds. 'Say you were a man who'd been deliberately crippled by the Gestapo, or you'd seen your wife tortured – well, you'd almost certainly be unable to reach a state of real forgiveness, even if you thought it was your duty to try to.'

'Vicarious pardon, may be?' Williams asks.

'What do you mean?'

'Someone who has endured what Tolkien describes might, well, entreat anyone who loved him to make an effort towards pardon on his behalf.'

'Exchange and Substitution again, Charles?' Lewis asks.

'An operation of it. But you know, we seem to forget that many Germans (including Hitler? possibly indeed) may feel that *they* have much to forgive *us*. And what sort of reconciliation can be achieved if we are prepared to forgive but not to be forgiven?'

Lewis sighs. 'Of course, Charles. You're quite right. But it's getting late, and as usual you're turning the whole issue topsy-turvy and discovering all sorts of complications that really needn't concern us now.' (Williams smiles.) 'As I see it, you want a straight answer (for the purposes of your book) to the question: what are we going to do about the Germans after the war is over? Now, I'd have thought that you can quite simply resign the whole issue to the civil authorities, whose task it is to decide such things. You can say that it is *our* duty to be in as best a state of forgiveness as we can manage, and that it is *their* job – the League of Nations, I mean – to do whatever they think fit.'

'Ah yes,' says Williams. 'The League of Nations: but it owes its existence to treaties, does it not? And the problem with the Germans is that they are breakers of treaties; they deny the League of Nations.'

'Well of course the League can respond by passing laws which declare the Germans guilty of various crimes,' Warnie says, 'and it can then punish them. They would of course be retrospective laws, but really it wouldn't be any more unjust than the Germans' own behaviour.'

'No more and no less unjust,' says Jack. 'We're back with an eye for an eye. It would only be legalised vengeance. And we're agreed that vengeance is out of the question.'

'I wonder,' Williams muses. 'We can surely take vengeance if we choose; but we must be honest; we must call it vengeance.'

'What are you suggesting?' Havard asks. 'Executions?'

'Execution? Yes; maybe sacrifice. It is dangerous, but it could be done. It is a responsibility we could accept if we chose.'

'I can't see how,' says Lewis.

'Shall we say, the new League of Nations – whatever form it may take – might rise not merely out of the blood that has been shed in the war. It might be definitely dedicated to the future with blood formally shed.'

'But we've already said that there'd be no justification for that,' says Tolkien.

'No justification, no. It would be a new thing. We should say in effect: "We have no right to punish you. But we are determined to purge our own hearts by sacrificing you." And indeed to execute our enemy after that manner would be an admission of our solidarity with him. We should execute him not because he was different from us, but because we were the same as he.'

'But this is quite impossible for Christians,' Lewis expostulates. 'It's forbidden to the Church. And after all, if bloody vengeance is a sin, bloody sacrifice is an outrage.'

'But if it were conceded outside the Church?' Williams asks. 'The Church, though refusing it in one sense, might allow it in another – as she does with divorce.'

'You amaze me, Charles,' Warnie bursts out. 'Sheer bloodthirstiness!'

Williams laughs, and lights a cigarette with hands that shake (as they always do). 'At the time of Munich,' he says, 'I was regarded as a cowardly wretch because I wanted peace and appeasement. Now I'm called a bloody wretch. A lonely furrower – that's what I am!' He gets up, says brief goodnights to the company, thanks Warnie for the tea ('Why does no one else – except my wife – provide tea at all hours? You spoil me') and is gone. Warnie and Havard follow a few minutes later, making for Havard's car, which is parked in the yard at the back of the college. Magdalen clock strikes midnight as they leave, and as the last strokes die away another sound reaches their ears from some distance away. Jack Lewis has accompanied Tolkien downstairs, and as they leave the cloisters of New Buildings and make their way across the grass, they have started to improvise their opera about Hamlet's father. It is a very strange noise.

4

'A fox that isn't there'

Charles Williams's book *The Forgiveness of Sins*, with its discussion of the difficulties of 'forgiving the Germans', was published in 1941. It was dedicated to the Inklings. Lewis found a setting for his floating islands and wrote a sequel to *Out of the Silent Planet*. Tolkien sometimes wrote and read aloud more chapters of *The Lord of the Rings*, but his progress on the book was slow and often came altogether to a halt. The war went on. The Inklings continued to meet.

Were the Inklings more than just a group of friends? Some people have suggested that Lewis, Tolkien and Williams saw their work as a movement which would in some way alter the course of literature, or which would at least encourage a particular kind of writing. It has also been suggested that Owen Barfield participated in this literary movement, and that the philosophical books which he wrote in the years after the 1939–45 war were in some way associated with the work of the other three men.[1] One critic has dubbed Lewis and his friends 'The Oxford Christians', explaining that he uses this term 'to suggest a shared outlook and to connote both an academic and a religious point of view common to them all'. Another has declared that the work of

[1] Barfield's later books are *Saving the Appearances* (1957), *Worlds Apart* (1963), *Unancestral Voice* (1965), *Speaker's Meaning* (1967), and *What Coleridge Thought* (1973). All are concerned to some extent with the propagation of Anthroposophy; the first three explore Steiner's teachings using different literary forms. *Saving the Appearances* is a conventionally-shaped philosophical dissertation; *Worlds Apart* is a symposium involving a number of fictional participants (the character of 'Hunter' is partly modelled on Lewis); *Unancestral Voice* might be described as a novel. Several of the books were published by Faber & Faber, and Barfield's work was admired by T. S. Eliot.

All these books were written during the period when partial retirement from his work as a solicitor permitted Barfield to devote his time to such things. In the pseudonymous *This Ever Diverse Pair* (published under the name of G. A. L. Burgeon in 1950) Barfield expressed his considerable unhappiness at the way in which his professional life in the legal business had prevented him from concentrating on writing.

Lewis, Tolkien, Williams and Barfield represents a conscious attempt to present religion through the medium of romanticism, while a third has talked about 'the common Inklings attitude'.

Was there any such thing as a 'common Inklings attitude'? Can the group of friends who met on Thursday nights really be called with any significance 'The Oxford Christians'? Or is any attempt to search out important links between the work of these people really, as Lewis himself put it, 'chasing after a fox that isn't there'?

*

If we are going to see whether or not the fox really exists, a good starting-point might be the expression 'The Oxford Christians', because certainly Lewis, Tolkien, Williams and Barfield were all Christians. But once that plain fact has been stated, even a superficial examination of their beliefs and attitudes shows that a number of strong qualifications have to be introduced – so strong that the statement rather loses its force.

Tolkien was a Roman Catholic of entirely traditional views. He thought that the sacraments were by far the most important part of a Christian's life. He did not believe that interpretation of Christianity was the crucial thing; what was required (in his view) was regular attendance at Mass, with Communion taken only after a preparatory Confession; and this, together with private prayer, was the centre of his spiritual life. Lewis, on the other hand, believed that the sacraments were important but did not regard them as the bedrock of his faith. He had come to Christianity after a long intellectual struggle: hence the great attention that he paid in his books to justifying Christianity intellectually. As for Williams, he certainly could and sometimes did turn his hand to the intellectual justification of Christianity – for example, in his book *He Came Down From Heaven*, where he shows himself quite as capable as Lewis of closely reasoned argument on the subject of doctrine and belief. But that was not where Williams's heart lay. His vision of Christianity was idiosyncratic for two reasons: first because he was a poet, and many of his writings on theology are in fact poetic vision rather than rational argument; and second because of his interest in the neo-magical fringes of the Church.[1] His principal doctrines – Co-inherence, Romantic Theology, Substituted Love – reflect his early involvement with Rosicrucianism and the Golden

---

[1] It is interesting to note how rarely Williams refers plainly to God, Christ, or the Devil. He prefers other terms. God is 'the High God', 'the One Mover'; Christ is 'the Crucified Jew', 'the Divine Hero', 'the Revealer', 'Messias'; the Devil is 'the Enemy', 'the Infamy'. Particularly characteristic of Williams are the phrases 'under the Protection', 'under the Mercy', 'under the Permission'.

Dawn. As a result there is scant resemblance between the breezy out-door Chestertonian Christianity of Lewis and the esoteric world occupied by Williams and his disciples. As for Barfield, his approach to Christianity had very little in common with any of the other three. While Lewis had reached a belief in God through his search for an exterior and objective idealism, Barfield had come to his Anthropo-sophical Christianity through delving inwards and exploring the inner nature of the human mind and imagination. If Chesterton had been one of Lewis's chief guides, the great influence on Barfield's 'conversion' was Coleridge. Moreover, before the 1939–45 war Barfield regarded himself solely as an Anthroposophist, and was not a practising member of any Christian church; after the war he did join the Church of Eng-land, but retained his belief (derived from Steiner) in reincarnation and continuing personal revelation from God. Lewis objected to both these doctrines, declaring that no Christian can possibly believe in reincarnation, and that personal revelation is a thing of the past which ceased once the canon of Scripture had been settled. When Lewis and Barfield published books about their beliefs it could be seen that they were far apart from each other. Lewis accepted the Christian world-picture as a literal truth (he was indeed very nearly a fundamentalist) and set about defending it. He also concerned himself frequently with the ethical problems of Christian behaviour, and with practical things such as prayer. Barfield devoted his attention to explaining and defend-ing Rudolf Steiner's view of existence without concerning himself seriously with ethical or practical problems. Lewis expressed this pro-found difference between himself and Barfield when he said of his friend, 'He has read all the right books but has got the wrong thing out of every one. It is as if he spoke your language but mispronounced it.'[1]

So 'The Oxford Christians' does not seem to be a term which holds much real meaning. Nor does the idea that there was an *academic* view-point common to Lewis and his friends stand up at all well to examina-tion. Certainly Lewis, Tolkien and Williams were all expert in English

---

[1] Owen Barfield feels that he might have found some common philosophical or theological ground with Charles Williams if he had ever had a chance to talk at length with him. But they never found the opportunity for a lengthy conversation. He recalls that at their first meeting, Williams, not knowing that Barfield was a disciple of Steiner, opened the conversation by saying: 'I have just been talking to someone who told me I was an Anthroposophist'.

Williams reviewed Barfield's volume of essays *Romanticism Comes of Age* in 1945 (*New English Weekly* XXVII no. 4, 10 May 1945, pp. 33–4). The review was admiring in tone, but Williams concentrated on what Barfield had to say about the Romantic poets and did not discuss any questions relating specifically to Anthropo-sophy. Moreover on the subject of personal revelation, Williams once remarked (in a letter to Thelma Shuttleworth): 'Intuition, or inner revelation, leads to anarchy.'

155

literature, but within this field their forms of expertise could scarcely have been more different. Tolkien's area of scholarship was confined to Anglo-Saxon and early Middle English, as well as related Germanic languages. Moreover he approached it primarily through philology. His academic work was distinguished by great insight, and there was nothing remotely pedantic about it, but it was none the less work of great precision and accuracy, involving a detailed study of the minutiae of early literature. Lewis, though he certainly had an interest in Anglo-Saxon and early Middle English, was expert in later literature, and there was nothing of the precise textual scholar about him. 'Lor' bless you,' he once told a former pupil. 'I can't *edit* any more than I can audit. I'm not accurate.' He was not. Though he quoted fluently it was often inaccurately. Of course he and Tolkien did have an important attitude in common with their shared feelings about 'Northernness', but Lewis was also susceptible (as *The Allegory of Love* shows) to the entirely different literary traditions of Southern Europe.

It might be supposed that Williams and Lewis had something in common as literary critics. Certainly Williams's Milton lectures at Oxford were the germ of Lewis's *Preface to Paradise Lost*. But apart from this it is surprisingly hard to find any similarity in their literary criticism. Indeed their attitudes reveal themselves as fundamentally different. Lewis liked to maintain that literature is ultimately no more than a recreation, though a very valuable one. In the essay 'Christianity and Literature' he declared that 'the salvation of a single soul is more important than the production or preservation of all the epics and tragedies in the world'. Though Williams, as a Christian, would perhaps have agreed with this with his rational mind, it is difficult to believe in his assenting to it emotionally. To him, great poetry was a thing of supreme importance, essential to a full spiritual life, and indeed itself a source of supernatural power. 'Love and poetry are powers,' he declared through the mouth of Roger Ingram in *Shadows of Ecstasy*; elsewhere in the same novel Ingram declares that Milton's verse is a form of 'immortal energy'. This is very far from Lewis's view of such things.

What remains that can be called a 'common Inklings attitude'? Certainly it seems a significant link that Tolkien, Lewis and Williams all wrote stories in which myth plays an important part. Yet each of the three uses myth in quite a different way. Williams takes the already existing Arthurian myth and uses it as a setting for metaphysical odes. Lewis uses the Christian 'myth' and reclothes it for his didactic purposes. Tolkien invents his own mythology and draws stories of many different kinds from it. The distinction needs to be emphasised as much as the similarity. On the other hand there is, of course, the belief shared by Tolkien and Lewis that myth can sometimes convey truth in a way that no abstract argument can achieve: a very important notion behind both men's work, and an idea that was certainly shared in some degree by Williams.

Where else might the 'fox' of shared ideas be found? Possibly in the area of magic and the occult, for as Adam Fox expressed it, when recalling his acquaintance with the Inklings, 'They all had a tendency to the occult in some way.' Certainly Tolkien's stories are concerned with such devices as the Silmarils and the One Ring, which contain immense supernatural power; and if one searches for comparisons two that suggest themselves are the Stone of Suleiman in Williams's *Many Dimensions* and the Graal in his *War in Heaven*. But the comparison does not go very deep. The Ring in Tolkien's story may be supernaturally endowed, but the story of Frodo Baggins carrying it to Mordor is a story more of natural than of supernatural events, a tale of courage and heroism and treachery rather than of actual magic. By contrast, in Charles Williams's novels the crucial events occur in the plane of the supernatural, while the terminology of magic and occult practices is part of Williams's basic vocabulary. He and Tolkien had nothing whatever in common in the way they used the supernatural in their stories. As for Lewis, he was by his own admission fascinated by the occult. It was a fascination that began in schooldays and was revived when he discovered Yeats's poetry. But Lewis was always very wary of it. When he met Yeats at Oxford in 1921 he was 'half fascinated and half repelled, and finally the more repelled because of the fascination'. Later, when he had become a Christian, he set his face firmly against anything smacking of the occult. Certainly magical events do occur in his stories, most notably in *That Hideous Strength,* where Merlin (a figure probably drawn, as the magician in *Dymer* certainly was, from Lewis's memories of Yeats) engineers the downfall of the villains by supernatural means. But Lewis never indulged in the kind of occultism that attracted Williams, believing that a passion for such things is (as he put it) a 'spiritual lust'. Nor would it be more than superficially true to say that Owen Barfield was interested in magic or the occult. The word 'occult' does occur in his writings in connection with Anthroposophy, but he is quick to emphasise that in this context the word merely means 'hidden' and has nothing to do with magic or witchcraft.

We are being driven to look for the fox in some rather unlikely places, and the next one looks distinctly unpromising: the fact that Tolkien, Lewis and Williams felt, to some extent, alienated from the mainstream of contemporary literature.

Though Tolkien lived in the twentieth century he could scarcely be called a modern writer. Certainly some comparatively recent authors made their mark on him: men such as William Morris, Andrew Lang, George MacDonald, Rider Haggard, Kenneth Grahame and John Buchan. There are also, perhaps, certain 'Georgian' characteristics about him. But his roots were buried deep in early literature, and the major names in twentieth-century writing meant little or nothing to him. He read very little modern fiction, and took no serious notice of it.

Lewis read much more widely than Tolkien among modern writers, and disliked much of what he saw. His projected crusade against T. S. Eliot in 1926 was the opening shot in what was to be years of sniping at that poet. He did come to have a guarded respect for Eliot's criticism, but he continued to attack his verse. At an Inklings in 1947 he declared one of Eliot's poems to be 'bilge', and in 1954, writing to Katherine Farrer, he defined his dislike of Eliot's image of evening 'like a patient etherised upon a table': 'I don't believe one person in a million, under any emotional stress, would see evening like that. And even if they did, I believe that anything but the most sparing admission of such images is a very dangerous game. To invite them, to recur willingly to them, to come to regard them as normal surely poisons us?' In 1921 he declared that 'our best moderns' were Brooke, Flecker, de la Mare, Yeats and Masefield; and he remained a Georgian all his life, both in his criticism and in his own poetry. He did approve of some of Edith Sitwell's verse, and he came to admire W. H. Auden's alliterative poems (which were themselves partly the result of Auden's admiration for Tolkien). But the great body of modern poetry remained outside his sympathy. Nor where prose was concerned was he any more generous in his comments. Predictably, he disliked D. H. Lawrence's novels for their attitude to sex; he dismissed such writers as James Joyce as '*steam of consciousness*', and categorised Virginia Woolf as one of 'the clevers'. E. M. Forster was almost the only serious novelist of the period whose work he admired. He declared that he preferred science fiction to the work of many accepted writers, and he said of the magazine *Fantasy & Science Fiction*: 'Some of the most serious satire of our age appears in it. What is called "serious" literature now – Dylan Thomas and Pound and all that – is really the most frivolous.'

Owen Barfield's sympathies can be seen to be strongly allied to Lewis's dislike of modernism. In *Poetic Diction* he agrees with the critic who declared that Eliot 'has done serious damage in his poetry to the structure of the English language'. Indeed the whole theory behind *Poetic Diction*, the notion that poetic language has *decayed* over the centuries, has moved from semantic unity towards fragmentation, carries the implication that modern poetry must of necessity be less rich in meaning than that of earlier centuries.

Williams's attitude was more subtle. His own early poetry and verse-dramas were scarcely modern in character, having a strong tendency towards the pastiche of earlier styles. Those poets who made a mark on him in his early work included Chesterton, Yeats, and Lascelles Abercrombie, as well as such diverse people as Kipling, the Pre-Raphaelites and Macaulay. His attitude to Eliot was at first largely one of puzzlement. Yet in his book *Poetry at Present* (1930) he was characteristically quick to find virtues in poets whose work was distinctly modern, and by that time he was aware that if he wished to achieve anything more than minor success as a poet he must find a more modern style. 'Better be modern than minor,' says a character in *War in Heaven*, and it was with this in mind that Williams set about remodelling his verse-rhythms. Yet, despite the apparent modernity of much of *Taliessin through Logres*, his style resembled Gerard Manley Hopkins far more than (say) Eliot, while his diction remained largely formal and never became thoroughly colloquial. He was perhaps never a true modern in his poetry.

As to prose, Williams's novels, or at least the early ones, are more like the Fu Manchu thrillers of Sax Rohmer or Chesterton's *The Man Who Was Thursday* than 'serious' modern fiction. Williams, however, did read widely among contemporary writers, partly because of his work as a reviewer; and he was always finding virtues in authors whose ideas were very different from his own. In an essay for the journal *Theology* in 1939 he examined D. H. Lawrence's attitude to sex, and recorded his admiration of Lawrence's glorification of the physical body, though he pointed out that Lawrence stopped short of developing this glorification to what he himself thought out to be its true (and Dantean) end. This essay, reprinted in *The Image of the City*, precisely expresses how much more subtle Williams's mind was than Lewis's when confronted with such issues. After reading what Williams has to say about Lawrence it is merely irritating to listen to Lewis's occasional snorts of disapproval about him.[1]

If there is very little that can be called a 'common Inklings attitude', what about the notion that Lewis and his friends made a deliberate attempt to organise a movement which would change the course of literature? One person close to them certainly thought that this was the case. In the late 1940s John Wain often came to the Inklings on

---

[1] For example in the fifth chapter of *Arthurian Torso* where Lewis declares that the wood of Broceliande in Williams's *Taliessin* cycle 'leads down to the world of D. H. Lawrence as well as up to the world of Blake'; and in the essay 'Four-Letter Words' (reprinted in *Selected Literary Essays*) when he writes: '*Lady Chatterley* has made short work of a prosecution by the Crown. It still has to face more formidable judges. Nine of them, and all goddesses' (p. 174).

Thursday nights, and some years later he wrote of them: 'This was a circle of instigators, almost of incendiaries, meeting to urge one another on in the task of redirecting the whole current of contemporary art and life.' This was undoubtedly an exaggeration, and Lewis took John Wain to task for it, replying: 'The whole picture of myself as one forming a cabinet, or cell, or coven, is erroneous. Mr Wain has mistaken purely personal relationships for alliances.' Perhaps the truth lay somewhere between the two. Lewis was not so naïve as to suppose that the Inklings could, merely by 'urging one another on', directly instigate a change of taste in art and life. On the other hand he undoubtedly believed that if a sufficient number of people were to read his friends' (and his own) books they would be significantly affected by them. For example he declared of *The Lord of the Rings*: 'Wouldn't it be wonderful if it really succeeded (in selling I mean)? It would inaugurate a new age. Dare we hope?'

Whether or not the Inklings can with any justification be called 'a circle of incendiaries', it must be remembered that the word 'influence', so beloved of literary investigators, makes little sense when talking about their association with each other. Tolkien and Williams owed almost nothing to the other Inklings, and would have written everything they wrote had they never heard of the group. Similarly, Tolkien's imagination was fully fledged and the fundamental body of his ideas was sketched out before he even met Lewis. As he himself declared, his debt to Lewis 'was not "influence" as it is ordinarily understood, but sheer encouragement'. Nor did Williams owe any crucial part of his thinking to Lewis or to others of the group. His work was almost finished by the time he came to Oxford, and though he did benefit from the contact with the Inklings, this was of small importance in his life compared to what had gone before. He appreciated the criticism of the group, but they and their remarks had little effect on the work he did in Oxford, and the books he wrote there are not greatly different or markedly superior to those written towards the end of his time in London. Lewis, on the other hand, had not written many of his books before the Inklings began to meet, and there are elements in his later work which can be easily identified as bearing the mark of Tolkien or Williams. Perhaps he even tried consciously to take up the mantle of both writers. He alone can be said to have been 'influenced' by the others[1] (he was as Tolkien said 'an impressionable man'), but for the rest it is sufficient to say that they came together because they already agreed about certain things. As Lewis put it, 'To be sure, we had a

---

[1] He was certainly influenced in many ways by Owen Barfield. Note also the effect that Barfield's *Poetic Diction* had on Tolkien (see above, p. 42).

common point of view, but we had it before we met. It was the cause rather than the result of our friendship.'

*

The question at the beginning of this chapter was 'Were the Inklings more than just a group of friends?' So far it has only received some rather patchy answers. Are we after the wrong fox? Should we not rather ask 'What sort of friends were they?'

There was nothing particularly unusual in the fact that they gathered together in this way. Oxford has always been peppered with unofficial and semi-official clubs of a similar kind. For example, Tolkien founded a short-lived dining club when he was an undergraduate, and a few years later Hugo Dyson was one of a group of undergraduates who met informally at an Oxford public house to read Elizabethan plays (these meetings, at the Jolly Farmers in Paradise Street, were initiated by Sir Walter Raleigh, the then Professor of English Literature, and were often visited by such literary notables living in the area as T. E. Lawrence, Edmund Blunden, Robert Graves, and John Masefield). Such things were the habit rather than the exception, and in this sense the Inklings were just one more Oxford club.[1] Yet they were certainly more than that to Jack Lewis. And one can perhaps begin to see why this was by looking at certain recurring patterns in his life.

As he himself pointed out, his first real friendship was with his brother Warnie, and this friendship was nourished twice, both by the persecution at their preparatory school and by the difficulties of home life in Belfast. 'We stood foursquare against the common enemy,' he wrote in his autobiography, adding, 'I suspect that this pattern, occurring twice and so early in my life, has unduly biased my whole outlook. To this day the vision of the world which comes most naturally to me is one in which "we two" or "we few" (and in a sense "we happy few") stand together against something stronger and larger.'

His attitude to friendship was also affected by his experience at Malvern when he found that the school was ruled by the unofficial clique of 'Bloods'. He saw this group as at once highly objectionable and infinitely enviable, and his feelings about it eventually became a

---

[1] They were scarcely even that. Their informality, the fact that they had no constitution or even definable membership, cannot be stressed too strongly. R. E. Havard says, in a letter to the present writer: 'We really had no corporate existence. In my view we were simply a group of C. S. L. 's wide circle of friends who lived near enough to him to meet together fairly regularly. I think, perhaps, this should be made clear, as there does seem to be some tendency to take us all much more seriously than we took ourselves.'

fixation. He called such groups 'Inner Rings'. He wrote, when describing the frequency of such things in society:

> There exist two different systems of hierarchies. The one is printed in some little book and anyone can easily read it up. A general is always superior to a colonel and a colonel to a captain. The other is not printed anywhere. Nor is it even a formally organised secret society with officers and rules which you would be told after you had been admitted. You are never formally and explicitly admitted by anyone. You discover gradually, in almost indefinable ways, that it exists and you are outside it; and then later, perhaps, that you are inside it. It is not constant. It is not easy, even at a given moment, to say who is inside and who is outside. Some people are obviously in and some are obviously out, but there are several on the border-line. People think they are in it after they have in fact been pushed out of it, or before they have been allowed in: this provides great amusement for those who are really inside. I believe that in all men's lives one of the most dominant elements is the desire to be inside the local Ring.

Whether or not this really corresponds to most people's experience of the world, circumstances conspired to embed the idea in Lewis's mind, for when he came up to Oxford as an undergraduate he found himself in a society where cliques really did play a large part. 'I have a holy terror of coteries,' he told his father when describing university life, but really the terror was of not belonging to one himself, and he gradually drew his own coterie around him – men such as Barfield, who shared his taste for traditional art-forms as opposed to modernism. Then came his fellowship at Magdalen, and his discovery that the college was ruled to a large extent by the unofficial junto of 'progressives' under the leadership of Harry Weldon. This really was an Inner Ring, and it inevitably increased Lewis's determination to gather his own friends around him for protection. Weldon was the perfect enemy for Lewis: militantly atheist, ruthless, subtle, everything that Lewis was not. He was in fact far too good an enemy, and he and Lewis never really joined battle. Instead Lewis to a large extent turned his back on his college and concentrated on the English Faculty. Here too he found something of an Inner Ring (though it was a poor one compared with Weldon and his allies) – the 'Literature' camp; and, after at first giving his allegiance to it, Lewis soon broke away and formed his own clique with Tolkien, a clique that actually managed to change the direction of the whole Faculty. It was to a large extent this clique – Lewis, Tolkien, Coghill and others of like mind – who were the nucleus of the Inklings when that group began to meet; and it might have been observed that the

Inklings too had certain resemblances to those Inner Rings which Lewis described with such detestation.

'There were no rules, officers, agendas, or formal elections,' Warnie Lewis declared of the Inklings, and the words are noticeably reminiscent of what his brother had to say about the Inner Ring (*Nor is it even a formally organised secret society with officers and rules*). 'From time to time we added to our original number,' Warnie recalled of the Inklings, 'but without formalities.' (*You are never formally admitted by anyone.*) And as for the indefinable membership of the Inner Ring (*It is not easy to say who is inside and who is outside*), nothing could be more characteristic of the Inklings. Even the hostility of the Inner Ring to uninvited intruders, or to earlier members whom it has rejected, is reflected in the Inklings' proceedings. 'Jack and I much concerned this evening by the gate crashing of ———,' Warnie wrote in his diary one Thursday night. 'Tollers, the ass, brought him here last Thursday, and he has apparently now elected himself an Inkling.' And on another occasion: 'Well attended Inkling in the evening with ———, whom we all thought had tacitly resigned' (and whose resignation, he might have added, they had clearly hoped for).

Certainly one of the few involvements of the Inklings in University affairs shows them behaving like an Inner Ring of the more unscrupulous sort. This was the election of Adam Fox to the Professorship of Poetry in 1938. The other candidate was E. K. Chambers, the distinguished Shakespearian scholar, whose candidature Lewis opposed on the grounds that 'we must have a practising poet'. It was ostensibly for this reason that the Inklings put up Adam Fox for election, even though he could scarcely be called a poet – his *Old King Coel*, a long narrative poem published in 1937, is hardly more than light verse – and though Fox himself thought the whole thing rather absurd. The election of the Professor of Poetry at Oxford is unique in that it is determined by a poll of all M.A.s, and Lewis and his friends gathered everybody they could muster to vote, with the result that Fox was elected, greatly to the disappointment of Chambers. Lewis could scarcely have had any real reason for doing this other than to demonstrate the power of his Ring.

On the other hand, a true Inner Ring (as Lewis described it) is held together exclusively by a desire for power rather than by friendship; and it was this which chiefly distinguished the Inklings from such power-groups, for friendship was the foundation upon which the group rested.

Strong male friendships were an inevitable characteristic of Oxford, a university that had been chiefly celibate until the late nineteenth century. In Lewis's era it was still customary for dons (even married dons) to spend a large part of their spare time in each other's company. All the same, Lewis paid far more attention than did his contemporaries to the actual *notion* of male friendship. From quite early in his life he had strong views on the subject. He believed that full intimacy with another man could only be achieved if women were completely excluded. 'A friend dead is to be mourned: a friend married is to be guarded against, both being equally lost,' he wrote in his diary in 1922. He also felt that it was not the done thing for male friends to discuss their domestic or personal problems. 'I speak of my own affairs with some difficulty,' he wrote to Barfield during their 'Great War' controversy, 'and don't think it conduces to the right sort of intimacy (male intimacy) to do so v. often.'

These were not just chance remarks. Each of them reflects very closely the sort of person he was. First of all, his statement that 'a friend married is to be guarded against' was part of his whole attitude to women, for he was firmly convinced from an early age that the female psychology was entirely different from – and largely inimical to – that of the male. In 1923 he and Barfield discussed the subject and agreed that 'either men or women are mad' – not that they themselves had any doubt as to which sex was sane. More seriously, he was well aware of the Greek doctrine that Form is masculine and Matter feminine, which he quoted with apparent approval; and after his conversion he adapted that doctrine into a Christian framework when he declared that the relationship of the created to the Creator is that of 'female to male'. Given this belief, it was inevitable that he should have strong views on the subject of marriage. He declared that 'Christian law' (as he put it) bestowed a necessity of 'headship' on the husband, and from biblical sources he deduced that 'the husband is the head of the wife just so far as he is to her what Christ is to the Church', adding: 'If there must be a head, why the man? Well, is there any very serious wish that it should be the woman?' And elsewhere: 'Do you really want a matriarchal world? Do you really like women in authority? When you seek authority yourself, do you naturally seek it in a woman?' One might note that in Lewis's *Perelandra* the Eve and Adam are referred to respectively as 'The Lady' and 'The King'.

It would be wrong to say that he despised women. He was no misogynist. But he did regard the female mind as inferior to the male, or at least as being incapable of the mental activities which he valued. He told Charles Williams that he thought women's minds 'not really meant for logic or great art', and he once wrote an uncharacteristically cruel short story called 'The Shoddy Lands' in which he is allowed, for a few moments, to see the world as it is seen through the eyes of what he clearly regards as a typically selfish and vain woman. What he did wish to find in women was clearly expressed in the characters of the Lady in *Perelandra* and Mrs Dimble in *That Hideous Strength*: intelligence certainly, but submissiveness to the male, and great motherliness. Not merely motherliness, moreoever, but fertility: one of Jane Studdock's sins in *That Hideous Strength* is her refusal to bear children.

To some extent these attitudes were typical of his social background, and of Oxford in particular. Until the reforms of the eighteen-seventies, holders of college fellowships were in general not allowed to marry and, though by Lewis's day marriage was common among dons, it had not been fully integrated into university life. Dons worked in their colleges and took a large proportion of their meals there. Their college was almost invariably the centre of their social life. In the meantime their wives were obliged to remain at home in the suburbs, superintending the servants and bringing up the children. Added to this was the fact that some of the wives were far less well educated than their husbands,[1] so that even when they were given a chance to talk to those male friends of their husband who came to the house they had very little to say, or at least very little that the men thought worth listening to. 'The men have learned to live among ideas,' wrote Lewis when he was discussing this very problem. 'They know what discussion, proof and illustration mean. A woman who has had merely school lessons and has abandoned soon after marriage whatever tinge of "culture" they gave her – whose reading is the Women's Magazines and whose general conversation is almost wholly narrative – cannot really enter such a circle [of male friends]. If the men are ruthless, she sits bored and silent through a conversation which means nothing to her. If they are better bred, of course, they try to bring her in. Things are explained to her: people try to sublimate her irrelevant and blundering observations into some kind of sense. But the efforts soon fail and, for manners' sake, what might have been a real discussion is deliberately diluted and peters out in gossip, anecdotes and jokes.' Cruel, but true of at least some women at Oxford in the years between the wars; though of course the very fact that Lewis and his contemporaries had this poor opinion of female conversation itself prevented such women from being given any conversational chances. It was a vicious circle. Moreoever many women found Lewis as unbearable as he found them. If they had no 'real conversation', he had no small talk whatever, and they often felt that he was blundering, brusque, or downright rude.

In this respect, then, he was merely typical of his contemporaries.

[1] Some, but by no means all. Many dons' wives were graduates, and in a few cases their scholarly ability equalled that of their husbands. Lewis's view of women was modelled more closely on Mrs Moore and on Tolkien's wife Edith than on university wives in general.

But it should be remembered that his own experience was worse than most people's. He was unmarried, but there was Mrs Moore, and even by Oxford standards her conversation was ruthlessly illogical. Her mind, as Warnie Lewis once remarked, was 'just the sort of mind Jack could not tolerate. I was dining alone with her one evening, and the meal opened with the following exchange:

> *Myself:* I see this is the coldest winter since 18——.
> *Mrs Moore:* No. It was much colder the year my grandfather died.
> *Myself:* Oh I'm not quoting from one of those chatty newspaper articles about the weather, but from the official statistics.
> *Mrs Moore:* Then the man who wrote them was a fool. It was much colder the year my grandfather died.

Mrs Moore's company cannot have improved Lewis's opinion of the female mind. His involvement with her perhaps also goes some way towards explaining his almost aggressive refusal to discuss deeply personal matters with his men friends. In the nineteen-twenties his private life had been a mystery to his friends, and he had refused to explain his feelings for Mrs Moore even to Warnie. During the thirties she became more and more demanding, and by the time war broke out she had grown into a tyrannical and perhaps not entirely sane old woman. Lewis continued to behave towards her with infinite and un-failing charity, scarcely ever complaining about her even to Warnie, let alone to anyone else. So why should he encourage other people to complain about their domestic difficulties or discuss their problems? Lewis's friends sometimes found this attitude tiresome. It annoyed Tolkien, who often wanted to find a sympathetic ear for the tale of his domestic troubles.

But despite this attitude to women and this desire to avoid talking about personal things, Lewis did not enter into male friendship in a manner that could be described as hearty or boorish. He was capable also of great delicacy and sensitivity, perhaps even feminine sensitivity. He once said: 'I can't bear "a man's man" or "a woman's woman". There ought spiritually to be a man in every woman and a woman in every man.' Indeed it might be said that the femininity in him con-tributed to the friendships of the Inklings.

This is not to say that he was homosexual. He does not appear ever to have felt any overt sexual attraction towards other men, and he said of this, 'How a man can feel anything but bewildering pity for the genuinely homosexual I've never been able to understand.' In *The Four Loves* he argued forcibly that it is ridiculous to suppose all male friend-ships to be founded on sexual attraction. On the other hand he was *disturbed* by homosexuality: the considerable space which he devotes to it in his account of school life in his autobiography shows as much. Perhaps (as has been suggested) one can also see in his shabby manner of dress – baggy trousers, old mackintosh, squashed hat – a wish to differentiate himself from the homosexual-dandy fashions of Oxford in the late twenties and early thirties.

Yet for somebody who did not experience overt homosexual feelings, and perhaps even feared them, Lewis was prepared to admit a considerable element of something like the erotic into his notions of friendship between man and man. In *The Allegory of Love* he discusses the nature of male friendship in early medieval society, this being an era when (as he believed) romantic heterosexual love played a negligible part in life as well as literature. 'The deepest of worldly emotions in this period', he declares, 'is the love of man for man, the mutual love of warriors who die together fighting against odds, and the affection between vassal and lord.' This last emotion he compared to 'a small boy's feeling for some hero in the sixth form', while he said of the friendships between warrior and warrior that they 'were themselves lover-like; in their intensity, their wilful exclusion of other values, and their uncertainty'. Whether or not this is a true picture of early medieval society, it has some resemblance to Lewis's own life. A king's man may or may not have regarded his feudal lord in the fashion of small boy looking up to an eighteen-year-old, but this was rather the way in which Lewis behaved towards Charles Williams. The feelings of one medieval fighting man for another may or may not have been 'lover-like in their intensity', but there was certainly a trace of this in the way that Lewis felt about his own men friends. And when towards the end of his life he wrote an essay on the topic of Friendship, he reverted to the image of warriors in an earlier society when trying to explain the history of male friendship. 'Long before history began we men have got together and done things,' he wrote. 'We enjoyed one another's society greatly; we Braves, we hunters, all bound together by shared skill, shared dangers and hardships, esoteric jokes – away from the women and children.' There is something absurd in his trying to explain his feelings for his friends in this way, and several of the Inklings actually thought the whole essay (in *The Four Loves*) was ill judged. Yet the very fact that Lewis had to resort to such far fetched comparisons suggests how intangible and inexplicable his feelings were.

Despite the exaggeration of some of the essay, it should be studied closely by anyone who wants to come near an understanding of the nature of the Inklings. There is much in it which relates closely to Lewis's life. His account of how true Friendship begins when two acquaintances discover that they have some common insight or taste inevitably recalls his and Tolkien's discovery of their mutual delight in 'Northernness'. His assertion that friendship thrives not so much on agreeing about the answers as on agreeing what are the important questions reminds one of the way in which he and Barfield continued on close terms long after they had disagreed on fundamental religious issues. His assertion that Friendship is not inquisitive – 'You become a man's Friend without knowing or caring whether he is married or single or how he earns his living' – is a statement of his own obstinate refusal to admit private matters into conversation with his friends. And his declaration that real friendship is not jealous, and that 'in each of my friends there is something that only some other friend can fully bring out', perhaps comes closest of all to explaining what the Inklings were fundamentally about. It comes closest, but it does not finally get there; and all attempts to analyse the nature of Lewis's feelings for his friends will ultimately come to nothing because these things cannot be explained. They can only be observed.

*

Friendship with other men played as important a part in Tolkien's life as it did in Lewis's. Unlike Lewis, Tolkien encountered romantic love at an early age, for when he was sixteen he fell in love with a girl of nineteen, a fellow orphan who lived in his Birmingham lodging house. But he and Edith Bratt were soon separated by his guardian, and in late adolescence Tolkien was thrown back on friendship with others of his own sex, so much so that by the time he was reunited with her he had, as it were, lost touch with her, and had devoted the greater part of his deepest affections to his male friends. He and Edith were eventually married and had four children, but family affairs (though of great interest and importance to Tolkien) seemed to him to be quite apart from his life with his male friends. This division of his life into water-tight compartments inevitably caused a strain, and Edith Tolkien resented the fact that such a large part of her husband's affections were lavished on Lewis and other men friends, while Tolkien himself felt that time spent with the Inklings and in other male company could only be gained by a deliberate and almost ruthless exclusion of attention to his wife. 'There are many things that a man feels are legitimate even though they cause a fuss,' he wrote to a son who was about to be married. 'Let him not lie about them to his wife or lover! Cut them out – or if worth a fight: just insist. Such matters may arise frequently – the glass of beer, the pipe, the non writing of letters, the other friend, etc. etc. If the other side's claims really are unreasonable (as they are at times between the dearest lovers and most loving married folk) they are much better met by above board refusal and "fuss" than subterfuge.' Edith

Tolkien was capable of responding to this attitude with equal obstinacy, and as a result the atmosphere in the Tolkien household at Northmoor Road was sometimes as difficult as that in the Lewis–Moore ménage at the Kilns.

It might be imagined that Tolkien adopted this attitude and divided his life in this fashion because, like Lewis, he regarded the female intellect as largely inferior to the male. Certainly he was quite capable of expressing such an opinion. In 1941 he wrote: 'How quickly an intelligent woman can be taught, grasp the teacher's ideas, see his point – and how (with some exceptions) they can go no further, when they leave his hand, or when they cease to take a personal interest in him. It is their gift to be receptive, stimulated, fertilized (in many other matters than the physical) by the male.' Yet Tolkien was not at all condescending to his many women pupils, and he helped several of them to achieve considerable academic distinction. Moreover, while he was capable of agreeing with the kind of view about female minds which Lewis held, he was also quite capable of sympathising with the plight of a clever woman who had been trapped by marriage into leading an intellectually empty life.

If the Inklings were for Lewis the culmination of patterns in his earlier life, there were precedents in Tolkien's earlier years too. At school he was one of a group of four friends who called themselves 'The Tea Club and Barrovian Society' (the latter after Barrow's Stores in Birmingham where they met for tea) and who read and criticised each other's writing much as the Inklings did many years later. The affections of the members of the 'T.C.B.S.' for each other were very strong, and Tolkien was profoundly distressed when two of them were killed in the Battle of the Somme. Like Lewis, he too had his 'set' of undergraduate friends at Oxford. Like Lewis he enjoyed the challenge of faction-fighting in the English School, and of forming a junto to achieve the syllabus reforms. But while Lewis felt that all his friendships were equally important in their way – Lewis cared as much for Barfield as for Williams, as much for Williams as for Tolkien – Tolkien was more selective with his affections.

This is not to say that he was not fond of many of the Inklings. He had much affection and respect for Warnie Lewis, whom he actually considered to be unfairly overshadowed by Jack. He was deeply fond of Havard, whose company he greatly valued especially in his later years, when Havard was a neighbour and a close confidant. The friendship of Barfield, Williams, Dyson, and the others played a large part in his life. But his affection for Jack Lewis was more profound; his feelings for the other Inklings never equalled it.

*

Warnie Lewis took friendships very much for granted. In his army days he had been obliged to spend most of his time with other men, and his Oxford life was merely a continuation of this. Above this there stood out one stronger emotion: his love for his brother, which was the emotional centre of his life. When one day Jack mentioned the question of what might happen if he were to predecease his brother, Warnie wrote in his diary that this was 'a subject which does not bear thinking about, for I dare not contemplate a life which does not centre round J.' For more than thirty years Warnie's life did indeed centre round Jack, and the Inklings were to him only an accidental result (though a valuable one) of this central attachment.

As to his brother's and Tolkien's attitude to women, Warnie Lewis to some extent shared this in that he had little enthusiasm for female company in general. But this was not because he had a contempt for the female intellect – his regard for his own mind was so modest as to rule out any such attitude – as because he was, by his own admission, very ill at ease in the company of women. He wrote in his diary in 1946: 'With all my army experience I am still as shy of women as a hobbledehoy.'

*

With Charles Williams there was, as always, a complexity of views. Williams was certainly aware (with Lewis) of masculine friendship as a specifically identifiable emotion. He also believed (with Tolkien) that it involved very different emotions than did marriage. On the other hand he did not think, as Tolkien did, that the two were largely incompatible. In his novel *All Hallows' Eve*, a book that he wrote after he had been among the Inklings for several years, he talked of the importance of 'the tide of masculine friendship'. Yet he went on to declare that (for the character in the novel called Richard Furnival) this tide had always 'swelled against the high cliff' of marriage: 'He had not lost at all the sense of great Leviathans, disputes and laughter, things native and natural to the male, but beyond them, and shining towards them had been that other less natural, and as it were more archangelic figure, the shape of the woman and his wife.'

Though this should not be taken too closely as autobiography – Williams's marriage was, after all, a source of stress as much as of happiness – he undoubtedly regarded romantic love as ultimately of far greater importance than 'things native and natural to the male'. This of course set him strongly apart from Lewis and Tolkien. Nor where the practical question of authority in marriage was concerned did he exactly share Lewis's view of the natural headship of the husband. When discussing Milton's view of marriage in *Paradise Lost* (a view that closely resembles Lewis's own) Williams declared: 'Milton's principles of the relations of the sexes may have been all wrong – probably because any principle of the relations of the sexes will be wrong, since there are, after all, no such things; there are an infinite number of women and an infinite number of men.'

*

Barfield, Dyson, Havard, and many of the others who were in the Inklings at one time or another were married men who did not depend so exclusively on male friendship as did Lewis. Yet for those of them who were close to Lewis friendship with him proved to be a uniquely rich experience. 'He gave one a warmth of friendship,' said Havard, 'which I have never met anywhere else.'

One day Tolkien, in a letter to his son Christopher, referred to the Inklings as 'the Lewis seance', and there was more than an element of truth in this. They were Lewis's friends: the group gathered round him, and in the end one does not have to look any further than Lewis to see why it came into being. He himself is the fox.

5
'Hwaet! we Inclinga'

'The war and Oxford make it impossible to *settle*,' Charles Williams wrote to his wife in December 1939. 'Poetry is different; poetry is still more me than I am; and the coming of great lines is less one's work than – something. If I could do as I chose and yet had to be down here, I would do nothing but think of the next *Taliessin* group. However – "all luck is good"; I think it even if I have not felt it – not habitually.'

'All luck is good' was the theme of Williams's play *The Death of Good Fortune*. It expressed his profound belief that every event, however apparently evil, will lead to some good. It was of course easier to say it than to apply it to his own life. Living a makeshift existence, moving daily between his temporary home in South Parks Road, his office at Southfield House and Lewis's rooms in Magdalen, he might still have been at ease had circumstances allowed him to devote his mind to the only form of writing he really cared about, the *Taliessin* poems. By the end of 1939 he had completed some verse for the next volume of the cycle; but there was still so much that he wanted to think about. Or rather, he wanted to be in a frame of thought where 'the coming of great lines' could be allowed to happen uninterrupted by more trivial concerns. However, that was not to be. He needed money, and he must do commissioned work. There were a good many commissions, too. T. S. Eliot, who was now his publisher, had contracted him to do a book for Faber's on the history of witchcraft, and as 1939 came to an end he worked wearily at it. 'It is a dull book,' he told his wife in one of his almost daily letters to her, 'and I have no interest in it whatever.' However, when it was eventually finished Eliot thought it acceptable, and that meant a cheque from the publishers. And as soon as it was done, there was *The Forgiveness of Sins* to be tackled for Ashley Sampson at Geoffrey Bles, as well as several plays that had been commissioned by religious drama groups. All the time there was also a steady flow of reviews and articles to be written. 'I am particularly taken with the idea', he told his wife, 'that the article on "The City in English Poetry"

172

will (a little late!) pay the last insurance almost exactly. Very useful!' And later, while writing a play for a missionary society: 'The Teeth Bill has come and is £16/16/-. It shall be paid as soon as the Play's done: this play will always mean Teeth to me.'

Most of his letters to his wife contained a pound note, which he sent to help her with housekeeping at their London flat where she was still living despite the danger of bombs. But sometimes he could not even afford that small sum. 'I had hoped that some cheque or other would have enabled me to send you another pound at once; however, there isn't one. A letter asking me if I will write a pamphlet for some religious views: 4000 words for £2.2.0 – I ask you! Nevertheless I think I shall do it, and make £2.2.0 instead of nothing.'

Quite why he had so little money it was difficult to say. The Press still paid him his salary, and the expense of living in Oxford was not very great. Moreover one of his female admirers, a woman called Margaret Douglas, had come to live in the Randolph Hotel with her mother, so as to be away from London and near C. W., and on Sunday nights the Douglases fed him at their table in the hotel. But, if that saved him a few shillings, he was always buying a drink or a meal for a friend, or he was giving away a pound or two to someone who had come to see him from a long distance and was in need of help. 'We have never lost by being free-handed,' he told his wife. 'I feel that we have done better, in freedom and friendship, than the more cautious kind of people. We are Elizabethans, not Victorians.'

Meanwhile he lived much of his life in cafés and pubs, eating a sandwich with a London friend who was passing through, drinking beer with one of the Inklings, or dealing with the emotional crisis of some complete stranger who had read his books and arrived without warning to ask his advice. And always there was more writing to plan. 'I have a kind of yearning towards a novel,' he told his wife in the summer of 1940, 'but I don't see my way yet.'

*

C. S. Lewis was an obvious choice as one of the contributors to Ashley Sampson's series of wartime books for his firm Geoffrey Bles, which was called 'Christian Challenge'. Lewis was known to be a comparatively recent convert to Christianity, and his *Pilgrim's Regress* (though it had not sold many copies) was generally admired. Sampson asked Lewis to tackle the difficult subject of the Christian justification of pain and suffering. Lewis agreed, began the book in the summer of 1939, read it to the Inklings – to whom it was eventually dedicated – and obtained their approval, asked Havard to contribute an appendix on the clinical effects of pain, and finished the book by the spring of 1940. When *The*

Problem of Pain was published the following autumn it was received enthusiastically by a large number of readers – larger, perhaps, than in peacetime, for the war had filled the churches. 'One unexpected feature of life at present,' Lewis noted shortly after the outbreak of war, 'is that it is quite hard to get a seat in church.' This apparent religious revival included the University, and as the war progressed it was noticeable that Christianity was being regarded much more sympathetically at Oxford than it had been in the thirties. The Oxford Union debated the motion 'That a return to God through organised religion is essential for the establishment of a new world order', and the majority in favour was seen to be so great that no division was taken. Meanwhile one day coming out of church at Headington Quarry on a summer Sunday morning, Lewis was 'struck by an idea for a book which I think might be both useful and entertaining. It would be called "As one Devil to another" and would consist of letters from an elderly retired devil to a young devil who has just started work on his first "patient". The idea would be to give all the psychology of temptation from the *other* point of view.' *The Screwtape Letters* were finished in a few months, and were passed to a Christian newspaper, which serialised them during 1941. Ashley Sampson published them in book form the following spring, and so great was the demand for copies that *Screwtape* had to be re-printed eight times that year alone. An American edition came out in 1943 and was soon a best-seller. Lewis's name had suddenly become known to thousands of readers.

'In 1943 I came across *Screwtape Letters*,' recalled an American admirer, one of many who wrote gratefully to Lewis. 'I was a Junior in college then and trying to find myself intellectually and spiritually. I resolved on that Sunday evening to live a positive life for Christ rather than one just out of the reach of evil.' And another American wrote 'to thank you for having turned me into a reasoning and fairly lovable Christian. It seems I was quite the simpering little demon before reading *Screwtape*.'

Lewis himself could not say quite why the book appealed so widely, except that the temptations it described were drawn closely from his personal experience. 'If one begins from the sin that has been one's own chief problem during the last week,' he observed, 'one is very often surprised at the way this shaft goes home.' Certain elements of *Screwtape* are indeed at times distinctly recognisable as relating to Lewis's own life, not least the figure of the mother, 'the sharp-tongued old lady at the breakfast table'. Life with Mrs Moore was no easier at this period than it had been before the war.

Lewis dedicated *Screwtape* to Tolkien, adding beneath the printed dedication in Tolkien's own copy, 'In token payment of a great debt'.

Tolkien himself was not altogether enthusiastic about the book, for as somebody who believed profoundly in the power of evil he thought it foolish to trifle rather facetiously with such things. Not that Lewis himself was much in doubt about the reality of evil. When discussing belief in the Devil or devils he said quite categorically, 'I do believe such beings exist.' Indeed, by temperament he inclined strongly towards dualism, the belief that God and the Devil are equal powers at war with each other. 'I have always gone as near Dualism as Christianity allows,' he admitted. Though as an orthodox Christian he had to reject the fully dualist view of the world, he did believe firmly that while the power of evil could *create* nothing, it could *infect* everything. In *The Problem of Pain* he even suggested (with dubious orthodoxy) that Satan might be the cause of certain pains and diseases.[1]

If he was not a dualist, was he a fundamentalist? *The Problem of Pain* and the many books of Christian 'apology' with which Lewis followed it certainly suggest that he came close to a belief in the literal truth of the entire Bible. Lewis himself said of this:

> I have been suspected of being what is called a Fundamentalist. That is because I never regard any narrative as unhistorical simply on the grounds that it includes the miraculous. Some people find the miraculous so hard to believe that they cannot imagine any reason for my acceptance of it other than a prior belief that every sentence of the Old Testament has historical or scientific truth. But this I do not hold, any more than did St Jerome did when he said that Moses described Creation 'after the manner of a popular poet' (as we should say, mythically).

But, although he did not believe the Bible to be the direct and flawless product of divine inspiration, he did declare himself to be 'a dogmatic Christian untinged with Modernist reservations and committed to supernaturalism in its full rigour'. He was in fact not a theologian in any true sense of the word, for he did not set about an investigation of doctrine, but rather made himself an apologist, a defender of the faith in its full orthodoxy. He was largely ignorant of the work of modern theologians, and was proud of this ignorance, because he thought it helped him to avoid taking sides in any faction-fights. 'A great deal of my utility', he wrote in 1963, 'has depended on my having kept out of all dog-fights between professing schools of "Christian

---

[1] *The Problem of Pain*, footnote to the first page of Chapter 6: 'I by no means reject the view that the "efficient cause" of disease, or some disease, may be a created being other than man. In Scripture Satan is specially associated with disease in Job, in Luke xiii, 16, I Cor. v, 5, and (probably) in I Tim. i, 20.'

175

thought".' He was, however, candid in his dislike of the 'demytholo-gisers', particularly (in the nineteen-sixties) John Robinson, the Bishop of Woolwich and author of *Honest to God*, whom Lewis named 'the Bishop of Woolworths'. To someone who had come to Christianity through a perception of its character as a myth, the notion of abandoning that myth was the ultimate absurdity.

If *Screwtape* was written with complete sincerity, the actual task of writing it proved to be remarkably unpleasant. 'Though I had never written anything more easily,' Lewis recalled, 'I never wrote with less enjoyment. Though it was easy to twist one's mind into the diabolical attitude, it was not fun, or not for long. The strain produced a sort of spiritual cramp. The world into which I had to project myself while I spoke through Screwtape was all dust, grit, thirst and itch. It almost smothered me before I was done.'

Although Charles Williams wrote extensively about black magic, and though his novels deal largely with the supernatural contention of good and evil, he did not share Lewis's precise and explicit belief in the Devil. 'The devil, even if he is a fact, has been an indulgence,' Williams wrote when discussing the problem of evil in *He Came Down From Heaven*. 'We have relieved our own sense of moral submission [to God] by contemplating, even disapprovingly, something which was neither moral nor submissive. While he [the devil] exists there is always something to which we can be superior.' Williams believed the cause of evil to lie not so much in direct supernatural influence as in the capacity of human beings to envisage something other than pure good. He wrote that the Fall 'was merely the wish to know an antagonism in the good, to find out what the good would be like if a contradiction were introduced into it'. However, he answered *Screwtape* in kind. Reviewing it in *Time & Tide* he wrote: 'My dearest Scorpuscle: It is a dangerous book, heavenly-dangerous. I hate it, this give-away of hell.' He signed the review 'Your sincere friend, Snigsozzle', and added as a postscript: 'You will send someone to see after Lewis? – some very clever fiend?'

*

'Hwæt! we Inclinga,' wrote Tolkien, parodying the opening lines of *Beowulf*, 'on ærdagum searoþancolra snyttru gehierdon.' 'Lo! we have heard in old days of the wisdom of the cunning-minded Inklings; how those wise ones sat together in their deliberations, skilfully reciting learning and song-craft, earnestly meditating. That was true joy!' The poem continued for two more lines:

> þara wæs Hloðuig sum, hæleða dyrost,
> brad ond beorhtword, cuþe he . . .

11 (a)   Hugo Dyson in 1969.

11 (b)   Magdalen College, Oxford: looking across to New Buildings, where Lewis's rooms were situated.

12 Jack and Warnie Lewis on holiday in 1949.

'One of them was Hlothwig, dearest of men, broad and bright of word; he knew . . .'. 'Hlothwig' was the Anglo-Saxon form of the Germanic name from which 'Lewis' was ultimately derived, and if Tolkien had not abandoned the poem at this point he might have gone on to portray all the Inklings in turn. Certainly that was what he attempted in a series of clerihews.

> Dr U. Q. Humphrey
> Made poultices of comfrey.
> If you didn't pay his bills
> He gave you doses of squills.

'Humphrey' Havard was called up in 1943 and served in the navy as a medical officer. When he appeared in Oxford on leave he was seen to have grown a surprisingly rust-coloured beard. The Inklings immediately gave him yet another nickname, 'the Red Admiral'. Later, Tolkien managed to put Havard in touch with a malaria research unit which was based in Oxford, and he was allowed to come home and work for the unit. 'Almost the only wire I have ever pulled that has rung a bell,' Tolkien remarked, and it was perhaps with this in mind (and recalling Tolkien's skill many years earlier in the syllabus reforms) that Lewis once referred to Tolkien as 'The Lord of the Strings'.

Tolkien's clerihews surveyed each of the Inklings in turn.

> Mr Owen Barfield's
> Habit of turning cartwheels
> Made some say: 'He's been drinking!'
> It was only 'conscientious thinking'.

The cartwheels were of an intellectual sort, and 'conscientious thinking' was one of Barfield's terms for the thought processes related to Anthroposophy. Barfield was only a rare visitor to the Inklings, but Tolkien recorded the proceedings one Thursday night when he was there: 'I reached the Mitre at 8 where I was joined by C. W. and the Red Admiral, resolved to take fuel on board before joining the well-oiled diners in Magdalen (C. S. L. and Owen Barfield). C. S. L. was highly flown, but we were also in good fettle; while O. B. is the only man who can tackle C. S. L. making him define everything, and interrupting his most dogmatic pronouncements with subtle *distinguo*'s. The result was a most amusing and highly contentious evening, on which had an outsider dropped he would have thought it a meeting of fell enemies hurling deadly insults before drawing their guns. Warnie was in excellent majoral form. On one occasion when the audience had flatly refused

177

to hear Jack discourse on and define "Chance", Jack said: "Very well, some other time, but if you die tonight you'll be cut off knowing a great deal less about Chance than you might have." Warnie: "That only illustrates what I've always said: every cloud has a silver lining." But there was some quite interesting stuff. A short play on Jason and Medea by Barfield, two excellent sonnets sent by a young poet to C. S. L.; and some illuminating discussion of "ghosts", and of the special nature of Hymns (C. S. L. has been on the Committee revising Ancient and Modern). I did not leave till 12.30, and reached my bed about 1 a.m.'

*

When the bombings of London began, Williams was deeply saddened by the damage done to his beloved City. 'Did you see that Bourne and Hollingsworth's was bombed?' he wrote to his wife in September 1940. 'To think that we were there a week ago today! O you my heart and London my love! it is shocking not to be there.' And a few months later: 'Things are a little gloomy here today because no-one knows whether anything of Amen House is left. When I had your letter about taxis and cinemas this morning *and* was thinking of A. H. being no more, I very nearly broke down altogether. It wasn't only A. H.; it was all my poor loved City! St Bride's and St Andrew's by the Wardrobe and the Guildhall! O well ——!'

Yet the City of his imagination and his writings did not ultimately depend on the City of London for its existence and its fertility as a symbol, and when he actually spent five nights in London during the height of the Blitz and, from the balcony of his Hampstead flat, watched the docks go up in flames, he experienced a curious sense of detachment. He told Anne Ridler: 'I said to myself, "London is burning", but produced no thrill, though there was a sense of crisis, due however (I fear) to the knowledge that it would make a good landmark that night. Living in history is as inconvenient as living in love.' His old association with London had been broken; to another friend he remarked: 'Do me the high favour to consider Oxford also as the City.'

London was no longer even tolerably safe for his wife Michal, and for a time she went to stay with her sister in Leicestershire. Later, during 1942, she came to Oxford and threw in her lot with the South Parks Road household. This time she was moderately happy there, though (as Williams remarked) 'a little conscious of being superfluous'. Life was not particularly easy for him with Michal living in Oxford, not least because 'Celia' had returned from Java and often came into Southfield House to do part-time work for the Press. 'It *is* a little nerve-racking,' he told Anne Ridler, 'for I never know which day in the week C. is likely to come in, and I refuse to tell Michal never to come to the office except on Saturday mornings. However I take refuge in the Holy Ghost – who limits my actual seeing of Celia to an hour in six weeks; so that my quiescence is fairly undisturbed.' He was also worried by the difficulty of looking after his son Michael, who was by now a rebellious and unhappy late-adolescent, and who spent some time with his father in the Spalding household in Oxford before a brief and miserable time in the R.A.F. One day at about this period, Williams rediscovered a horoscope which somebody had cast for him many years before. 'Venus is weak,' he noted ironically; 'I might be "happier ar.d more successful unmarried" (only I should have done nothing) . . .' And indeed just at this time, when he was beginning a long-planned book on Dante and Romantic Theology (which had been commissioned for Faber & Faber by T. S. Eliot) he found, as he had so often found, his wife's presence a strangely stabilising influence. After the book was finished, he reminded Michal that it 'was written with You about, and it's been the only good book I've done since '39.'

The Figure of Beatrice was indeed one of the finest books he had written: an interpretation of Dante's writings as a poetic account of that Way of Affirmation by which romantic love may lead to the truly selfless love of God. Before he began writing it, Williams made the 'hideous confession' that 'I do *not* want to read Dante through again!' (He did not share Lewis's delight in re-reading masterpieces of literature in their entirety, preferring to concentrate on what he considered the most important passages.) And when the book was finished he reported that Eliot 'is being a Pest' in saying that the introductory chapter was obscure and should be rewritten. 'Now Lewis says it is the clearest thing I have ever written and forbids me to touch it. He even told my wife that the whole book was extraordinarily clear, "which has not always been, Mrs Williams, a virtue of your husband's work".'

Lewis had no notion that Williams's marriage was anything other than entirely happy. He took at face value Williams's elaborately chivalrous manner of referring to Michal, and told Arthur Greeves that Williams 'is, I think, youthfully in love with his wife still.' Later he wrote of Williams's 'brilliantly happy marriage'. It was an understandable error, for to most of his friends Williams made much of his devotion to Michal – in contrast with the reserved or even off-hand manner with which Lewis's other married acquaintances often referred to their wives. Indeed, had Lewis been privy to any of the six hundred and eighty or so letters written by Williams to his wife during the war, he would have found scarcely a word to suggest that all was not well with the marriage. Quite the opposite, for the letters (signed with the pet-name 'Serge') were full of poetic endearments. 'It is fresh fire, as well as fresh springs, which leap in you,' he wrote to Michal in a typical passage. 'Your Excellency is to consider that few women retain the fresh fire of nature and super-nature so long. It is on such beauty of sanctity as yours that the whole Church depends.' It is only when one finds him using almost identical terms when writing to many of his female disciples and friends, and when one discovers him referring almost brusquely to Michal when addressing someone who was truly in his confidence ('Separation is bad for her, and I dare say not too good for me'), that one realises that these letters of devotion were in a sense little more than another image thrown up by Williams's kaleido-scopic mind. Not that they were in any way an act of hypocrisy or self-deception. Despite the tension and unhappiness that coloured much of his married life, he still, by his most candid admission, needed Michal. He wrote to Raymond Hunt, a faithful follower from London days who was fully in his confidence about 'Celia' and the true state of the marriage: 'My great difficulty with her [Michal] has been that she is always uncertain whether I shouldn't do very well without her. The answer (I have always maintained) is that I should *if* in that case I "did" at all. Rather like religion, perhaps; one would be better without it, only then one would not "be".' And very near the end of the war he spoke to Thelma Shuttleworth about the sense of impoverishment caused by his separation from Michal during much of the time between 1939 and 1945: 'More than one ever dreamed or thought – though one thought it a good deal – one, or at least I know *I*, depended on my wife; and flying visits, however frequent, are not the mutual exchange of unseen life. And one's distinguished friend at Magdalen – however good and useful – is *not* that steady unnoticeable nourishment and repose . . .'

*

The success of Williams's Oxford lectures on Milton, especially the one on Chastity, was not merely a passing phenomenon. 'I have seen his impress on the Milton papers when I examined,' Lewis reported to a friend some months after the lectures. 'Fancy an Oxford student, and a girl, writing about Mammon's speech in Book II: "Mammon pro-poses an ordered state of sin with such majesty of pride that but for the words *live to ourselves* which startle our consciences we should hardly recognise it as a sin, so natural it is to man." Compare that with the sort of bilge you and I were proud to write in Schools.'

On no one was the effect of the lectures more marked than on Lewis himself. Since his conversion, his own orthodox and supernaturalist Christian faith had already inclined him to accept the theology of *Paradise Lost* almost in its entirety, and to dismiss as irrelevant the reservations held by many modern critics of the poem. Then came Williams's own lectures, which Lewis attended and which (as he reported) 'partly anticipated, partly confirmed, and most of all clarified and matured, what I had long been thinking about Milton'. Shortly afterwards, Lewis wrote *A Preface to Paradise Lost*.

It was in fact not so much a 'preface' to a reading of the poem as a defence of it against contemporary critics. In passing, it also included an attack on modern poetry, delivered in Lewis's most Chestertonian manner: 'While the moderns have been pressing forward to conquer new territories of consciousness, the old territory, in which alone man can live, has been left unguarded, and we are in danger of finding the enemy in our rear.' The book was in fact far more characteristic of Lewis than of Williams. Nevertheless it had a very real debt to Williams's ideas, and Lewis acknowledged that debt with characteristic generosity in the dedication: 'Apparently the door of the prison was really unlocked all the time; but it was only you who thought of trying the handle. Now we can all come out.'

When Williams read this, he remarked: 'I will go so far as to say I have turned a few handles – let us pray, heavenly.' Writing to Raymond Hunt about Lewis, he added: 'I should never have written the book, and in scholarship he is far more competent than I; after all, he was struggling towards the truth when I was flung across his path.' Later, when the book was published, Williams was a little distressed to find that the reviews treated Lewis rather than Williams himself as the critic who was restoring the poem to its former place. But he declared, 'The main point is Milton, and whether C. S. L. or I is of no importance.' He also told Raymond Hunt, with a characteristically half-mocking half-serious use of the ceremonial plural: 'The restoration of Milton criticism to its proper balance is but a side-accident of Our existence; not Our chief affair.' His 'chief affair' was of course the writing of *Taliessin* and, as the months passed, further poems for the second volume came into existence, but only slowly. 'Meanwhile,' he told Anne Ridler, 'Mr Eliot thinks I should do a novel.' But still he could not think of a subject.

Lewis meanwhile *could* think of a novel. Indeed it arose partly out of his writing *A Preface to Paradise Lost*. When considering Milton's treatment of the Fall and pondering the *purpose* of the 'fruit of that forbidden tree', he came to the conclusion that 'the only point of forbidding it was to instil obedience'. In fact at one point in his book on Milton he moved into the realm of fiction with an imaginative account of what might have happened had Adam and Eve remained unfallen and immortal, and had the later peoples of the world made an occasional pilgrimage to Eden:

To you or to me, once in a lifetime perhaps, would have fallen the almost terrifying honour of coming at last, after long journeys and ritual preparations and slow ceremonial approaches, into the very presence of the great Father, Priest, and Emperor of the Planet Tellus; a thing to be remembered all our lives.

To this preoccupation with the nature of an unfallen Adam and Eve was added his recurring mental picture of floating islands; the two merged, and the result was the planet Perelandra, where the human pair have not yet fallen, where there are floating islands and a forbidden 'fixed land', and where (even as the story begins) the power of evil, dwelling in a human space-voyager, arrives to attempt to bring about yet another Fall.[1]

Perelandra was begun soon after the completion of the Milton book, but it was not published until 1943.[2] For many years, Lewis considered it to be his best piece of fiction, and Tolkien shared this high opinion of it, telling his daughter that he thought it a great work of literature. The Fall was indeed a subject that occupied Tolkien's imagination as much as it did Lewis's – as Tolkien himself said, his own books were largely about it – and in 1945 he wrote to his son Christopher: 'Partly as a development of my own thought, partly in contact with C. S. L., and in various ways, not least the firm guiding hand of Alma Mater Ecclesia, I do not now feel ashamed or dubious on the Eden "myth". It has not, of course, historicity of the same kind as the New Testament, but certainly there was an Eden on this very unhappy earth. We all long for it, and we are constantly glimpsing it: our whole nature at its best and least corrupted, its gentlest and most humane, is still soaked with the sense of "exile".'

When Tolkien's daughter Priscilla read *Perelandra*, she told her father that she thought the hero, the philologist Ransom who had also played a central part in *Out of the Silent Planet*, was surely meant to be a portrait of him. Tolkien replied: 'As a philologist, I may have some part in him, and recognize some of my opinions and ideas Lewisified in him.' And he was quite sure that the names which Lewis gave the Adam and Eve of *Perelandra*, 'Tor and Tinidril', were 'certainly an echo' of his own 'Tuor and Idril' in *The Silmarillion*. He might have added that Ransom's first name, 'Elwin', was a version of the Old English *Ælfwine* or 'elf-friend', a name that appeared in early versions

[1] The floating islands are mentioned by Lewis as the source of *Perelandra* in the transcript of a tape-recorded conversation with Kingsley Amis and Brian Aldiss, printed in *Of Other Worlds*.

[2] Williams's letters indicate that Lewis finished *A Preface to Paradise Lost* in the spring of 1941. In November of that year Lewis was writing the chapter of *Perelandra* in which Ransom meets the Lady.

of *The Silmarillion*. Lewis often liked to make such faint allusions to his friends, and *Perelandra* contained an even more direct example in the naming of the doctor as 'Humphrey', a kind of private tribute to Havard. The book was also deeply concerned with Tolkien and Lewis's notion that mythology can be 'true'. Indeed, the story was largely arranged to demonstrate the possibility that 'what was myth in one world might always be fact in another'.

By the time that *Perelandra* was published, Lewis was becoming well known as a speaker on Christianity. The BBC's Religious Broadcasting Director much admired *The Problem of Pain*, and he invited Lewis to give a series of radio talks on Christian belief. Lewis accepted, though not without misgivings, and he delivered a series of four broadcasts entitled 'Right and Wrong: A Clue to the meaning of the Universe?' from the studio in London on Wednesday evenings in August 1941. The talks began, as did *The Problem of Pain*, by 'proving' the existence of God, or at least by advancing Lewis's profound belief that the existence of Reason or Conscience in the human mind indicates that we are not merely slaves to instinct but are fundamentally aware of a Moral Law that comes from God. They also included a characteristic attack on Progress. 'If you look at the present state of the world,' Lewis told his listeners, 'it is pretty plain that humanity has been making some big mistake. We are on the wrong road. And if that is so, we must go back. Going back is the quickest way on.'

Lewis was not exactly at his best at the microphone; or rather, his use of the medium emphasised the more dogmatic side of his character. Radio brought out neither his stentorian power nor his flashes of wit, and his broadcasting manner was formal and rather restrained. But he spoke clearly and unhesitatingly, and the talks were considered a great success, not least because of the large number of letters which resulted from them, and which Lewis answered with characteristic patience and promptness. Indeed anybody, adult or child, who ever wrote to him to thank him for his books, or to raise a point relating to them, or to ask his advice on a personal or spiritual problem, always found that he replied virtually by return of post, writing briefly and to the point but with limitless sympathy and patience. As he became better known for his Christian apologetics, letter writing came to take up a large proportion of his time, but he never delayed in answering, so that it might be said that he did as much to help people in this way as he did by writing his books.

Following the radio talks, Lewis was asked to address young men at a number of Royal Air Force stations around the country. He accepted, and found the task exhausting and by no means to his liking, but he undertook it whenever he could manage to do so. He told a friend that the first of these lectures on Christianity was 'a complete failure', but consoled himself by 'remembering that God used an *ass* to convert the prophet'. He was also asked by Sister Penelope of the Community of St Mary the Virgin at Wantage, with whom he had corresponded for some time, to address the junior nuns at the convent. 'What very odd tasks God sets us!' he remarked to her. 'If anyone had told me ten years ago that I should be lecturing in a convent——! The doors do open outwards as well, I trust?' He remained lifelong friends with Sister Penelope, and it was to her and her fellow nuns that *Perelandra* was dedicated in the words 'To some ladies at Wantage'. The translator of the Portugese edition delighted the sisters by mistranslating this 'To some wanton ladies'.

In 1942 and 1944 Lewis gave more radio talks, on 'What Christians Believe', 'Christian Behaviour', and 'The Christian View of God'. They met with an even greater success than the first series, not least because of the popularity of *Screwtape* which was now in print. These later broadcasts, like the first ones, were not notable for their subtlety. Lewis said of them, 'I had to go like a bull at a gate', and in many of them he adopted a very bellicose manner. 'Christianity is a fighting religion,' he declared. 'This moment is our chance to choose the right side. God is holding back to give us that chance. It will not last for ever. We must take it or leave it.'

Charles Williams listened to these broadcasts, and was not entirely enthusiastic about Lewis's rather broad approach to the subject. 'I do not think the BBC is my medium,' he remarked. 'One has to be too rashly general. I have observed how even C. S. L. has to omit (because of time) points of some seriousness. For example, he made some play with this business of trusting Reason: "If you trust Reason . . ." and so on. I reminded him of the pure agnostic answer – "But I do not trust reason, not so far". But there was not "time". Quite true, but if I had been a listener I should have lost real interest when I realized that he had just left it out.' Williams was aware of a certain difference of manner between himself and Lewis where the 'preaching' of Christianity was concerned. Writing to Anne Ridler, he referred to this (in a fashion that trod his usual narrow line between pride and humility). He had, he told her, been helping two young women. One of them 'had been, it appeared, praying for "grace to believe", but the grace had not consciously shown itself; and so what? I could not resist making the suggestion that, in the circumstances, might not I (most unworthily) be the grace? Anyhow she is now labouring to believe. Both of them began by admiring C. S. L.; both of them (he said blushing) convey somehow a faint impression of advancing in the grades – absurd but flattering.'

Tolkien was not entirely enthusiastic about Lewis's broadcasts, or at least about the sort of attention they attracted. 'Lewis is as energetic and jolly as ever,' he told his son Christopher, who in the later part of the war went to South Africa to train as an Air Force pilot, 'but getting too much publicity for his or any of our tastes. "Peterborough", usually fairly reasonable, did him the doubtful honour of a peculiarly misrepresentative and asinine paragraph in the *Daily Telegraph* of Tuesday last. It began "Ascetic Mr Lewis——"!!! I ask you! He put away three pints in a very short session this morning, and said he was "going short for Lent".'

*

Towards the end of the war the morning sessions of the Inklings were by no means restricted to Tuesdays at the Bird and Baby. Indeed they were likely to meet on almost any morning at almost any pub. The 'Bird' was closed for a time because of the beer shortage, itself caused largely by thirsty American troops waiting for D-Day; and the Inklings often gathered in the King's Arms opposite the Bodleian Library, in the tap room of the Mitre Hotel, or in the White Horse in Broad Street, a small pub next to Blackwell's book shop which offered almost as much seclusion as the 'Bird'.

When some of Lewis's teetotal American readers heard of his fondness for drinking beer, and asked him how he could square the consumption of alcohol with his Christianity, they received the reply: 'I strongly object to the tyrannic and unscriptural insolence of anything that calls itself a Church and makes teetotalism a condition of membership. Apart from the more serious objection (that Our Lord Himself turned water into wine and made wine the medium of the only rite He imposed on all His followers), it is so provincial (what I believe you people call 'small town").'

Talking, rather than reading aloud, was the habit at these morning sessions in a pub. 'The fun is often so fast and furious', Lewis told Arthur Greeves, 'that the company probably thinks we're talking bawdy when in fact we're very likely talking theology.'

By the later part of the war the composition of the Inklings had changed a little. The nucleus still consisted of the Lewis brothers, Tolkien, Williams and Havard, together with the rarer visitors Dyson and Barfield; but Coghill and Adam Fox had entirely ceased to attend (Fox had now left Oxford), and Charles Wrenn (who was working in London) only came very rarely to the Thursday meetings. Others stepped in, so to speak, to fill their places, men who never became part of the true inner ring of Lewis's friends but whose company was generally welcomed by the other Inklings. R. B. McCallum, the History

Tutor at Pembroke College and a friend of Tolkien, often came along, though his manner was too formally 'donnish' to make him an entirely congenial member of the group. Indeed McCallum was among those who to some extent invited themselves to be Inklings, rather than waiting for the invitation, as was Gervase Mathew, a Catholic priest and academic polymath from Blackfriars, the Oxford house of the Dominicans, situated near the Bird and Baby. This extraordinary man, the brother of Archbishop David Mathew, smoked a continual succession of cigarettes in a nicotine-stained holder and talked in a kind of breathless mutter, speaking at such speed that even Tolkien, until then the champion among the Inklings for haste and inaudibility, was left far behind. Tolkien wrote:

> The Rev. Mathew (Gervase)
> Made inaudible surveys
> Of little-read sages
> In the dark Middle Ages.

This was entirely true, for Gervase Mathew was an expert on English medieval history; he was also a specialist in Byzantine art and architecture. He was very enthusiastic about Charles Williams's imaginative use of Byzantium in the *Taliessin* poems, and he did his best to spread Williams's fame about Oxford and further afield. He took a particular delight in fact in 'pulling strings' and in assisting his friends' lives in all kinds of ways, a characteristic that made Warnie Lewis once refer to him rather sardonically as 'the universal Aunt'. As Jack Lewis remarked, 'he knows everyone and will put you onto the right people (if there are any)'. It was perhaps this desire to be in touch with spheres of influence that made Gervase Mathew seek out the Inklings and virtually elect himself a member; not that he was unwelcome.[1]

One or two of Lewis's other Oxford friends sometimes came to Magdalen on Thursday evenings or drank beer with the Inklings on a weekday morning. One was the shock-headed theological philosopher Donald MacKinnon from Keble College, a Tuesday morning but never a Thursday evening man. Another was Lord David Cecil, then the English Tutor at New College, who was always a most welcome visitor whenever Lewis or Tolkien could persuade him to attend. 'Visitor', perhaps, Cecil always remained, for his friendships were too wide-ranging and his literary tastes too broad to make him (so to speak) 'spiritually an Inkling'. He read aloud to the Inklings from his book *Two Quiet Lives* which he was then writing, and he was impressed by

[1] Gervase Mathew told Walter Hooper that he had attended Inklings meetings as early as 1939 or 1940, but there is no record of his attendance until 1946.

Williams and attended his lectures. 'Listening to those oracular imaginings,' he recalled of them, 'delivered in that delightfully characteristic voice, one couldn't help wondering a little whether Blake might have been like that.'

If Cecil was intrigued by Williams, Williams was almost childishly delighted by making the acquaintance of Cecil. He told his wife to tell a snobbish London neighbour 'that Lord David Cecil and I are now on Christian name terms! He came into Magdalen last night and in the course of conversation addressed me as Charles and then kind of half-not-apologised, rather sweetly; so I made a suitable answer and proceeded to say in a few minutes "David" – very odd! but he feels I am a husband and a father where the Lewises are not, and we talk of the difficulties of Babies. But he also told the others that his pupils now, when he lays down the law, look up at him and say "I'm not sure that Mr Williams would agree with that", and he has to say: "O well if Mr W. thinks differently . . ." and get out of it as best he can.'

Williams's mark on the English School was now considerable. He followed his Milton lectures with a course on Wordsworth, and then with another on the eighteenth century. 'His lectures were crowded out,' recalled John Wain, who was an undergraduate at St John's reading English at this time. 'Even I, who chose to be very supercilious about lectures, seldom missed one.' Besides the official lectures, Williams gave talks to undergraduate societies. Later, he was asked by a couple of the women's colleges to give tutorials, and he began to be visited by groups of two or three pupils, whom he sometimes taught in his makeshift bathroom-cum-office at Southfield House. His employer, Sir Humphrey Milford, observed to a colleague that C. W. was now not only using Press time but Press *premises* for his private work, but merely sighed and said, 'What can I do?'.

In the summer of 1943 Williams's book on Dante and Romantic Theology, *The Figure of Beatrice,* was published. Tolkien wrote:

> The sales of Charles Williams
> Leapt up by millions,
> When a reviewer surmised
> He was only Lewis disguised.

This was deliberate nonsense, for the book did not sell vastly and it did not remotely resemble anything Lewis had written. But undoubtedly Lewis's persistent praise of Williams was having effect, for *The Figure of Beatrice* began to bring Williams something for which he had waited a long time: public recognition. It would be an exaggeration to say that until now nobody had read his books; the novels had their small but

187

enthusiastic public, and *The Descent of the Dove,* Williams's 'History of the Holy Spirit in the Church', had brought him enthusiastic letters from unlikely places. 'I had an extraordinarily moving note from W. H. Auden in America,' Williams told his wife in the spring of 1940. 'He said he just wanted to tell me how moved he was by the *Dove* (and he no Christian) and he was sending me his new book "as a poor return".'[1] But such praise had until now been a rare thing, and the success of *The Figure of Beatrice* was therefore doubly welcome to Williams.

Christopher Hollis, reviewing *Beatrice* in *The Tablet,* said that it was a book 'to be read and re-read until it becomes part of the furniture of the mind'. The Oxford theologian Austin Farrer declared himself 'allured' by it; Gervase Mathew forthwith lost no time in introducing Williams to Farrer. Indeed Williams found that the book had conferred a true academic respectability upon him, even in Oxford's cynical eyes. He was invited to a meeting of the august Dante Society, with Father Martin d'Arcy in the chair, where his book was discussed, and a paper was read on it by Lewis's friend Colin Hardie; and when it was discovered that Williams could not be elected a member because he did not hold a fellowship at any college Maurice Bowra the Warden of Wadham told Williams that he thought it 'scandalous' and 'a condemnation of our whole system' that no college had offered him a fellowship.

No fellowship was forthcoming, but early in 1943 the University did award Williams the degree of Honorary Master of Arts. Williams himself remarked to his disciple Raymond Hunt that this was not really because Oxford had recognised his achievement, nor even because Lewis and his friends had arranged it, but simply because the University regularly honoured long-serving employees of the Press at its Oxford headquarters in this fashion; and now that the London branch was in Oxford it was thought courteous to extend the gesture to them. 'And', said Williams, 'it's obvious that I'm the best person to start on.' He carried himself with his usual grace and poise at the degree-giving; afterwards, Lewis told him that he had appeared to be 'the only graduand who seemed to understand what a ceremony was'.

Not all who read *The Figure of Beatrice* and were struck by Williams's

---

[1] Auden and Williams met briefly before the war, on publishing business. Auden was greatly impressed by Williams's personality. When he came to read Williams's books he found the novels 'the least satisfactory' and at first 'could not make head or tail' of the *Taliessin* poetry. But he thought *The Figure of Beatrice* 'magnificent', and regarded *The Descent of the Dove* as Williams's masterpiece. See Auden's introduction to *The Descent of the Dove* in the edition published by Living Age Books (Meridian Books, New York, 1956). Auden told Williams (as reported by Williams to his wife in a letter of 17 October 1940) that 'he feels that I have a divine gift, and he seems to be regarding me as the father of his present verse; at least he says I am responsible for a good deal of it'.

exposition of Romantic Theology had themselves read the works of
Dante. One such was Dorothy L. Sayers, who had already achieved a
reputation as a writer of detective stories and more recently of religious
plays: her radio cycle on the life of Christ, *The Man Born to be King*, had
been broadcast with great success by the BBC. She had met Williams
before the war, but she began to pay serious attention to him only after
spending some hours in his company at the Spaldings' house in South
Parks Road late in 1943 or early in 1944. Anne Spalding remembers:
'When she arrived, she was very much the successful author, lecturing
C. W. on how he ought to get his books into mass circulation by doing
this and that with publishers and agents. Twenty-four hours later she
was his disciple, sitting at his feet.' She went away and read *The Figure
of Beatrice*, as she herself said, 'not because it was about Dante, but because it was by Charles Williams'.

As for Williams himself, 'I got in from Magdalen last night about 12
and found her sitting up,' he told Michal after another of Dorothy
Sayers's visits to South Parks Road. 'We conversed till 2.15. I like the
old dear, but she's rather heavy going. I should find 2.15 late for one's
dearest friends – but what can one do? She is beginning to think in
terms of my Doctrine (Mine? O no!), and consulted me on her deductions.' A few months later she sent him a thirty-six page letter. 'She has,
under the compulsion of *Beatrice*,' Williams told his wife, 'been reading
Dante and Milton, and feels she must write to someone, and to whom
but me? Quite a sincere letter; I begin to admire Dorothy seriously as
a human being, which I never did before!'

Dorothy Sayers was also impressed by Lewis's writings on Christianity, and she wrote to him to say so. 'She was the first person of importance who ever wrote me a fan-letter,' he recalled, and he added, 'I liked
her, originally, because she liked me; later, for the extraordinary zest
and edge of her conversation – as I like a high wind.' She did not, however, come to any meetings of the Inklings. No woman ever did. 'She
never met our own club,' Lewis said, 'and probably never knew of its
existence.' Indeed the Inklings did not approve of all her work. Lewis
and Tolkien greatly admired *The Man Born to be King*; Lewis said he
thought it 'has edified us in this country more than anything for a long
time'. Lewis also considered her *Mind of the Maker* 'good on the whole'.
But when as a result of this enthusiasm he tried her Oxford detective
story *Gaudy Night* he 'didn't like it at all'; while Tolkien, though he
liked Dorothy Sayers personally, wrote of it and its hero Lord Peter
Wimsey: 'I could not stand *Gaudy Night*. I followed P. Wimsey from
his attractive beginnings so far, by which time I conceived a loathing
for him not surpassed by any other character in literature known to me,
unless by his Harriet.'

189

Two other writers of some reputation were made thoroughly welcome by the Inklings. One was E. R. Eddison, one of the very few authors of the time whose fiction might be said to have even the faintest resemblance to the stories of Tolkien and Lewis. Tolkien thought Eddison 'a great writer' and read everything that he published, though he declared that he disliked Eddison's 'peculiarly bad nomenclature and his personal philosophy'. It was not, however, on Tolkien's recommendation but after seeing it mentioned in a book on the Novel that Lewis read Eddison's fantasy *The Worm Ouroboros* in the autumn of 1942. As usual when he was delighted by a book, Lewis wrote to the author. His letter to Eddison was in a pastiche of Middle English, which suited the style of Eddison's romances, and was also something that Lewis enjoyed doing for its own sake. He declared that the *Worm* was 'the most noble and ioyous book I have read these ten years', far and above better than 'all the clam jamfrey and whymperinges of the raskellie auctours in these latter daies, as the Eliots, Poundes, Lawrences, Audens, and the like'. He concluded by suggesting that Eddison (who lived in Wiltshire) should visit 'my poor house and colledge of Sta. Marie Maudlin' to meet 'oon or two faste frendes of myne who still, in this duncial age, delight in noble books, that is in straunge adventures, heroicall feates, good maneres, and the report of feyre londes'. They would, he promised, offer him 'the beste chere and feste we can or mai deuyse'. Eddison replied, also in medieval English, with much enthusiasm; and in February 1943 he came to Oxford and attended a Thursday Inklings, staying the night in his old college, Trinity. He wrote a letter of thanks to Lewis a few days later:

'Certeyn it is, you have given me a memorie to chew upon, as beeves cheweth cudd, beginning with yourself & your brother; your good canarie afore dinner; dinner itself in your great shadowy hall with good & honourable company, good ale & good meats set forth upon shining board; thence to your Common Roome, with puss by the fire & a voidee of fruits & spices; & so to that Quincunciall symposium, at ease about your sea-cole fire, in your privat chaumbre, where (as it seemed to mee) good discourse made night's horses gallop too faste; & so to our goodnight walke & adieux in the gate under your great Towre. For my self, I tasted wisdome as wel as good ale at your fireside, all be it, I am much afeared, pouring you out on my parte some provokements in exchange. If our talk were battledore & shuttlecock, what matter? 'Twas merry talk, & truth will sometimes appere, better than *in statu*, in the swift flying to & again of the shuttlecock. So, praying you to convey my duetie to Maister Tolkien & Maister Williams & to yr. worship's Brother, & in great hope ere many months of our renewed meeting, I rest yr. honour's most Obedient Humble Servant, E. R. Eddison.'

There was indeed a renewed meeting between Eddison and the Inklings, in the early summer of 1944. On this occasion Eddison heard Tolkien read aloud from the newly completed Book IV of *The Lord of the Rings,* and himself read part of his romance *The Mezentian Gate,* which Tolkien found to be 'of undiminished power and felicity of expression'. A year later Eddison died, aged sixty-three, leaving this story incomplete.

A few months after Eddison's second visit to the Inklings, another and rather less likely person was made welcome by them. On 6 October 1944 Tolkien wrote to his son Christopher: 'On Tuesday I looked in at the Bird and B. with C. Williams. There to my surprise I found Jack and Warnie already ensconced. (For the present the beer shortage is over, and the inns are almost habitable again.) The conversation was pretty lively – though I cannot remember any of it now except C. S. L.'s story of an elderly lady that he knows. (She was a student of English in the past days of Sir Walter Raleigh.[1] At her *viva* she was asked: "What period would you have liked to live in, Miss B?" "In the fifteenth century," said she. "Oh come Miss B., wouldn't you have liked to meet the Lake poets?" "No, sir, I prefer the society of gentlemen." Collapse of *viva*.) – and I noticed a strange tall gaunt man half in khaki half in mufti with a large wide-awake hat, bright eyes and a hooked nose, sitting in the corner. The others had their backs to him, but I could see in his eye that he was taking an interest in the conversation quite unlike the ordinary pained astonishment of the British (and American) public at the presence of the Lewises (and myself) in a pub. It was rather like Trotter at the Prancing Pony, v. like in fact. All of a sudden he butted in, in a strange unplaceable accent, taking up some point about Wordsworth. In a few seconds he was revealed as Roy Campbell (of *Flowering Rifle* and *Flaming Terrapin*). Tableau! Especially as C. S. L. had not long ago violently lampooned him in the *Oxford Magazine*, and his press-cutters miss nothing. After that things became fast and furious and I was late for lunch. It was (perhaps) gratifying to find that this powerful poet and soldier desired in Oxford chiefly to see Lewis (and myself). We made an appointment for Thursday night.'

Roy Campbell, born in South Africa in 1901, had been a professional jouster and bullfighter in Provence. After establishing his reputation as a poet in the twenties, he fought on the side of Franco's right-wing forces in the Spanish Civil War. Now that he was in Oxford, Father Martin d'Arcy had told him to search out Lewis and company in the Bird and Baby.

[1] Raleigh was Professor of English Literature at Oxford before the First World War.

When the Inklings met on the Thursday night with Campbell as their guest, there was a division of opinion which revealed a deep-seated difference between Lewis and Tolkien. Both men were strongly conservative in their politics, but Lewis believed in the democratic control of power while Tolkien did not. 'I am a democrat,' Lewis once said, 'because I believe in the Fall and therefore think men too wicked to be trusted with more than the minimum power over other men.' Tolkien declared: 'I am not a "democrat", if only because "humility" and equality are spiritual principles corrupted by the attempt to mechanize and formalize them, with the result that we get not universal smallness and humility, but universal greatness and pride.' Lewis and Tolkien both feared the rise of Communism and the growing power of the Left; they also hated and feared the growth of fascism in pre-war Britain – Lewis included Blackshirts among the forces of intellectual evil in *The Pilgrim's Regress* – as well as sharing their countrymen's enmity to Hitler and Mussolini. But during the Spanish Civil War, Tolkien largely sympathised with Franco's cause in Spain, not because he approved of fascism but because he saw Franco as the defender of the Catholic Church against Communist persecution. Roy Campbell had not only fought on Franco's side but had become a Catholic in the process, so that Tolkien had a large area of agreement with him. Lewis on the other hand declared fervently: 'I loathed and loathe Roy Campbell's particular blend of Catholicism and Fascism, and told him so.' Observing this, Tolkien suspected that it was not the Fascism which Lewis hated about Campbell so much as the Catholicism. He reported to his son Christopher that on the Thursday night Lewis, who (he said) 'had taken a fair deal of port and was a little belligerent', insisted on reading his lampoon to Campbell, and that after listening to Campbell's stories of Communist outrages against Catholic clergy in Spain, Lewis's 'reactions were odd'. Tolkien continued: 'If a Lutheran is put in jail he is up in arms; but if Catholic priests are slaughtered – he disbelieves it, and I daresay really thinks they asked for it. There is a good deal of Ulster still left in C. S. L., if hidden from himself.'

Roy Campbell reappeared at the Bird and Baby once or twice, and came to the Inklings again in 1946. But another visitor made an even briefer appearance, and not strictly at an Inklings meeting. This was T. S. Eliot, whom Charles Williams had been eager to introduce to Lewis for some time. They met over tea at the Mitre Hotel one day in the last months of the war. Eliot's opening remark scarcely delighted Lewis: 'Mr Lewis, you are a much *older* man than you appear in photographs.' The tea party progressed poorly, and was enjoyed by no one except Charles Williams, who seemed to be immensely amused.

*

Williams had intended since 1940 to write another novel. His last, *Descent into Hell*, had been published in 1937, and T. S. Eliot had been trying for some time to get another commissioned for publication by Faber's. Indeed Eliot now regarded himself as Williams's patron. 'I really launched him,' he told a friend; and he tried to see that Williams concentrated on major work rather than wasting his energies in pot-boilers. For a long time Williams stalled on the novel, for he was still unable to make up his mind about a subject, and it was not until 1943 that at last he had 'a kind of ghostly skeleton of a novel' in his mind. He wanted to progress beyond the achievement of *Descent into Hell*, and a logical sequel to that book with its graphic account of damnation would be (as he remarked to a friend) a kind of *Paradiso*, an account of heaven. He was after all approaching his sixtieth birthday, and as he said to his wife in February 1940, he did have 'a hovering sense that my work is now all but done'. Yet he said of the new novel, 'I doubt if I can do heaven. An account of the Timeless in terms of time is bound to seem silly.' And when he eventually began to write, the book seemed not so much like a fitting conclusion to his series of novels as like his early and rather mediocre work.

He began work on it in the late summer of 1943, and by the beginning of September he was writing the third chapter. The story told how the body of a young woman is found in an empty London house during the blitz, a body that dissolves into dust and water when a post-mortem is held. This strange corpse is the product of an attempt by some demonic power to create a human being, this being an idea that had long interested Williams; he mentioned it in his book *Witchcraft*. The opening chapters of this new novel were read to Lewis and Tolkien. Williams also showed the manuscript to his wife, whose opinion he always respected in such matters; and she was quite firm. She thought the whole draft was poor stuff: as indeed it was, by the standard of his recent work. Williams agreed, and had few regrets. 'Three quarters of my mind is delighted that we are so at one about my discarded chapters,' he told her; 'the other quarter is sad about the wasted work. Two months almost thrown away! But perhaps something better may come.'

A few days later he began the novel all over again from the beginning. 'I am not much happier,' he told Michal. 'It's all so *dull*.' It was not dull; it was one of the finest things he had written.

It opened with a girl standing on Westminster Bridge, a dead girl (though she scarcely knows it at first), who has just been killed by an aeroplane which has crashed down on the Embankment; a surprising accident, for the war is over. 'It was true that formal peace was not yet in being; all that had happened was that fighting had ceased.' Sudden death was no longer expected; yet Lester Furnival is dead, and the novel tells of her strange adventures in that other and supernatural City which, as Williams had long believed, lies alongside the physical London and occasionally crosses paths with it. The novel was not precisely about heaven, but if it was not his *Paradiso, All Hallows' Eve* (as he named it) proved to be Williams's triumphant *Purgatorio*.

He was reading the new draft aloud to the Inklings in November 1943. 'I heard two chapters of a new novel by Charles Williams, read by him, this morning,' Tolkien told his son Christopher. Years later he recalled of those readings: 'I was in fact a sort of assistant midwife at the birth of *All Hallows' Eve*, read alound to us as it was composed, but the very great changes made in it were I think mainly due to C. S. L.' They were in fact mainly due to Michal Williams.

Williams found it hard work writing the book. The considerable attention which he had paid to problems of style while composing the poems for his second *Taliessin* volume (now almost complete) made him self-conscious about his prose style in the novel, and he was severely critical. 'A style suitable to us in our last period takes some finding,' he told Michal. 'I have (you will excuse this) a dark feeling that there is something I ought to be saying, a kind of unity of all – but don't know what it is.' Yet he progressed. 'I have pushed slowly on,' he told Michal in January 1944, adding, 'I have read some of it to C. S. L.–Tolkien (you will forgive that; and excuse its technical usefulness) who admire and approve.'

Lewis too was writing a story concerned with Purgatory, or at least with the point of balance between Heaven and Hell. Tolkien recorded of a meeting of the Inklings in April 1944 (by which time Warnie Lewis was at work on the first of his books of French history): 'All turned up except Cecil, and we stayed until after midnight. The best entertainment proved to be the chapter of Major Lewis' projected book – on a subject that does not interest me: the court of Louis XIV; but it was most wittily written (as well as learned). I did not think so well of a chapter of C. S. L.'s new moral allegory or "vision", based on the mediæval fancy of the Refrigerium, by which the lost souls have an occasional holiday in Paradise.'

Lewis modelled his story (at first entitled 'Who Goes Home' but eventually published as *The Great Divorce*) at least in part on Dante, whose works he had known very well since he and Colin Hardie, the Classical Tutor at Magdalen, had read them aloud together in weekly evening sessions just before the war.[1] But this in itself was not calculated

---

[1] Lewis wrote of *The Great Divorce:* 'The meeting of the "Tragedian" with his wife is consciously modelled on that of Dante and Beatrice at the end of the *Purgatorio:* i.e. it is the same predicament, only going wrong. I intended readers to spot these resemblances' (letter to W. Kinter, 29 September 1951).

to please Tolkien, who remarked, albeit in old age: 'Dante doesn't attract me. He's full of spite and malice. I don't care for his petty relations with petty people in petty cities.'

Tolkien himself was now once again in full spate with *The Lord of the Rings*. A lengthy period of mental dryness came to an end when Lewis persuaded him to tackle the story again; he reported in March 1944 that Lewis 'is putting the screw on me to finish', and a few days later: 'I have begun to nibble at Hobbit again.' He began work on what was eventually to be Book IV of the story, recounting Frodo, Sam and Gollum's journey to Mordor. He was soon reading the new chapters aloud to the Inklings, and was receiving the usual mixed reactions of great enthusiasm from some and considerable reservations from others, the latter including Hugo Dyson, who had never cared for the story – not that Dyson liked *any* readings on Thursday nights; his preference for talk was well known. Tolkien wrote on 14 May: 'I saw C. S. L. from 10.45 to 12.30 this morning, heard two chapters of his "Who Goes Home?", and read my sixth new chapter "Journey to the Cross Roads" with complete approval.' And on 31 May: 'The Inklings meeting was very enjoyable. Hugo was there: rather tired-looking, but reasonably noisy. The chief entertainment was provided by a chapter of Warnie Lewis's book on the times of Louis XIV (very good I thought it); and some excerpts from C. S. L.'s "Who Goes Home?" – a book on Hell, which I suggested should have been called rather "Hugo's Home".'

All Hallows' Eve was sent to the publishers in May 1944. Five months later, the second volume of Williams's *Taliessin* cycle was published under the title *The Region of the Summer Stars*. This volume consisted of eight long poems in which Williams came near to perfecting his style, and in which the themes of the myth were handled with the kind of 'purged' understatement reminiscent of Shakespeare's last plays, which Williams had always regarded with special awe. Characteristic was Taliessin's farewell to his Household in the poem 'The Prayers of the Pope':

> Taliessin gathered his people before the battle.
> 'Peers of the household,' the king's poet said,
> 'dead now, save Lancelot, are the great lords
> and the Table may end to-morrow; if it live,
> it shall have new names in a new report.
> Short is Our time, though that time prove eternal.

*   *   *

> Therefore now We dissolve the former bonds –'
> the voice sounded, the hands descended – 'We dissolve

the outer bonds; We declare the Company still
fixed in the will of all who serve the Company,
but the ends are on Us, peers and friends; We restore
again to God the once-permitted lieutenancy.'

The sales of the first volume of the cycle, *Taliessin through Logres*, had been so poor that Williams's own employers the Oxford University Press, who had published it, declined to handle *The Region of the Summer Stars*, and it was passed to another publisher. Yet Williams had a suspicion that the success of *The Figure of Beatrice* and his high reputation in Oxford might improve matters this time. Even so, he was not prepared for the response to the new volume of poems. Pupils began to arrive for tutorials bearing copies for him to sign. Edith Sitwell wrote to say how impressed she was with it. The publishers of the book wrote to say that they had sold eight hundred copies in a month out of a first printing of one thousand, and would bring out a new edition next year. They also said that they would like more poems from Williams, and hoped that a further *Taliessin* volume could be published. Williams told Michal: 'This selling of and passion for my verse is something altogether new, and I want to cry a little. I don't say it's much – but we have waited so long. Kiss me; you were the first to believe, and you always have.'

He did indeed plan a third volume in the cycle. Its poems were to be largely concerned with the Dolorous Blow and its relevance to the quest of the Graal. But he reported: 'There are no more than 20 or 30 lines written', and there was much else occupying his mind. He wanted to write a book on Wordsworth and 'the Romantic Way in English verse', and he offered the idea to his old friend and employer Sir Humphrey Milford at the Press. He was embittered when Milford turned it down on the grounds that Williams's agent was demanding terms that were too high. 'This, after so many years, seems to me a little unkind,' Williams remarked to Anne Ridler. Not that he had any inflated idea of his status at the Press. He knew very well that his achievements passed for comparatively little there, and he was amused as well as saddened when, at a routine meeting at Southfield House, he and Milford and the others solemnly discussed whom they should ask to write a book on Shakespeare for the Home University Library. 'Would you think there could be – *here* – more than one answer?' he told Michal. 'There could; there could, in fact, be any answer but that. We discussed A, B, and C, anyone except – Except – Of course they may think of me yet, but I think it unlikely. It's a little strange to be superfluous when one has been Someone; in all the literary world there is no place where I am as negligible – in the most charming way – as here.'

His work in the editorial department at the Press was dull and sterile, and he himself knew that he had outstayed his usefulness. He felt he was wanted at Oxford by the university: no definite proposals had been made, but hints were frequently dropped that an academic job might be found for him after the war. Even Humphrey Milford 'said he had heard a rumour that something was to be offered me'; Williams supposed that it might be a Readership in the English Faculty, or something similar which Lewis and his friends might have engineered. By now he knew that he would gladly stay in Oxford. He had no illusions about academic life, and in many ways he hated what he called Oxford's 'pseudo-culture'; but, as he said, the Inklings avoided all that. 'How different the Magdalen feeling is from anywhere else in Oxford,' he told Michal. And he no longer had any wish to go back to London. 'I have no place-attachment now,' he said. 'This Oxford period has broken all that.'

Meanwhile there was a lot of work to be done, and he was tired. 'I cannot quite describe the extreme effort which the act of writing seems to demand,' he told Thelma Shuttleworth. 'Verse now has to be thought and planned and considered and re-considered; prose needs writing two or three times when once was formerly enough. Like the Red Queen one has to run so very fast to remain in the same place.' Eliot was waiting for a book on the history of the Arthurian myth. Dean Close School had commissioned, through the mediation of Sir Humphrey Milford, a biography of their founder Flecker: 'For cash,' Williams remarked wryly, adding, 'All Caesar's fault, bless him! He is always Caesar, but really, he and Celia do make all this Myth-living very difficult.' And there were also the regular teaching commitments of lectures and tutorials, both of which were now more wearisome than enjoyable to Williams.

An old friend from Amen House days, Alice Mary Hadfield, came to see him in Oxford. 'He had not changed at all,' she said. 'He was rather more thin and a little more withdrawn behind his face, and over the grey suit he wore a heel-length M.A.'s gown, since he came to meet me from his lecture. But he was still erect, swift, intent, the beautiful hands quick to mark and define, the forehead's line unmarred by falling hair, the blue eyes behind their thick glasses as full of amusement and gentleness as ever.' And he was soon at work on his next book, *The Figure of Arthur*, an account of the Arthurian legends in history and literature, together (as he planned) with an interpretation of his own Arthurian poems. On a couple of Monday mornings he read aloud what he had written to Tolkien and Lewis. Tolkien recalled of one of these morning sessions: 'It was a bright morning, and the mulberry tree in the grove outside Lewis's window shone like fallow gold against the cobalt blue sky.' Lewis too described the scene: 'Picture to yourself an upstairs sitting-room with windows looking north into the "grove" of

197

Magdalen College on a sunshiny Monday morning in vacation at about ten o'clock. The Professor and I, both on the Chesterfield, lit our pipes and stretched out our legs. Williams in the arm-chair opposite to us threw his cigarette into the grate, took up a pile of the extremely small, loose sheets on which he habitually wrote – they came, I think, from a twopenny pad for memoranda – and began . . .'

Lewis himself had written yet another book. It was the third of the 'Ransom' stories, but it was very different in character from *Out of the Silent Planet* and *Perelandra*. It was in fact a celebration of everything that had happened in his life up to now. His old tutor Kirkpatrick was in it, as MacPhee, the sceptical Ulster Scot – 'I have no *opinions* on any subject in the world. I state the facts and exhibit the implications.' The Bloods of Malvern were in it, as the Inner Ring at the scientific research station Belbury, which threatens to overpower England. Lewis's old Magdalen foe Harry Weldon was in it, as Lord Feverstone, taunting the hero Mark Studdock in the very words with which Weldon had mocked Lewis twenty years earlier – 'Incurable romantic!' Williams's Arthurian mythology was in it, with Merlin's supernatural powers ranged against Belbury, and the little company at the village of St Anne's standing out against evil just as Logres in Williams's poems stood out against the darkness of disordered Britain. 'Something we may call Britain is always haunted by something we may call Logres,' Ransom tells his friends. 'After every Arthur, a Mordred; behind every Milton, a Cromwell. Is it any wonder they call us hypocrites? But what they mistake for hypocrisy is really the struggle between Logres and Britain.' Barfield was in it, for just a brief moment – 'It is one of Barfield's "ancient unities",' says Ransom, explaining the feelings between Mr Bultitude the bear and Pinch the cat. Tolkien's mythology was in it: Merlin's art is explained as 'something brought to Western Europe after the fall of Numinor'. ('A hearing error,' remarked Tolkien, for *he* spelt the word 'Númenor'.) And in a sense Charles Williams himself was in it, in the character of Ransom as now portrayed: a man of great spiritual strength, a man who easily earns obedience from his followers but is aware that this obedience may be dangerously seductive, a man of quietness and at the same time of great vigour. And on top of this the whole book had a schoolboy, almost pantomime quality, so much so that when Tolkien began to hear it read aloud by Lewis he thought it trivial. Yet when Tolkien had heard it right through he remarked that though it was scarcely a proper conclusion to Lewis's trilogy it was certainly 'good in itself'. Good or bad – the book was damned by reviewers and hugely enjoyed by many readers – *That Hideous Strength* was the essence of Lewis and of his feelings about the Inklings.

*

The war gradually drew to an end. Blackout curtains were removed and street lighting was switched on. 'I actually went out to an Inklings on Thursday night and rode in almost peacetime light all the way to Magdalen for the first time in five years,' Tolkien noted. 'Both Lewises were there, and C. W.; and beside some plesant talk, we heard the last chapter of Warnie's book and an article of C. S. L., and a long specimen of his translation of Virgil.' Lewis and Tolkien thought they might collaborate on a book. It was, Tolkien recorded, to be on the nature, origins, and function of language. The company also made plans to celebrate peace. 'The Inklings have already agreed', Tolkien told his son Christopher, 'that their victory celebration, if they are spared to have one, will be to take a whole inn in the countryside for at least a week, and spend it entirely in beer and talk, without reference to any clock!' They also began to organise contributions to a volume of essays which they were to present to Williams, to mark his return to London. For though he had no wish to leave Oxford, Williams had now reluctantly decided that he must go with the Press when it returned to Amen House after the war was finished, and continue to work there for the few years that remained until his retirement. He would after all lose his Press pension if he did anything else, and though his novel *All Hallows' Eve,* just published, was proving very popular in Oxford, he could not seriously contemplate making ends meet for the rest of his life solely by writing books. He might perhaps be able to get himself elected Professor of Poetry at Oxford while still working in London; that was one hope. At all events he knew he must return to Amen House. 'I am to have my old office – which on the whole I think I should prefer,' he told Michal on 2 May 1945. 'I shall linger there, a superfluous but kindly-treated – O well, don't let's be bad-tempered and resentful. We shall see how everything works out. Till Saturday. All love . . .'

*

On 9 May the war in Europe came formally to an end. 'How did *you* feel on V-Day?' Lewis asked Dom Bede Griffiths. 'I found it impossible to feel either so much sympathy with the people or so much gratitude to God as the occasion demanded.' On the following Tuesday, the usual meeting-day for the Inklings at the Bird and Baby, the day dawned particularly fine. 'It was the middle of the summer term,' recalled John Wain, who was just coming to the end of his undergraduate career. 'Beautiful weather, with a stir of hopefulness in the air. I was walking from Longwall Street, where I lodged, towards St John's, and had just reached the Clarendon Building when a girl I knew by sight came pedalling fast and agitatedly on her bicycle round

199

the corner from New College Lane. "John," she called out, "Charles Williams is dead." '

*

Williams had been taken into hospital a few days earlier suffering from adhesions in the digestive system, a legacy from his operation some years earlier. There was nothing to cause alarm, except that he was a very tired man and not strong. There was an operation, but he never recovered consciousness.

On that day, Tuesday 15 May 1945, Warnie Lewis wrote in his diary: 'At 12.50 this morning I had just stopped work on the details of the Boislève family, when the telephone rang, and a woman's voice asked if I would take a message for J. – "Mr Charles Williams died in the Acland this morning". One often reads of people being "stunned" by bad news, and reflects idly on the absurdity of the expression; but there is more than a little truth in it. I felt just as if I had slipped and come down on my head on the pavement. J. had told me when I came into College that Charles Williams was ill, and it would mean a serious operation: and then went off to see him. I haven't seen him since. I felt dazed and restless, and went out to get a drink: choosing unfortunately the King's Arms, where during the winter Charles and I more than once drank a pint after leaving Tollers at the Mitre, with much glee at "clearing one's throat of varnish with good honest beer" as Charles used to say. There will be no more pints with Charles: no more "Bird and Baby": the blackout has fallen, and the Inklings can never be the same again.'

PART FOUR

I

'No one turned up'

The railway line from Oxford to Fairford is closed now, but in 1945 it was still operating. At nine thirty-five each weekday morning a tank engine would haul two or three coaches northwards from Oxford station, along the edge of Port Meadow, and then sharp west at Wolvercote and over the fields to Witney. In the summer months the train would often be quite full, carrying (besides its usual complement of local people) families setting off for a holiday by the Upper Thames or in the Cotswolds, or maybe a group of men from the University armed with knapsacks and sticks and about to begin a walking tour. But in winter only a few people used the train.

One Wednesday morning in December 1945 Jack Lewis was on board, looking out of the carriage window at the fields and streams and villages as they passed. The countryside through which the branch line meandered was not, as he observed, dramatically beautiful: just a fine English winter beauty of haystacks and stubble, ploughed land, bare trees and rooks. From Witney the train carried him on until it passed not far from William Morris's old home at Kelmscott, and came at last to the end of the line and the station that served the small quiet town of Fairford. Warnie Lewis was on the platform to meet him, with Tolkien. They had already spent a day and a night staying at the Bull Hotel in Fairford. It was the long-planned Inklings' celebration of victory ('To take a whole inn in the countryside for at least a week, and spend it entirely in beer and talk'). But none of them could spare even as much as a week, let alone more; and they were only a small party. Dyson could not come, Owen Barfield was ill, Havard was only able to get to Fairford for lunch one day, Jack Lewis himself had not been able to arrive until after the others; and Charles Williams was dead.

On the morning that Williams died, Lewis went straight from the hospital where he heard the news to the Bird and Baby, where the other Inklings had already gathered for their Tuesday beer. It was only a couple of minutes' walk, 'but I remember the very streets looked different,' he said. When he got to the pub he had difficulty in making the others believe or even understand what had happened. In the days that followed, Warnie Lewis reacted simply with grief. 'There is something horrible, something *unfair* about death,' he said, 'which no religious conviction can overcome.' Tolkien too was greatly saddened. 'In the far too brief years since I first met him,' he told Michal Williams, 'I had grown to love and admire your husband deeply, and I am more grieved than I can express.' As for Jack Lewis, after the initial shock he experienced 'great pain but no mere depression'. And he wrote to Michal Williams: 'My friendship is not ended. His death has had the very unexpected effect of making death itself look quite different: I believe in the next life ten times more strongly than I did. At moments it seems quite tangible. Mr Dyson, on the day of the funeral, summed up what many of us felt. "It is not blasphemous," he said, "to believe that what was true of Our Lord is, in its less degree, true of all who are in Him. They go away in order to be *with* us in a new way, even closer than before." A month ago I would have called this silly sentiment. Now I know better. He seems, in some indefinable way, to be all around us now. I do not doubt he is doing and will do for us all sorts of things he could not have done while in the body.' Williams himself had described this very sensation of experiencing the presence of a recently dead loved one, in the first (rejected) draft of *All Hallows' Eve*: 'She was dead, but her very death heightened that word "supernatural"; it was what she, not being, was.'

The Fairford party made the best of it. They walked. They argued. They found a pub called the Pig and Whistle. They admired the flat countryside. 'I don't remember ever seeing more exquisite winter colouring, both of sky and landscape, of the subdued type,' Warnie Lewis wrote in his diary. 'Down on the river was a perfect mill house where we amused ourselves by dreaming of it as a home for the Inklings.' Then, on Friday afternoon, they took the train back to Oxford.

*

The Thursday meetings of the Inklings continued. There was, after all, no reason why they should not.

To talk of filling Charles Williams's place would have been absurd. But a few new people were asked to come along on Thursday nights. Gervase Mathew was already in the habit of putting in appearances, and now he became a fairly regular member. At about this time the Inklings were also joined by Colin Hardie, a Fellow of Magdalen and a friend of Jack Lewis's – he was the brother of the Hardie who had been a Magdalen don in the twenties. At first Colin Hardie was inclined towards Harry Weldon's atheist-progressive junto in Magdalen, but later he married a Catholic and was received into that church himself. Two other Magdalen dons sometimes turned up: C. E. ('Tom') Stevens, the Ancient History Tutor, and J. A. W. Bennett, the Anglo-Saxon and medieval scholar who came to Magdalen after the war to relieve Lewis by teaching the 'language' side of the English course, there now being a considerably larger number of undergraduates than before the war.

These men were all senior members of the University, but one person who was invited to become an Inkling late in 1945 was only twenty-one. Tolkien's third son Christopher had been known to the Lewis brothers and to Havard since he was a schoolboy; they also knew that he was deeply involved with the writing of *The Lord of the Rings*. He had read the first chapters in manuscript, and had drawn maps and made fair copies of the text for his father. Later, when he was abroad with the R.A.F., his father sent him the new parts of the story as they were written, telling him: 'I don't think I should write any more, but for the hope of your seeing it.' After the war Christopher Tolkien returned to Oxford and resumed his undergraduate career, with Lewis as his tutor for several terms. In the autumn of 1945 his father told him that the Inklings proposed 'to consider you a *permanent member*, with right of entry and what not quite independent of my presence or otherwise'. Once Christopher had become an Inkling it grew to be the custom that he, rather than his father, should read aloud any new chapters of *The Lord of the Rings* to the company, for it was generally agreed that he made a better job of it than did Tolkien himself. 'Chris gave us an admirable chapter of the Hobbit, beautifully read,' Warnie wrote in his diary in February 1947. And on another Thursday: 'Tollers gave us a chapter of Hobbit; but I think we all missed Christopher's reading.'

Another young man who was made welcome by the Inklings at this time was John Wain. He had been Lewis's pupil, and after taking his degree he held first a junior research fellowship at his old college, St John's, and then a lecturership at Reading University. Wain had discovered (as others had discovered) that the only way to survive being Lewis's pupil was to copy Lewis's manner, and he was certainly able to counter his old tutor's dogmatic pronouncements with an equal torrent of assertion, proof, illustration and metaphor. Warnie wrote in his diary in January 1949: 'A good Inklings after dinner: present, J., McCallum, Gervase, Tom Stevens, John Wain, and myself. We started on the Lays of Ancient Rome and thence to poetry in general, on which Wain talked an amazing amount of nonsense – even going so far as to illustrate his point by reciting a song of Harry Champion's, which he claimed was as good as Macaulay. If I got him aright, his point is that poetry whose meaning can be apprehended at a first reading is not poetry at all: I should say for my part that exactly the reverse is true.

The sense of the House was strongly against him. He recited a pretty good poem of his own composing on the death of the John's porter,[1] and then read to us from the first two chapters of his book on Arnold Bennett: absolutely first class, and I enjoyed them greatly.'

Wain's difference of outlook from the other Inklings was fundamental. 'I admired Lewis and his friends tremendously,' he wrote some years later, 'but already it was clear that I did not share their basic attitudes. The group had a corporate mind, as all effective groups must; the death of Williams had sadly stunned and impoverished this mind, but it was still powerful and clearly defined. Politically conservative, not to say reactionary; in religion, Anglo- or Roman Catholic; in art, frankly hostile to any manifestation of the "modern" spirit. There was very little here that I could fit myself into.' Moreover Wain did not share the belief, very precious to Tolkien and Lewis, that the practice of 'mytho-poeia', the invention of myth-like stories, was a valuable (indeed invaluable) form of art. One evening he was unable to keep silent while Lewis aired this view. 'A writer's task, I maintained', Wain recalled, 'was to lay bare the human heart, and this could not be done if he were continually taking refuge in the spinning of fanciful webs. Lewis retorted with a theory that, since the Creator had seen fit to build a universe and set it in motion, it was the duty of the human artist to create as lavishly as possible in his turn. The romancer, who invents a whole world, is worshipping God more effectively than the mere realist who analyses that which lies about him. Looking back, I can hardly believe that Lewis said anything so manifestly absurd.'

John Wain, like many others of his generation, believed and hoped that the Labour victory in the 1945 general election would set in motion a long-delayed wave of social justice in Britain. Lewis on the other hand thought that the Labour government and its prime minister Attlee were the very devils of Hell incarnate. He lamented that heavy taxation would liquidate the middle classes, or would at least prevent them from educating their children privately, declaring that only if a man were so educated could he have 'the freeborn mind'. He poured scorn on the use of 'Brotherhood' as a social maxim, declaring that it was a hypocritical disguise for self-advancement; and he maintained that while democracy was a necessity this was only because of the Fall. 'I do not believe', he wrote, 'that God created an egalitarian world. I believe that if we had not fallen, patriarchal monarchy would be the sole lawful government.' Nor did he support those who, some years after the war, began to campaign for nuclear disarmament, for the prospect of mass destruction did not greatly alarm him. 'As a Christian I take

[1] i.e. the porter of St John's, Wain's own college.

it for granted that human history will end some day,' he said, and he was irritated by 'young people who make it [the bomb] a reason for poisoning every pleasure and evading every duty in the present. Didn't they know that, Bomb or no Bomb, all men die? There is no good moping and sulking about it.'

These views are perhaps more understandable when one remembers that he was brought up in middle-class Belfast society, where constant vituperation was poured upon the then equivalent of the Left, the Liberals, for their Irish Home Rule Bill; and also when one realises that such things did not really interest him very much. His attention was directed towards the salvation of the individual soul rather than to the solution of communal problems. Indeed, reading the newspapers as little as he did, he really knew next to nothing about contemporary affairs. 'Jack's ignorance in some directions amazes me as much as his knowledge in others,' Warnie wrote in his diary in 1950. 'Last night at dinner I mentioned Tito's volte-face in Jugoslavia, where there is a state-fostered return to Christianity. I thought J. very stupid about the whole affair, and we had talked for a minute or two before I found out that he was under the impression that Tito was the King of Greece!'

Not surprisingly, Lewis started to find himself out of touch with the post-war generation of undergraduates, many of whom, like John Wain, were beginning to be politically aware and to take the state of society rather more seriously than their predecessors had done. Lewis lamented this. 'The modern world is so desperately serious,' he remarked to Arthur Greeves. He also regretted that the post-war undergraduates rarely took the long country walks which he himself had felt to be such an important part of his development. Gone too were the small coteries and cliques of friends which had mattered so much to his generation. He remarked that the modern undergraduate lived in a crowd. 'Caucus,' he said, 'has replaced friendship.'

He was also increasingly out of sympathy with his fellow dons, but this was for rather a different reason. It might or might not be true to say that Christians were in the minority in the senior common rooms of Oxford; but certainly those dons who did profess Christianity generally kept their religion to themselves, attending their college chapel or parish church but not making any display of the fact, and certainly not writing popular books in the hope of converting others to their beliefs. Lewis, in fact, had offended against Oxford etiquette not by becoming a Christian, but by making a public matter of his conversion. He had refused to adopt the detached irony which Oxford has always regarded as an acceptable manner of cloaking one's true beliefs. He had indeed guyed this ironical detachment in the character of 'Mr Sensible' in *The Pilgrim's Regress*. 'He must have irritated many by the lack of any ironic view of himself,' wrote John Bayley of New College when discussing Lewis's life some years later in the *Times Literary Supplement*. 'In all innocence, he took over areas which others assume cannot be *owned*. Faith, belief, affections, sorrows – they are areas which most prefer to assume than to demonstrate knowledge of, and people were not endeared to Lewis by his downright occupation of them.' There was also the plain fact that some of Lewis's colleagues resented the sheer success of such books as *Screwtape*. 'Academicism cherishes a knowing anonymity,' wrote John Bayley. 'Contrary to what is often supposed, dons do not like drawing colleagues' attention to themselves, and regard with a mixture of envy and resentment any of their number who achieve public notoriety on the scale that Lewis did.' (As to the matter of financial success, from an early stage – and this was not known to his colleagues – Lewis paid more than two-thirds of all royalties from his books into a trust fund, from which he then gave generously, and usually anonymously, to persons in need.) What many in Oxford resented most of all was the breadth of appeal of such things as *Screwtape*. Lewis's books (and Tolkien's too, after the publication of *The Lord of the Rings*) were read eagerly by children, by working people, by the poorly educated, and by many other categories very alien to the world of professional scholarship in general and 'literary criticism' in particular. A good many at Oxford did not much care for this. They resented the remarkable capacity of Lewis and Tolkien for getting themselves across to an enormous range of readers, a capacity for climbing the walls that surround academicism and communicating with the world outside.

But if Oxford was censorious and envious, it was also rather proud of Lewis. He and the Inklings were now part of the scenery. One morning during the war, John Wain was walking towards the Bird and Baby when he met a friend coming away from it. ' "Who's in there?" I asked. "Nothing much," he answered, "just the poet Williams and the theologian MacKinnon disputing in a corner." ' The phrase stuck in Wain's mind as an indication of the atmosphere of the period. Similarly when another graduate of St John's College, Bruce Montgomery, published one of his first detective stories under the name of Edmund Crispin, he set one scene in the Bird and Baby, and made his professor-detective Gervase Fen remark: 'There goes C. S. Lewis – it must be Tuesday.'

Tuesdays at the 'Bird' continued unabated, and at these morning sessions the Thursday company was usually augmented by one or two of Lewis's other friends, such as 'D-G.', Commander Jim Dundas-Grant, a Scotsman who had been quartered in Magdalen during the war to supervise the University Naval Division, and who was still

13 (a) J. R. R. Tolkien and Colin Hardie in
        1972, at the conferment of an Honor-
        ary D.Litt. on Tolkien. Hardie was
        the University's Public Orator at
        this time.

13 (b) C. S. Lewis, circa 1951 – 'dung-
        coloured mackintosh and old cloth
        hat'.

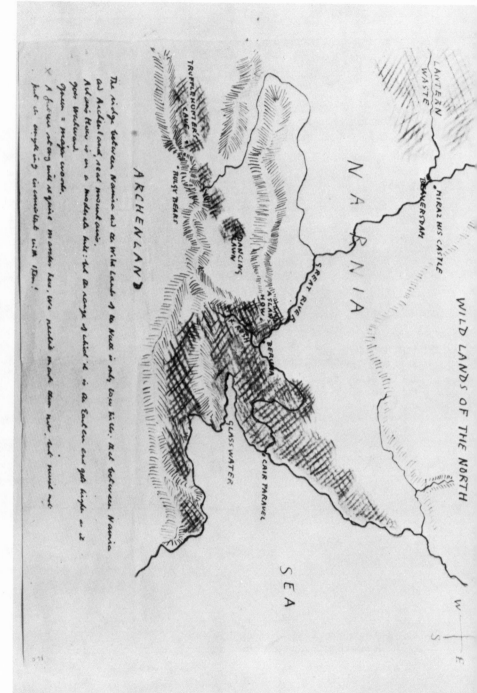

14   A map of Narnia drawn by C. S. Lewis.

living in Oxford. Another who put in a very occasional appearance was a friend of Havard's named Edward Robinson, whom Lewis, recalling Beatrix Potter's *The Tale of Little Pig Robinson*, christened 'Little Pig'. These and others occupied the back parlour of the 'Bird' on Tuesdays, a parlour whose seclusion and whose coal fire (especially lit for the Inklings by Charles Blagrove, the landlord) was one of the attractions of that pub, another being the very potent draught cider, which the company inexplicably referred to as 'Bung Misery'.[1] Indeed the only pub which became a rival to the 'Bird' was the Trout, on the river at Godstow, to the north of Oxford. 'An exquisitely lovely spring day,' Warnie wrote in his diary in 1946. 'To the Bird and Baby as usual in the morning, where I had started on my second pint before J. arrived. When Humphrey came, he suggested an adjournment to the Trout at Godstow: which, picking up Christopher Tolkien on the way, we did, and there drank beer in the sunlight. The beauty of the whole scene was almost theatrical, and that nothing might be lacking to show off the warm grey of the old inn, there was a pair of peacocks.'

Another variation in the Inklings' routine was caused by the frequent arrival, between 1947 and 1950, of lavish food parcels from one of Lewis's American admirers, Dr Warfield M. Firor of Maryland. As post-war food rationing was making life almost more drab than it had been during the war itself, these parcels were most welcome, and they invariably included something that could scarcely be bought in England then, a large ham. In consequence, 'ham suppers' in a private dining-room at Magdalen became quite a frequent event for the Inklings, with Colin Hardie as carver, neither of the Lewis brothers being able to wield a carving knife with any skill. 'We sat down eight to dinner,' Warnie wrote on the first occasion, 'all in the highest spirits: J. and Colin at top and bottom respectively, Tollers, Humphrey and Christopher on one side, Hugo, David, and I on the other.' After dinner they adjourned to Lewis's rooms. An American admirer had sent Lewis a tuxedo, and this was raffled, it being far too narrowly cut for Lewis. Warnie recorded: 'Proceedings opened with the great Tuxedo raffle – for an American dinner jacket suit, won by Colin, whom it didn't fit, and who with great generosity waived his claim in favour of Christopher, who looked admirable in it.' Some months

---

[1] John Wain says that Lewis actually preferred the public bar of the Bird and Baby to the back parlour, which was really a private sitting-room offered only by kindness of Blagrove; but another of the Inklings rather officiously 'booked' the parlour for use on Tuesdays, and Lewis regretfully fell in with this arrangement. John Wain adds that Blagrove looked remarkably like Lewis, and that Lewis owned a photograph of Blagrove serving him across the bar with a pint of beer, the effect being of Lewis observing his reflection in a mirror.

later, after a number of further hams had been consumed with due ceremony, Lewis wrote to the donor Dr Firor: 'To all my set you are by now an almost mythical figure – Firor-of-the-Hams, a sort of Fertility god.' There were of course other things in Dr Firor's parcels besides hams, and indeed there were other parcels from other admirers. Lewis gave a good many of the contents to the Inklings and, as John Wain recalled, his method of distribution was to scatter the tins and packets on his bed, cover them with the bedspread, and allow each of them to pick one of the unidentifiable humps. Wain said: 'It was no use simply choosing the biggest, which might turn out to be prunes or something equally dreary.'

*

On several occasions after the war the Lewis brothers took one of their fellow Inklings on holiday with them. In August 1946 Tolkien accompanied them to Malvern, where (despite Jack Lewis's unhappy schooldays there) they often took holidays. This was partly because Mrs Moore's daughter Maureen was now married to a member of the Malvern College teaching staff, and they could simply exchange houses with her and her husband, Maureen going to Oxford to look after her mother. But the Malvern countryside itself was an attraction, and Lewis's former pupil George Sayer who taught at the College was much liked by both brothers. Tolkien reported of this 1947 holiday:

'Only one *really* good inn, The Unicorn, which is all that you could desire in looks and otherwise. The Herefordshire cider is astringent and thirst quenching. The great brethren are in good form and not too energetic. Warnie's attempts to control his irascibility and do *all* the work so as to give Jack a rest are quite touching – and also very efficient. We are living well and economically.'

Despite Tolkien's dislike of the Lewis brothers' 'ruthless' speed of walking, 'we managed two good days with him,' Warnie wrote in his diary, 'including one to the top of the Camp, where I was more than ever impressed with the beauty of the northward view. Our nice bar lady has left the Camp, and been replaced by a sulky Glaswegian with a patch of plaster on his forehead, who was truculent at our disapproval of his abominable beer: as Tollers said after the encounter, it was easy to see how he came by his patch! Much more enjoyable was our morning draught at the Wych, where they keep Sprackley's Ale, a beer still brewed by one of the old fashioned family concerns, now alas almost all gone. From time to time I contrasted this holiday with the Hugo one, and was struck with the diversity of taste and interest we have in the Inklings: particularly when Tollers stopped one day and gave us a talk on the formation of the Spanish chestnut at the identical spot

210

which prompted Hugo to tell us of the scandalous circumstances under which the late Earl Beauchamp was ordered out of England by George V. Tollers left us on Saturday. His visit added a private piece of nomenclature to Malvern – the christening of the mysterious and ornate little green and silver door in the walls of the old cab rank in Pring Road as "Sackville-Baggins's".'

The Malvern holiday with Hugo Dyson was not recorded in Warnie Lewis's diary, but he did keep a note of the trip that he, Jack, and Dyson made to Liverpool in the spring of 1946. Jack had to make the journey so as to take part in a Brains Trust, and this was extended into a short holiday.

On the train journey from Oxford, Warnie recorded that 'Hugo and I behaved over engines like a couple of school boys. He had brought nothing to read with him, but this we sternly corrected at a later period. From Bletchley to Rugby we had a crowded corridor train, and reached the latter in time for a cup of tea: here we lost Hugo, who, as J. said, should always have a collar and lead when one travels with him. Hugo behaved heroically after dark, singing and telling stories: "If I stopped I should become hysterical" he said.' They slept at Birkenhead, and next evening Warnie noted: 'I was the unhappy and inadvertent cause of launching an argument on the difference between Art and Philosophy; towards the end of the first hour J. and Hugo discovered that they were talking about different subjects. Each side then restated its war aims, and then set to again. When or how the argument ended I don't know, for it was still going strong when I went to bed at eleven.'

The next day: 'Hugo has developed a passion for ferry voyaging, which is indeed the best diversion this place affords, so nothing loathe we all set out after breakfast to Liverpool, and from there took the other ferry to Wallasey. After lunch Hugo, who has become a ferry addict, went for another voyage, and I, after a siesta, went for a more extended stroll in Birkenhead than I have yet had in it; it is exactly Hell as described by J. in the opening chapter of *The Great Divorce*. How can any government expect content from the inhabitants of such a place?' In the evening Lewis went to his Brains Trust, and Hugo and Warnie explored Liverpool. 'Our evening began badly by finding the theatrical pub so crowded that there was no prospect of a drink there, and mercurial Hugo decided that there was nothing for it but to go straight home. However, on the way down to Pier Head, we saw a still blacked out pub called the "Angel", which proved to be comfortable and nearly empty, and there we rapidly revived under the stimulus of bottled Guinness, and had much talk about army life. Hugo, who was by now completely restored to his best spirits, suggested another voyage to Wallasey, and I was nothing loathe, so off we went. We

211

found J. in the lounge when we got home, and a conversation started on the wit of the seventeenth century. Hugo quoted an epigram of Suckling's on the birth of Nell Gwyn which was the most disgusting thing of the sort I have ever heard.'

*

The Inklings' ham suppers continued until late in 1949, by which time food supplies in England had returned to something like normal. At the last ham supper, Warnie Lewis recorded that Hugo Dyson 'bellows uninterruptedly for about three minutes, and as he shows no sign of stopping, two guests at the bottom of the table begin a conversation: which being observed by Hugo, he raises his hand and shouts reproachfully – "Friends, friends, I feel it would be better if we keep the conversation *general*." '

Dyson was now, at least in theory, able to attend the Inklings more frequently, for in 1945 he was elected a Fellow of Merton College, and he and his wife left Reading University where they had been for twenty-two years and came to live in Oxford, taking a house just round the corner from Magdalen. In practice however he still only put in comparatively rare appearances on Thursdays. 'This evening Hugo carried me to dine with him in Merton,' Warnie wrote in his diary in August 1946. 'He was in high spirits when I met him, and his spirits rose steadily for the rest of the evening. I was more than ever struck with his amazing knowledge of Shakespeare; I don't suppose there is a man in Oxford – with the possible exception of Onions – who can quote so happily, e.g. tonight, apropos of J. – "O cursed spite that gave thee to the Moor": poor J.'s whole catastrophe epitomized in nine words! I saw tonight why Hugo rarely gets to an Inkling; every one he meets after dinner he engages in earnest conversation, and tonight, even with steady pressure from me, it took him forty minutes to get from Hall to the gate.' And on another occasion, when the Inklings were meeting not in Magdalen but (as they sometimes did during this period) in Tolkien's rooms in Merton – Tolkien also being a Fellow of that college since 1945 when he became Professor of English Language and Literature: 'When I arrived Hugo's voice' (noted Warnie) 'was booming through the fog in the Quad, inviting a party of undergraduates up to his rooms; he really can be very irritating at times.'

Dyson was certainly 'irritating at times' to the Tolkiens, both father and son; for his impatience with *The Lord of the Rings* (and indeed with all Thursday night readings, as opposed to conversation) had been voiced so often that eventually he was allowed a veto. 'A well attended Inkling this evening,' Warnie wrote in April 1947; 'both the Tolkiens,

J. and I, Humphrey, Jervase [sic], Hugo; the latter came in just as we were starting on the Hobbit, and as he now exercises a veto on it – most unfairly I think – we had to stop.'

Inevitably, Dyson's pupils at Merton either loved him or found him unbearable. One of the latter was P. J. Kavanagh, who in 1951 came back wounded from Korea, and misunderstood his tutor's manner from the start. 'We took you from the trenches! The trenches!' Hugo Dyson chortled at him, and Kavanagh shrank back, later revenging himself by a rather cruel cameo of Dyson in his autobiography. What Kavanagh failed to appreciate was that though Dyson used his wit like a broad-sword, roaring his jokes across the room in sheer exuberance, that wit was itself rapier-keen.

Long before, Lewis had described Dyson as 'a burly man, both in mind and body, with the stamp of the war upon him'. By the time Dyson had taught for a few years at Merton he was no longer burly. Arthritis had its grip on him, and he walked lamely, with a silver-topped stick. 'He could sometimes seem as he perched on his chair almost birdlike,' recalled one of his pupils, Stephen Medcalf. 'But he still had the thrust and apparent mass of burliness, and I never rid myself of the feeling that the arthritic lameness was really a wound from the '14–18 war. "I'm Hugo Dyson," he introduced himself, "I'm a bore"; and once at dinner when the menu announced Roast Duck and the scouts brought Roast Lamb, "Le Malade Imaginaire", he said.'

Dyson published virtually nothing, and what there is of his in print – Augustans and Romantics, an article on Wordsworth, an introduction to Pope, a British Academy lecture on Shakespeare – captures almost nothing of his volatile personality. He had, in his work as well as in the Inklings, a strong preference for talk rather than the written word, and it was in lectures and tutorials that the best of him came out. When he lectured (as Stephen Medcalf recalled) 'he would stare out over the heads of his audience as if seeing another world, sink himself in the cross-currents of Shakespeare's mind, and himself, sometimes, become one of Shakespeare's images. I remember his acting Death with "rotten mouth – iron teeth".' In tutorials he would begin by dispensing beer – 'Bring out the buckets, men' – yet he rarely drank it himself, wishing merely to raise his pupils to his own normal level of eloquence. He did not often allow them to read more than a few lines of their essays without interrupting with some enthusiastic comment or suggestion. He told them: 'Write an essay. Write an essay. Must have something to stop me talking.' Some were maddened by him. Others, such as Medcalf, left the tutorial hour 'joyful under the impetus of irresistible gusto'.

In the nineteen-sixties Dyson was seen briefly by a wider audience when he gave half a dozen unscripted television talks on Shakespeare for the BBC, at the instigation of the producer Patrick Garland who had been his pupil. He also introduced Garland's television series *Famous Gossips*, and as a result of all this made a third and much more surprising appearance on screen in John Schlesinger's film *Darling*, which starred Julie Christie and Dirk Bogarde. Dyson was by his own admission no actor, but he performed with charm in his one scene, where he portrayed an elderly writer whose friendship and advice is sought by the principal characters. Dyson said of all this: 'I think I've never been happier. The mere fact of being on television or in the cinema is so enormously flattering to a vain man; and though a timid man I have my vanity. I did enjoy it; my *word* I enjoyed it.' His only complaint was about a scene in *Darling* where his funeral took place. 'That I was sorry about. First of all I was not paid for it – you aren't paid if you don't appear – and second, well, there was Julie Christie saying what a lot I'd meant to her, you know, and I knew I hadn't, and there was just a coffin brought on, and it was said to contain me, and I didn't believe it did, you know. No, one doesn't like being buried. I'm not ambitious, a quiet, timid man, but I didn't like being buried.'

*

Lewis aroused equally strong reactions in his pupils as did Dyson. For every one of them who (like John Wain) managed to enjoy and to ape Lewis's forceful logic, there were at least as many who were alarmed and cowed by the heavy-handedness of his manner, combined with his general refusal to put his relationship with his pupils on anything like a personal footing. A few lapped it up, but some very nearly ran away. 'If you think that way about Keats you needn't come here again!' Lewis once roared down the stairs to a departing pupil. And on another occasion when an Australian student professed that he could never read Arnold's *Sohrab and Rustum*, and refused to admit its good qualities even after Lewis had chanted a hundred lines of it at him, Lewis declared. 'The sword must settle it!' and reached for a broadsword and a rapier which (according to J. A. W. Bennett, who was there) were inexplicably in the corner of the room. They fenced – Lewis of course choosing the broadsword – and, said Bennett, 'Lewis actually drew blood – a slight nick.'

Lewis's intellectual pugnacity found yet another outlet in the nineteen-forties. When the wave of wartime enthusiasm for Christianity was at its height in Oxford, Stella Aldwinckle, who was active in University church affairs, founded a Socratic Club, which was to be an open forum for religious argument and in particular an arena where Christians could dispute their beliefs with atheists. Lewis accepted the invitation to be President, and the Socratic Club quickly became popular with undergraduates. It could however hardly be said to be truly Socratic, for though it was supposed to be without doctrinal bias and was allegedly committed to following arguments wherever they led, it was in actual fact almost exclusively Christian in its membership; Christian, moreover, in a highly orthodox and sometimes aggressive manner.

The usual pattern of meetings was that an atheist (or an agnostic, or sometimes a 'liberal churchman') would read a paper which would then be disputed, the discussion being opened by someone who held the opposite point of view. In practice, after the visiting speaker had been given his chance it was very often Lewis who opened the discussion; or rather, engaged the visitor in intellectual combat, refuting everything that had been said, to the delight of what was usually a highly partisan audience.

John Wain sometimes observed these performances at the Socratic: 'It was in practice a kind of prize-ring in which various champions appeared to try conclusions with Lewis, who week after week put on a knock-down-and-drag-out performance that was really impressive.' Lewis was of course a highly skilled debater. Yet, even if he had not been, with the Socratic audience so heavily on his side he could hardly have failed to win the day. For example, when C. E. M. Joad, best known for his part in the BBC's Brains Trust, visited the club in 1944 and read a paper that was mildly critical of some Christian notions, no sooner had he finished than according to Wain 'the society's Secretary, a formidable crop-haired young woman, was on her feet with the announcement, "Mr C. S. Lewis will now *answer* Dr Joad." Lewis gently corrected her: "Open the discussion, I think, is the formula". But to this Secretary and her like, those performances were no mere polite "opening" of discussions. An enemy had invaded the very hearthstone of the faithful, and it was a matter of "Christian, up and smite them!" – Christian, in this case, being Lewis.'

The same pattern was repeated with other visitors, such as J. B. S. Haldane, whose views on science and the progress of humanity had often raised Lewis's righteous wrath in print, and the Oxford philosopher A. J. Ayer, who recalled of his appearance at the Socratic that he and Lewis 'engaged in a flashy debate, which entertained the audience but did neither of us much credit'. But if Ayer was not impressed by the proceedings of the club, Lewis probably was. Certainly he was encouraged by the success and the popularity of his argumentative methods on these occasions, for during the early years of his Presidency of the Socratic his writings on Christianity were coloured by the kind of rhetoric that he used in the club's debates. In his broadcast talks, in numerous articles, and in particular in his book *Miracles* he came to rely largely on the sheer force of argument.

He skated on thin ice in the opening chapter of *The Problem of Pain*, where he offered his readers a 'proof' of the existence of God which, as Austin Farrer remarked, tackled this immense issue 'on the scale of a pamphlet in a church porch'. This 'proof' was based first upon Man's apprehension of the 'Numinous' or spiritual, and secondly on human awareness of an abstract Moral Law. Lewis repeated this argument in his BBC talks on Christianity, where he alleged that Reason, the part of the human mind which makes moral decisions, is directly related to the Moral Law and hence to God. And some years later in *Miracles* he took this even further, attempting to prove the existence of God by demonstrating the existence of Reason as something quite independent of the rest of human mentality.

Philosophy changes faster than almost any other academic subject. By the 1940s Lewis was simply behind the times as a philosopher. He still argued along the lines taken by the post-Hegelians who had been fashionable in his undergraduate days; but among Oxford philosophers it was now as if Hegel and his disciples had never been. 'Logical Positivism' dominated, and Lewis's methods seemed old fashioned.[1] Moreover there were many passages in *The Problem of Pain* and *Miracles* where his dubious logic simply did not do justice to his standpoint.

Lewis's friends had observed the dangers of his methods. Charles Williams, listening to his wartime broadcasts, had expressed serious reservations about his tendency to make Reason the primary basis for belief in God, while Tolkien was aware of Lewis's too close reliance on supposedly infallible dialectics. Tolkien remarked that, while Lewis was certainly a great debater who had the art of making points brilliantly and tellingly, he had distinct weaknesses. 'He was keen-witted rather than clear-sighted,' Tolkien wrote, 'logical within some given position, but in ranging argument neither lucid nor coherent. On the fallacies, verbal subterfuges, and false deductions of his opponents (and of his friends) he could dart like a hawk; yet he was himself often confused, failing to make essential distinctions, or seeming unaware that his immediate contention had been already damaged by some "point" that he had made elsewhere.'

Miracles was published in 1947. Early the following year, its third chapter, in which Lewis proved that human Reason is independent of the natural world, was publicly attacked at the Socratic Club, not by an atheist but by a fellow Christian, the Catholic philosopher Elizabeth Anscombe. Lewis was unprepared for the severely critical analysis to

[1] Lewis himself would have laughed at this comment, on the grounds that it accepts uncritically the notion that change means improvement.

which she submitted his arguments, for she proved in her turn that his 'proof' of theism was severely faulty. It is true that Lewis's most fervent supporters felt that she had not demonstrated her point successfully, but many who were at the meeting thought that a conclusive blow had been struck against one of his most fundamental arguments. Certainly after it was all over Lewis himself was in very low spirits. He and Hugo Dyson had organised an informal dining club with four of their pupils, Philip Stibbe, Tom Stock, Peter Bayley and Derek Brewer, and the club happened to meet a couple of days after the Socratic duel. Brewer wrote in his diary: 'None of us at first very cheerful. Lewis was obviously deeply disturbed by his encounter last Monday with Miss Anscombe, who had disproved some of the central theory of his philosophy about Christianity. I felt quite painfully for him. Dyson said – very well – that now he had lost everything and was come to the foot of the Cross – spoken with great sympathy.' Brewer added that Lewis's imagery when talking about the debate 'was all of the fog of war, the retreat of infantry thrown back under heavy attack'.

Lewis had learnt his lesson: for after this he wrote no further books of Christian apologetics for ten years, apart from a collection of sermons; and when he did publish another apologetic work, *Reflections on the Psalms*, it was notably quieter in tone and did not attempt any further intellectual proofs of theism or Christianity. Though he continued to believe in the importance of Reason in relation to his Christian faith, he had perhaps realised the truth of Charles Williams's maxim, 'No-one can possibly do more than decide what to believe.'

*

Lewis's next book after *Miracles* was published three years later, in 1950. It was *The Lion, the Witch and the Wardrobe,* the first of his seven 'Narnia' stories for children. What kind of mind was it that could switch from rigorous theological argument to children's fantasy?

Any attempt to describe a man's mental attributes by dividing them into compartments will be artificial; yet to do this with Lewis does at least seem to give us some idea of how his mind worked. Certainly there are four aspects of his mind and work that deserve to be examined: let us call them the 'Chestertonian', the 'boyish', the 'debater' and the 'poet'.

This was Lewis's estimate of G. K. Chesterton: 'A great Roman Catholic, a great writer, and a great man'. And in *Surprised by Joy* he makes it clear how much Chesterton's writings and in particular *The Everlasting Man* helped him to become a Christian. So it was scarcely surprising that he took Chesterton for a model in many of his own attitudes to his faith. 'Christianity is a fighting religion' – 'I don't want

217

retreat; I want attack' – 'We shall probably fail, but let us go down fighting for the right side'. This is Lewis, but it might easily be Chesterton; and Lewis adopts the same persona when he refers to his Socratic Club atheist opponents as 'the enemy', when he declares that Christianity is 'manly', and when he talks of his deep regard for 'common things and common men'.

Yet the Chestertonian cap did not really fit Lewis. It was indeed more 'the sort of thing a man might say' rather than the expression of his real feelings. For example, he might declare roundly that the business of writing poetry did not require so much courage as the act of stepping into a cold bath, but from his own experience as a poet he must have known that this was absurd. So why did he adopt this Chestertonian manner?

Perhaps the answer has something to do with a remark by Charles Williams. He, too, was much influenced by Chesterton (particularly in his early poetry and in *War in Heaven*), but he had serious reservations about him. Chesterton, he once declared, was 'adult by inspiration at great moments; hardly wholly so'. And indeed there is something very like a schoolboy about much of Chesterton's work. Is this why he appealed to Lewis? For there was a very boyish element in Lewis too.

In his literary criticism Lewis liked to adopt a childlike posture. He told his audience at a British Academy Shakespeare Lecture that he felt 'rather like a child brought in at dessert to recite his piece before the grown-ups', and he said that in talking about *Hamlet* he would 'bestow all my childishness upon you' – would in fact remind his audience that, to a child, *Hamlet* is an exciting play, and not an 'artistic failure' as T. S. Eliot had called it. Similarly, when he was writing about *The Faerie Queene* he said, 'It demands of us a child's thirst for adventures, a young man's passion for physical beauty. The poem is a great palace, but the door into it is so low that you must stoop to go in.' He also said: 'Beyond all doubt it is best to have made one's first acquaintance with Spenser in a very large – and, preferably, illustrated – edition of *The Faerie Queene*, on a wet day, between the ages of twelve and sixteen.'

Once again, all this was a guise. When the *Hamlet* lecture really got into its stride it became a serious and scholarly argument which no child could have formulated. Similarly, Lewis's real contribution to Spenserian studies depended on his considerable scholarship rather than on any childlike instinctive appreciation. Nor indeed did the remarks about a child's responses make much sense in themselves. Although Lewis himself had loved *The Faerie Queene* and *Hamlet* when he first met them in boyhood, comparatively few other modern children could really be expected to do the same. These remarks are chiefly interesting not so much as literary criticism but because they show how important

Lewis thought it was to remain spiritually a child – or at least to retain something of the child's responses to the world.

A superficial observer of his life might suppose that in some ways he never grew up. He himself said he felt his youth to have been 'of immense length', and certainly his autobiography gives the impression that he was, at the comparatively late age when he wrote it, still deeply concerned with the crises of childhood – an odd father, a cruel head-master, schoolfellows who bullied him – for these take up a lot of space in the book. Such an observer might also conjecture that since most of his adult years were spent with a woman whom he called 'my mother', he himself remained largely the childlike or adolescent son. This sort of observation would, of course, be trivial in that it ignores the maturity of his scholarly work, and of much of his writing on Christianity, beside the sheer shrewdness and wisdom of what he had to say about human behaviour. It also ignores the plain fact that though he behaved as 'son' to Mrs Moore he treated her with a far more adult patience than most real sons would have displayed in the circumstances. And yet one cannot observe his mind without remarking on the very large part that boyishness did play in it.

This boyishness can be seen in quite small details: in his handwriting, for example, which looked bold and confident but had (as Peter Bayley remarks) 'something uncertain or incomplete about it'. His sense of humour, too, showed itself in schoolboy jokes, like his fondness for referring to his book as *The Alligator of Love*; while his slang was often (though perhaps deliberately) that of an Edwardian schoolboy – he called one author 'a corking good writer', another story 'a tip-top yarn', and yet another 'an absolute corker'.

These are rather trivial examples; more revealing is his much-vaunted fondness for re-reading childhood favourites such as *The Wind in the Willows* and the works of Rider Haggard and Beatrix Potter – or indeed for re-reading anything, for he once declared: 'An unliterary man may be defined as one who reads books only once'. David Cecil says of this: 'Lewis's taste in *light* literature was that of an imaginative Victorian schoolboy'.[1]

When one comes to Lewis's own stories, boyishness is immediately apparent. Often it is an asset. The poet Ruth Pitter has praised his

---

[1] Cecil adds: 'His *serious* literary taste was also nineteenth century; but that of a mid-nineteenth century scholar and man of letters. He liked the grand, the noble, or the Romantic: Homer, Virgil, Milton, also Spenser, Malory, etc. – though he also did get a great deal of pleasure from writers as different as Lamb and Jane Austen. But his taste did stop about 1890. It was not just that he disliked the post-1914 writers – Joyce, Lawrence, etc. I don't think he cared for Henry James or Hardy or Conrad. This always interested me.' (Letter to the present writer, January 1978.)

'child's sense of glory and nightmare', and the success of *Screwtape* is largely due to the splendidly childish characterisations of Screwtape and Wormwood, who are every schoolboy's idea of devils. But the serious themes of *Out of the Silent Planet* come dangerously near to being lost in farce when Weston and Devine behave like a cartoon-strip caricature of the Englishman among the natives in their encounter with the Oyarsa of Malacandra; while Ransom's fight with the diabolical Un-man in *Perelandra* is (though splendidly written in itself) the intellectual battle of *Paradise Lost* reduced to fisticuffs. The third 'Ransom' novel, *That Hideous Strength*, is both the worst and the most enjoyable book of the trilogy, worst because its central action around the Inner Ring at Belbury is Lewis working out his schoolboy resentment of bullies, and most enjoyable because it is on a full-bloodedly schoolboy level, and this is the level on which Lewis is at his best. It might even be argued that the whole Ransom trilogy is really a series of children's books in disguise. The unfallen worlds of Malacandra and Perelandra are largely characterised by the fact that their inhabitants include furry animals who can talk, a baby dragon which sports at Ransom's feet, and a fleet of dolphin-like fish who will carry humans about at their bidding. In *That Hideous Strength*, Ransom's household includes a tame bear and a troop of mice who gather the crumbs when he summons them. The Un-man's grossest crime is not his tempting of the Eve of *Perelandra* but his wanton destruction, schoolboy fashion, of the frogs which inhabit the floating islands; and when he wants to annoy Ransom he chants his name over and over again, like 'a nasty little boy at a pre-paratory school' as Lewis says, and performs unnamed obscenities 'like a very nasty child'. And at the conclusion of the trilogy, when Mark Studdock finally comes to his senses and rejects the villainy of Belbury, he goes to a hotel, has a boiled egg for his tea, and discovers in bound volumes of *The Strand Magazine*

> a serial children's story which he had begun to read as a child but abandoned because his tenth birthday came when he was half-way through it and he was ashamed to read it after that. Now, he chased it from volume to volume till he had finished it. It was good. The grown-up stories to which, after his tenth birthday, he had turned instead of it, now seemed to him, except for *Sherlock Holmes*, to be rubbish.[1]

It is of course very easy to sneer at Lewis's boyishness, and any

[1] *That Hideous Strength*, Chapter 17; omitted in the version of the book that Lewis himself abridged for the paperback edition.

accusation of immaturity must be accompanied by a clear definition of maturity. It is no good just saying that Lewis wrote like a schoolboy without determining which writers can, by comparison, really be called adult. One might suggest Charles Williams as an example of maturity, both in his fiction and his theology, at least in comparison with Lewis. His mind held belief and scepticism in a balance that was arguably more adult that Lewis's rather boyish enthusiasm. F. R. Leavis has, however, called Williams's supposed preoccupation with evil 'evidence of arrest at the schoolboy (and -girl) stage rather than of spiritual maturity', which shows how subjective all such judgements are. Moreover, it needs to be realised that Lewis's best and most characteristic work sprang from this very boyishness, and also that he was largely conscious of both the spiritual and literary value of it. He willed it, and knew its effect.

These two aspects of Lewis's mind, the 'Chestertonian' and the 'boyish', were closely reflected in the two distinct kinds of writing he produced. He was both a debater and a poet – 'poet' in the sense of imaginative writer, for his actual poetry is of negligible importance compared with the rest of his work. At times the debater had the upper hand, and showed the mark of Chesterton. Often the poet was in charge, and then it was the boyishness that became apparent.

The poet was, of course, always present to assist the debater. Though the *logic* of Lewis's Christian apologetics may be fallible, the imagination of the writing with its brilliantly-conceived analogies is itself enough to win a reader to his side. As Austin Farrer expressed it, 'We think we are listening to an argument; in fact we are presented with a vision; and it is the vision that carries conviction.'

Moreover, while the 'poet' in Lewis is often a very attractive figure, the debater frequently is not. There is often an unnecessarily bullying weight to his arguments, particularly if he is putting down an opponent. When he disagrees with a remark he tends to tear it from its context and wave it all at the reader, blinded by his feelings from considering the real meaning of the writer. One case of this is the opening of his *Abolition of Man*, the 1943 lectures that he gave to Durham University,[1] where he bases an attack on modern ethics chiefly on a handful of remarks about subjectivity made by the authors of a school text-book for the teaching of English. Even supposing these remarks to be truly representative of modern thought, Lewis does not give them a chance.

---

[1] Lewis took advantage of the journey to explore Durham, and from what he saw there came at least something of the description of 'Edgestow' in *That Hideous Strength*. Warnie Lewis, who accompanied his brother, wrote in his diary (on 24 February 1943) that Durham's 'exquisite beauty came upon us with an impact I shall long remember. The University lies all about and around the cathedral, and was of a totally unexpected attractiveness.'

221

He removes them from the context and brandishes them furiously, declaring that they prove that the old belief in objective values has now been entirely lost. He does not discuss the work of any modern ethical philosopher (except C. H. Waddington, who gets a brief mention in a footnote), and he bases his argument entirely on what he *supposes* to be his opponents' case, taking that supposed case to its extreme and producing a *reductio ad absurdum* which of course he has no difficulty in demolishing. He is not prepared to examine those elements in his opponents' case which have a potential for good (unlike Charles Williams); and he selects, as typical of the achievements of science, the aeroplane, the radio, and the contraceptive, entirely ignoring (for example) the advance of medicine. The result is not an argument but a harangue.

Such a manner of dealing with a subject grew largely from Lewis's susceptibility to prejudices. Among these prejudices were the closing of his mind towards the avant-garde in literature, his deep suspicion of anything 'liberal' in theology, and his notions about certain aspects of Roman Catholicism: he was convinced, despite the attempts of his Catholic friends to persuade him otherwise, that Catholics do not merely revere but actually worship the Virgin. In contrast with Lewis, Charles Williams was always on his guard against prejudice. 'Prejudice must be regarded as sinful,' he declared; and he once remarked, 'Hell is always inaccurate.'

Neither the bullying tone of his arguments nor the basing of a substantial part of his thought on prejudice rather than knowledge helped to improve Lewis's work as a debater, and it was as well that in the late nineteen-forties the argumentative side of his writing did begin to give place to the poetic or imaginative. Lewis himself was well aware of the poetic element in his mind as something indentifiable. In 1954 he wrote: 'The imaginative man in me is older, more continuously operative, and in that sense more basic than either the religious writer or the critic. It was he who made me first attempt (with little success) to be a poet. It was he who, in response to the poetry of others, made me a critic, and in defence of that response, sometimes a critical contro-versialist. It was he who, after my conversion, led me to embody my belief in symbolic or mythopoeic form, ranging from *Screwtape* to a kind of theologised science-fiction. And it was, of course, he who has brought me, in the last few years, to write the series of Narnia stories for children.'

*

One day in the early spring of 1949, Lewis began to read aloud to Tolkien the beginning of a new book he was writing: 'Once there were four children whose names were Peter, Susan, Edmund and Lucy. This story is about something that happened to them when they were sent away from London during the war because of air-raids . . .'

Lewis said that the immediate cause of *The Lion, the Witch and the Wardrobe* was a series of nightmares that he had been having about lions. On a deeper level the story was, he explained, an answer to the question, 'What might Christ be like if there really were a world like Narnia and he chose to be incarnate and die and rise again in that world as he actually has done in ours?' So arose the story of four children and the great Lion, Aslan, who perhaps also owed a little of his origin to Williams's *The Place of the Lion*. And in one sense *The Lion, the Witch and the Wardrobe* was simply an extension of Lewis's three 'Ransom' novels. For, as in the earlier books Ransom travelled to other planets to discover the truth of the Christian 'myth', so the children who journey into Narnia experience, in *The Lion* and its sequels, many of the chief events of the Christian story, described as they might happen in another world. But the fact that the Narnia stories are 'about' Christianity does not mean that they are allegorical. The characters exist in their own right and are not mere allegorical types. The events of the Christian story are reimagined rather than allegorised, and the reader is left free, as he never is with allegory, to interpret in whatever fashion he pleases.

The Narnia stories are therefore entirely in keeping with Lewis and Tolkien's shared belief that Story (especially of the mythical type) can in itself give nourishment without imparting abstract meaning. They have, it is true, a far more specifically Christian colouring than does *The Lord of the Rings*; indeed at times they have something very near a didactic purpose. But so do *Out of the Silent Planet* and *Perelandra*, and Tolkien had been extremely enthusiastic about those books. Why then did he totally reject the Narnia stories?

For reject them he did. Lewis told his former pupil Roger Lancelyn Green, who sometimes drank with the Inklings at the Bird and Baby, that after listening to the opening chapters of *The Lion, the Witch and the Wardrobe* Tolkien had said he 'disliked it intensely'. And when Green met Tolkien shortly afterwards, Tolkien said to him, 'I hear you've been reading Jack's children's story. It really won't do, you know!'

Why wouldn't it 'do'? Tolkien was, by his own admission, a man of limited sympathies. He lacked Lewis's habitual urge to be enthusiastic about a friend's work simply because it *was* a friend's. He judged stories, especially stories in this vein, by severe standards. He disliked works of the imagination that were written hastily, were inconsistent in their details, and were not always totally convincing in their evocation of a 'secondary world'. This was one reason why it had taken him the past eleven years to write *The Lord of the Rings*, which was still not finished at the time that Lewis began to write *The Lion*. Every loose end, every detail of the story – the chronology, the geography, even the meteorology of Middle-earth – had to be consistent and plausible, so that the reader would (as Tolkien wished) take the book in a sense as history.

The Lion, the Witch and the Wardrobe offended against all these notions. It had been very hastily written, and this haste seemed to suggest that Lewis was not taking the business of 'sub-creation' with what Tolkien regarded as a proper seriousness. There were inconsistencies and loose ends in the story, while beyond the immediate demands of the plot the task of making Narnia seem 'real' did not appear to interest Lewis at all. Moreover, the story borrowed so indiscriminately from other mythologies and narratives (fauns, nymphs, Father Christmas, talking animals, anything that seemed useful for the plot) that for Tolkien the suspension of disbelief, the entering into a secondary world, was simply impossible. It just *wouldn't* 'do', and he turned his back on it.

*

While Lewis was dashing off *The Lion, the Witch and the Wardrobe*, the Inklings were meeting as usual on Tuesdays and Thursdays regularly in term-time and often in vacation. There had been much of late to give them a corporate identity in the public eye. *Essays Presented to Charles Williams*, the book intended as a *Festschrift* but which became a memorial volume, had been published in 1947, while the joint Lewis-Williams *Arthurian Torso* followed a year later. The first, besides including articles by several of the Inklings (as well as one outsider, Dorothy L. Sayers, whose essay on Dante Lewis thought 'a trifle vulgar in places') had for an introduction Lewis's memoir of Williams and a brief account of the Inklings themselves. Moreover, two of the essays, by Lewis and Tolkien, were a clear expression of their deep belief in the value of Story in general and mythical fairy-stories in particular. The second book, *Arthurian Torso*, consisted of those chapters which Williams had written for his study of the Arthurian legends, followed by a detailed commentary by Lewis on the *Taliessin* cycle. In this commentary, Lewis did not stint his praise of Williams. He called the cycle 'among the two or three most valuable books of verse produced in the century', and declared that in certain poems Williams had produced 'word music equalled by only two or three in this century and surpassed by none'.

Yet only a small public bought *Arthurian Torso*, and both it and Williams's two *Taliessin* volumes soon went out of print, to reappear only sporadically at the discretion of the publishers. Williams had left his mark on contemporary poets – one critic, George Every, has cited

Norman Nicholson, W. H. Auden, Sidney Keyes, John Heath-Stubbs and Anne Ridler as those who bear Williams's mark to a greater or lesser extent – but his fame dwindled rather than increased in the years immediately following his death, and Lewis's energetic praise perhaps did as much harm as good. Certainly some critics were irritated by it. Kenneth Allott wrote in *The Penguin Book of Contemporary Verse* (1950) that he considered Lewis's estimate of the importance of Williams's poetry to be 'wildly off the mark', adding: 'Mr Lewis has in my opinion been hypnotised by his memories of the man, and by his conviction of the importance and wisdom of the things Williams had to say, into imagining that they are said (and happily) in the poems.' He concluded by judging the poems to be 'a literary oddity of great interest'. F. R. Leavis was even less enthusiastic; in *The Common Pursuit* (1952) he declared that Williams 'hadn't begun to be a poet'. And even David Jones, who was largely sympathetic to Williams's poetry and whose own work bore certain resemblances to it, judged of the *Taliessin* cycle: 'Somehow, somewhere, between content and form, concept and image, sign and what is signified, a sense of the contemporary escapes.'

Certainly Williams's work no longer had any great appeal in Oxford. A number of undergraduates attended Lewis's lectures on *Taliessin* when they were delivered in the autumn of 1945 (it was these lectures which went to make up Lewis's contribution to *Arthurian Torso*) but they were soon succeeded at the University by other young men and women many of whom had never heard of Williams. Moreover, the apparent religious revival at Oxford in the forties was now seen to have been largely a wartime phenomenon. The religious societies, including the Socratic Club, continued to exist; but now, as one historian of the University has remarked, 'they attracted only a few men of intellectual distinction, and served as a refuge for the shy and sensitive', while the vast majority of undergraduates and dons maintained towards Christianity an attitude of incurious tolerance.

The Inklings continued to meet. Their Thursday routine had not changed outwardly. 'I can see it now,' recalled John Wain; 'the electric fire pumping heat into the dank air' (coal fires were no longer lit in most colleges), 'the faded screen that broke some of the keener draughts, the enamel beer-jug on the table, the well-worn sofa and armchairs, and the men drifting in (those from distant colleges would be later), leaving overcoats and hats in any corner and coming over to warm their hands before finding a chair.' Yet things were not quite the same.

As he approached the end of *The Lord of the Rings*, Tolkien's pace of work slowed almost to a standstill. Moreoever, after October 1947 he did not read any more of the story to the Inklings. Whether it was that Hugo Dyson's objections had finally offended him into silence, or

225

simply that he was now progressing so slowly as to make it impossible to achieve any continuity with the readings, he did not bring the final chapters with him on Thursday nights. This, together with the fact that Lewis no longer read any major part of his own 'work in progress' to the Inklings (the Narnia stories were never read aloud to the group) meant that Thursday nights now depended chiefly on conversation. Occasionally somebody would produce a poem, either his own or someone else's, and there would be a discussion about it; and sometimes Lewis would take Amanda Ros's eccentric novel *Irene Iddesleigh* from the shelves and set a competition to see who could read the longest passage without breaking into helpless laughter. But for much of the time talk was the staple diet. This meant that the success of the evening was rather less certain, depending entirely on the mood of those present. 'A very pleasant meeting,' Warnie Lewis wrote in his diary one Thursday in November 1947. 'We talked of Bishop Barnes, of the extraordinary difficulty of interesting the uneducated indifferent in religion: savage and primitive man and the common confusion between them: and how far pagan mythology was a substitute for theology.' But on another Thursday not very long afterwards, 'A very poor Inklings in Merton this evening. J. was worn out with examining, Tollers had a bad cold, Chris was moody: and the talk was slack and halting. We talked of philology, various ways of saying "farewell", and of the inexplicable problem of why some children are allowed to die in infancy. Home by midnight.'

The end came almost imperceptibly, and for no apparent reason. The last Thursday Inklings to be recorded in Warnie Lewis's diary was on 20 October 1949, when there was a 'ham supper' in his brother's rooms. The next Thursday, 'No one turned up after dinner, which was just as well, as J. has a bad cold and wanted to go to bed early.' And the week after that: 'No Inklings tonight, so dined at home.' So vanished the Thursday Inklings. 'The best of them,' said John Wain, 'were as good as anything I shall live to see.'

*

Tuesdays at the Bird and Baby continued, but that was not quite the same thing, and the word 'Inklings' no longer appeared in Warnie Lewis's diary.

Later in 1949 Tolkien finished *The Lord of the Rings*, and he immediately passed the complete typescript to Lewis, who read it all through and wrote an enthusiastic critique. He told Tolkien that in its mounting levels of grandeur and terror it was 'almost unequalled in the whole range of narrative art'. But his remarks were not without censure. 'There are many passages I could wish you had written otherwise or omitted altogether,' he said. 'If I include none of my adverse criticisms in this letter that is because you have heard and rejected most of them already (*rejected* is perhaps too mild a word for your reaction on at least one occasion!).'

After Lewis had finished reading the typescript, he passed it to his brother. Warnie took three weeks to read it and then wrote in his diary: 'Golly, what a book! The inexhaustible fertility of the man's imagination amazes me. A great book of its kind, and in my opinion ahead of anything that Eddison did.'

The Inklings naturally hoped that, now that the twelve years' labour of writing *The Lord of the Rings* was over, the book would soon get into print. Gervase Mathew, 'the universal Aunt', suggested to a friend and fellow Catholic, Milton Waldman of the publishing house of Collins, that he should read the manuscript. Waldman did so, and was enthusiastic; but the resulting negotiations between Tolkien, Collins, and the publishers of *The Hobbit* (Allen & Unwin) became so confused that for a long time nothing definite happened towards publication.

In the meanwhile, Lewis was hard at work on his 'Narnia' stories. *The Lion, the Witch and the Wardrobe* was quickly snapped up by a publisher, and long before it had reached the bookshops Lewis had written three more stories in the series, *Prince Caspian*, *The Voyage of the Dawn Treader*, and *The Horse and his Boy*. All three were finished in less than a year, and *The Silver Chair* followed soon afterwards. A sixth, *The Magician's Nephew*, was virtually completed by the autumn of 1951, and in March 1953 Lewis told his publisher that he had written the seventh and final book in the series, *The Last Battle*. The Narnia stories were not, of course, published with quite such speed as they were written, and were issued at a more sedate pace; nevertheless Lewis was soon being reckoned among the most prolific and respected writers of children's fiction.

The Narnia series was rather uneven in quality. Lewis began to write the first two books with little forethought, and with nothing like the elaborately prepared background upon which Tolkien had been able to draw for *The Hobbit* and *The Lord of the Rings*. As a result, the earlier Narnia stories largely lacked that special quality of atmosphere which Lewis himself declared was such a vital ingredient of stories. They showed signs, too, of hasty writing, and had little of the careful pacing of Tolkien's work; for Lewis threw in any incident or colouring that struck his fancy. Yet by the time he wrote the third story, *The Voyage of the Dawn Treader*, he had developed something like Tolkien's sense of decorum, while the very existence of the first two Narnia books gave him a certain degree of 'history' to draw upon. In the four remaining stories he did full justice to his imagination, and produced some of his best and most moving work, drawing not just on the traditions of children's literature but enriching his writing from such 'adult' sources as Plato and Dante, and infusing the whole with his own deeply-held Christian beliefs.

But Tolkien's views on the Narnia books continued to be as unfavourable as when he had listened to the opening chapters of *The Lion, the Witch and the Wardrobe*. In 1964 he wrote to an admirer of his own books: 'It is sad that "Narnia" and all that part of C. S. L.'s work should remain outside the range of my sympathy.'

*

By 1946 Lewis had been a Fellow of Magdalen College for twenty-one years. It was not unnatural to regard him as a strong candidate for a professorship. Indeed early in 1945 Tolkien told Christopher: 'Five years ago my ambition was to get C. S. L. and myself into the two Merton chairs. It would be marvellous to be both in the same college.' He was referring to the Professorship of English Language and Literature and the Professorship of English Literature at Oxford, which are both attached to Merton College. Half of this ambition was gratified later the same year when Tolkien went to Merton as the holder of one of the two professorships, and there was a chance that the other half could be achieved when, the next year, the retirement was announced of David Nichol Smith, the then Professor of English Literature. Moreover, as one of the seven persons responsible for electing the new professor, Tolkien was theoretically in a position to help to bring it about. But he did not give his support exclusively to Lewis's candidature, and he suggested to David Cecil that he too should put in his name. He wrote to his publisher Sir Stanley Unwin: 'We are about to elect another Merton professor (of modern literature). It ought to be C. S. Lewis, or perhaps Lord Devid Cecil, but one never knows.'

It would in fact be groundless to suppose that Lewis's failure to be elected was due to lack of support from Tolkien. His chances were poor at the outset. The widespread antipathy of many senior members of the University to such books as *The Screwtape Letters* had not been modified by Lewis's openly contemptuous attitude towards much of the academic work done in Oxford, and in particular his dislike (strongly shared by Tolkien) of specialised 'research' degrees, which he regarded as a very poor substitute for wide knowledge in the subject. Lewis liked to remark that there were three categories at Oxford: the literate, the illiterate, and the B. Litt-erate, and he preferred the first two. This attitude 'may well' (said W. W. Robson, another member of the English Faculty) 'have cost him a professorship'. Moreover, the board of electors responsible for choosing the new professor included, besides Tolkien, three particularly severe stalwarts of the English School, H. W. Garrod, C. H. Wilkinson and Helen Darbishire, none of whom is likely to have approved of the popular nature of many of Lewis's books. It was presumably because he realised how hopeless were Lewis's chances that Tolkien supported David Cecil. In the event both Lewis and Cecil were passed over, and the chair was given to Lewis's former tutor F. P. Wilson.

Shortly afterwards, Cecil was elected Goldsmiths' Professor of English Literature. But Lewis remained without a chair. Then in 1951 his friends put up his name for the Professorship of Poetry, which had again fallen vacant. This time the other candidates were C. Day Lewis and Edmund Blunden, but Blunden stood down before the election. Lewis's friends campaigned energetically on his behalf. Warnie Lewis recorded of a Tuesday morning at the Bird and Baby: 'Present, Hugo Dyson, Colin Hardie, Dundas-Grant, Humphrey Havard, David Cecil, J. and I. Hugo, who has been canvassing for J. in the poetry chair, was at his most effervescent ("If they offer you sherry, you're done, they won't vote for you: I had lots of sherry").' And on Thursday 8 February 1951: 'While we were waiting to dine at the Royal Oxford – Barfield, Humphrey, David, J. A. W. Bennett, J. and I – came the bad news that J. had been defeated by C. Day Lewis for the Poetry Chair, by 194 votes to 173. J. took it astonishingly well, much better than his backers. Hugo told me that one elector whom he canvassed announced his intention of voting for C. D. L. on the ground that J. had written *Screwtape*!' Ironically, Day Lewis's chief backer in the election, Enid Starkie, had put up his name on the same grounds that Jack Lewis had used in 1938 when proposing Adam Fox for the poetry chair: 'We must have a practising poet'.

Neither of the two professors of English Literature now holding office, F. P. Wilson and David Cecil, shared the views so energetically held by Lewis and Tolkien in the nineteen-thirties that Victorian literature should be excluded from compulsory examination papers in the English School so as to leave room for Anglo-Saxon and medieval studies; and at about this time they set up a committee, which also included Humphry House and Helen Gardner, to make recommendations about possible changes in the syllabus. As Professor of English Language and Literature, Tolkien was an inevitable choice to be a fifth member of the committee, and he was eventually persuaded by his colleagues on it that the time had come to restore Victorian literature to the syllabus, and indeed to extend the period of study into the twentieth century. This was what the committee recommended to the full Faculty in their report.

Lewis was still passionately devoted to the syllabus that he and Tolkien had created. He was now deeply upset that Tolkien had deserted their cause. 'He at least should have supported me,' he told Roger Lancelyn Green. But he did not give in so easily. Before the Faculty meeting which was to vote on the report, he campaigned energetically; and at the meeting he made an impassioned speech championing the present syllabus and opposing any changes. He achieved his aim, for the proposals were voted down for the time being, despite opposition led by David Cecil, who was fervently in favour of restoring the nineteenth century to the syllabus. Moreover, among those who voted against them was Tolkien, for Lewis had persuaded him to change his mind; so the Faculty was presented with the spectacle of Tolkien voting in the full meeting against proposals which he himself had helped to draft in committee. Lewis had not lost his old power of marshalling his friends.

*

In 1954 Cambridge University advertised a new Professorship of Medieval and Renaissance English. There could be few scholars as well qualified for the post as Lewis, for besides *The Allegory of Love* his academic reputation rested largely on his Oxford lectures which introduced undergraduates to the intellectual background of medieval and Renaissance writings. He had also just finished a lengthy study of sixteenth-century poetry and prose for the *Oxford History of English Literature* series, and his 700-page book on the subject, with its brilliant introductory summary of the period, was as one reviewer remarked a 'triumphant refutation' of the notion that his popular books had been a distraction from his academic work. Helen Gardner declared in the *New Statesman* that the book 'is continuously enjoyable, provocative and stimulating, yet satisfying', and concluded that it would remain a standard work of reference for some time. Donald Davie called it 'far and away the best piece of orthodox literary history that has appeared for many a long year' (though he remarked that almost all the judgements in the book were unsympathetic to modern taste). A. L. Rowse called the book 'magnificent', and said that it showed 'such intellectual vitality, such sweep and imagination, such magnanimity'. John Wain declared that Lewis wrote 'now as always, as if inviting us to a feast', and I. A. Shapiro writing in the *Birmingham Post* asked: 'Can Oxford really afford to let him migrate to Cambridge?'

For, to the accompaniment of this chorus of praise, Lewis was leaving Oxford, having accepted the Cambridge chair. He had not taken the decision lightly. His admirers at Cambridge made it clear that they wanted him for the new professorship, particularly in the hope that he would be a counterblast to the influence of F. R. Leavis. Basil Willey, the Professor of English Literature, tried to move him by saying, 'Come over into Macedonia and help us!' But Lewis took a lot of persuading, and it was not until his Oxford friends (including Tolkien) had convinced him that it would be for the best that he accepted.[1] Even so, he had no wish to leave his Oxford house, and Cambridge agreed that it would be acceptable if he returned to the Kilns for long weekends during term, as well as living there during the vacation.

On Thursday 9 December 1954 the English Faculty at Oxford gave a farewell dinner for Lewis in Merton. The company included Warnie Lewis, Tolkien, Christopher Tolkien, Hugo Dyson, David Cecil and 'Humphrey' Havard. Shortly afterwards, Lewis left the rooms in Magdalen which he had occupied for very nearly thirty years, and settled in at Cambridge, where he was made a Fellow (appropriately) of Magdalene College. He was enthusiastic about his new home. 'Many of my colleagues are Christians,' he said, 'more than was the case in my old College.' Because of this he had soon named Magdalene 'the penitent', as compared to its impenitent Oxford namesake. 'My rooms are comfortable, and Cambridge, unlike Oxford, is still a country town, with a farming atmosphere about it,' he reported. 'My new College is smaller, softer, more gracious than my old. The only danger is lest I grow too comfortable and over-ripe.' Nor did he lose touch with his Oxford friends. The Bird and Baby meetings continued, though they were now moved to Monday so as to fit his timetable; and the custom was established that after the lunchtime beer, and perhaps a snack at the Trout at Godstow, Havard and one or two of the others would drive with him to Oxford station and see him off for his week in Cambridge, sitting in the train with him and talking until the whistle blew. Occasionally they would take him out into the country after their visit to the Trout, to pick up the Cambridge train at the wayside station of Islip; and sometimes they would come to Cambridge with him, dining in Magdalene before a long evening of conversation, and sleeping in the college guest rooms.

Tolkien was not among them on these occasions. Though he often

---

[1] The detailed history of the Cambridge election is rather complicated. There were two Oxford men on the Cambridge board of electors, Tolkien and F. P. Wilson. It appears that initially Lewis was regarded as the obvious choice, and Tolkien was asked to sound him out. He presumably reported that Lewis was unwilling to leave Oxford, for on 18 May 1954 Helen Gardner was offered the chair. She was uncertain whether to accept, having just been elected to a readership at Oxford. Meanwhile Lewis apparently heard that she was being considered, and this seems to have moved him to change his mind, for rumour reached her that he was now prepared to accept. Hearing this, she declined the chair, and he was elected.

appeared in the Bird and Baby his feelings were, by the mid-nineteen-fifties, more cool towards Lewis than they had once been. Lewis knew it to be so, and once, walking away from the Bird and Baby, he asked Christopher Tolkien (who was now teaching in the University) why his father's manner had altered. Christopher was unwilling to try and give an answer.

The arrival of Charles Williams had perhaps begun it. 'We saw less and less of one another after he came under the dominant influence of Charles Williams,' Tolkien wrote of Lewis in 1964. Lewis's continuing lack of sympathy towards Tolkien's Catholicism, together with his almost vulgar level of success as what Tolkien once called 'Everyman's Theologian,' had possibly hardened it. Then came 'Narnia', which did not help; though when *The Lord of the Rings* was eventually published in 1954 and 1955 Tolkien's reputation as a storyteller rose to a height that certainly equalled Lewis's and eventually surpassed it. Moreover Lewis did everything he could to contribute to the success of *The Lord of the Rings*, writing a note of praise for the 'blurb', and contributing richly enthusiastic reviews to *Time & Tide*. So it might be true to say that none of these things, by themselves, were the cause of the friendship's decay – or rather, of the cooling in Tolkien's feelings, for Lewis behaved as warmly and magnanimously towards Tolkien as he had ever done. It was in part perhaps the complex nature of Tolkien's emotions and affections. And if external causes are still sought, few events in the nineteen-fifties upset Tolkien as much as Lewis's marriage.

2
Till We Have Faces

Mrs Moore died in January 1951, aged nearly eighty. Always a demanding woman, during the last years of her life she became tyrannical, forbidding Lewis to light a fire in his study at the Kilns so as to save fuel, engendering quarrels among the maids, and, as Warnie Lewis described it in his diary, 'going mad through trying to live on hate instead of love'. In 1944 she had a stroke, and thereafter she kept to her bed, but not until April 1950 was her condition sufficiently poor for her to be removed to a nursing home. Jack visited her every day. 'She is in no pain but her mind has almost completely gone,' he said. 'What traces of it remain seem gentler and more placid than I have known for years.' When the winter was at its most severe she caught influenza and died.

'So ends the mysterious self-imposed tyranny in which J. has lived for at least thirty years,' Warnie wrote in his diary. And of life at the Kilns without Mrs Moore he declared, 'Gosh, how I am loving it all!' Even Jack was obliged to admit that life was easier. 'I specially need your prayers,' he wrote to Sister Penelope at Wantage, 'because I am (like the pilgrim in Bunyan) travelling across "a plain called Ease". Everything without, and many things within, are marvellously well at present.' And in the autumn of the year following Mrs Moore's death he told Arthur Greeves that he had just passed through 'what has perhaps been the happiest year of my life'.

A few months before Mrs Moore was taken into the nursing home there came, among Lewis's invariably large mail from readers of his books, a letter from a Mrs Joy Gresham who lived in the neighbourhood of New York. 'Just another American fan,' remarked Warnie, 'with however the difference that she stood out from the rut by her amusing and well-written letters, and soon J. and she had become "pen-friends".' In 1952 she told Lewis that she was coming to England for a time, and he invited her to Oxford.

*

233

Joy Davidman was born in New York City in 1915. Her parents were Jews who had come to America from eastern Europe in their childhood, and her mother brought her up on tales of Jewish village life in the Ukraine, a life where more than six hundred ritual laws governed daily conduct, and religion was of the letter rather than the spirit. Her father and mother had abandoned Judaism; Joy declared herself an atheist at the age of eight, after reading H. G. Wells's *Outline of History*. 'In a few years', she recalled, 'I had rejected all morality as a pipe dream. If life had no meaning, what was there to live for except pleasure? Luckily for me, my preferred pleasure happened to be reading, or I shouldn't have been able to stay out of hot water as well as I did.'

If she had any philosophy in her childhood, it was a belief in American prosperity. But that faith was destroyed by the Depression, and by 1930 she believed in nothing. 'Men, I said, are only apes. Love, art, and altruism are only sex. The universe is only matter. Matter is only energy. I forget what I said energy was only.' Yet she was also a poet, and in her verse she asked whether life was really no more than just a matter of satisfying one's appetites:

> Come now all Americans
> kiss and accept your city, the harsh mother,
> New York, the clamor, the sweat, the heart of brown land.

> This is New York,
> our city; a kind place to live in; bountiful – our city
> envied by the world and by the young in lonely places.
> We have the bright-lights, the bridges, the Yankee Stadium
> and if we are not contented then we should be
> and if we are discontented we do not know it,
> and anyhow it has always been this way.

She read eagerly: ghost stories, science fiction, the tales of George MacDonald and Lord Dunsany. She revelled in the supernatural. 'It interested me above all else,' she said. But she did not believe in it.

After school she went to Hunter College in New York and then to Columbia University where she received her M.A. in English Literature. She took a job teaching English in New York high schools, and she joined the Communist Party. 'All I knew was that capitalism wasn't working very well, war was imminent – and socialism promised to change all that. And for the first time in my life I was willing to be my brother's keeper. So I rushed round to a Party acquaintance and said I wanted to join.' She became an energetic worker for the Party, and she published a volume of poems entitled *Letter to a Comrade*.

> Now with me,
> bow and set your mouth against America
> which you will make fine and the treasure of its men,
> which you will give to the workers and those who turn land
>   over with the plough.
>
> There is no miracle of help
> fixed in the stars, there is no magic, no savior
> smiling in blatant ink on election posters;
> only the strength of men.

Yet there was a delicacy of imagery in her poetry too, and the volume won two awards. She gave up teaching to devote her time to writing, and her first novel, *Anya*, was published in 1940. It was based on her mother's childhood memories, and gave a vivid account of Jewish village life in the Ukraine during the late nineteenth century, as seen through the eyes of Anya, the shopkeeper's daughter who rejects the strict conventions of her people and goes in search of love, wherever she may find it. The book had something about it of D. H. Lawrence.

For a few months Joy Davidman had a job with Metro-Goldwyn-Mayer in Hollywood, as a junior scriptwriter. Then in 1942 she married a fellow Communist, William Lindsay Gresham. Born in 1909, in his time Bill Gresham had worked as office boy, copywriter, singer in Greenwich Village clubs, and reviewer for a New York newspaper. Brought up an agnostic, he toyed for some time with Unitarian theology, but later became an atheist and joined the Communist Party. In 1937 he went out to Spain to fight on the Communist side; he spent fifteen months there, never fired a shot, and came home in a state of mind so bad that shortly afterwards he tried to hang himself. Psychoanalysis restored him to some degree of self-confidence, but he became a heavy drinker. He managed, however, to hold down a series of editorial jobs on popular story-magazines. It was at this stage that his first marriage was ended by divorce and he married Joy Davidman.

They set up home in upstate New York, and two sons were born to them, David and Douglas. Neither Joy nor Bill Gresham now had much time or inclination for Party activities, though they still called themselves Communist and, out of habit, accepted Marxist philosophy. Meanwhile Joy's taste for books about the supernatural led her to *The Screwtape Letters* and *The Great Divorce*. 'These books stirred an unused part of my brain to momentary sluggish life,' she said. 'Of course, I thought, atheism was *true*; but I hadn't given quite enough attention to developing the proof of it. Someday, when the children were older, I'd work it out. Then I forgot the whole matter.'

235

Bill Gresham was still going through mental difficulties, and one day he rang Joy from his New York office to say he was having a nervous breakdown. He felt his mind going; he could not stay where he was and he could not bring himself to come home. Then he rang off. For hours, Joy tried frantically to find out what had happened to him. In the end she gave up and waited. 'I put the babies to sleep. For the first time in my life I felt helpless; for the first time my pride was forced to admit that I was not, after all, "the master of my fate" and "the captain of my soul". All my defences – the walls of arrogance and cocksureness and self-love behind which I had hid from God – went down momentarily. And God came in. There was a Person with me in the room, directly present to my consciousness – a Person so real that all my previous life was by comparison mere shadow play. I understood that God had always been there, and that, since childhood, I had been pouring half my energy into the task of keeping him out. My perception of God lasted perhaps half a minute. When it was over I found myself on my knees, praying. I think I must have been the world's most astonished atheist.'

When Bill Gresham finally came home, he accepted his wife's experience without questioning it, largely because he himself had become interested in the supernatural. Together they began to study the outlines of theology. Joy considered becoming a practising Jew of the 'Reformed' persuasion, but soon decided that she must accept Christianity. Then in the summer of 1948, Bill Gresham, frightened by his alchoholism, prayed for help to stop drinking. 'And my prayer was answered,' he wrote in 1951. 'Up until now I have never taken another drink.' This gave him the final spur to accepting Christianity, and he and Joy became Presbyterians.

They were both having some success as writers. Bill Gresham's first thriller, *Nightmare Alley*, was published in 1946. It sold well and was bought up for the cinema. Joy's second novel, *Weeping Bay* (dealing with the miseries of an impoverished community in Canada), came out in 1950 and was well reviewed. In 1951 the Greshams each contributed an account of their conversion to Christianity to a Protestant anthology. But their marriage continued to go through difficulties, and in 1952 Joy decided to travel to England, in the hope that some months of separation would help it. During her English trip, C. S. Lewis invited her to Oxford and gave a lunch party in her honour at Magdalen.

*

Warnie Lewis met her for the first time on that occasion. 'I was some little time in making up my mind about her,' he wrote in his diary. 'She proved to be a Jewess, or rather a Christian convert of Jewish race, medium height, good figure, horn rimmed specs., quite extraordinarily uninhibited.' At the Magdalen lunch 'she turned to me,' wrote Warnie, 'in the presence of three or four men, and asked in the most natural tone in the world, "Is there anywhere in this monastic establishment where a lady can relieve herself?" But her visit was a great success, and we had many merry days together; and when she left for home in January 1953, it was with common regrets, and a sincere hope that we would meet again.'

Lewis was astonished by her. 'Her mind was lithe and quick and muscular as a leopard,' he wrote of her. 'Passion, tenderness and pain were all equally unable to disarm it. It scented the first whiff of cant or slush; then sprang, and knocked you over before you knew what was happening. How many bubbles of mine she pricked! I soon learned not to talk rot to her unless I did it for the sheer pleasure of being exposed and laughed at.'

Joy went home to her husband in January 1953, but it quickly became apparent that the marriage was at an end. Allowing him to divorce her for desertion, she came back to England, bringing the two boys and setting up home in London. Thanks to financial help from her parents she was able to send the boys to a preparatory school in Surrey. Then, in the winter of 1953, she and her sons came to stay with the Lewises at the Kilns.

'Last week we entertained a lady from New York for four days, with her boys, aged nine and seven respectively,' Lewis wrote to a friend in December. 'Can you imagine two crusted old bachelors in such a situation? It however went swimmingly, though it was very, very exhausting; the energy of the American small boy is astonishing. This pair thought nothing of a four mile hike across broken country as an incident in a day of ceaseless activity, and when we took them up Magdalen tower, they said as soon as they got back to the ground, "Let's do it again!" Without being in the least priggish, they struck us as being amazingly adult by our standards and one could talk to them as one would to "grown-ups" – though the next moment they would be wrestling like puppies on the sitting room floor.' Lewis dedicated the Narnia story that was just about to be published, *The Horse and his Boy*, to the two boys.

Joy was writing another book, rather on the model of Lewis's Christian apologetics. With her Jewish origins in mind she chose as her subject an interpretation of the Ten Commandments in terms of contemporary life. The book, *Smoke on the Mountain*, was published in 1955 with a foreword by Lewis. Though it did not equal his brilliance it was the product of much thought and imagination, and it was enriched by her own experience of life.

In the first weeks of 1954 she helped Lewis move to Cambridge. 'Poor lamb,' she wrote to friends, 'he was suffering all the pangs and qualms of a new boy going to a formidable school – he went around muttering, "Oh, what a fool I am! I had a good home and I left!" and turning his mouth down at the corners most pathetical. He always makes his distresses into a joke, but of course there's a genuine grief in leaving a place like Magdalen after thirty years; rather like a divorce, I imagine. Even *I* feel I shall miss those cloisters after a mere dozen visits! The Cambridge college is nothing like so beautiful, though pleasant enough; and Lewis has just written to say that they only get *one* glass of port after dinner, instead of Magdalen's three! In spite of the move, he keeps on working as hard as usual; has finished his auto-biography – I've got the last chapters here now and must get my wits to work on criticism.' The autobiography was entitled, apparently without any intention of a double meaning, *Surprised by Joy*.

At Cambridge, Lewis marked his arrival with an inaugural lecture. Discussing his new title as Professor of Medieval and Renaissance Literature, he told his audience that 'the great divide' was not between those two supposed periods of history but somewhere between the early nineteenth century and the present day, between (as he believed) the greater part of civilised history and what he regarded as the 'post-Christian' mechanised society of the present day. 'That,' he declared, 'really is the greatest change in the history of Western Man.' He also alleged that there were still alive some specimens of the 'Old Western Culture' that had existed before this change, and that he himself was one such specimen. 'I read as a native texts that you must read as foreigners,' he told his audience. 'Where I fail as a critic, I may yet be useful as a specimen. I would even dare to go further. Speaking not only for myself but for all other Old Western men whom you may meet, I would say, use your specimens while you can. There are not going to be many more dinosaurs.'

In the summer of 1955 Joy Gresham (or Joy Davidman as she preferred to be known) moved to Oxford. She rented a house not far from the Kilns, in the Old High Street of Headington, and she began to see Lewis almost every day. Some time later, Warnie Lewis remarked in his diary: 'It was obvious what was going to happen.'

Yet the progress of the friendship was not without its difficulties. Warnie, who was certainly a little jealous of Joy's invasion of his brother's life, may have warned Jack about what he supposed to be her intentions, which (he remarked in his diary) 'were obvious from the outset'. Certainly there were stories of Lewis hiding upstairs and pretending to be out when he saw her coming up the drive. It was perhaps a case such as he described in *The Four Loves*: 'What is offered as Friendship on one side may be mistaken for Eros on the other, with painful and embarrassing results.' But if so, his feelings had apparently changed by the spring of 1956.

Early in that year the Home Office refused to renew Joy's permit to stay in Great Britain. With a home established and a school found for the boys, she was appalled at the prospect of having to return to America. There was, however, one method of securing her right to remain, and on 23 April 1956 she was married at the Oxford registry office to C. S. Lewis.

Two days after the ceremony, Lewis told Roger Lancelyn Green that the marriage was 'a pure matter of friendship and expediency'. Warnie wrote in his diary: 'J. assured me that Joy would continue to occupy her house as "Mrs Gresham", and that the marriage was a pure formality designed to give Joy the right to go on living in England.' Moreover, the marriage was largely kept secret – or at least was simply not mentioned to Lewis's friends, apart from Barfield.

Lewis had in no way compromised his principles. In his wartime broadcasts he had made the distinction between a purely civil marriage and the sacrament of the Church. 'There ought to be two distinct kinds of marriage,' he had said: 'one governed by the State with rules enforced on all citizens, the other governed by the Church with rules enforced by her on her own members. The distinction ought to be quite sharp, so that a man knows which couples are married in a Christian sense and which are not.' Clearly he now believed that he and Joy were *not* married in a Christian sense.

But it was not so simple. When Joy's sons were home for the holidays, Lewis could only manage to see much of her by spending long evenings at her house, often not leaving until a late hour; and Joy pointed out to him that her reputation with the neighbours was suffering as a result. Meanwhile he was no longer being so secretive about the marriage, and began to speak about it to one or two of his friends. He and Joy even discussed the possibility of her moving to the Kilns, for apart from other considerations she was suffering from acute rheumatism in the hip and would be glad of help with keeping house. Arrangements were made for the move. Then the rheumatism grew worse and she had to go into hospital for treatment. In hospital it was discovered that she was suffering from bone cancer.

'No one can mark the exact moment at which friendship becomes love,' Lewis wrote to one of his regular correspondents shortly after he had heard this news. In some ways he did not *want* to love this woman who was so near to death. He once said: ' "Don't put your goods in a leaky vessel. Don't spend too much on a house you may be turned out of" – there is no man alive who responds more naturally than I to such canny maxims. I am a safety-first creature. Of all arguments against love none makes so strong an appeal to my nature as "Careful! This might lead you to suffering!" ' Yet the days of talking about the marriage as a mere expediency were over, and Lewis and Joy determined that they must be married in the eyes of the Church. Warnie too had been won over. 'Never have I loved her more than since she was struck down,' he wrote in November 1956, shortly after the cancer had been diagnosed. 'Her pluck and cheerfulness are beyond priase, and she talks of the disease and its fluctuations as if she was describing the experiences of a friend of hers. God grant that she may recover.'

A church marriage was not so easy to arrange: Joy was, after all, divorced, and the Church of England, to which Lewis belonged, did not normally sanction remarriage. Official permission was refused. But Lewis had felt for many years that Christ's teachings seemed to forbid remarriage only to a guilty party in a divorce where adultery was concerned, and not to an innocent person.[1] And in *Smoke on the Mountain* Joy Davidman declared: 'There are marriages which *God* puts asunder, cases of danger to body and soul, cases where children must be saved at all costs from a destructive parent.' She implied that in such cases remarriage should be allowed. A priest was found who shared these views – he was a former pupil of Lewis's – and on 21 March 1957 he celebrated their marriage at Joy's bedside in hospital.

'One of the most painful days of my life,' Warnie wrote in his diary after the ceremony. 'At 11 a.m. we all gathered in Joy's room, and the marriage was celebrated. I found it heartrending, and especially Joy's eagerness for the pitiable consolation of dying under the same roof as J.' One reason for the ecclesiastical ceremony was that she did not want to die in hospital, and Lewis wished her to be married to him in the sight of God before he brought her home. 'She is to be moved here next week,' Warnie added, 'and will sleep in the common-room, with a resident hospital nurse installed. Sentence of death has been passed, and the end is only a matter of time.'

The priest who conducted the marriage ceremony also laid hands on Joy and prayed for her recovery. Lewis recorded Joy's physical state at this time: one femur was eaten through and the hip was partially destroyed, and the cancer had spread to her other leg and to the shoulder. She was moved to the Kilns. A few weeks later Lewis told Roger Lancelyn Green that, though her case was still considered to be terminal, she was sleeping well and had no pain. Moreover the cancerous

---

[1] See *Letters of C. S. Lewis*, p. 240, where he discusses this view; also the chapter on 'Christian Marriage' in *Mere Christianity*.

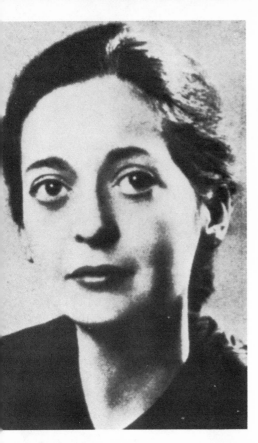

15 (a)   Joy Davidman as a young woman.

15 (b)   Jack and Joy Lewis in 1958.

16 C. S. Lewis.

spots in the bones had ceased to multiply. A little later, the existing spots were found to be healing, as was the fracture in the femur. In September 1957 she was able to move about in an invalid chair. By December she could walk with the aid of a stick, limping badly but otherwise quite strong. In the summer of 1958 she wrote to a friend, 'My case is definitely arrested for the time being.'

Lewis had never doubted the possibility of healing by faith, but he was also aware that the cure might have been the result of radiotherapy or hormone treatment. Only rarely did he use the word 'miraculous' when talking about Joy's recovery. But Warnie was in no doubt. 'Joy is busy in the kitchen cooking our dinner,' he wrote in his diary in November 1958. 'A recovery which was in the truest sense a miracle – admitted to be such by the doctors.'

And so it was that Jack Lewis could begin something he had never contemplated: a marriage, founded on love. At this time he was at work on a series of recorded lectures for America, which he later revised as *The Four Loves*. Writing about Eros or romantic love, he looked back to what he had said in *The Allegory of Love* in 1936, and remarked: 'Years ago when I wrote about medieval love-poetry and described its strange, half make-believe, "religion of love", I was blind enough to treat this as an almost purely literary phenomenon. I know better now.'

*

At the Kilns, Joy organised redecorations and renovations, which were certainly badly needed ('We were afraid to move the bookcases,' Lewis said, 'in case the walls fell down'). She managed to do a little digging in the garden, and she took to shooting pigeons in the wood, as well as firing a starting pistol to drive off trespassers, for she was certainly a determined woman. Lewis told his friends about these and other domestic incidents with great glee. He also gave a series of lunch parties in Magdalen so that they could meet her, for the marriage was now public knowledge. He made it clear to his friends how much the marriage meant to him. Walking across the quadrangle with Nevill Coghill and Peter Bayley he said, 'Do you know, I am experiencing what I thought would never be mine. I never thought I would have in my sixties the happiness that passed me by in my twenties.'[1]

His friends, however, responded with something a little less than enthusiasm. They could see that Joy was witty and clever; but several of them also thought that there was something 'hard' about her.

---

[1] There seems to be no conclusive evidence as to whether the marriage was consummated.

Moreover, Lewis (as it were) thrust her forward at them, almost demanding that they should like her. He, who had expected his men friends to leave their own marriages entirely on one side when they came to the Inklings, now assumed that they would all accept her as an equal without a moment's questioning.

He did not help matters by overpraising her, rather as he had overpraised Charles Williams. He spoke of her almost as if she were an angelic being; whereas in their sight she looked, it had to be admitted, physically unattractive. And to those who knew something of her background she seemed to represent everything that Lewis had strenuously opposed: she had been a Communist, she wrote *vers libre*, she had published a novel somewhat in the style of D. H. Lawrence, and she was that thing which Lewis had always attacked, a voluble woman. She was also, which did not recommend her to the more insular among them, American and Jewish. Had Charles Williams been there to observe, he would undoubtedly have remarked with delight that in choosing a wife for Lewis the Omnipotence had displayed its 'usual neat sardonic touch'. But to Tolkien the marriage seemed 'very strange'.

Tolkien, like many of Lewis's friends, had not heard of the marriage until some time after it took place. When he did learn of it, probably at second hand rather than from Lewis himself, he was profoundly injured by the fact that Lewis had concealed it from him. He was also distressed by the fact that Lewis had married a divorcee, for his own views on divorce and remarriage were much less liberal than Lewis's. In his eyes, Joy was still Mrs Gresham. But there was, perhaps, some other and deeper reason why he resented it. His friend Robert Murray noticed that when he talked about Lewis and the marriage it seemed almost as if he felt that some deep tie of friendship had been betrayed by it.

There was of course somebody else who might have responded to the marriage with the same resentment and even hostility that Tolkien showed. No one had been closer to Lewis or depended on his company so much as his brother Warnie. And indeed when it first became apparent that Joy's recovery would make it possible for her to establish a married life at the Kilns with Jack, Warnie's reactions were as might be expected. 'For almost twenty years,' he wrote, 'I had lived under a matriarchy at the Kilns. Then had followed a few years of unfettered male liberty. And now the Kilns was once more to have a mistress. Upon one thing my mind was absolutely made up, and that was that never again for any consideration would I submit to the domestic conditions which had prevailed under our *ancien régime* – and I sketched out provisional arrangements for an unobtrusive withdrawal from the home after the marriage, and the establishing of a home of my own in Eire. However, before I could even hint at my intention I discovered that it had never entered the heads of either Jack or Joy that I should do otherwise than continue to be one of the family at the Kilns; so obviously I had to give the new *régime* a trial before committing myself to my Irish plans. I found all my apprehensions permanently and swiftly dispelled. What Jack's marriage meant to me was that our home was enriched and enlivened by the presence of a witty, broad-minded, well-read, tolerant Christian whom I had rarely heard equalled as a conversationalist and whose company was a never ending source of enjoyment. And to crown all, one who had a deep interest in and a considerable knowledge of the seventeenth century, my own pet hobby horse. Indeed at the peak of her apparent recovery she had already started work on a life of Madame de Maintenon.'

Warnie was perhaps painting in this retrospective picture (it was written some years later) a rather rosier portrait of his feelings towards Joy and the marriage than was entirely the case at the time. One evening in March 1960, when Joy was away fetching one of the boys from school, he wrote laconically in his diary: 'J. spent the evening with me in the study. With the exception of the 15 minute walk back from St Mary's twice a month, this has been the only time I have spent with him since the end of March 1957 – just three years ago.'

But if Warnie did enjoy less of Jack's company than he would have wished, he had more than enough to occupy him, for between 1953 and 1962 he wrote and published six books on seventeenth-century France, books whose readability, wit and good sense almost equalled his brother's work; Tolkien, despite his lack of interest in French history in general, read them avidly and much admired them.[1] Warnie still indulged in bouts of heavy drinking, particularly during his annual holiday in Ireland; but this was probably as much the result of old habits as a reflection of his feelings about the marriage.

*

Was it, then, a 'real' marriage, or was Lewis merely imagining himself

---

[1] Warnie Lewis's books are: *The Splendid Century: some aspects of French life in the reign of Louis XIV* (Eyre & Spottiswoode, 1953); *The Sunset of the Splendid Century: the life and times of Louis Auguste de Bourbon, Duc de Maine, 1670–1736* (Eyre & Spottiswoode, 1955); *Assault on Olympus: The Rise of the House of Gramont between 1604 and 1678* (Andre Deutsch, 1958); *Louis XIV: An Informal Portrait* (Andre Deutsch, 1959); *The Scandalous Regent: A Life of Philippe, Duc d'Orleans, 1674–1723, and of his family* (Andre Deutsch, 1961); *Levantine Adventurer: the travels and missions of the Chevalier d'Arvieux, 1653–1697* (Andre Deutsch, 1962); and an edition of the *Memoirs of the Duc de Saint-Simon* (B. T. Batsford, 1964). The author's name is given as W. H. Lewis.

to be in love? Probably the question is meaningless, for there is usually some element of conscious choice in the business of 'being in love' – or so, at least, Lewis thought. 'When we meet someone beautiful and clever and sympathetic,' he wrote, 'of course we ought, in one sense, to admire and love these good qualities. But is it not very largely in our own choice whether this love shall, or shall not, turn into what we call "being in love"?'

On the other hand one can see much of Lewis's life as a series of masks or postures which he adopted, consciously or unconsciously, as his way of dealing with the world. He himself was certainly aware that he had to penetrate many layers before he could discover his real feelings. He once wrote a poem on this subject, which he called 'Posturing':

> Because of endless pride
> Reborn with endless error,
> Each hour I look aside
> Upon my secret mirror
> Trying all postures there
> To make my image fair.

The poem declared that only God's shadow glimpsed in the mirror could bring about the death of this self-love, and the birth of a real Love. Ironically the poem itself was a posture, a pastiche of the seventeenth-century metaphysical poets.

Indeed one can regard all Lewis's most successful literary work as pastiche. He chose a form from one source, an idea from another; he played at being (in turns) Bunyan, Chesterton, Tolkien, Williams, anybody he liked and admired. He was an impersonator, a mimic, a fine actor; but what lay at the heart of it all? Who was the real C. S. Lewis?

Again, the question is meaningless, or very nearly so. Lewis was what he was. Yet during this undeniably strange marriage which came at the close of his life, and which itself may have begun as yet another self-deception, there became visible what may have been a more 'real' Lewis than before. Certainly those who saw him at this period noticed a change in his manner. 'He seemed very different,' recalls Peter Bayley, 'much more muted, much more gentle and much more relaxed. Even his voice seemed quieter.'

Out of all this there came a book. It was written in 1955, and in many respects it was like Lewis's other fiction, being both a myth retold and a story written didactically with relevance to Christianity. Yet there was also something very different about it.

It was founded on the Cupid and Psyche myth, which had fascinated

244

Lewis since he first read it in Apuleius. But, though he derived the story from a classical source, he invented much that was entirely his own, most notably the central figure of the book. This is Orual, the king's daughter and sister to Psyche. Plain looking, rather masculine in her agility, but deeply loving to those who earn her affection, Orual has been supposed by some readers to be in part a portrait of Joy Davidman. It may have been; but was it not also a self-portrait of Lewis? 'There ought spiritually to be a man in every woman and a woman in every man,' he had said; and in the character of Orual he perhaps found, at last, an expression of his whole nature. Like Orual with her veil, a veil which both protects her and is a source of her reputation among her people, his manner, all his postures, had brought him success but had also, perhaps, hidden his inner nature not merely from others but from himself. It was only when his marriage somehow removed that veil that he found his true nature.

He wanted to call the book *Bareface*, but the publisher objected that this sounded like a Western; so he took a title from Orual's words in the closing chapter: 'Lightly men talk of saying what they mean. A glib saying. When the time comes to you at which you will be forced at last to utter the speech which has lain at the centre of your soul for years, which you have, all that time, idiot-like, been saying over and over again, you'll not talk about joy of words. I saw well why the gods do not speak to us openly, nor let us answer. Till that word can be dug out of us, why should they hear the babble that we think we mean? How can they meet us face to face till we have faces?'

Till We Have Faces is possibly Lewis's best book. He himself thought so, preferring it even to his earlier favourite, *Perelandra*. Ironically it had a poorer reception than any other story he had written.

*

Lewis's Cambridge friends had hoped that he would prove a real opponent to the leading critic in that university at the time, F. R. Leavis of Downing College, whose demand for social earnestness in literature and literary criticism had for many years greatly coloured the thinking of undergraduates. But they had left it too late. Lewis was, by his own admission, past his intellectual prime; he told Professor Basil Willey, when he was still hesitating to accept the Cambridge chair: 'We Lewises burn out quickly.' At Cambridge he made little attempt to set up in opposition to Leavis. He continued to lecture on the background to medieval and Renaissance literature, and published the lectures as *The Discarded Image*; but his audiences were rather smaller than they had been in Oxford, though just as enthusiastic. His only real attempt to answer Leavis was *An Experiment in Criticism*, which he published in

1961 and which suggested that we should 'scrutinise' not books and writers in the manner of Leavis and his followers, but should rather categorise the readers. It was ingenious, but too oblique to make any real impact. A few Cambridge undergraduates were impressed by it. 'Can it be that the tide *is* turning at last?' Lewis asked hopefully after receiving fan-letters from one or two of them; and he also remarked: 'Some of the younger men express great dissatisfaction at the rule of Downing.' But it was a vain hope. In truth Lewis, who had for years attacked (openly or by implication) Leavis's notions of 'culture', who regarded Leavis's mode of criticism as fundamentally wrong because of its subjective basis, and who had perhaps hoped ever since his essay 'Christianity and Literature' to help to establish a school of criticism based on objective (and ultimately Christian and traditional) criteria, was no longer a fighter. Indeed, when he actually met Leavis he found him to be 'quiet, charming and kindly'. There were one or two unhappy incidents when, at question-and-answer sessions after Lewis had addressed undergraduate societies, the more fervent disciples of Leavis would ask pointed questions about the 'social relevance' of Lewis's own works of fiction, and Lewis's temper might flare up. But he did not confuse the disciples with the master, and when it was suggested that he might like to accept the post of Chairman of the Faculty Board he not only refused but suggested that a good candidate might be Leavis.

At this time he made his peace too with another old adversary, or at least someone whom he had seen as an adversary. He and T. S. Eliot were both on the commission to revise the language of the Psalter, and they were soon on the friendliest terms. One day in the summer of 1959 Lewis and Joy had lunch with Eliot and his new wife Valerie. It was an event which the pre-war Lewis would have declared to be in every respect impossible.

*

Lewis was no longer in good health. During the period of Joy's recovery he too contracted a bone disease, and although it was not malignant and was soon brought under control he was obliged to live carefully. 'I wear a surgical belt and shall probably never be able to take a real walk again,' he told a friend, 'but it somehow doesn't worry me. The intriguing thing is that while I (for no discoverable reason) was losing the calcium from my bones, Joy, who needed it much more, was gaining it in hers. One dreams of a Charles Williams substitution! Well, never was gift more gladly given; but one must not be fanciful.'

As to Joy's condition, though she still limped badly ('the doctors, rather than the disease, shortened one leg'. Lewis said) she was otherwise in good health. The bones had rebuilt themselves firmly. 'Of course the sword of Damocles hangs over us,' Lewis often remarked; but there was much ground for optimism. Not long after her recovery they went for a brief holiday ('you might call it a belated honeymoon', he said) to Ireland, travelling by air so as to avoid the sudden jolts likely on board ship. For both of them it was their first flight. 'We found it – after our initial moment of terror – enchanting,' Lewis said. 'The cloud-scape seen from above is a new world of beauty – and then the rifts in the clouds through which one sees "a glimpse of that dark world where I was born" . . .' At home, Joy sometimes helped Lewis with his correspondence, especially to American readers of his books:

Dear Mary,

Perhaps you won't mind a letter from me this time, instead of Jack? He is having his first go at examining for the Cambridge tripos, and is fairly drowning in examination papers. He can't even get home for the next fortnight; our longest separation since our marriage, and we're both feeling it badly!

Of course we're both praying for you – and don't be too afraid, even if you turn out to need an operation. I've had three, and they were nothing like so bad as my fears.

Blessings,
Yours,
Joy Lewis.

Then in October 1959 an X-ray check revealed that cancerous spots were returning to many of her bones.

'This last check is the only one we approached without dread,' Lewis told Roger Lancelyn Green. 'Her health seemed so complete. It is like being recaptured by the Giant when you have passed every gate and are almost out of sight of his castle.'

There was still some hope. 'Meanwhile you have the waiting,' Lewis said. 'And while you wait, you still have to go on living – if only one could go underground, hibernate, sleep it out. And then the horrible by-products of anxiety: the incessant, circular movement of the thoughts, even the Pagan temptation to keep watch for irrational omens. And one prays; but mainly such prayers are themselves a form of anguish.' He asked Father Peter Milward: 'Can one without presumption ask for a *second* miracle?'

Joy began to experience slowly increasing amounts of pain; yet, as Warnie Lewis recorded in his diary, 'her courage and vitality were such that one was able to forget the grim fact for hours and even days at a time'. She was even determined that she and Jack should go on the holiday to Greece that they had planned to take with Roger Lancelyn

Green and his wife June; and though Joy was by that time suffering considerably the party left London Airport on 3 April 1960 and flew to Athens. During the following fortnight the Lewises did not join in the more strenuous expeditions (they were travelling as part of a 'package' tour), but they climbed the Acropolis, visited Mycenae and Rhodes, and went with the Lancelyn Greens in a private hired car on a day's expedition to the Gulf of Corinth. The Greek trip – Lewis's first journey abroad since the First World War – had been Joy's greatest remaining ambition, and on their return Lewis told Chad Walsh, 'She came back in a *nunc dimittis* frame of mind, having realized, beyond hope, her greatest, lifelong, this-worldly desire.'

Secondary cancer had now developed, and Joy had to go to hospital. During this time, Tolkien's wife Edith who was also in hospital met her and became friendly with her; this helped at least in some degree to reconcile Tolkien to Lewis's marriage. On 20 May Joy had to have her right breast removed. The operation went well, and a fortnight later she was sent home in good spirits, though she could now only move about in a wheelchair. She was still able, though, to make a few short expeditions. Warnie wheeled her about the garden so that she could inspect her plants, and late in June (after another spell in hospital following a severe relapse) she and Jack were even able to go out to dinner at Studley Priory hotel. 'It is incredible,' he recalled, 'how much happiness, even how much gaiety, we sometimes had together after all hope was gone.'

On the night of Tuesday 12 July Warnie took the usual evening cups of tea to Joy and Jack, and found them playing Scrabble. 'Before I dropped off to sleep,' he wrote in his diary, 'they sounded as if they were reading a play together.' ('How long, how tranquilly, how nourishingly, we talked together that last night!' Lewis later wrote). Next morning Warnie was woken at a quarter past six by Joy's screams: she had severe pains which seemed to be in the stomach but were really in the spine. Warnie woke Jack who called the doctor; he arrived before seven and drugged her, 'but even now she has tremendous resistance', Warnie wrote in his diary, 'and this and subsequent dopings did no more than make her drowsy'. After a nightmare morning of telephoning and argument with the hospital authorities, Lewis at last managed to arrange for the surgeon to give her a bed in his private ward at the Radcliffe Infirmary. She was taken there by ambulance, still conscious. Jack went with her.

Once during these days he had written a poem.

All this is flashy rhetoric about loving you.
I never had a selfless thought since I was born.

I am mercenary and self-seeking through and through:
I want God, you, all friends, merely to serve my turn.

Peace, re-assurance, pleasure, are the goals I seek,
I cannot crawl one inch outside my proper skin:
I talk of love – a scholar's parrot may talk Greek –
But, self-imprisoned, always end where I begin.

Only that now you have taught me (but how late) my lack.
I see the chasm. And everything you are was making
My heart into a bridge by which I might get back
From exile, and grow man. And now the bridge is breaking.

Late the same night, a few hours after Joy had been taken into hospital, Warnie wrote in his diary: 'When I was in my bath about 11.40 p.m. I heard J. come into the house and went out to meet him. Self: "What news?" J.: "She died about twenty minutes ago." '

*

'No one ever told me that grief felt so like fear. The same fluttering in the stomach, the same restlessness, the yawning. I keep on swallowing.
'There are moments, most unexpectedly, when something inside me tries to assure me that I don't really mind so much, not so very much, after all. Love is not the whole of a man's life. I was happy before I ever met her. I've plenty of what are called "resources". People get over these things. Come, I shan't do so badly. One is ashamed to listen to this voice but it seems for a little to be making out a good case. Then comes a sudden jab of red-hot memory and all this "commonsense" vanishes like an ant in the mouth of a furnace.'
Writing had always been Lewis's way of coping with life, and now he began to write once again, recording his thoughts in the days and weeks after Joy's death. This was not like the loss of Charles Williams, when there had been easy assurances of his supernatural presence. 'I had for some time a most vivid feeling of certainty about *his* continued life; even his enhanced life. I have begged to be given even one hundredth part of the same assurance. There is no answer. Only the locked door, the iron curtain, the vacuum, absolute zero. "Them as asks don't get." I was a fool to ask. For now, even if that assurance came, I should distrust it. I should think it a self-hypnosis induced by my own prayers.'
There was also the danger not of ceasing to believe in God, but of going back to his old belief in a cruel God, the belief that had haunted him in his early days before his conversion to Christianity. 'The

conclusion I dread is not "So there's no God after all", but "So this is what God's really like. Deceive yourself no longer." ' And again: 'Sooner or later I must face the question in plain language. What reason have we, except our own desperate wishes, to believe that God is, by any standard we can conceive, "good"? Doesn't all the *prima facie* evidence suggest exactly the opposite?'

The grief slowly eased. After a time his prayers ceased to be the same desperate demands for help. 'I have gradually been coming to feel that the door is no longer shut and bolted. Was it my own frantic need that slammed it in my face?' One night, quite unexpectedly, he thought he felt some sense of Joy's presence. He had said that even if such a thing did happen, he would regard it as self-hypnosis. But now, 'Easier said than done. It was quite incredibly unemotional. Just the impression of her *mind* momentarily facing my own.' Her mind, not her emotions. 'Didn't people dispute once whether the final vision of God was more an act of intelligence or of love? That is probably another of the nonsense questions.' And he remembered her last words in hospital, spoken not to him but to the chaplain. 'I am at peace with God', she had said. 'She smiled, but not at me. *Poi si torno all'eterna fontana.*'[1]

*

And after that there is really nothing more to be said. Lewis published these thoughts pseudonymously under the title *A Grief Observed*. He continued to work at Cambridge. He met his friends regularly in the Bird and Baby, reluctantly changing the meeting-place to the Lamb and Flag across the road when the Bird was disagreeably 'modernised'. He wrote *Letters to Malcolm: Chiefly on Prayer*, a wise and gentle book whose subject he had attempted before, but for which he only now found the form. Occasionally he saw Tolkien, who lived not very far away on the other side of Headington; but their meetings were rare. He contributed an essay to the *Festschrift* published in 1962 to mark Tolkien's seventieth birthday. In November of that year, Tolkien wrote him a letter (which does not survive) asking him whether he would be at the dinner to mark its publication. He replied to Tolkien, on a postcard:

> What a nice letter. I also like beer less than I did, tho' I have retained the taste for general talk. But I shan't be at the Festschrift dinner. I wear a catheter, live on a low protein diet, and go early to bed. I am, if not a lean, at least a slippered pantaloon. All the best. Yours, Jack.

[1] Dante of Beatrice: 'Then she turned to the eternal fountain.' *Paradiso*, XXXI, 93.

He was supposed to be having an operation on his prostate, but the surgeon would not perform it until his heart and kidneys were in a better condition; and after a time the plans for the operation were abandoned. In the summer of 1963 he had a heart attack, but recovered. 'I can't help feeling it was rather a pity I did survive,' he remarked. 'I mean, having glided so painlessly up to the Gate it seems hard to have it shut in one's face and know that the whole process must some day be gone through again, and perhaps less pleasantly. Poor Lazarus!'

Reluctantly, he gave up his Cambridge professorship, and kept to a ground-floor room at the Kilns. A young American, Walter Hooper, came to live in the house for a time as companion and secretary, but had to go home in September 1963 to wind up his affairs before returning (as he intended) on a permanent basis. By this time Warnie was away, drinking heavily on his annual Irish holiday, and for a long time failing to return despite appeals from Jack's friends. Jack was left in the care of the housekeeper and the gardener, not greatly happy in this near-solitude but certain that at least he would not have long to wait. He was, he told Arthur Greeves, 'quite comfortable and cheerful. The only real snag is that it looks as if you and I shall never meet again in this life.'

At last Warnie came home. 'The wheel had come full circle,' he said. 'Once again we were together in the little end room at home, shutting out from our talk the ever-present knowledge that the holidays were ending, and that a new term fraught with unknown possibilities awaited us both.'

On the afternoon of Friday 22 November 1963, not long after taking Jack his tea, Warnie heard a crash and found his brother lying unconscious at the foot of his bed. Jack Lewis died a few minutes later. He was not quite sixty-five. The news of his death was a little overshadowed by the fact that on the same day President Kennedy was assassinated.

The funeral was held four days later at Headington Quarry parish church. Among those in the congregation were Barfield, Havard and Tolkien. 'The coffin was carried out into the churchyard and set down,' recalled Peter Bayley, who was also there. 'It was a very cold, frosty morning, but the winter sun coming through the yews was brilliantly bright. One candle stood on the coffin. The flame burned steadily. Although out in the open air, it did not so much as flicker.'

*

Some years earlier, Havard had remarked to Lewis that the Inklings would come to an end if he was not there. Lewis replied that this was nonsense; and now, after his death, there was some attempt to keep up the meetings at the Lamb and Flag. But they were soon abandoned as being absurd without Lewis. As Havard said, 'He was the link who bound us all together.'

*

Warnie Lewis lived for another ten years, remaining for most of that time at the Kilns. He died in the same year as Tolkien, 1973.

*

Not long after Lewis's death, Tolkien began a letter to one of his children:

'I am sorry that I have not answered your letters sooner; but Jack Lewis's death on the 22nd has preoccupied me. It is also involving me in some correspondence, as many people still regard me as one of his intimates. Alas! that ceased to be some ten years ago. We were separated first by the sudden apparition of Charles Williams, and then by his marriage. But we owed each a great debt to the other, and that tie, with the deep affection that it begot, remained. He was a great man of whom the cold-blooded official obituaries have only scraped the surface.'

THE END

APPENDICES

APPENDIX A
Biographical notes

These are short outlines of the careers of those who often came to the Thursday evening gatherings at Magdalen. The list is by no means comprehensive, and does not include those who were occasional visitors. It also omits many who joined the Inklings at the Bird and Baby on Tuesdays.

OWEN BARFIELD   Born in 1898, the son of a London solicitor. His parents were 'free-thinkers' and (wrote Lewis in *Surprised by Joy*) 'he had hardly heard of Christianity itself until he went to school'. After attending Highgate School he served in the Royal Engineers, 1917–19, and then read English at Wadham College, Oxford, where he got a First Class. He later took a B. Litt. After leaving Oxford, Barfield worked for seven years as a freelance writer, holding various appointments on editorial staffs and contributing to the *New Statesman, London Mercury*, and other journals. In about 1922 he became interested in the teachings of Rudolf Steiner, and, together with Lewis's friend Cecil Harwood, joined the Anthroposophical Society. His book *Poetic Diction*, which in its original form was his B. Litt. thesis, was published in 1928. In 1931 lack of sufficient income from writing (he now had a wife and children to support) made him enter his father's legal firm while studying for the B.C.L. at Oxford. The work was hard and demanding, and his literary output became small until, nearly thirty years later, a gradual retirement from legal practice allowed him to write a number of books which are largely concerned with Anthroposophy: *Saving the Appearances* (1957), *Worlds Apart* (1963), and *Unancestral Voice* (1965), as well as *Speaker's Meaning* (1967) and *What Coleridge Thought* (1971). Interest in these books was aroused in several American universities, and Barfield has made a number of visits to the United States to give lectures. He lives in Kent.

J. A. W. BENNETT   Born in New Zealand in 1911. After taking his degree in Auckland, he read English at Merton College, Oxford, and became a Research Fellow at Queen's College, 1938–47. In 1947 he was elected Fellow and Tutor at Magdalen College. In 1964 he succeeded C. S. Lewis as Professor of Medieval and Renaissance Literature at Cambridge. He has now retired, and continues to live in Cambridge.

LORD DAVID CECIL   Born in 1902, the youngest son of the fourth Marquess of Salisbury. Educated at Eton and Christ Church. Became Fellow and Lecturer in Modern History at Wadham College in 1924, but left this post

255

in 1930 to devote himself to writing. He soon became known as a biographer and critic, his first published book being a life of Cowper, *The Stricken Deer*. This was followed by numerous biographical and literary studies. In 1939 he returned to Oxford as a Fellow of New College, where he taught English Literature. He was elected Goldsmiths' Professor of English at Oxford in 1948. He retired in 1969, and now lives in Dorset.

NEVILL COGHILL   Born in 1899, the younger son of an Anglo-Irish baronet. Educated at Haileybury. After war service, he read English at Exeter College, Oxford, and was elected a Fellow of that college in 1924. In 1957 he was elected Professor of English Literature at Oxford. He retired in 1966 and now lives near the Severn estuary. Outside Oxford, he is best known for his popularisation of Chaucer through his translation of the *Canterbury Tales* into modern English. At Oxford he was much admired for his theatrical productions; among the undergraduate actors who took part in these was Richard Burton.

COMMANDER JIM DUNDAS-GRANT   Always known to the Inklings as 'D-G'. Educated at Eton and served in the Navy during the First World War, remaining in the service after 1918. A member of the Catholic Church. In the Second World War he was given command of the Oxford University Naval Division, and he took up residence in Magdalen College, where he became friends with Lewis. After the war he and his wife were in charge of a residential house for Catholic students in Oxford. They now live in Surrey.

HUGO DYSON   Born in 1896, and christened Henry Victor Dyson Dyson. Educated at Brighton College and Sandhurst. Commissioned in the Royal West Kent regiment, and seriously wounded at Passchendaele. Came up to Exeter College, Oxford, in 1919 and read English. In 1924, after taking a B. Litt. at Oxford, he became Lecturer in English at Reading University, but often came to Oxford to lecture for the University Extension Courses and the W.E.A. In 1945 he was elected Fellow and Tutor in English Literature at Merton College, Oxford, where he remained until his retirement in 1963. He died in 1975.

ADAM FOX   Born in 1883. Educated at University College, Oxford. Was ordained before the First World War. He became a public school master, taught at Lancing, and from 1918 to 1924 was Warden of Radley. In 1929 he became a Fellow of Magdalen College and Dean of Divinity. In 1938 he was elected Professor of Poetry at Oxford. He left Oxford in 1942 to become a Canon of Westminster Abbey. His publications include the narrative poem *Old King Coel* (1937), *Plato for Pleasure* (1945), *Meet the Greek Testament* (1952), and *Dean Inge* (1960). He died in 1977.

COLIN HARDIE   Born in 1906. Educated at Edinburgh Academy and Balliol College, Oxford. From 1930 to 1933 he was Fellow and Classical Tutor of

Balliol. In 1933 he became Director of the British School at Rome. In 1936 he returned to Oxford as Fellow and Classical Tutor at Magdalen. He was Public Orator of the University from 1967 to 1973, and since 1971 has been Honorary Professor of Ancient Literature at the Royal Academy of Arts. He retired from his Oxford fellowship in 1973, and he and his wife now live in Sussex.

R. E. ('HUMPHREY') HAVARD Born in 1901, the son of an Anglican clergyman. He read Chemistry at Keble College, Oxford, then studied medicine and became a doctor. He was received into the Catholic Church when he was thirty. After working in Leeds, and marrying, he came to Oxford in 1934 and took over a medical practice with surgeries in Headington and St Giles. He now lives in the Isle of Wight.

CLIVE STAPLES ('JACK') LEWIS Born on 29 November 1898 in Belfast, the son of Albert Lewis, a solicitor specialising in police court work, and Flora Hamilton. He was at first educated at home, but after the death of his mother in 1908 he was sent to Wynyard School in Hertfordshire. He left Wynyard when the school was closed in 1910, and after spending one term at Campbell College, Belfast, was sent to Cherbourg preparatory school at Malvern. In 1913 he entered Malvern College, but left after the summer term of 1914. From then until 1917 he was taught privately by W. T. Kirkpatrick at his home at Great Bookham in Surrey. He won a scholarship to University College, Oxford, and began to study there during 1917, but was called up into the army in June. In September he was gazetted to the Third Battalion, Somerset Light Infantry, and after training in the West Country he embarked for France in November. In April 1918 he was wounded during the Battle of Arras, and was transported to hospital in London. After convalescence, he returned to Oxford in January 1919. In 1920 he took a First Class in Classical Moderations, and in 1922 another First in Literae Humaniores ('Greats'). He then studied English Language and Literature and took a First in this in 1923. In 1925 he was elected Fellow and Tutor in English at Magdalen College, where he remained until 1954. In that year he was elected Professor of Medieval and Renaissance English at Cambridge. He married Helen Joy Gresham (Davidman) in 1956. In the autumn of 1963 he retired from his Cambridge chair. He died on 22 November 1963, aged sixty-four.

WARREN HAMILTON ('WARNIE') LEWIS Born in 1895, and, like his younger brother C. S. Lewis, was at first educated at home. He later attended Wynyard School and Malvern College. He won a prize cadetship to Sandhurst in 1914, then became an officer in the Royal Army Service Corps, serving in France. He remained in the army after the war, serving largely in England but also in the Far East, and holding the rank of Captain. In 1932 he retired from the army and came to live in Oxford with his brother, depending on his army pension and on small private means for his income. In 1939 he returned to the R.A.S.C. and served for some months in France with the rank of Major, but left the army again in 1940. In his later years he published a number of

257

books of seventeenth-century French history and biography. After his brother's death in 1963 he continued to live in Oxford, chiefly at the Kilns. He himself died in 1973.

GERVASE MATHEW   Born in 1905. Educated privately, then at Balliol College, Oxford. Joined the Catholic order of Dominicans in 1928 and was ordained priest in 1934, residing at Blackfriars in Oxford for the rest of his life. He travelled widely, often taking part in archaeological surveys in Africa and the Middle East. In Oxford he lectured for the Modern History, Theology, and English Faculties, and published books on Byzantium and medieval England. He died in 1976.

R. B. MCCALLUM   Born in 1898. Read Modern History at Worcester College, Oxford, and was elected to a Fellowship at Pembroke College, where he remained until his retirement in 1967. He was elected Master of Pembroke in 1955. He died in 1973.

C. E. ('TOM') STEVENS   Born in 1905. Educated at Winchester, where he acquired the nickname 'Tom Brown Stevens' – his real Christian names were Courteney Edward – and at Oriel College, Oxford. Became Fellow and Ancient History Tutor at Magdalen College in 1934. He died in 1976.

CHRISTOPHER TOLKIEN   Born in 1924, the third son of J. R. R. Tolkien. Educated at the Dragon School, Oxford, and at the Oratory School. During the Second World War he served as a pilot in the Royal Air Force. After the war he read English at Trinity College, Oxford. Later he lectured at Oxford in Anglo-Saxon, Middle English and Old Norse, and was elected a Fellow of New College. In 1975 he resigned his Fellowship to devote his time to editing his father's unpublished works, and he prepared *The Silmarillion* for publication in 1977. He now lives in France.

JOHN RONALD REUEL TOLKIEN   Born on 3 January 1892 in Bloemfontein, Orange Free State, the son of Arthur Reuel Tolkien, a bank manager, and Mabel Suffield; both his parents were themselves born in Birmingham. His father died in 1896, while he and his mother, together with his younger brother Hilary, were visiting England on leave. In the years that followed he was at first educated at home by his mother; in 1900 he entered King Edward's School, Birmingham, where he remained until 1911 (with a short interval in which he attended another Birmingham school). His mother died in 1904. In 1911 he went up as an Exhibitioner to read Classics at Exeter College, Oxford. After taking a Second Class in Moderations in 1913 he read English Language and Literature, taking a First Class in this in 1915. In 1916 he married Edith Bratt. In 1915 he was commissioned in the Lancashire Fusiliers, and in 1916 he served, from July to November, in the Battle of the Somme. He was sent home from France suffering from 'trench fever', and continued to be ill for much of the time until the end of the war, though during this period he also served in various camps in England. In November

1918 he took up a job on the New English Dictionary at Oxford. His first son, John, was born in 1917; the second and third children, Michael and Christopher, were born in 1920 and 1924 respectively; a daughter, Priscilla, was born in 1929. In 1920 Tolkien was appointed Reader in English Language at Leeds University, and he worked there until 1925, when he was elected Professor of Anglo-Saxon at Oxford. He held this chair until 1945, when he became Professor of English Language and Literature, retiring from university work in 1959. In 1968 he and his wife moved to Bournemouth; Mrs Tolkien died in 1971, and Tolkien returned to Oxford and lived in Merton College. He was awarded the C.B.E. in 1972. He died on 2 September 1973, aged eighty-one.

JOHN WAIN Born in 1925 in Stoke-on-Trent. Educated at Newcastle-under-Lyme High School. Failed his medical test for the army because of poor eyesight and came up to Oxford in 1943 to read English at St John's College. Because of wartime arrangements, C. S. Lewis was his tutor. Got a First Class, then held a research fellowship at St John's. In 1947 he became Lecturer in English at Reading University, where he remained until 1955. His first book to achieve popular success was the novel *Hurry On Down* (1953), and this was followed by other novels, volumes of poetry, and criticism. He was elected Professor of Poetry at Oxford from 1973 to 1978. He lives in Oxford.

CHARLES WALTER STANSBY WILLIAMS Born on 20 September 1886, the son of Walter Williams, clerk, and Mary Wall. He was at first brought up in Holloway, north London, but in 1894 the family moved to St Albans. Charles was educated at St Albans Grammar School, to which he won a Junior County Scholarship. In 1901 he won an award to University College, London, and began to study there the following year; but in 1904 he was obliged to leave because of the lack of family funds. He began work in the Methodist New Connexion Bookroom in Holborn, and moved to the Oxford University Press in 1908. In 1917 he married Florence Conway. A son, Michael, was born in 1922. In 1939 Williams moved to Oxford, together with the staff of the Press. In 1943 Oxford University conferred upon him the honorary degree of M.A. He died on 15 May 1945, aged fifty-eight.

CHARLES WRENN Born in 1895. Educated at Queen's College, Oxford. Between 1917 and 1930 he lectured at Durham, Madras, Dacca, and Leeds. He returned to Oxford in 1930 as University Lecturer in Anglo-Saxon. In 1939 he was elected to a professorship at King's College, London. He returned to Oxford in 1946 to succeed J. R. R. Tolkien as Professor of Anglo-Saxon. He died in 1969.

APPENDIX B
Bibliography

The abbreviations in **bold type** are those used in the notes (Appendix C) which give the sources of quotations. All books were first published in London unless otherwise stated.

A   The principal writings of Lewis, Tolkien and Williams A highly selective list. For full bibliographical information see *Light on C. S. Lewis* (by Owen Barfield and others, edited by Jocelyn Gibb) (Geoffrey Bles, 1965); the present writer's *J. R. R. Tolkien: a biography* (Allen & Unwin, 1977); and *The Image of the City* (essays by Charles Williams, edited with an introduction and bibliography by Anne Ridler) (Oxford University Press, 1958).

C. S. LEWIS
Spirits in Bondage: A Cycle of Lyrics Heinemann, 1919 (as Clive Hamilton)
Dymer J. M. Dent, 1926 (as Clive Hamilton; reissued 1950 as by C. S. Lewis)
The Pilgrim's Regress: An Allegorical Apology for Christianity, Reason and Romanticism J. M. Dent, 1933; Sheed & Ward, 1935. 2nd edition, Geoffrey Bles, 1943
The Allegory of Love: A Study in Medieva. Tradition Oxford, Clarendon Press, 1936
Out of the Silent Planet John Lane the Bodley Head, 1938
Rehabilitations and other essays Oxford University Press, 1939
(with E. M. W. Tillyard) *The Personal Heresy: A Controversy* Oxford University Press, 1939
The Problem of Pain Geoffrey Bles, 1940
The Screwtape Letters Geoffrey Bles, 1942
A Preface to 'Paradise Lost' Oxford University Press, 1942
Broadcast Talks ('Right and Wrong as a Clue to the Meaning of the Universe' and 'What Christians Believe') Geoffrey Bles, 1942
Christian Behaviour: A Further Series of Broadcast Talks Geoffrey Bles, 1943
Perelandra John Lane the Bodley Head, 1943. Also published as *Voyage to Venus*, Pan Books, 1953
The Abolition of Man, or Reflections on Education with Special Reference to the Teaching of English in the Upper Forms of Schools Oxford University Press, 1943
Beyond Personality: the Christian Idea of God Geoffrey Bles, 1944
That Hideous Strength: a modern fairy-tale for grown-ups John Lane the Bodley Head, 1945. Abridged version, Pan Books, 1955.

The Great Divorce: A Dream Geoffrey Bles, 1946

Miracles: A Preliminary Study Geoffrey Bles, 1947. With revision of Chapter III, Fontana Books, 1960

(with A. O. Barfield, W. H. Lewis, Gervase Mathew, Dorothy Sayers and J. R. R. Tolkien) *Essays presented to Charles Williams* Oxford University Press, 1947 [**EPCW**]

Arthurian Torso [see under Charles Williams, 1948]

Transposition and Other Addresses Geoffrey Bles, 1949 (Published in America as *The Weight of Glory*)

The Lion, the Witch and the Wardrobe Geoffrey Bles, 1950

Prince Caspian: The Return to Narnia Geoffrey Bles, 1951

Mere Christianity (a revised and enlarged edition of *Broadcast Talks, Christian Behaviour*, and *Beyond Personality*) Geoffrey Bles, 1952

The Voyage of the 'Dawn Treader' Geoffrey Bles, 1952

The Silver Chair Geoffrey Bles, 1953

The Horse and His Boy Geoffrey Bles, 1954

English Literature in the Sixteenth Century, excluding Drama (The Oxford History of English Literature, Volume III) Oxford, Clarendon Press, 1954

The Magician's Nephew The Bodley Head, 1956

Surprised by Joy: the shape of my early life Geoffrey Bles, 1955 [**SBJ**]

The Last Battle The Bodley Head, 1956

Till We Have Faces: A Myth Retold Geoffrey Bles, 1956

Reflections on the Psalms Geoffrey Bles, 1958

The Four Loves Geoffrey Bles, 1960

Studies in Words Cambridge, Cambridge University Press, 1960

The World's Last Night and other essays New York, Harcourt, Brace & Co, 1960

A Grief Observed Faber & Faber, 1961 (as N. W. Clerk; reprinted 1964 as by C. S. Lewis)

An Experiment in Criticism Cambridge, Cambridge University Press, 1961

They Asked for a Paper: Papers and Addresses Geoffrey Bles, 1962

Letters to Malcolm: Chiefly on Prayer Geoffrey Bles, 1964

The Discarded Image: An Introduction to Medieval and Renaissance Literature Cambridge, Cambridge University Press, 1964

Poems (edited by Walter Hooper) Geoffrey Bles, 1964

Screwtape Proposes a Toast and Other Pieces Fontana Books, 1965

Studies in Medieval and Renaissance Literature (collected by Walter Hooper) Cambridge, Cambridge University Press, 1966

Letters of C. S. Lewis (edited with an introduction by W. H. Lewis) Geoffrey Bles, 1966 [**Letters**]

Of Other Worlds: essays and stories (edited by Walter Hooper) Geoffrey Bles, 1966

Christian Reflections (edited by Walter Hooper) Geoffrey Bles, 1967

Spenser's Images of Life (edited by Alistair Fowler) Cambridge, Cambridge University Press, 1967

Letters to an American Lady (edited by Clyde S. Kilby) Hodder & Stoughton, 1969

Narrative Poems (edited by Walter Hooper) Geoffrey Bles, 1969

Selected Literary Essays (edited by Walter Hooper) Cambridge, Cambridge University Press, 1969

Undeceptions: Essays on Theology and Ethics (edited by Walter Hooper) Geoffrey Bles, 1971 (Published in America as *God in the Dock*)

Fern-seed and Elephants, and other essays on Christianity (edited by Walter Hooper) Fontana Books, 1976

The Dark Tower and other stories (edited by Walter Hooper) Collins, 1977

(In preparation: an edition of C. S. Lewis's letters to Arthur Greeves, to be edited by Walter Hooper and published by Collins; see note in section D, below.)

J. R. R. TOLKIEN

A Middle English Vocabulary Oxford, Clarendon Press, 1922

(co-edition with E. V. Gordon) *Sir Gawain and the Green Knight* Oxford, Clarendon Press, 1925

'Ancrene Wisse and Hali Meiðhad', *Essays and Studies by members of the English Association*, Volume XIV, pp. 104–26 Oxford, Clarendon Press, 1929

'Beowulf: the Monsters and the Critics', *Proceedings of the British Academy*, 22 (1936), pp. 245–95 Oxford University Press, 1937

The Hobbit: or There and Back Again Allen & Unwin, 1937

Farmer Giles of Ham Allen & Unwin, 1949

'The Homecoming of Beorhtnoth Beorhthelm's Son', *Essays and Studies by members of the English Association*, New Series Volume VI, pp. 1–18 John Murray, 1953

The Fellowship of the Ring: being the first part of The Lord of the Rings Allen & Unwin, 1954

The Two Towers: being the second part of The Lord of the Rings Allen & Unwin, 1954

The Return of the King: being the third part of The Lord of the Rings Allen & Unwin, 1955

The Adventures of Tom Bombadil and other verses from The Red Book Allen & Unwin, 1962

Ancrene Wisse: the English Text of the Ancrene Riwle, edited from MS. Corpus Christi College Cambridge 402, Early English Text Society No. 249 Oxford University Press, 1962

Tree and Leaf Allen & Unwin, 1964

Smith of Wootton Major Allen & Unwin, 1967

Sir Gawain and the Green Knight, Pearl, and Sir Orfeo translated into modern English (edited by Christopher Tolkien) Allen & Unwin, 1975

The Father Christmas Letters (edited by Baillie Tolkien) Allen & Unwin, 1976

The Silmarillion (edited by Christopher Tolkien) Allen & Unwin, 1977

CHARLES WILLIAMS

The Silver Stair Herbert & Daniel, 1912

Poems of Conformity Oxford University Press, 1917

Divorce Oxford University Press, 1920

Windows of Night Oxford University Press, 1924

The Masque of the Manuscript Privately printed by Henderson & Spalding, 1927

A Myth of Shakespeare Oxford University Press, 1928

The Masque of Perusal Privately printed by Henderson & Spalding, 1929

War in Heaven Gollancz, 1930

Heroes and Kings The Sylvan Press, 1930

Poetry at Present Oxford, Clarendon Press, 1930

    (edited) *The Poems of Gerard Manley Hopkins* Oxford University Press, 1930

Many Dimensions Gollancz, 1931

Three Plays Oxford University Press, 1931

The Place of the Lion Gollancz, 1931

The Greater Trumps Gollancz, 1932

The English Poetic Mind Oxford, Clarendon Press, 1932

Shadows of Ecstasy Gollancz, 1933

Bacon Arthur Barker, 1933

Reason and Beauty in the Poetic Mind Oxford, Clarendon Press, 1933

James I Arthur Barker, 1934

Rochester Arthur Barker, 1935

    (edited) *The New Book of English Verse* Gollancz, 1935

Queen Elizabeth Duckworth, 1936

Thomas Cranmer of Canterbury Oxford University Press, 1936

Descent into Hell Faber & Faber, 1937

Henry VII Arthur Barker, 1937

He Came Down From Heaven Heinemann, 1938

Taliessin Through Logres Oxford University Press, 1938

Judgement at Chelmsford Oxford University Press, 1939

The Descent of the Dove: A Short History of the Holy Spirit in the Church Longmans, 1939

Witchcraft Faber & Faber, 1941

The Forgiveness of Sins Geoffrey Bles, 1942

The Figure of Beatrice: a study in Dante Faber & Faber, 1943

The Region of the Summer Stars Poetry (London) Editions, 1944

All Hallows' Eve Faber & Faber, 1945

The House of the Octopus Edinburgh House Press, 1945

Flecker of Dean Close Canterbury Press, 1946

Seed of Adam and other plays Oxford University Press, 1948

Arthurian Torso (containing 'The Figure of Arthur' (unfinished) by Charles Williams and 'Williams and the Arthuriad' by C. S. Lewis) Oxford University Press, 1948

The Image of the City and other essays (selected by Anne Ridler, with a critical introduction and bibliography) Oxford University Press, 1958

Collected Plays of Charles Williams (edited by John Heath-Stubbs) Oxford University Press, 1963

Taliessin Through Logres, The Region of the Summer Stars, and Arthurian Torso (qq.v. above) published in one volume by William B. Eerdmans, Grand Rapids, Michigan, 1974 (introduction by Mary McDermott Shideler)

B   *Biographical studies*
The following are the principal studies of the lives of Lewis, Tolkien and Williams:

Roger Lancelyn Green and Walter Hooper, *C. S. Lewis: a biography* Collins, 1974 [**Green & Hooper**]
Douglas Gilbert and Clyde S. Kilby, *C. S. Lewis: Images of His World* William B. Eerdmans, Grand Rapids, Michigan, 1973
Humphrey Carpenter, *J. R. R. Tolkien: a biography* Allen & Unwin, 1977
A. M. Hadfield, *An Introduction to Charles Williams* Robert Hale, 1959 [**Hadfield**]
Anne Ridler, critical introduction to *The Image of the City and other essays* by Charles Williams Oxford University Press, 1958

Memoirs of Charles Williams are sometimes published in the Newsletter of the Charles Williams Society. Inquiries should be addressed to the Editor at 13 Princess Road, London NW1.

C   *Other relevant books*
Light on C. S. Lewis (edited by Jocelyn Gibb, with contributions by Owen Barfield and others) Geoffrey Bles, 1965
John Wain, *Sprightly Running: Part of an Autobiography* Macmillan, 1963

D   *Unpublished material*
1 *C. S. Lewis* The two principal collections of letters and papers are in the Bodleian Library, Oxford, and the Wade Collection, Wheaton College, Wheaton, Illinois. Each of these libraries also possess photocopies of most of the other's holdings, so that the greater part of the material is accessible in each place. These are the principal items held in these institutions (some items are reserved, but the majority are available for public consultation):

The Lewis Papers The title generally given to eleven volumes of typescript, compiled by W. H. Lewis and actually titled 'Memoirs of the Lewis Family'. A transcript of letters, diaries, and other family papers covering the early history of the family and also giving a detailed account of the lives of Jack, Warnie, and their father up to 1930. The originals are in the Wade Collection. [**LP**]
Letters from C. S. Lewis to Arthur Greeves The originals are in the Wade Collection, and the Bodleian has photocopies. The letters are shortly to be published by Collins in an edition by Walter Hooper. [**CSL to Greeves**]
The Great War Correspondence between C. S. Lewis and Owen Barfield during the nineteen-twenties. The originals are in the Wade Collection, and the Bodleian has photocopies.
Letters from C. S. Lewis to W. H. Lewis The originals are in the Wade collection, and the Bodleian has photocopies. [**CSL to WHL**]

Several hundred other letters from C. S. Lewis to miscellaneous correspondents are available for consultation in both the Wade Collection and the

Bodleian. Because of this dual accessibility, I have not specified in my notes (Appendix C) which library houses the originals.

2 *W. H. Lewis* The diaries of Warnie Lewis [**WHL diary**] are housed in the Wade Collection, Wheaton College, Wheaton, Illinois. At the present time they are not available for public consultation. The Wade Collection also houses a typescript by Warnie Lewis entitled 'C. S. Lewis: A Biography', which is in effect his first draft for *Letters of C. S. Lewis*, but which contains substantially more biographical information about his brother than appears in the printed volume [**WHL biography of CSL**].

3 *J. R. R. Tolkien* The majority of Tolkien's unpublished papers are in the keeping of his Estate and are not available for public consultation. In this book, quotations from his letters (except those to Christopher Tolkien) have generally been taken from carbons retained by him or from first drafts which he retained.

Letters from J. R. R. Tolkien to Christopher Tolkien [**JRRT to CRT**]
The Ulsterior Motive An unpublished essay by Tolkien written in 1964, which originated as a critique of Lewis's *Letters to Malcolm* [**UM**]

4 *Charles Williams* The principal collections of unpublished papers relating to Williams are housed as follows:

Williams's letters to his wife, 1939 to 1945 Wade Collection, Wheaton College, Wheaton, Illinois. [**CW to MW**]
Williams's letters to Raymond Hunt Wade Collection. [**CW to RH**]
Williams's letters to Thelma Shuttleworth Bodleian. [**CW to TS**]

Williams's letters to Anne Ridler [**CW to AR**] are in the possession of Anne Ridler, and I am particularly grateful to her for allowing me to consult them.

APPENDIX C
Sources of quotations

The quotations used in the text are identified in this list by the number of the page on which they appear, and by the first few words quoted. When two or more quotations from the same source follow each other in a brief space, I have generally only used the first words of the first quotation for identification. Abbreviations refer to the Bibliography (Appendix B) where the full title of the work or source is given.

Except on rare occasions, I have not indicated elisions within quotations, and have omitted the row of dots customary in such circumstances.

In cases where a number of different editions of a work are available, I have given a reference to a chapter number or title rather than to a page number.

page 3   'My Life during . . .', LP iii, p. 80 ff.
page 4   'It was sea and islands . . .', SBJ chapter 1.
page 5   'Pure "Northernness" engulfed me', SBJ chapter 5. 'Not only does this persecution . . .', LP iv, p. 152.
page 6   'Please take me out of this . . .', LP iv, p. 152. 'Stop! What do you mean . . .', SBJ chapter 9.
page 7   'I have no *opinions* . . .', SBJ chapter 9. 'I had thought that you were . . .', LP v, p. 130. 'How one does want to read everything', CSL to Greeves, 15 February 1917.
page 8   'Those mystic parts . . .', LP v, p. 127. 'a great literary experience', *Letters*, p. 27. 'While admirably adapted . . .', LP v, p. 74. 'Lewis and Moore . . .', WHL diary, 16 February 1934. 'I don't think . . .', CSL to Greeves, 15 February 1917.
page 9   'hadn't got on at all well', WHL diary, 29 April 1950. 'to look after me . . .', LP vi, p. 45. 'the horribly smashed men . . .', SBJ chapter 12. 'What, brother, brother . . .', 'Dymer', *Narrative Poems*, p. 39.
page 10   'It is too cut off . . .' and 'At that moment . . .', SBJ chapter 12. 'the Beast', LP vii, p. 116. 'our hired house' and 'After lunch . . .', CSL to Greeves, 26 January 1919.
page 11   'He is as good . . .', *Letters*, p. 16. 'The hopeless business . . .', LP viii, p. 152. 'He has read more classics . . .' and 'He is a student . . .', LP v, p. 74.
page 12   'Jack's affair', Green & Hooper, p. 62. 'most of them vile', LP viii, p. 134. 'she was quite convinced . . .', LP vii, p. 284. 'I'm afraid I shall . . .', CSL to Greeves, 15 October 1918.
page 13   'it really made no difference . . .', Green & Hooper, p. 67. 'the exclusive subject . . .' and 'I do not blame D . . .', LP viii, p. 142.

page 14   'Minto's mares' nests', LP x, p. 231. 'the perpetual interruptions . . .' and 'This sounds as if . . .', LP x, p. 231. 'The atmosphere of the English school . . .', LP vii, p. 254. 'Very good stuff . . .', LP vii, p. 267.

page 15   'In spite of many . . .' and 'We were neither of us . . .', LP viii, pp. 74–5. 'Hige sceal . . .', *The Battle of Maldon*, 312–3. (The translation is taken from Tolkien's *Homecoming of Beorhtnoth*.)

page 16   'Everyone may allegorise . . .', *Narrative Poems*, p. 3. 'old, old, matriarchal dreadfulness', ibid. p. 32.

page 17   'Several Univ. people . . .', *Letters*, p. 87. 'beautiful beyond compare', ibid. p. 104. 'I am beginning to be rather disillusioned . . .', LP x, p. 75.

page 18   'He thinks of himself . . .', LP ix, p. 125. 'He has great abilities . . .', ibid. p. 123. 'He practises what . . .', CSL to Owen Barfield, 27 May 1928. 'A country club . . .' and 'I really don't know . . .', LP x, p. 95.

page 19   'Balkan Sobranies . . .', John Betjeman, *Summoned by Bells*, John Murray, 1960, p. 93. 'Betjeman and Valentin . . .', *Letters*, p. 108. 'Thus Æ to E . . .', *Letters*, p. 164.

page 20   'I cut tutorials . . .', *Summoned by Bells* (see above), p. 93. 'While in College . . .', LP ix, p. 144. 'in his arid room' and 'You'd have only . . .', *Summoned by Bells*, p. 109. 'indebted to Mr. C. S. Lewis . . .', John Betjeman, *Continual Dew*, John Murray, 1937, preface.

page 21   'Objectively our Common Room . . .', ibid. p. 20. 'Bridget is the elder . . .', LP ix, p. 110.

page 22   'only real line', Green & Hooper, p. 89. 'I wish there was . . .', CSL to A. K. H. Jenkin, 4 November 1925. 'Tolkien managed to get . . .', LP ix, pp. 89–90.

page 26   'jettisoning certainly . . .', 'The Oxford English School', *Oxford Magazine*, 29 May 1930, pp. 778–82.

page 28   'When we were enrolled . . .', conversation with the author, 10 December 1975. 'Spent the morning . . .', LP ix, p. 155. 'One week I . . .', CSL to Greeves, 3 December 1929. 'What? You too? . . .', *The Four Loves*, chapter 4.

page 29   'the nameless North' and 'desired dragons . . .', EPCW p. 63.

page 30   Quotations from Tolkien's poem, from Lewis's letter to Tolkien, and Lewis's suggested emendations: MSS, Estate of J. R. R. Tolkien.

page 32   'Tolkien is the man . . .', CSL to Greeves, 30 January 1930. 'The unpayable debt . . .', JRRT to Dick Plotz, 12 September 1965. 'Friendship with Lewis . . .', diary of J. R. R. Tolkien, 1 October 1933.

page 33   'one of my friends . . .', CSL to Greeves, 22 September 1931.

page 34   'given tea by a postmistress . . .' and 'ham and eggs', LP ix, p. 229. 'This time we . . .', LP x, p. 40 ff.

page 35   'Some of the others . . .', CSL to Greeves, 29 April 1930. 'We had a long, tiresome . . .', WHL diary, 11 August 1933. 'Owen's dark . . .', CSL to W. O. Field, 10 May 1943.

page 36   'got through the serious . . .', LP ix, p. 126. 'a re-assuring Germanic . . .', SBJ chapter 13.

page 37   'Imaginative vision . . .', 'The Great War' (correspondence between CSL and Barfield).

page 38   'I wonder can you . . .', *Letters*, p. 152. 'Dear Warnie . . .', CSL to Greeves, 27 December 1940. 'To-day, I got up . . .', WHL diary, 21 December 1932.

page 39   'I reviewed . . .', LP xi, p. 179. 'to postulate . . .', CSL to Leo Baker, September 1920. 'our ideas are . . .', LP viii, p. 172. Quotations referring to Lewis's developing philosophical ideas are from SBJ chapter 14.

page 40   'Joy was not . . .', SBJ chapter 14. 'All my ideas . . .', LP ix, pp. 96–7.
'One needn't be . . .', LP ix, p. 109. 'the danger of . . .', LP ix, p. 144.
'showing an alarming tendency . . .', *Letters*, p. 141. 'became aware
that . . .', SBJ chapter 14. 'admitted that God was God', ibid.

page 41   'gave in and knelt and prayed', ibid. 'My outlook is now . . .', CSL to
A. K. H. Jenkin, 21 March 1930.

page 42   'You might like to know . . .', CSL to Barfield, undated (? 1928).
'Languages are a disease of mythology', EPCW, p. 50. 'liked him so
much . . .', CSL to Greeves, 29 July 1930. 'a man who really . . .', ibid.
The account of the conversation between Lewis, Tolkien and Dyson is
based on Lewis's letter to Greeves of 22 September 1931 and on Tolkien's
poem 'Mythopoeia' (MS., Estate of J. R. R. Tolkien), which was written
to commemorate the conversation.

page 43   'lies and therefore . . .', 'Mythopoeia' (see above). These words of Lewis's
are quoted by Tolkien in one of the MSS of the poem, and he also refers
to them in EPCW, p. 71. 'a rush of wind . . .', CSL to Greeves, 22
September 1931. Paragraph beginning 'You look at trees, he said . . .':
an exact paraphrase of 'Mythopoeia' (see above). 'myth-woven . . .',
'Mythopoeia' (see above).

page 44   'we continued on Christianity', CSL to Greeves, 22 September 1931.
'nearly certain . . .', CSL to Greeves, 18 October 1931. 'how the life . . .',
ibid. 'right in the centre . . .', ibid.

page 45   'Dyson and I . . .', CSL to Greeves, 22 September 1931. 'I have just
passed on . . .', CSL to Greeves, 10 October 1931.

page 46   'perhaps I had said too much' and 'Perhaps I was not . . .', CSL to
Greeves, 18 October 1931. 'There must perhaps . . .', CSL to Sheldon
Vanauken, 17 April 1951. 'How could I . . .', CSL to the same, 22 April
1953. 'Even assuming . . .', 'Myth Became Fact', MS of article by Lewis
(Bodleian Library). Printed in *World Dominion* xx, September/October
1944, pp. 267–70; reprinted in *Undeceptions* (known in America as *God
in the Dock*).

page 47   'the *spontaneous* appeal . . .', CSL to Greeves, 8 November 1931. 'now, as
never before . . .', *Selected Literary Essays*, p. 147. 'It's such fun . . .',
CSL to Ruth Pitter, 29 September 1945.

page 48   'He was indeed . . .', MS note by Tolkien (Estate of J. R. R. Tolkien).

page 49   'My ethics . . .' and 'learn from your . . .', *The Pilgrim's Regress*, pp. 97,
102. 'What I am attacking . . .', Green & Hooper, p. 130. 'poacher
turned gamekeeper', *The Pilgrim's Regress*, p. 108. 'Though Mr Lewis's . . .',
Times Literary Supplement, 6 July 1933, p. 456.

page 50   'It was not . . .', UM. 'My father . . .', SBJ chapter 1. 'We were obliged . . .',
LP iii, p. 536.

page 51   'I wouldn't for the world . . .', *The Pilgrim's Regress*, pp. 118–9. 'bog-
trotters': 'By my father and his friends the Roman Catholic Nationalist
was dismissed as a poor ignorant bogtrotter who was too stupid and
priest-ridden to understand the blessings of English rule.' WHL biography of CSL, fol. 28. WHL often uses the term 'bog-rat' in his diary.
'We were coming down the steps . . .', UM.

page 52   'besides giving . . .', Diary of J. R. R. Tolkien, 1 October 1933. 'On
Saturday last . . .', WHL diary, 13 May 1931. 'a conviction . . .', ibid.

page 53   'I am delighted . . .', WHL diary, 19 January 1932. 'What a mercy . . .',
CSL to Greeves, 25 March 1933. 'We discussed how useful . . .', WHL
diary, 3 January 1935.

page 54 'in came J's friend . . .', WHL diary, 18 February 1933. 'At about half past . . .', ibid, 17 November 1933. 'This is one . . .', *Letters*, p. 145.

page 55 'a vast medieval erection', recalled by Derek Brewer. 'must have nothing . . .', CSL to WHL, 25 December 1931. 'my party and I . . .', ibid., 24 October 1931. 'Two at the table . . .', MS. (Estate of J. R. R. Tolkien). 'In fact during . . .', ibid. 'Confound Tolkien! . . .', WHL diary, 4 December 1933.

page 56 'where we had fried . . .' and 'and finished . . .', ibid., 26 March 1934. 'Dyson and Tolkien . . .', ibid., 26 July 1933.

page 57 'a real discovery . . .', ibid., 30 November 1933. 'Since term . . .', CSL to Greeves, 4 February 1933. 'Whether it is . . .', ibid.

page 58 'His one fault . . .', WHL diary, 19 August 1947. 'We were talking . . .', *Rehabilitations*, p. 122. 'The occasion . . .', quoted in Lewis's *Selected Literary Essays*, p. 18n.

page 59 'is really about . . .', *The Personal Heresy*, p. 2. 'A poet does . . .', ibid., p. 26.

page 60 'To know how bad . . .', *Rehabilitations*, p. 20. 'Man, please thy Maker . . .', quoted in *English Literature in the Sixteenth Century* (Oxford History of English Literature), p. 97. 'Looking back . . .', introduction to *Light on C. S. Lewis* (ed. Jocelyn Gibb), p. ix. 'deliberately ceased . . .', ibid., p. xxvi. 'with a certain underlying . . .', ibid., p. x.

page 61 'common things . . .', *The Personal Heresy*, p. 96. 'the life of the . . .', ibid., p. 106. 'What meditation . . .', ibid., p. 107. 'It left me . . .', *Light on C. S. Lewis*, p. xi. 'From about 1935 . . .', ibid., p. xiv.

page 62 'a half-hearted materialist . . .', *The Personal Heresy*, p. 28. 'If the world is . . .', ibid., p. 30. 'a disquieting contrast . . .', *Rehabilitations*, p. 185. 'What are the key-words . . .', ibid., p. 186. 'Applying this principle . . .', ibid., p. 192.

page 63 'Man, Sub-creator . . .', EPCW, pp. 71–2. 'Man without art . . .', 'The Emergence of Shakespeare's Tragedies', *Proceedings of the British Academy* xxxvi (1950), p. 72. 'our mortality catches . . .', *Poetic Diction*, p. 181.

page 64 'sufficient measure . . .', *Education and the University*, Chatto & Windus (1943), p. 18. 'tradition of educated infidelity' and 'one phase . . .', *Christian Reflections*, p. 19. 'like trying to lift . . .' and 'Unless we return . . .', ibid., p. 81. 'Since the real wholeness . . .', CSL to George Every, 4 February 1941. 'Leavis demands . . .', *Of Other Worlds*, p. 96.

page 65 'How I hate . . .', G. A. L. Burgeon (pseud. Owen Barfield), *This Ever Diverse Pair*, Gollancz (1950), p. 19. 'All who love . . .', *The Times*, 8 October 1937. 'No common recipe . . .', *Times Literary Supplement*, 2 October 1937. 'Mr Lewis and my . . .', JRRT to Allen & Unwin, 18 February 1938. 'Lewis said to me . . .', JRRT to Charlotte & Denis Plimmer, February 1967.

page 66 'first suggested to me . . .', CSL to W. Kinter, 29 September 1951. 'I read the story . . .', JRRT to Stanley Unwin, 4 March 1938. 'heard it pass . . .', ibid., 18 February 1938.

page 67 'You may not have noticed . . .', ibid., 4 June 1938. 'On Thursday . . .', *Letters*, p. 170. 'was then transferred . . .', JRRT to William Luther White, 11 September 1967; printed in White's *Image of Man in C. S. Lewis*. 'It was a pleasantly . . .', ibid.

page 68 'Yet our spirits . . .' and subsequent quotations from R. E. Havard are taken from his unpublished memoir of Lewis (Wade Collection).

page 69 'regards this as sealing . . .', *Letters*, p. 168. 'along with these . . .', ibid.

page 73   'The telephone . . .', *War in Heaven*, chapter 1.

page 74   The description of Williams at Amen House is largely based on 'Charles Williams as I knew him' by Ralph Binfield, Charles Williams Society newsletter, 2 (Summer 1976), p. 9.

page 77   'had too many brains for him', Hadfield, p. 21.

page 78   'rather like an ancient . . .', ibid., p. 36.

page 79   'O rooms . . .', *Poems of Conformity*, p. 21. 'For the first five minutes . . .', *Image of the City* (ed. Anne Ridler), p. xvii. 'a face which . . .', *Divorce*, p. 61. 'So lovely . . .', *Image of the City*, p. xvii. 'whether love were not . . .', *Shadows of Ecstasy*, chapter 13. 'put off love for love's sake', *The Silver Stair*, p. 63.

page 80   'the steep whence I see God', ibid., p. 44. 'But this is *true*', quoted by Dorothy L. Sayers, *The Poetry of Search and the Poetry of Statement*, Gollancz (1963), p. 73. 'At bottom . . .', Hadfield, p. 181.

page 81   'bridged the gap . . .', quoted on cover of John Symonds, *The Great Beast*, Mayflower Books (1972), p. 142. 'a dull and inaccurate . . .', Aleister Crowley, *Moonchild*, Sphere Books (1972), p. 142. 'My soul is wandering . . .', Symonds, op. cit., p. 35. Williams's recollections of the Golden Dawn as told to Anne Ridler are in *Image of the City*, p. xxiv.

page 82   'It is not in competition . . .', A. E. Waite, *The Brotherhood of the Rosy Cross*, William Rider (1924), pp. 627–8. 'It is a House . . .', ibid.

page 83   'No one can possibly . . .', *War in Heaven*, chapter 9. 'Our Father . . .', *Windows of Night*, pp. 114–16.

page 84   'My mind possessed . . .', ibid., p. 56. 'To keep the Mass . . .', *Divorce*, p. 69.

page 85   'dispersed in ancient pain . . .', Hadfield, p. 61. 'firmer under-stone', *Divorce*, p. 24.

page 87   'even the most precious . . .', *The Masque of the Manuscript*, p. 18. 'He found the gold . . .', *The Bookseller*, 24 May 1945.

page 88   'wilful, insolent' and 'part scornful . . .', *Poems of Conformity*, p. 37.

page 89   'labour and purity and peace', *The Masque of Perusal*, p. 21. 'Nothing at all . . .', *Troilus and Cressida* v, 2.

page 90   'undergoes an entire subversion . . .', *The English Poetic Mind*, p. 58. 'the passing of the poetic . . .', ibid., p. 200. 'When one reads . . .', letter to the author, 5 March 1977.

page 91   'This she? . . .' *Troilus and Cressida* v, 2. 'How dreadful . . .', Hadfield, p. 110. 'There can be few . . .', CW to RH, 1 March 1940. 'great period', ibid.

page 92   'The Duchess, sir . . .', 'The Chaste Wanton', *Three Plays*, p. 123. 'I would be somebody . . .', ibid., p. 124. 'good works . . .', ibid., p. 126. 'The void! . . .', ibid.

page 93   'all such a mad mixture . . .', *Shadows of Ecstasy*, chapter 12. 'You've nearly killed it . . .', ibid., chapter 7. 'I have poured the strength . . .', ibid., chapter 5. 'If this pain . . .', ibid., chapter 13.

page 95   'I saw Shakespeare . . .', *Windows of Night* p. 91.

page 97   'painfully incredible', quoted by Williams, CW to TS, undated (? 1932). 'There are no novels . . .', *The Listener*, xxxvi no. 936 (19 December 1945), pp. 894–5. 'I remember a man . . .', Introduction to *All Hallows' Eve*, Pellegrini & Cudahy edition (New York, 1948), p. x. 'I feel a real apology . . .', *Poetry at Present*, p. 7. 'If only we could neglect it . . .', ibid., p. 163–73.

page 98   Eliot's mention of his debt to *The Greater Trumps*: unpublished journal of Mary Trevelyan (in possession of the author).

page 99   'I have just read...', CSL to Greeves, 26 February 1936. 'noble fusion...', *The Allegory of Love*, p. 21. 'My dear Mr Lewis...', Green & Hooper, p. 134.

page 101   'He is of humble origin...', CSL to Greeves, 30 January 1944.

page 102   'his curious accent...', Lois Lang-Sims, *A Time to be Born*, Andre Deutsch (1971), p. 196. 'Love – obey...', ibid., p. 197. 'God bless you...', memoir of Williams by Thelma Shuttleworth, Charles Williams Society newsletter, 6, p. 10. 'And thus the Filial Godhead...', *Paradise Lost* vi, 722. 'Felt in the blood...', 'Tintern Abbey', 28. 'There has been a great deal...', *The English Poetic Mind*, p. vii. 'It isn't what poetry...', *Shadows of Ecstasy*, chapter 4. 'submitted his obedience...', ibid., chapter 13.

page 103   'Grounded in the Acts...', 'The Founding of the Company', *The Region of the Summer Stars*. 'Sin is the preference...', *He Came Down From Heaven*, chapter 3. 'an explanation of the whole...', ibid., chapter 5.

page 104   'I have a point...', Hadfield, pp. 139–40. 'bear ye one another's burdens', Galations vi. 2.

page 105   'a tremendous flow of words', Lang-Sims, op. cit., p. 201. 'My dear Thelma...', CW to TS, 18 March 1930.

page 106   'We were together...', Charles Williams Society newsletter, 6, p. 8. 'I was by this time...', Lang-Sims, op. cit., p. 206. 'to teach them...', *Letters*, p. 208. 'held me in a strange stillness...', Lang-Sims, op. cit., p. 203. 'seemed to control...', *Shadows of Ecstasy*, chapter 5. 'You'll copy out...', CW to TS, 28 June 1932.

page 107   'God forbid...', ibid., 2 April 1940. 'St Paul knew...', ibid., 1 September 1930. 'Whether his personal life...', *Descent into Hell*, chapter 4. 'We do not know...', *The Figure of Beatrice*, chapter 1. 'He seemed to me to approximate...', *The Listener*, xxxvi no. 936 (19 December 1945), pp. 894–5. 'What finally convinced me...', *Theology* xxxviii, April 1939, p. 275.

page 108   'kidneys enclosed...', EPCW, p. viii. 'almost Platonic...', ibid. 'one of the most important...', *He Came Down From Heaven*, chapter 5.

page 109   '*Taliessin through Logres* contained...', *New Statesman*, xviii no. 459 (9 December 1939), pp. 864–6. 'He always boiled...', Introduction to *All Hallows' Eve*, Pellegrini & Cudahy edition (New York, 1948), p. xii. 'The poor benefit...' and 'One would hardly think...', *The Spectator*, clv, 13 September 1935, pp. 400–1.

page 110   'To think we said...', Hadfield, p. 109.

page 113   'Outside Lewis...', CW to MW, 4 October 1939. 'I was just saying...', ibid.

page 114   'Can you cook?...' Recalled by Anne Spalding in conversation with the author, 7 March 1977. 'I sympathise with her...', CW to RH, 13 September 1939. 'I am in...', CW to MW, 21 June 1940. 'if he had to choose...', *Shadows of Ecstasy*, chapter 11. 'I have fled...', quoted by C. S. Kilby, *Tolkien and the Silmarillion*, Illinois, Harold Shaw (1976), p. 72.

page 115   'There is no-one here...', CW to MW, 6 October 1939. 'Things are not too bad...', CW to RH, 17 October 1939. 'unusually intelligible', *Letters*, p. 170. 'We had an unusually...', CSL to WHL, 4 May 1940. 'He is largely...', *Letters*, p. 197.

page 116   'He has an undisciplined mind...', CSL to Dom Bede Griffiths, 25 May 1942. 'Don't imagine...', *Letters*, p. 212. 'a cheering proof...', EPCW, p. xi. 'Before he came...', ibid.

page 117 'Much was possible . . .', *The Place of the Lion*, chapter 15. 'one of the most . . .' and '*almost* seriously . . .', *Letters*, p. 169. 'They are good for my mind', CW to MW, 30 August 1940. 'I brood on and off . . .', CW to AR, 30 September 1942.

page 118 'or rather not "read" . . .', CSL to WHL, 18 November 1939. 'to smuggle him in . . .', ibid., 28 January 1940. 'The vulgarest . . .', ibid. 'We cannot make him real . . .', T. S. Eliot, *Selected Prose*, Penguin Books (1953), p. 123. 'To-morrow I go . . .', CW to MW, 28 January 1940.

page 119 'On Monday . . .', CSL to WHL, 11 February 1940. 'Am I only . . .', CW to MW, 5 March 1940.

page 120 'a very impressionable . . .', JRRT to Anne Barrett, 7 August 1964. 'had already become . . .', EPCW, p. x. 'If you were going up . . .' and 'To my eyes . . .', unpublished memoir of Lewis by Peter Bayley.

page 121 'In every circle . . .', EPCW, p. v. 'No, I think not', MS comment in Tolkien's copy of EPCW (Estate of J. R. R. Tolkien). 'I was and remain . . .', JRRT to Dick Plotz, 12 September 1965. 'a witch doctor', recalled by Paul Drayton from a conversation with Tolkien in 1967 (personal communication to the author). 'This morning I reached . . .', JRRT to CRT, 29 November 1944.

page 122 'Had a glass . . .', ibid., November 1943. 'I did not start . . .', ibid., 23 September 1944. 'The only freedom . . .', *The Image of the City*, p. 115. 'In her heart . . .', 'The Departure of Dindrane', *The Region of the Summer Stars*.

page 123 'C. Williams who is reading . . .', JRRT to CRT, 13 December 1944. 'Our dear Charles Williams . . .', MS (Estate of J. R. R. Tolkien).

page 127 (and following pages) The imaginary conversation: as I have not transcribed verbatim from the sources, but have adapted them freely to suit the context, I do not give detailed references. Among the sources used are CSL to Greeves, CSL to WHL, JRRT to CRT, WHL diary, early drafts of *The Lord of the Rings*, JRRT letter to Daphne Cloke (from which the Berúthiel story is taken), EPCW ('On Fairy-Stories'), JRRT to W. H. Auden, Lewis's *Of Other Worlds*, JRRT to Milton Waldman, Lewis's *Poems* (pp. 55–6), his discussion of 'progress' in *Fern-Seed and Elephants* and *Screwtape Proposes a Toast*, his review of *The Lord of the Rings* in *Time & Tide*, and Charles Williams's *The Forgiveness of Sins*.

page 153 'to suggest a shared outlook . . .', Charles Moorman, *The Precincts of Felicity, the Augustinian City of the Oxford Christians*, University of Florida Press (1966), p. 15n.

page 154 'the common Inklings attitude': J. S. Ryan, *Tolkien: Cult or Culture?* Australia, University of New England (1969), p. 54. 'chasing after a fox . . .', *Letters*, p. 287.

page 155 'He has read . . .', SBJ chapter 13.

page 156 'Lor' bless you . . .', CSL to Derek Brewer, 16 November 1959 (courtesy of Derek Brewer). 'the salvation . . .', *Rehabilitations*, p. 196. 'Love and poetry . . .', *Shadows of Ecstasy*, chapter 7. 'immortal energy', ibid., chapter 5.

page 157 'They all had a tendency . . .', Adam Fox interviewed by Stephen Schofield, recorded in 1975 (courtesy of Stephen Schofield). 'half fascinated . . .', *Narrative Poems*, p. 5. 'spiritual lust', SBJ chapter 4.

page 158 'bilge', WHL diary, 25 September 1947. 'I don't believe . . .', CSL to Katherine Farrer, 9 February 1954. 'steam of consciousness', *The Dark Tower*, p. 11. 'our best moderns', CSL to Leo Baker, undated (Hilary term 1921). 'Some of the most . . .', CSL to Arthur C. Clarke, 26 January 1954. 'has done serious damage . . .', *Poetic Diction*, Connecticut, Wesleyan University Press (1973), p. 36.

page 159   'Better be modern than minor', *War in Heaven*, chapter 8.

page 160   'This was a circle . . .', John Wain, *Sprightly Running: Part of an Autobiography*, Macmillan (London) (1963), p. 181. 'The whole picture . . .', letter to *Encounter*, January 1963, p. 81. 'Wouldn't it be wonderful . . .', CSL to Katherine Farrer, 4 December 1953. 'was not "influence" . . .', JRRT to Dick Plotz, 12 September 1965. 'To be sure . . .', *Letters*, p. 288.

page 161   'We stood foursquare . . .', SBJ chapter 2.

page 162   'There exist two different systems . . .', 'The Inner Ring', *Screwtape Proposes a Toast*, p. 29. 'I have a holy terror . . .', *Letters*, p. 48.

page 163   'There were no rules . . .', ibid., p. 13. 'Jack and I . . .', WHL diary, 22 August 1946. 'Well attended Inkling . . .', ibid., 26 February 1948.

page 164   'A friend dead . . .', LP vii, p. 174. 'I speak of my own . . .', CSL to Barfield, undated letter in 'The Great War'. 'either men or women . . .', LP vii, 169–70. 'female to male', *The Problem of Pain*, chapter 3. 'the husband is the head . . .', *The Four Loves*, chapter 5. 'If there must be a head . . .', 'Christian Marriage', *Mere Christianity*. 'Do you really want . . .', *Letters*, p. 184. 'not really meant . . .', quoted in CW to MW, 25 October 1939.

page 165   'The men have learned . . .', *The Four Loves*, chapter 4.

page 166   'just the sort of mind . . .', WHL biography of CSL, fol. 102. 'I can't bear . . .', *Letters*, p. 237. 'How a man can feel . . .', 'Philia', *Four Talks on Love by C. S. Lewis*, Episcopal Radio–TV Foundation, Atlanta, Georgia. (The original version of *The Four Loves*.)

page 167   'The deepest of worldly emotions . . .', *The Allegory of Love*, p. 9. 'were themselves lover-like . . .', ibid., p. 10. 'Long before history began . . .', *The Four Loves*, chapter 4.

page 168   'There are many things . . .', JRRT to Michael Tolkien, 12 March 1941.

page 169   'How quickly an intelligent woman . . .', ibid., 6 March 1941.

page 170   'a subject which does not . . .', WHL diary, 21 August 1934. 'With all my army experience . . .', ibid., 25 July 1946. 'the tide of masculine friendship . . .', *All Hallows' Eve*, chapter 5.

page 171   'Milton's principles . . .', *Reason and Beauty in the Poetic Mind*, pp. 97–8. 'He gave one a warmth . . .', letter to the author, 12 December 1977. 'the Lewis seance', JRRT to CRT, 23 April 1944.

page 172   'The war and Oxford . . .', CW to MW, 4 December 1939. 'It is a dull book . . .', ibid., 17 October 1940. 'I am particularly taken . . .', ibid., 15 May 1940.

page 173   'The Teeth Bill . . .', ibid., 1 September 1944. 'I had hoped . . .', ibid., 1 July 1940. 'We have never lost . . .', ibid., 21 August 1944. 'I have a kind . . .', ibid., 9 July 1940.

page 174   'One unexpected feature . . .', CSL to WHL, 18 September 1939. 'That a return to God . . .', quoted in V. H. H. Green, *Religion at Oxford and Cambridge*, SCM Press (1964), p. 353. 'struck by an idea . . .', *Letters*, p. 188. 'In 1943 . . .', letter to CSL from Edward T. Dell, 1 February 1949 (Bodleian). 'to thank you . . .', letter to CSL from Vera Matthews, 10 May 1949 (Bodleian). 'If one begins . . .', *Undeceptions*, p. 70. 'the sharp-tongued . . .', *The Screwtape Letters*, letter 3.

page 175   'I do believe . . .', *Undeceptions*, p. 33. 'I have always gone . . .', *Letters*, p. 301. 'I have been suspected . . .', *Reflections on the Psalms*, chapter 11.

'a dogmatic Christian . . .', *Christian Reflections*, p. 44. 'A great deal of my utility . . .', CSL to Edward T. Dell, 29 April 1963.

page 176 'Though I had never . . .', *Screwtape Proposes a Toast*, introduction to 'Screwtape Proposes a Toast'. 'The devil, even if he . . .', *He Came Down From Heaven*, chapter 2. 'My dearest Scorpuscle . . .', *Time & Tide*, xxiii no. 12, 21 March 1942, pp. 245–6. 'Hwæt! we Inclinga' and the clerihews by Tolkien throughout this chapter: MS (Estate of J. R. R. Tolkien).

page 177 'Almost the only wire . . .', JRRT to CRT, 1 March 1944. 'The Lord of the Strings', recalled by Christopher Tolkien. 'I reached the Mitre . . .', JRRT to CRT, 18 November 1944.

page 178 'Did you see . . .', CW to MW, 18 September 1940. 'Things are a little . . .', ibid., 31 December 1940. 'I said to myself . . .', CW to AR 26 September 1940. 'Do me the high favour . . .', CW to RH, 29 April 1942. 'a little conscious . . .', CW to AR, 5 January 1942. 'It *is* a little . . .', ibid., 23 December 1941.

page 179 'Venus is weak . . .', ibid., 25 March 1942. 'written with You about . . .', CW to MW, 5 December 1944. 'hideous confession . . .', CW to RH, 12 February 1942. 'is being a Pest . . .', CW to AR, 30 September 1942. 'is, I think, youthfully . . .', CSL to Greeves, 30 January 1944. 'brilliantly happy marriage', chapter 3 of 'Williams and the Arthuriad' in *Arthurian Torso*. 'It is fresh fire . . .', CW to MW, 11 November 1943.

page 180 'Separation is bad for her . . .', CW to RH, 29 April 1942. 'My great difficulty . . .', ibid. 'More than one ever dreamed . . .', CW to TS, 20 December 1944. 'I have seen his impress . . .', *Letters*, p. 197.

page 181 'partly anticipated . . .', *A Preface to Paradise Lost*, p. v. 'While the moderns . . .', ibid., p. 57. 'Apparently the door . . .', ibid., p. v. 'I will go so far . . .', CW to RH, 29 April 1942. 'I should never have written . . .', ibid., 29 March 1941. 'The main point is Milton . . .', ibid., 21 December 1942. 'The restoration . . .', ibid., 29 March 1941. 'Meanwhile Mr Eliot . . .', CW to AR, 13 July 1943. 'the only point . . .', *A Preface to Paradise Lost*, p. 86.

page 182 'To you or to me . . .', ibid., p. 118. 'Partly as a development . . .', JRRT to CRT, 29 January 1945. 'As a philologist . . .', ibid., 31 July 1944.

page 183 'what was myth . . .', *Perelandra*, chapter 8. 'If you look . . .', 'We Have Cause To Be Uneasy', *Mere Christianity*.

page 184 'a complete failure' and 'God used an *ass* . . .', Green & Hooper, p. 205. 'What very odd tasks . . .', *Letters*, p. 193. 'I had to go . . .', Green & Hooper, p. 209. 'Christianity is a fighting religion': 'The Rival Conceptions of God', *Mere Christianity*. 'This moment is . . .', 'The practical Conclusion', ibid. 'I do not think the BBC . . .', CW to RH, 31 July 1942. 'had been, it appeared . . .', CW to AR, 30 September 1942.

page 185 'Lewis is as energetic . . .', JRRT to CRT, 1 March 1944. 'I strongly object . . .', *Letters*, p. 262. 'The fun is often . . .', CSL to Greeves, 30 January 1944.

page 186 'the universal Aunt', WHL diary, 1 November 1949. 'he knows everyone . . .', CSL to Mr Hutter, 30 March 1962.

page 187 'Listening to those . . .', 'Is there an Oxford "School" of Writing?', *The Twentieth Century*, clvii, June 1955, p. 562. 'that Lord David . . .', CW to MW, 1 December 1944. 'His lectures . . .', *Sprightly Running*, p. 149.

page 188 'I had an extraordinarily . . .', CW to MW, 5 March 1940. 'to be read . . .', quoted in CW to MW, 6 September 1943. 'allured', ibid., 15 October 1943. 'scandalous' and 'a condemnation . . .', ibid., 15 November 1944.

'And it's obvious . . .', CW to RH, 20 February 1943. 'the only graduand . . .', CW to MW, 30 March 1943.

page 189   'when she arrived . . .', conversation with the author, 7 March 1977.
'not because . . .', EPCW, p. 1. 'I got in . . .', CW to MW, 10 February
1944. 'She has, under the compulsion . . .', CW to MW, 24 August 1944.
'She was the first . . .', letter to *Encounter*, January 1963, p. 81. 'She never
met . . .', ibid. 'has edified us . . .', CSL to Edward T. Dell, 25 October
1949. 'good on the whole', CSL to Greeves, 23 December 1941. 'didn't
like it . . .', ibid. 'I could not stand . . .', JRRT to CRT, 25 May 1944.

page 190   Tolkien's remarks about Eddison: JRRT to Daphne Cloke, 'the most
noble and ioyous . . .', CSL to E. R. Eddison, 16 November 1942.
'Certeyn it is . . .', E. R. Eddison to CSL, 21 February 1943 (Bodleian).

page 191   'of undiminished power . . .', JRRT to CRT, 10 June 1944. 'On Tuesday . . .', ibid., 6 October 1944.

page 192   'I am a democrat . . .', draft of letter by JRRT to an unknown recipient,
1956. 'I loathed and loathe . . .', letter to *Encounter*, January 1963, p. 81.
'had taken a fair deal . . .', JRRT to CRT, 6 October 1944. 'Mr Lewis . . .',
Green & Hooper, pp. 223–4.

page 193   'I really launched him': unpublished journal of Mary Trevelyan (in
possession of the author). 'a kind of ghostly skeleton', CW to MW, 15
June 1943. 'a hovering sense . . .', ibid., 9 February 1940. 'I doubt if . . .',
CW to TS, 30 July 1940. 'Three quarters . . .', CW to MW, 3 September
1943. 'I am not much happier . . .', ibid., 6 September 1943. 'It was
true . . .', *All Hallows' Eve*, chapter 1.

page 194   'I heard two chapters . . .', JRRT to CRT, 10 November 1943. 'I was in
fact . . .', JRRT to Anne Barrett, 7 August 1964. 'A style suitable . . .',
CW to MW, 13 December 1943. 'I have pushed . . .', ibid., 12 January
1944. 'All turned up . . .', JRRT to CRT, 10 April 1944.

page 195   'Dante doesn't attract . . .', quoted by Clyde S. Kilby, op. cit., p. 30. 'is
putting the screw . . .', JRRT to CRT, 30 March 1944. 'I have begun . . .',
ibid., 3 April 1944. 'I saw CSL . . .', ibid., 14 May 1944. 'Taliessin
gathered . . .', 'The Prayers of the Pope', *The Region of the Summer Stars*.

page 196   'This selling . . .', CW to MW, 23 November 1944. 'There are no
more . . .', ibid. 'This, after so many . . .', CW to AR, 13 July 1943.
'Would you think . . .', CW to MW, 24 April 1945.

page 197   'said he had heard . . .', ibid., 14 October 1944. 'pseudo-culture', ibid.,
15 January 1944. 'How different . . .', ibid., 21 February 1945. 'I have
no place-attachment . . .', ibid., 14 July 1944. 'I cannot quite describe . . .',
CW to TS, 23 March 1943 and 20 December 1944. 'For cash . . .', CW
to AR, 21 September 1943. 'He had not changed . . .', Hadfield, p. 199.
'It was a bright morning . . .', JRRT to CRT, 7 November 1944.
'Picture to yourself . . .', introduction to 'The Figure of Arthur' in
Arthurian Torso.

page 198   'I have no *opinions* . . .', *That Hideous Strength*, original Bodley Head
edition, p. 202. 'incurable romantic', ibid., p. 135. 'It is one of Barfield's . . .', ibid., p. 321. 'Something we may call Britain . . .', ibid.,
p. 459. 'something brought to Western Europe . . .', ibid., p. 246. 'a
hearing error', JRRT to Dick Plotz, 12 September 1965. 'good in
itself', undated draft of letter by JRRT, 1964.

page 199   'I actually went out . . .', JRRT to CRT, 23 September 1944. 'The
Inklings have . . .', ibid. 'I am to have . . .', CW to MW, 2 May 1945.
'How did you feel . . .', CSL to Dom Bede Griffiths, 10 May 1945. 'It

was the middle . . .', *Sprightly Running*, p. 152. 'At 12.50 this morning . . .',
WHL diary, 15 May 1945.

page 203 'but I remember . . .', EPCW, p. xiv. 'There is something horrible . . .',
WHL diary, 15 May 1945. 'In the (far too brief) years . . .', JRRT to
Michal Williams, 15 May 1945 (Wade Collection). 'great pain but . . .',
CSL to Barfield, 18 May 1945. 'My friendship is not ended . . .', CSL to
Michal Williams, 22 May 1945. 'She was dead . . .', draft of first version
of *All Hallows' Eve* (Wade Collection). 'I don't remember . . .', WHL
diary, 15 December 1945.

page 205 'I don't think I should . . .', JRRT to CRT, 30 September 1944. 'to
consider . . .', ibid., 9 October 1945. 'Chris gave us . . .', WHL diary,
6 February 1947. 'Tollers gave us . . .', ibid., 23 October 1947. 'A good
Inklings . . .', ibid., 27 January 1949.

page 206 'I admired Lewis . . .', *Sprightly Running*, p. 180. 'A writer's task . . .',
ibid., p. 182. 'I do not believe . . .', *Fern-Seed and Elephants*, p. 19. 'the
freeborn mind', *Undeceptions*, p. 262. 'As a Christian . . .' and 'young
people . . .', *Undeceptions*, p. 160.

page 207 'Jack's ignorance . . .', WHL diary, 27 September 1950. 'The modern
world . . .', CSL to Greeves, 5 January 1947. 'Caucus has replaced . . .',
Fern-Seed and Elephants, p. 12. 'He must have irritated . . .', *Times Literary
Supplement*, 12 July 1974, pp. 747–8.

page 208 'Who's in there ? . . .', *Sprightly Running*, p. 152. 'There goes C. S. Lewis . . .',
Edmund Crispin, *Swan Song*, chapter 8.

page 209 'An exquisitely lovely . . .', WHL diary, 26 March 1946. 'We sat down
eight . . .', ibid., 11 March 1948. 'Proceedings opened . . .', ibid.

page 210 'To all my set . . .', *Letters*, p. 215. 'It was no use . . .', *Sprightly Running*,
p. 184. 'Only one *really* good . . .', JRRT to CRT, August 1947. 'we
managed two . . .', WHL diary, 19 August 1947.

page 211 'Hugo and I . . .', ibid., 19 March 1946.

page 212 'bellows uninterruptedly . . .', ibid., 20 October 1949. 'This evening . . .',
ibid., 8 August 1946. 'When I arrived . . .', ibid., 4 March 1948. 'A well
attended Inkling . . .', ibid., 24 April 1947.

page 213 'We took you from the trenches . . .', P. J. Kavanagh, *The Perfect Stranger*,
Chatto & Windus (1966), p. 105. 'a burly man . . .', *Letters*, p. 145. 'He
could sometimes . . .' and other quotations from Stephen Medcalf:
obituary of Dyson in *Postmaster* (journal of Merton College, Oxford),
v, no. 3, January 1976. 'Bring out the buckets . . .' and 'Write an
essay . . .', ibid.

page 214 'I think I've never . . .' and 'That I was sorry . . .', interview with Roger
Green, BBC Radio Oxford, May 1971. 'If you think . . .', recalled by
J. A. W. Bennett. 'The sword . . .', ibid. 'Lewis actually drew . . .', ibid.

page 215 'It was in practice . . .', *Sprightly Running*, p. 140. 'the Society's secretary . . .', ibid., p. 141. 'engaged in a flashy debate . . .', A. J. Ayer, *Part
of My Life*, Collins (1977), p. 297.

page 216 'on the scale . . .', *Light on C. S. Lewis* (ed. Jocelyn Gibb), p. 31. 'He was
keen-witted . . .', UM.

page 217 'None of us . . .', MS memoir of Lewis by Derek Brewer. 'A great
Roman Catholic . . .', *Selected Literary Essays*, p. 116. 'Christianity is a
fighting religion': see reference to p. 184 above. 'I don't want retreat . . .',
They Asked for a Paper, p. 118.

page 218 'We shall probably fail . . .', *Fern-Seed and Elephants*, p. 93. 'The enemy',
CSL to Dom Bede Griffiths, 22 April 1954. 'manly', 'The Invasion' in

Mere Christianity. 'common things . . .', *The Personal Heresy*, p. 96. 'adult by inspiration . . .', CW to RH, 31 July 1942. 'rather like a child . . .', *Selected Literary Essays*, p. 92. 'bestow all my childishness . . .', ibid. 'It demands of us . . .', *Studies in Medieval and Renaissance Literature*, pp. 132–3. 'Beyond all doubt . . .', ibid., p. 146.

page 219   'of immense length', *Letters*, p. 266. 'my mother', Green & Hooper, p. 228. 'The Alligator of Love', CSL to Barfield, 28 June 1936. 'a corking good writer', CSL to Sheldon Vanauken, 14 December 1950. 'a tip-top yarn', *Letters*, p. 147. 'an absolute corker', CSL to Joy Gresham, 22 December 1963. 'An unliterary man . . .', *Of Other Worlds*, p. 17. David Cecil on Lewis's literary tastes: letter to the author, January 1978.

page 220   'child's sense of glory and nightmare', MS note accompanying letters from CSL to Ruth Pitter (Bodleian). 'a nasty little boy . . .', *Perelandra*, chapter 9. 'like a very nasty child', ibid., chapter 10.

page 221   'evidence of arrest . . .', F. R. Leavis, *The Common Pursuit*, London (1952), p. 253. 'We think we are listening . . .', *Light On C. S. Lewis* (ed. Jocelyn Gibb), p. 37.

page 222   'Prejudice must be regarded . . .', *The Image of the City*, p. 157. 'Hell is always inaccurate', ibid., p. 30. 'The imaginative man . . .', *Letters*, p. 260.

page 223   'What might Christ . . .', CSL to Mrs Heck, 29 December 1958. 'disliked it intensely' and 'I hear you've been . . .', Green & Hooper, p. 241.

page 224   'a trifle vulgar . . .', CSL to Barfield, 16 December 1947. 'among the two or three . . .', EPCW, p. vii. 'word music equalled . . .', chapter 6 of 'Williams and the Arthuriad' in *Arthurian Torso*.

page 225   'Mr Lewis has . . .', *The Penguin Book of Contemporary Verse*, ed. Kenneth Allott, Penguin Books (1950), p. 85. 'hadn't begun . . .', Leavis, op. cit., p. 252. 'Somehow, somewhere . . .', *The Tablet*, cxcii, no. 5666, 25 December 1948, p. 421. 'they attracted only . . .', V. H. H. Green, op. cit., p. 359. 'I can see it now . . .', *Sprightly Running*, p. 184.

page 226   'A very pleasant meeting . . .', WHL diary, 27 November 1947. 'A very poor Inklings . . .', ibid., 4 March 1948. 'No one turned up . . .', ibid., 27 October 1949. 'The best of them . . .', *Sprightly Running*, p. 184. 'almost unequalled' and 'There are many passages . . .', CSL to Tolkien, 21 October 1949 (Estate of J. R. R. Tolkien). Quoted at greater length in the present writer's *J. R. R. Tolkien: a biography*, p. 204.

page 227   'Golly, what a book! . . .', WHL diary, 12 November 1949. 'It is sad that . . .', JRRT to Fr. David Kolb, S.J., 11 November 1964.

page 228   'Five years ago . . .', JRRT to CRT, 30 January 1945. 'We are about . . .', JRRT to Stanley Unwin, 21 July 1945. 'may well have cost . . .', *The Cambridge Quarterly*, i, no. 3, Summer 1966, p. 271.

page 229   'Present, Hugo Dyson . . .', WHL diary, 30 January 1951. 'While we were waiting . . .', ibid., 8 February 1951.

page 230   'He at least . . .', Green & Hooper, p. 280. 'is continuously enjoyable . . .', *New Statesman*, 30 October 1954. 'far and away . . .', *Essays in Criticism*, April 1955. 'magnificent' and 'such intellectual vitality . . .', *Sunday Times*, 16 January 1955. 'now as always . . .', *Spectator*, 2 October 1954. 'Can Oxford . . .', *Birmingham Post*, 5 October 1954.

page 231   'Come over . . .', Basil Willey to Walter Hooper, 20 September 1970 (Bodleian). 'Many of my colleagues . . .', CSL to Mrs E. O. Allen, 17 January 1955. 'My new College . . .', CSL to E. A. Allen, 5 December 1955.

page 232   'We saw less . . .', JRRT to Christopher Bretherton, 16 July 1964. 'Everyman's Theologian', UM.

page 233   'going mad through trying . . .', WHL diary, 14 October 1946. 'She is
in . . .', CSL to Sister Penelope, CSMV, 30 December 1950. 'So ends . . .',
WHL diary, 17 January 1951. 'I specially need . . .', *Letters*, p. 232. 'what
has been . . .', CSL to Greeves, 11 October 1952. 'Just another American
fan . . .', WHL diary, 5 November 1956.

page 234   'In a few years . . .', Joy Davidman, 'The Longest Way Round', *These
Found the Way*, ed. David Wesley Soper, Philadelphia, Westminster Press
(1951), p. 15. 'Men, I said . . .', ibid., p. 16. 'Come now all Americans . . .',
Letter to a Comrade, Yale University Press (1938), pp. 25–8. 'It interested
me . . .', *These Found the Way*, p. 17. 'All I knew . . .', ibid., p. 19.

page 235   'Now with me . . .', *Letter to a Comrade*, p. 47. 'These books stirred . . .',
These Found the Way, p. 22.

page 236   'I put the babies . . .', ibid., p. 23. 'And my prayer . . .', ibid., p. 80. 'I
was some little time . . .', WHL diary, 5 November 1956.

page 237   'Her mind was lithe . . .', *A Grief Observed*, p. 8. 'Last week we entertained . . .', CSL to Mrs Vera Gebbert, 23 December 1953.

page 238   'Poor lamb . . .', Joy Davidman to 'Bod and Jackie', 19 January 1954.
'That really is the greatest change . . .', *Selected Literary Essays*, p. 11. 'I
read as a native . . .', ibid., p. 13. 'Where I fail . . .', ibid., p. 14. 'It was
obvious . . .', WHL diary, 5 November 1956. 'were obvious from the
outset', ibid. 'What is offered . . .', *The Four Loves*, chapter 4.

page 239   'a pure matter . . .', Green & Hooper, p. 268. 'J. assured me . . .', WHL
diary, 5 November 1956. 'There ought to be two . . .', 'Christian
Marriage', *Mere Christianity*. 'No one can mark . . .', *Letters to an American
Lady*, p. 65. 'Don't put your goods . . .', *The Four Loves*, chapter 6.

page 240   'Never have I loved . . .', WHL diary, 5 November 1956. 'There are
marriages . . .', *Smoke on the Mountain*, p. 83. 'One of the most painful . . .',
WHL diary, 21 March 1957.

page 241   'My case is definitely . . .', Green & Hooper, p. 269. 'Do you know . . .',
unpublished memoir of Lewis by Peter Bayley.

page 242   'usual neat sardonic touch', CW to AR, 21 September 1943. 'very
strange', JRRT to Christopher Bretherton, 16 July 1964. 'For almost
twenty years . . .', WHL biography of CSL, fol. 440.

page 243   'J. spent the evening . . .', WHL diary, 16 March 1960.

page 244   'When we meet . . .', 'Christian Marriage', *Mere Christianity*. 'Because of
endless pride . . .', *Poems*, p. 89. 'He seemed very different . . .', unpublished memoir of Lewis by Peter Bayley.

page 245   'Lightly men talk . . .', *Till We Have Faces*, p. 305. 'We Lewises . . .',
Basil Willey to Walter Hooper, 20 September 1970 (Bodleian).

page 246   'Can it be . . .', CSL to Kathleen Raine, 5 December 1958. 'Some of the
younger men . . .', CSL to Basil Willey, 22 October 1963. 'quiet, charming and kindly', Green & Hooper, p. 289. 'I wear a surgical belt . . .',
CSL to Sheldon Vanauken, 27 November 1957. 'the doctors . . .', ibid.,
26 April 1958. 'Of course the sword . . .', ibid., 27 November 1957.

page 247   'You might call it . . .', Green & Hooper, p. 269. 'We found it . . .',
ibid. 'Dear Mary . . .', *Letters to an American Lady*, p. 76. 'This last
check . . .', Green & Hooper, p. 270. 'Meanwhile you have . . .', *Letters
to Malcolm*, p. 44. 'Can one ask . . .', CSL to Fr. Peter Milward, 25
December 1959. 'her courage . . .', WHL diary, 21 June 1960.

page 248   'She came back . . .', Green & Hooper, p. 276. 'It is incredible . . .', *A
Grief Observed*, p. 14. 'Before I dropped off . . .', WHL diary, 13 July

1960. 'How long . . .', *A Grief Observed*, p. 14. 'but even now . . .', WHL diary, 13 July 1960. 'All this is flashy . . .', *Poems*, p. 109.

page 249   'When I was . . .', WHL diary, 13 July 1960. 'No one ever told me . . .', *A Grief Observed*, p. 7. 'I had for some time . . .', ibid., p. 11. 'The conclusion . . .', ibid., p. 10. 'Sooner or later . . .', ibid., p. 26. 'I have gradually . . .', ibid., p. 38. 'Easier said . . .', ibid., p. 57. 'Didn't people dispute . . .', ibid., p. 59. 'I am at peace . . .', ibid., p. 60. 'What a nice letter . . .', CSL to Tolkien, 20 November 1962 (Estate of J. R. R. Tolkien).

page 251   'I can't help . . .', CSL to Greeves, 11 September 1963. 'quite comfortable . . .', ibid. 'The wheel had come . . .', *Letters*, p. 24. 'It was very cold . . .', unpublished memoir of Lewis by Peter Bayley.

page 252   'he was the link . . .', unpublished memoir of Lewis by R. E. Havard. 'I am sorry . . .', draft of letter by JRRT to ? (Estate of J. R. R. Tolkien).

APPENDIX D
Acknowledgements

This book was undertaken at the suggestion of Rayner Unwin of George Allen & Unwin Ltd, and I am grateful to him for his help and advice throughout the project. I could not have written it had not those people who have charge of the unpublished material relating to its subjects allowed me to consult it and to quote freely from it. C. S. Lewis's literary executor the Rev. Walter Hooper has, with his fellow Trustee, Owen Barfield, generously permitted me to make use of the full resources of Lewis's literary estate and to print many quotations whose copyright is in their keeping. Further material relating to Lewis and to Charles Williams has been collected by Dr Clyde S. Kilby, the founder of the Marion E. Wade Collection at Wheaton College, Illinois; and he has generously allowed me access to everything in his charge, as well as permitting me to study and quote from the diaries of W. H. Lewis, whose copyright he controls. Charles Williams's son, Michael Williams, has with similar generosity allowed me to quote from his father's unpublished letters. Finally in this group I must thank Christopher Tolkien, who as his father's literary executor has kindly allowed me to quote from unpublished writings by J. R. R. Tolkien.

Permission to quote from published material has been given by the following. For the works of C. S. Lewis: Collins (Publishers), the Delegates of the Oxford University Press, the Syndics of the Cambridge University Press, and Faber & Faber. For the works of Charles Williams: David Higham Associates and the Oxford University Press. For *Summoned by Bells* and *Continual Dew* by John Betjeman: John Murray. For *Sprightly Running* by John Wain: Macmillan & Co. and Curtis Brown Ltd.

All surviving Inklings have responded with great kindness to my request for information, and I owe a considerable debt of thanks to the following: Owen Barfield, Professor J. A. W. Bennett, Lord David Cecil, Professor Nevill Coghill, Commander Jim Dundas-Grant, Colin Hardie, Dr R. E. Havard, Christopher Tolkien, and John Wain. Several of them have also read the book in manuscript, and it has benefited greatly from their comments; though it should not be assumed that everything in it necessarily represents their own views.

Many other people who were associated with the persons and events described in the book have responded generously with information, the loan of letters and photographs, and personal memoirs. Here too, several of them have read the book in manuscript and have given me much valuable advice. In this category I owe many thanks to Peter Bayley, Dr Derek Brewer,

280

Margaret Dyson, Dame Helen Gardner, Roger Lancelyn Green, Alice Mary Hadfield, the Rev. Walter Hooper, Phyllis McDougall, Stephen Medcalf, Anne Ridler, Anne Spalding, Priscilla Tolkien, and Michael Williams.

My thanks also go to others who have helped me in various ways: Sir John Betjeman, the Rev. Frederick Black, Ann Bonsor, Keith Brace, the Rev. Peter Cornwell, Anthony Curtis, C. Talbot d'Alessandro, Wayne De Young, Roger Green, Christian Hardie, the Rev. Dr Brian Horne, Richard Jeffery, Charles Noad, Ruth Pitter, Billett Potter, the President of Magdalen College, Oxford, Stephen Schofield, and T. A. Shippey. My wife Mari Prichard has given her usual valuable help and advice.

I have of course depended for much of my information on the published biographical studies of Lewis and Williams, especially *C. S. Lewis, a biography* by Roger Lancelyn Green and Walter Hooper, *An Introduction to Charles Williams* by A. M. Hadfield, and Anne Ridler's critical introduction to *The Image of the City and other essays* by Charles Williams.

I owe a particular debt of thanks to the Phoenix Trust for a generous grant which made it possible for me to visit the Wade Collection at Wheaton College, Illinois, a journey without which the book could not have been written. My work at Wheaton was made much easier by the transcriptions from Warnie Lewis's diaries and Charles Williams's letters which had been typed by Linda La Breche and Barbara McClatchey. Nor can I close without mentioning with much affection the staff and students of Wheaton College, and in particular Barbara Griffin, Charlyn Johnson, Marjorie Mead, and Douglas Woods. Making such friends as these has been one of the many delights of writing the book.

INDEX